1) pg 458 ATlas Supply
2) pg 514 Minto Management
Due, thurs, Dec 1, 5pm

THE RULE of LAW

BUSINESS LAW FOR CANADIAN COLLEGES

STEVEN N. SPETZ GLENDA S. SPETZ

THE RULE of LAW

BUSINESS LAW FOR CANADIAN COLLEGES

Copp Clark Pitman Ltd.
A Longman Company
Toronto

ISBN 0-7730-5089-2

Cover and text design: Smart work/Steve MacEachern
Photo research: Melanie Sherwood
Typesetting: Spetz Publishing Ltd.
Printing and binding: John Deyell Company Limited.
Chapter illustrations: Greg White

CANADIAN CATALOGUING IN PUBLICATION DATA

Spetz, Steven N., 1940-
The rule of law
Includes index.
ISBN 0-7730-5089-2

1. Commercial law - Canada. I. Spetz, Glenda S.
II. Title.
KE919.S64 1992 346.71'07 C91-095631-6
KF889.S64 1992

Copp Clark Pitman Ltd.
2775 Matheson Boulevard East
Mississauga, Ontario
L4W 4P7

Printed and bound in Canada
1 2 3 4 5 5089-2 96 95 94 93 92

CONTENTS

REVIEWERS:

Mitch Wise
Southern Alberta Institute of Technology
Calgary, Alberta

Gus Mullings
Vancouver Community College
Vancouver, British Columbia

LEGAL CONSULTANT:

Margaret E. Rintoul, LL.B.
Carson, Gross & McPherson
Toronto, Ontario

PHOTO CREDITS

CSA, p. 262; Canapress, pp. 160, 220, 376, 440, 462; Carbolic Smoke Ball Co., p. 122; Jack Chang, p. *viii*; Foster Advertising Ltd., p. 72; Paul Godin, p. 34; *The Lawyer's Weekly*, p. 336; Provincial Archives of Alberta, Accession No. 67. 133, p. 416; Tom Shields / Creative & Editorial Services p. 300.

TEXT CREDITS

Permission to reprint the article, "We Were Wrong", *Toronto Sun*, 9 June, 1981 courtesy *Toronto Sun*

DEDICATION

To the families of all military personnel,
Missing in Action or held as Prisoners Of War,
in conflicts throughout the world.

Save a place for men gentle and kind,

For those noble heroes we left behind,

And when we learn that war is insane,

The bravest of brave will come home again.

CHAPTER ONE

THE CANADIAN LEGAL SYSTEM

"The Upper House should never set itself against the understood wishes of the people."

Sir John A. Macdonald,
Canada's first
Prime Minister

ORIGINS OF CANADIAN LAW

Canada derived its legal system from the two European nations that influenced its early settlement: Great Britain and France. The systems in these two countries were very different. The system of law used in France was based upon Roman law, under which all legal power rested upon the power and personage of the emperor. The French system relied heavily upon the codification of law. **Codification** is a system of organizing all laws into numbered volumes according to topic. In Quebec, the French *Code Civil* is the basic foundation of law in that province today.

Under the British system, which is the basis for today's law in the rest of Canada, the law existed independently of the ruler. The British monarchy was the fountain of justice, but it was not the fountain of law. This system was, for the most part, unwritten, and was based upon the customs and practices of the people. Written laws, or **statutes**, were added only when absolutely necessary and they were not organized into codes of any type.

The system of law based on the customs and practices of people is called **common law**. It operates on a principle called ***stare decisis***, or the **rule of precedent,** which can be loosely translated to mean "stand by that which has been decided." The rule of precedent requires that "like cases be decided alike." A judge attempting to reach a decision in one case relies upon previous cases involving the same kind of circumstances. If the judge can find such a case, the decision made in it will be followed, provided the issues in the two cases are similar. Once established, a precedent remains in force until overturned by a higher court or changed by the passage of a new statute (written law).

DEVELOPMENT OF CASE LAW

A system relying so much on previous decisions requires that cases be recorded for future reference. The practice of recording cases was begun in the twelfth century by King Henry I of England, who required judges to keep written records of all the cases they heard. These records formed the beginning of the first law library in England. The collection of cases for reference earned the name of **case law**. By referring to these recorded cases, lawyers and judges know what precedents should be applied to a case before the court. Precedent provides three main benefits to the legal system:

1. **Uniformity**: Without precedent, similar cases would result in unlike decisions. This would be unfair to someone and would be confusing.
2. **Predictability**: A lawyer can advise a client about the probable outcome of a case based upon past cases.
3. **Impartiality**: A judge cannot show favouritism because the judge is bound by the rule of precedent. The judge must apply the accepted principles of law to all cases before the court.

EQUITY BALANCES CASE LAW

If the rule of precedent is applied rigidly, then a decision might go unchanged for centuries. Judges are reluctant to overturn a previous ruling or refuse to follow what is believed to be the established law. In early England, some critics argued that precedent was a bad principle because it resulted in the "dead hand of the past wringing the neck of the future." Disgruntled people had the right to petition the monarch personally because of what they felt was an unfair ruling. The monarch usually referred such matters to an official, known as the Chancellor, who would make rulings. As the number of petitions grew, a separate court, the Court of Chancery, was established to deal with all appeals based upon complaints that the courts were applying outdated law. This concept, that precedent could be overturned if the result was unfair, became known as **equity**, which can be defined as a system of decision making that seeks a fair and just result.

For several hundred years, England had a dual system of courts of law, with common law in one and equity in the other. Today, the double system of courts is gone and the appeal courts of Canada apply both common law and equity.

When a judge concludes that a precedent cannot be applied fairly to a case at hand, there is ample support for reaching a totally new decision. In a 1963 case, a judge of the British House of Lords said:

> *The common law ought never to produce a wholly unreasonable result; nor ought existing authorities to be read so literally as to produce such a result never contemplated when they were decided.*

CANADIAN GOVERNMENT

The power to make and enforce Canadian laws is held exclusively by the federal and provincial governments. The provinces control legal activities at the municipal government level. There are three branches of the federal government: the legislative branch, the executive branch, and the judicial branch. Legislative power at the federal level belongs to the Parliament of Canada; at the provincial level it is held by the provincial legislatures. Executive power in Canada is exercised by the Sovereign (king or queen) as represented by the Governor General. The federal Cabinet carries out many of the executive duties under the authority of the Governor General.

At the provincial level, executive power is held by the Lieutenant Governors. Judicial power is exercised by the federal and provincial courts established by the legislative branch under the authority of the *Constitution Act, 1867.*

ROLE OF PARLIAMENT

The Canadian Parliament is modelled very much upon the traditions and processes of the British Parliament. Under the British system, Parliament is supreme. In power and authority, it stands above the executive and judicial branches of government. The historical view was that Parliament could do everything that is not naturally impossible. If the Parliament of Canada passed a law that ordered the earth to stand still, it would be of no force and effect. At one time there was no legal basis upon which any person could challenge in court what Parliament had enacted, except to argue that the federal government had intruded into the power of a province, or vice versa. This principle differs greatly from the U. S. system of government, which holds that the *Constitution of the United States* is the supreme authority, and that under the Constitution the three branches of government are equal in power, having been arranged in an elaborate "checks and balances" system.

In Canada, in 1982, the principle of the supremacy of Parliament was greatly altered by the enactment of the *Canadian Charter of Rights and Freedoms,* which is part of the Canadian Constitution. Although there is nothing in the Charter that specifically changes the principle of the supremacy of Parliament, the Supreme Court of Canada made a series of rulings that declared the principle was no longer true. These decisions centred around section 7 of the Charter, which reads as follows:

7. Everyone has the right to life, liberty and security of the person and the right not to be deprived thereof except in accordance with the principles of fundamental justice.

One of the first important rulings of the Supreme Court under the Charter centred around a basic argument about the power of the courts to review a statute. There were two very different schools of thought:

1. The courts could examine only the procedural aspects of a law.
2. The courts could examine both the procedural aspects and the substance of the law.

The lawyers and judges who believed that the courts had the power to consider only the procedural aspects of a law meant that a court could never consider if the law was too harsh, unnecessary, ill-conceived, or contrary to Canadians' legal heritage. A court could only consider if the law was being properly administered.

Using an exaggerated, hypothetical example, assume that a provincial legislature passed a law imposing a heavy fine upon all people who are left-handed. Failure to pay the fine would result in a jail sentence of 10 years. Such a vicious, unreasonable law would, of course, bring protest. Assume that Mr. Citizen is arrested and prosecuted for non-payment of the fine. He wants to argue that the law is stupid and unjust. Those who support the procedural concept would say that the court would have no power to hear such an argument. The court would simply want to know if Mr. Citizen was indeed left-handed. The court might also ask if other left-handed people were being excused from paying the fine. The law should be applied equally to all left-handed people.

Under procedural law, the court has no power to ask whether the legislature has lost its senses. The supremacy of Parliament principle prevents the court from examining the substance of the law. The worst law in the world would be constitutional as long as it was passed by the legislative body having authority and was applied according to the procedure stipulated by the legislature.

If the court hearing Mr. Citizen's case was also allowed to take into consideration the substance of the law, it would be able to refer to other laws that protect the basic human rights of people. Citizens should not be punished for being left-handed. As well, the court could consider whether fines should be levied for behaviour that does not represent any problem to society.

The obvious reality was that, following the passage of the Charter, section 7 had to be interpreted by the Supreme Court of Canada as supporting either school of thought. Only one view could prevail. Two cases decided the issue.

OPERATION DISMANTLE v. THE QUEEN

Supreme Court of Canada, 1985

The appellants took their case from the Federal Court of Appeal to the Supreme Court of Canada, alleging that a decision made by the government of Canada to allow the United States to test Cruise missiles in Canada violated section 7 of the *Charter of Rights and Freedoms*.

The development of the missile, it was argued, heightened the risk of nuclear war and the increased U.S. presence and interest in Canada made Canada a more likely target for nuclear attack. Declaratory relief, an injunction, and damages were sought. The Court dismissed the appeal.

However, the most important argument was whether a person, or group of people, could ask the courts to overturn a decision of the federal Cabinet and Prime Minister. Before the Charter was enacted, no such challenge could be made. The Court concluded that Cabinet decisions are reviewable under section 32(1) of the Charter and the executive branch of the Canadian government bears a general duty to act in accordance with the dictates of the Charter. Section 7 could give rise to a duty on the part of the executive branch to refrain from permitting the testing if it could be said that a deprivation of life or security of the person could be proven to result from the government act. However, the Court concluded that the appellants had not proven the existence of the alleged danger.

The decision in this case clarified one important issue: no government action, taken within its constitutional authority, is totally above the Charter or judicial review. This applies to the executive and legislative branches of government. It also had the effect of greatly increasing the power of the judiciary, for it would be the courts that would decide whether the Charter had been violated.

REFERENCE RE B. C. MOTOR VEHICLE ACT

Supreme Court of Canada, 1986

The province of British Columbia passed a law that provided a tough penalty, including a jail sentence, for any person caught operating a motor vehicle without a valid driver's permit. The law specifically ruled out any defence by the motorist that he or she did not know his or her permit had been suspended. There were immediate questions about whether the law violated the Charter, so a special reference was made to the Supreme Court of Canada. The opponents of the law believed the law violated section 7 of the Charter. An important issue was whether the Court had any power to consider the substance of the law.

In a unanimous decision, the Court ruled that it could consider both the procedural and substantive fairness of any law because the courts are the guardians of the legal system. The Court struck down the law as a violation of the Charter.

It is a reasonable inference that these two decisions greatly weakened the principle of supremacy of Parliament. Every action taken by government is subject to judicial review and may be declared contrary to the Charter and of no effect. The Charter contains a unique section, section 33, which allows a legislature to pass a law that, by its own declaration, is not to be subject to judicial review. A legislature can avoid judicial review by passing a law "notwithstanding" section 2 or sections 7 to 15 of the Charter. This would place the law outside the requirements of the Charter. The law would stand for only five years, after which it could be renewed. In 1986, Saskatchewan became the first province to pass such a law, a bill imposing a legislated contract agreement upon provincial employees. However, the other sections of the Charter are not subject to a notwithstanding clause and there is nothing the legislature can do to prevent a court from reviewing laws that seemingly violate these sections.

CONSTITUTION ACT, 1867

A country is governed according to the powers and duties expressly stated in its constitution. A constitution serves two purposes: it extends power to the government and, at the same time, limits the power of the government. A constitution can be defined as:

> *The supreme organic and fundamental law of a nation or state, establishing the character and conception of its government, laying the basic principles to which its internal life is to be conformed, organizing the government, and regulating, distributing and limiting the functions of its different departments, and prescribing the extent and manner of the exercise of sovereign powers.*

The Dominion of Canada was the legal creation of the *British North America Act, 1867*, which was later renamed the *Constitution Act, 1867*. Canada is a constitutional monarchy with a federal system of government. Specific powers have been assigned to the federal government, while other powers have been assigned to the various provincial governments. Any power not specifically delegated to one level of government or the other falls to the federal government by virtue of the "Peace, Order and Good Government" clause found in section 91 of the Act. This is called residual power. As well, the federal government, acting through the Governor General, has the power to disallow any provincial law within one year. Some of the more important powers of the federal government under section 91 relate to:

- Public debt
- Trade and commerce
- Postal services
- Penitentiaries
- Defence
- Navigation and shipping
- Currency
- Marriage and divorce
- Unemployment insurance
- Patents and copyrights
- Banks
- Bills of exchange
- Citizenship
- Criminal law
- Taxation
- Indian affairs
- Old age pensions
- Foreign affairs

Some of the powers of the provincial legislatures under section 92 relate to:

- Compensation to injured workers
- Property and civil rights
- Education
- Labour and trade unions
- Provincial courts and laws
- Hospitals and asylums
- Solemnization of marriage
- Direct taxation within the province

Some of these powers were added by later amendments or by judicial interpretations.

INDEPENDENCE OF THE JUDICIARY

Another tradition of the British legal system that was continued in the Canadian system is the independence of the judiciary. On numerous occasions, British monarchs tried to order judges to make certain decisions. The judges nearly always refused, despite threats of removal from office or imprisonment. Judges are free to decide cases as they see fit, according to their interpretation of the applicable statutes and case law. Even though judges may be appointed by the government, once appointed they obey no ruler in making legal decisions.

The tradition has very strict rules. A government official must not contact a judge to suggest how a case should be decided. It would be improper for any official to even ask how and when the case will be decided. The reverse side of the tradition is also very strict. Judges should not make any political statements or take part in activities that even hint of political involvement. Judges give few speeches, except to law students. For most of Canadian history, judges were prohibited from voting as this might suggest political involvement. That law has been repealed.

In recent years, the tradition has been softened somewhat; judges are speaking out more boldly about matters that affect the legal system. Mr. Justice John Sopinka of the Supreme Court of Canada publicly rebuked law firms for working young lawyers too hard for the sake of money, thereby destroying the meaning of the profession. Madam Justice Bertha Wilson, before her retirement from the Supreme Court of Canada, in a speech at the Osgoode Hall Law School, said that judges have their own agendas and that gender bias is deeply entrenched in the law and courts.

EFFECT OF THE CHARTER ON JUDICIAL DECISIONS

When it was adopted in 1982, the *Charter of Rights and Freedoms* did not contain express wording regarding judicial power. However, the Charter changed not only the constitutional law of Canada, but also the manner in which the courts examine the law. Prior to 1982, the majority of constitutional law cases brought before the courts asked one basic question: Did the government that passed a particular law have the power to do so? Disputes were primarily territorial disputes. If the court upheld the law, it ruled that the law was *intra vires* (within the power) of the government that passed it. If the law was struck down, the court declared it *ultra vires* (beyond the power) of the government that passed it. The merits or content of the law were not closely examined, only the constitutional authority to enact it.

Hundreds of examples exist. In 1982, for example, in *Schneider v. The Queen,* the Supreme Court of Canada heard a challenge to a provincial law, the British Columbia *Heroin Treatment Act, 1978*. This law permits provincial authorities to detain any person addicted to heroin for a period of up to four years for mandatory treatment for addiction. A person could be incarcerated for four years without trial and without having committed an offence. Ms. Schneider challenged the law, arguing that the province had invaded the federal constitutional sphere of criminal law. The province defended the law, saying it was not criminal law in nature, but pertained to health, which was under provincial jurisdiction. The Court ruled that the law was *intra vires* the province, stating that the substance of the Act was the medical treatment of heroin addicts and within the competence of the provincial legislature.

In *Morgan v. Jacobson and A.G. of P.E.I.* (1975) the province of Prince Edward Island passed a law that non-resident people, whether Canadian citizens or not, require permission to purchase land exceeding 10 acres or that has shore frontage exceeding 5 chains. This was challenged by a resident of Alberta who wanted to buy land in Prince Edward Island. The argument was that the effect of the Canadian *Citizenship Act* is such that any Canadian may move freely from province to province and that the law was directed against other Canadians. The Supreme Court of Canada ruled that the law was *intra vires* the province. The Court held that the law was not discriminatory because no one was prevented from entering the province and taking up residence there.

In *Winner v. SMT (Eastern) Ltd. and the A.G. of Canada* (1951) the Supreme Court of Canada heard a case involving interprovincial transportation. SMT had an exclusive bus licence in the province of New Brunswick. Israel Winner, who lived in the state of Maine, operated an international bus line. He was granted a licence by the province of New Brunswick that allowed him to pass through the province, but not to pick up or let off passengers. That right was exclusively given to SMT. The province argued that it had the constitutional power to "regulate its highways." Winner argued that Canadians and people legally doing business in Canada must be given free and unlimited travel rights in the country.

The Court declared the law *ultra vires* and struck it down, saying that every Canadian citizen has certain constitutional rights, including the right to travel, move, and work. A province cannot interfere with the lawful conduct of business by Canadians, and the same prohibition would apply to non-Canadians legally conducting business in Canada. To uphold the provincial law would result in Canada being divided into "enclaves," which is totally contrary to the union that the original provinces sought.

In all of these cases, the primary issue was constitutional power. The court's task was to determine if one government had trespassed into the exclusive field of another government.

After 1982, the situation changed. As was previously mentioned, the courts could now consider the substance of the law as well as the administration of the law. The primacy of the Constitution is declared in Part VII of the *Constitution Act:*

52. (1) The Constitution of Canada is the supreme law of Canada, and any law that is inconsistent with provisions of the Constitution is, to the extent of the inconsistency, of no force and effect.

However, the Charter begins with a reaffirmation that there are no *absolute* rights or freedoms in Canada:

1. The *Canadian Charter of Rights and Freedoms* guarantees the rights and freedoms set out in it subject only to such reasonable limits prescribed by law as can be demonstrably justified in a free and democratic society.

The effect of section 1 is to turn any Charter challenge to a law into a two-tier trial. The person alleging that his or her rights or freedoms have been infringed must prove that there has been an infringement. The Crown must then defend the law by showing that the infringement is both reasonable and justified.

A law might first be declared an infringement of rights, but be upheld nonetheless because it is a reasonable one. For example, many aspects of the breathalyzer law in Canada have been subjected to Charter challenge. These challenges include the right to counsel, the right not to be arbitrarily detained, the right not to give self-incriminating evidence, and many other issues. The Supreme Court of Canada has consistently held that these laws *do* violate the rights of citizens, *but* that they are reasonable and demonstrably justified because of the terrible problem of alcohol-related motor vehicle accidents. The Supreme Court has held that any infringement of a person's rights or freedoms must be the least possible intrusion. The Court has also ruled that the objectives of the law must be as important as, or greater than, the rights and freedoms being restricted. It cannot be for mere convenience.

While a government can limit rights and freedoms, it cannot totally deny them. In *Quebec Association of Protestant School Boards v. Quebec* (1984) the Supreme Court of Canada reviewed a Quebec law that restricted admission to its English-language schools to the children of people who had been educated in English in Quebec. The Court struck down the law, saying that it was a total denial rather than a limit of the language rights in the Charter. Denial of a right cannot be saved under section 1.

Most of the Charter pertains to matters that fall under criminal law. However, some sections have direct bearing upon civil law. For example, section 2 guarantees freedom of assembly. Cases have been brought that challenge restrictions upon joining a union and upon strike activity. Section 6 guarantees mobility rights, but this has not been interpreted to mean that a person can take employment anywhere in Canada without interference.

CLASSIFICATIONS OF LAW

There are many ways to classify law according to its particular purpose or form. These classifications do not fit into some overall plan or chart: they only suggest various terms that are understood to refer to a particular field.

CRIMINAL LAW

Criminal law covers the area of law that specifically prohibits certain acts and provides penalties for people committing such acts. Canadian criminal laws are codified in the *Criminal Code of Canada*, which is uniform throughout Canada, although there are some variations from province to province. As well, certain federal statutes contain penalties for violators and are generally considered part of the criminal law. An example would be the *Narcotic Control Act*.

CIVIL LAW

Civil law generally refers to private matters between individuals that do not directly involve the Crown. Such matters are non-criminal in nature and include such areas as contracts, property, torts, and many others. The civil law is not uniform across Canada, as each province has enacted statutes that apply specific terms only to that province. Civil law encompasses both statute law and case law.

CONSTITUTIONAL LAW

A constitution is a body of basic principles stating the powers and limitations of a government and the way those powers are to be exercised. In Canada, these powers are granted under the *Constitution Act, 1867*. There are also many customs and conventions that make up the unwritten section of the Canadian Constitution. There have been numerous amendments to the Constitution, but the most significant changes were effected in 1982, which included the adoption of the *Charter of Rights and Freedoms*.

STATUTE LAW

Many laws are enacted by the elected legislative bodies. The laws passed by the federal and provincial legislatures are called **statutes** or **Acts**. Statutes can be amended or repealed by the same legislature that originally passed them. Municipalities can enact ordinances and by-laws under power granted to them by the provincial legislatures.

INTERNATIONAL LAW

Numerous treaties, signed by many of the nations of the world, have such universal acceptance that they comprise a body of law viewed as binding upon all nations. The centre of international law is the World Court, located at den Hague, Holland. The Court has no power to enforce its judgments, but the judgments have a great moral weight and can be cited in courts within a particular country. In 1985, the World Court ruled that the United States had no legal right to mine the harbours of Nicaragua in order to try to weaken the government of that country. The United States eventually ceased the mining. There are many international agreements involving a wide variety of subjects including patents, trade, child abduction, migratory birds, and mining of the ocean floor.

The United Nations (UN) also has exercised power and influence in the area of international law by passing resolutions that require a member nation to cease a particular activity as a violation of international law. In 1990, the United Nations Security Council passed several resolutions condemning the invasion of Kuwait by Iraq and eventually applied military force to back up the resolutions. As well, Iraq's assets in foreign banks were frozen under the authority of UN resolutions.

ADMINISTRATIVE LAW

One of the most difficult things for the legislative branch to do is to enact laws that completely govern or regulate a particular subject. The complexity of Canadian society puts a great burden upon Parliament to enact legislation about matters that the Members of Parliament do not fully understand. Also, new bills cannot be of such enormous length that the Members do not have time to read them. To resolve complex problems, Parliament usually passes a basic statute governing a subject, then provides authority within the Act for a Cabinet Minister to establish further regulations under the Act. These regulations have the same force of law as the basic law itself.

Parliament also creates partly or completely independent boards or commissions to regulate certain industries, or to carry out specialized work. Matters such as unemployment insurance, workers' compensation, aviation safety, gas and oil marketing, telephone rates, product safety, and many other matters are regulated by boards and commissions.

The statute that creates the board or commission is called the **enabling Act.** The regulations issued under the authority of the statute are called **subsidiary legislation**. The difference between a statute and a regulation is often difficult to understand. For example, a dairy farmer must put milk into a certain type of container, be prepared for it to be inspected, and produce only the authorized amounts. These are all examples of regulations, not statutes. There are labour regulations, safety regulations, teaching regulations, meat inspection regulations, and thousands more.

Another source of administrative law is the executive branch of government. At the federal level, Cabinet Ministers issue many regulations and directives under the authority of the Governor General. These documents are referred to as **orders-in-council**. These decisions are made under the authority of existing statutes and are not debated in Parliament. They often come into existence with little or no public awareness.

The justification for these actions is much the same as for subsidiary legislation—there is no time to debate every decision of government. In 1983, the federal government became aware of the growing problem of dangerous martial arts weapons being imported into Canada. The existing law did not prohibit these weapons. In order to act quickly, an order-in-council was signed by the Governor General banning these weapons.

To a certain extent, boards and commissions have invaded the power of the legislative and judicial branches. They create regulations that have the force of law of a statute. These same agencies sometimes take on what appears to be judicial power in the sense that they can order people to appear and explain their actions to determine whether these actions were contrary to regulations. These agencies can also impose fines. There are appeal boards, set up by statute, to hear cases involving citizens who believe they were unjustly treated by regulatory bodies. More and more these appeal boards resemble courts, making decisions that can have a powerful effect upon individuals. For example, nearly every business requires a licence of some type for legal operation. If the regulatory board revokes that licence, the individual will suffer economic loss. The owner of a bar or restaurant could not stay in business if his or her liquor licence were revoked.

On some occasions, the boards are given so much power by the legislature that they equal the powers of superior courts. This power will eventually be challenged, for only the Governor General can appoint judges of a superior court. In *Re Residential Tenancies Act of Ontario* (1981) the Supreme Court of Canada struck down an Ontario law that established a board to handle landlord and tenant disputes. The Court found that the appointed officials of these boards would have powers so extensive that they would be equal to superior court judges. When a government agency has a decision to make, the requirements are that it:

1. Make decisions only within its jurisdiction;
2. Make a decision only on the basis of the evidence before it;
3. Make a decision fairly and not on the basis of bias;
4. Grant a hearing to the people whose interests will be affected by a decision and give fair notice to those people.

NICHOLSON v. HALDIMAND-NORFOLK BOARD of COMMISSIONERS of POLICE

Supreme Court of Canada, 1979

Nicholson was a probationary police constable in Ontario when he was dismissed without notice and without reasons. He was not given an opportunity to make representations and answer criticisms. Under the terms of his employment, Nicholson could be fired at any time during the first 18 months as a police officer. The Supreme Court of Canada agreed that a probationary police officer does not have the same rights and protections of a permanent officer, but that it would be wrong to suggest that a probationary officer has *no* rights. Such an officer should be treated fairly, not arbitrarily. The Court also stated that "in the administrative or executive field there is a general duty of fairness." The decision to fire Nicholson was **quashed** (declared void).

FEDERAL GOVERNMENT STRUCTURE

In a federal democracy, such as Canada, the national Constitution distributes the powers between the federal and provincial governments. In Canada this is the case insofar as constitutional provisions for the four original provinces of the union of 1867 are concerned. The federal government of Canada, although it has some similarities to the British government, is unique in many ways. It represents a compromise between British traditions and the need to have structures that are specifically appropriate for Canada.

THE GOVERNOR GENERAL

The chief executive of Canada is the Sovereign, represented by the Governor General. The Governor General is appointed by the king or queen and holds office for six years, but traditionally a new appointment is made every five years.

The Constitution gives the Governor General very extensive powers, as the following partial list illustrates:

1. To give assent to or reject all bills passed by the Canadian Parliament;
2. To appoint and dismiss the Lieutenant Governors for all the provinces;
3. To appoint and dismiss all superior court judges;
4. To exercise the prerogative of mercy and pardons for criminals;
5. To appoint and dismiss Cabinet Ministers;
6. To dissolve Parliament and call general elections;
7. To disallow provincial legislation within one year of its passage.

Although the Governor General holds these powers, they are generally exercised without question in the manner requested by the Prime Minister. The Governor General will not make a decision that opposes the will of the elected Canadian Parliament.

Initially, the people appointed as Governors General were British, usually retired military officers. Since 1952, all the Governors General have been Canadian. If the Governor General falls ill and cannot carry out his or her constitutional duties, the Chief Justice of the Supreme Court of Canada temporarily assumes signing authority.

THE SENATE

The Senate, the Upper House of the legislature, was created as a result of a compromise reached at the Charlottetown Conference of 1864. It was decided that Senators would be appointed, not elected, and would hold office for life or until retirement. All provinces and political parties should be fairly represented.

The Senate is an independent legislative body, sometimes referred to as the "House of Second Reflection," which means that it carries out the role of criticizing controversial legislation passed by the House of Commons. Seldom has the Senate totally blocked legislation, but it can do so. When the Senate blocked the *Free Trade Bill* with the United States, it precipitated a general election that saw the re-election of the Conservative party. The Senate then passed the bill as the elected House had a mandate to proceed with free trade.

THE HOUSE OF COMMONS

The House of Commons, sometimes called the Lower House, is the elected legislative body of the Canadian government. The House is presided over by the Speaker of the House who is elected by the Members. Seats in the House are apportioned to the provinces by a formula based on population.

Bills (proposed laws) are brought before the House by all elected Members, but the bills which receive the most attention are those proposed by Members who are also Cabinet Ministers. If consent to major legislation, such as proposed spending bills, is not given by the House of Commons, custom requires that the government resign and that elections be held.

THE CABINET

The *Constitution Act, 1867* mentions a "Council" that is to advise the Governor General. The Act also refers to a "Privy Council." This council does exist in Canada, but almost never meets. Appointment to the Privy Council is a ceremonial honour for long government service.

The Cabinet is not the "Council." There is no specific mention in the constitution of any such body called a "Cabinet." However, the Cabinet is the real executive authority in Canada. Cabinet Ministers are appointed by the Governor General at the request of the Prime Minister and hold office at the pleasure of the Governor General. However, it is the Prime Minister who may fire his or her Ministers and have new ones appointed. The Cabinet formulates policies, prepares legislation, is responsible for the administration of the departments of government, and has assumed control over all financial matters.

Canadian tradition requires that Cabinet Ministers be Members of the House of Commons so that they may be accountable to the House for their actions. Occasionally, a Cabinet Minister may be chosen from the Senate to represent a province that has not elected any Members to the majority party.

Cabinet Ministers must defend the actions of public servants working in their departments, must support the policies of the Prime Minister, and must support each other. This is called the principle of **Cabinet solidarity**. The principle must be upheld because the defeat of any major program represents a defeat of the Prime Minister, who must resign. In such an event, the entire Cabinet may have to resign, thus precipitating an election because the government no longer has the confidence of the people. A Cabinet Minister who cannot publicly defend the government's policies must resign his or her Cabinet position, but need not resign from the House of Commons.

THE JUDICIARY

The *Constitution Act, 1867* created no courts, but it empowered the federal government to "create a general court of appeal and any additional courts for the better administration of the laws of Canada." The provincial legislatures may establish whatever courts are desired for the "administration of justice within the province." The Supreme Court of Canada was established in 1875 by the Parliament of Canada. The intent was that this court would be the highest court of appeal in Canada. However, the highest British court still had the authority to hear Canadian cases and overrule the Supreme Court of Canada. This situation existed until 1949 when a special statute was passed declaring the Supreme Court of Canada as the final appeal authority.

The primary function of the judiciary is to settle the disputes that come before it. However, the judiciary also has the duty to interpret laws and give them fuller meaning, to protect the people from arbitrary acts of government, and to ensure that the rule of law is maintained. Since 1982, the Supreme Court of Canada has been very active in interpreting and applying the many sections of the *Charter of Rights and Freedoms.*

PROVINCIAL GOVERNMENT

The structure of the 10 provincial governments is similar to that of the federal government. Provincial governments exercise different powers and, in addition, the provincial governments delegate some authority to the municipalities.

THE LIEUTENANT GOVERNOR

The most obvious difference in the structure of the provincial governments is that the Lieutenant Governor, the chief executive officer of the province, is appointed by the Governor General on the advice of the Prime Minister of Canada. He or she must give assent to all bills that are passed and is also a representative of the federal government.

THE PROVINCIAL LEGISLATURE

All provinces have one house. There is no second level corresponding to the Canadian Senate. In the legislature, the provincial Premier and his Cabinet exercise the same authority as their counterparts in Ottawa. The provincial legislatures cannot sit for more than five years without a provincial election.

MUNICIPAL GOVERNMENTS

In Canada, the basic unit of municipal government is the municipality. The municipalities have no specific powers under the *Constitution Act, 1867.* Therefore, they can exercise only the power given to them by the provinces. In *Shell Canada v. Vancouver* (1990) the Supreme Court of British Columbia struck down a Vancouver by-law that prohibited the city from doing business with Shell Canada until it divested its South African holdings. The Court said the province had given the city a charter to run the affairs of the city, not to run the affairs of another country.

A municipality may be either rural or urban. In most provinces, a municipality must have a population of 10 000 to 15 000 before it can obtain a charter to call itself a city.

CANADA'S COURT SYSTEM

The *Constitution Act, 1867* did not create any courts, but continued the existing court structure and also provided a plan for Canada to establish courts as needed. Parliament was empowered to establish a court of appeal and any additional courts for the "better administration of the laws of Canada." The provincial legislatures were given jurisdiction over the "administration of justice within the province" including the power to create and maintain courts to enforce both civil and criminal laws. Under this system, the provincial courts have the power to enforce both provincial and federal statutes. This is a bit unusual because in most countries federal laws can be enforced only by federal courts, and state laws by state courts.

All superior court judges are appointed by the Governor General, to hold office during good behaviour. In Canada, judges are not elected. Provincial court judges are appointed by the Lieutenant Governors. Judges have no responsibility to Parliament, which reinforces the principle of the independence of the judiciary.

A judge may be removed for misconduct. Removal requires an address to both Houses of Parliament, followed by an order for removal by the Governor General. This has never happened in Canadian history as judges who admit to misconduct have always resigned.

The court structure in each province is unique to that province and the names and authority of the courts are constantly changing. The courts generally fall into three levels: at the bottom are the various provincial courts, which deal with family law, small civil disputes, and less serious crimes. In the middle are the superior courts, which deal with major civil disputes and crimes. The third level is the court of appeal, which hears appeals from all the provincial courts. Ontario has undertaken a vigorous restructuring to change this to just two levels: the Ontario Court of Justice and the Court of Appeal.

There are two significant courts at the federal level: the Federal Court of Canada and the Supreme Court of Canada. The Federal Court hears claims directly against the federal government or any of its departments. It has jurisdiction over appeals against rulings by federal regulatory agencies such as the Canadian Radio-television and Telecommunications Commission. It has authority over intellectual property and admiralty (shipping) matters. Like a provincial supreme court, the Federal Court has a trials division and an appeals division.

The Supreme Court of Canada is the highest appellate court in Canada for both civil and criminal cases. It hears appeals against decisions of the provincial courts of appeal. The Court also hears appeals where the validity of federal and provincial statutes is in dispute, hears appeals from the Federal Court, and gives advisory opinions when asked by a Lieutenant Governor or the Governor General by way of special reference. In recent years, it has provided crucial interpretations of the various sections of the *Charter of Rights and Freedoms.*

CIVIL COURT PROCEDURE

Civil law can be defined simply as the part of the law concerned with non-criminal matters. It regulates and protects people's private rights in several areas. There are three main branches of civil law: tort law, contract law, and property law. These will be discussed in later chapters.

The trial of a civil action is a process whereby private parties come before a court and ask that the court determine matters such as obligations, liability, or fault. The procedure is considerably different from a criminal trial. For one thing, the Crown is not a party in a civil case, unless the Crown is suing or being sued by someone. In a criminal case, the Crown is the prosecutor.

The burden of proof in a civil case is different from that in a criminal case, as are the rules of evidence. However, both types of trial use the adversary system. A civil case is not merely an inquiry, but a contest.

INITIATING AN ACTION

Civil cases are generally initiated in a particular court, depending on the nature of the case and the amount of money involved. Each province establishes its own civil courts and the names and jurisdiction vary from province to province. A **civil action** is also referred to as **litigation** or a **suit.** Even the terms generally used in a civil action are subject to provincial variations. Ontario, for example, in an attempt to streamline civil cases, has renamed many of the traditional documents and terms. In each province, the procedure is governed by a lengthy document called the *Rules of Civil Procedure* or the *Rules of Practice*.

The person who initiates a civil action is called the **plaintiff**. The person against whom the action is brought is called the **defendant**. If the case is later taken to an appeal court, the person appealing is called the **appellant** and the other party is called the **respondent.**

A special procedure is necessary in the case of an **infant**, who is a person who has not reached the age of majority. An infant cannot sue personally except in a few special cases, such as a suit for unpaid wages. In Alberta, Manitoba, Ontario, Prince Edward Island, Quebec, and Saskatchewan, the age is 18. In all other provinces, the age is 19.

A suit must be brought on behalf of an infant by a **next friend**, who is usually the parent or guardian, or any responsible adult. This requirement is to ensure that there is someone of legal age present to answer to the court regarding the necessity of a suit and to pay any costs or judgment that might result.

The court issues a **Writ of Summons** or **Notice of Action** on the defendant. This document is prepared by the plaintiff's lawyer and served by a court **bailiff**. It informs the defendant of the action, names the plaintiff, sets out his or her claim, and cites a statutory time limit in which to file a notice to defend the action. If a defendant does not file a **Defence,** sometimes called an **Appearance** or **Dispute**, a **Judgment** (decision of the court) will be entered against the defendant by default. A Writ of Summons is usually served personally on the defendant, but in some cases substitute service, such as registered mail, will be authorized by the court.

If the defendant wants to contest the suit, he or she files a Dispute, entering it in the same court where the Writ of Summons was issued. The clerk of the court sends a copy of it to the plaintiff. The plaintiff then files with the court a **Statement of Claim** in which are outlined the demands being made on the defendant. A copy is sent to the defendant.

In Ontario, proceedings are one of two types: actions or applications. An **Action** is usually initiated by a **Claim** or **Notice of Action**. An **Application** is started by a **Notice of Application**. Generally, a civil lawsuit for damages is an action and is therefore introduced by a Notice of Action.

BARS TO A CIVIL ACTION

Certain matters might prevent a plaintiff from bringing an action. The first potential bar to an action is a time limitation. Each province has a period of limitations for bringing a civil action. For example, in most provinces a lawsuit arising from an automobile accident must be initiated within two years. The same time limit applies for lawsuits against doctors for malpractice. Simple contract debts are outlawed in six years in most provinces.

Another bar is based on a common law rule called **laches** which means "lax." This is a principle that permits the defendant to show that the plaintiff has been unreasonable in delaying the assertion or enforcement of a right. A court may refuse to allow the action if the plaintiff has "slept on his or her rights" and has made it very difficult for the defendant to defend the action. In *Kennedy v. Saskatchewan Cancer Foundation* (Saskatchewan, 1990) the plaintiff sued the defendant for injuries received by radiation treatment when she was a child. The injury occurred in 1955 and the plaintiff brought the action 33 years later. The Court held that the delay was unreasonable. The period of limitations generally does not run against an infant who could not bring an action until becoming an adult, but even then the time period involved must be reasonable.

A plaintiff cannot succeed in a civil action if the alleged injury arose from illegal and immoral conduct between the parties.

NORBERG v. WYNRIB

British Columbia Court of Appeal, 1990

The plaintiff became addicted to painkillers while being treated for a condition of chronic headache. The defendant doctor recognized the addiction and promised the plaintiff drugs in return for sexual favours. The plaintiff eventually entered a drug treatment program and then sued the doctor for negligence and breach of his professional duties. The Court dismissed the case on the ground that the alleged injury occurred out of the plaintiff's own immoral or illegal conduct.

An action will also be barred if the plaintiff's action will allow him or her to profit from criminal acts. For example, after Toronto real estate developer Peter Demeter was convicted of the murder of his wife, he brought an action to collect on the $1-million life insurance policy he held on his wife. The Court refused to hear the case, holding that Demeter could not profit from his own crime.

A case may also be barred if the court finds it **vexatious** or **frivolous**. A lawsuit cannot be silly and it cannot be brought just to annoy someone. Under Ontario's *Vexatious Proceedings Act* a man was barred from filing suit anywhere in Ontario because he was using civil suits to harass people. In *The Law Society of Upper Canada v. Zikov* (Ontario, 1985) the defendant had sued 18 government officials, the Law Society (three times), the Ombudsman, and the Premier of another province. The Court found that the defendant had engaged in "relentless litigation" and barred him from any further actions.

THE CIVIL JURY

If the case is to be tried before a superior court, because of the amount of money involved, it is possible that a civil jury will be called to hear the case. In certain types of cases, including libel, false arrest, or false imprisonment, a jury is nearly always called.

If one party wishes a jury trial, a jury notice is sent to the other party. If the other party does not want a jury trial, he or she petitions the judge to strike the notice. The judge makes the final decision.

Where a case involves a great deal of technical evidence that a jury might not understand, a judge may refuse to grant a jury trial on the ground that a jury could not reach a proper verdict. In Ontario, a civil jury consists of six people, five of whom must agree in order to reach a verdict. If more than one issue must be decided, it is not necessary that the same five jurors agree on each issue. If a juror is later discharged for some reason, the case may continue with five jurors and all five remaining jurors must agree.

Alberta and Manitoba also have six jurors. In British Columbia, there are eight and Nova Scotia has five. Newfoundland has nine jurors, who deliberate for three hours. If they are not unanimous at that time, a majority of seven may then return a verdict. Quebec abolished civil juries in 1977.

The burden of proof in a civil case is not as stringent as in a criminal case. While the burden of proof generally lies upon the plaintiff, he or she does not have to prove the claim "beyond a reasonable doubt," as required in a criminal case. In a civil case, the burden is upon the plaintiff to prove the claim "on a balance of probabilities."

An interesting illustration of the different principles occurred in a single incident. In *Higgins v. State Farm* (Nova Scotia, 1973) the plaintiff sued the defendant for the proceeds of a fire insurance policy. After his property was destroyed by fire, the plaintiff had been charged with arson. He was acquitted in criminal court because the Crown could not prove beyond a reasonable doubt that the plaintiff had deliberately started the fire.

However, in the civil action, the insurance company raised the same point, saying that it was not required by the terms of the policy to pay the proceeds where the loss was caused by the deliberate acts of the insured. The civil court judge agreed that, on a balance of probabilities, the plaintiff had started the fire, and dismissed the action.

PRE-TRIAL PROCEDURE

Each party in a civil action is entitled to examine all documents that the other side intends to introduce at the trial. The rule is that there should be full disclosure of relevant witnesses and materials. It is improper to try to surprise the other side in court. Most provinces permit either party to request a pre-trial meeting called an **Examination for Discovery**. This is not a hearing, but an attempt to put the other party's case on the record and get the other party to admit certain facts.

The two litigants (plaintiff and defendant) may be questioned and a formal transcript is made of their testimony. This record may be used as evidence during the trial. If the parties only wish to discover (examine) documents, this can be done without actually holding a meeting.

Quite often after the examination, the two parties are able to settle out of court. In Ontario, strong pressure is brought upon the parties to settle by virtue of the fact that the judge can deny the successful party his or her costs if the case goes to trial. For example, if the defendant offers to settle at least seven days before trial and the plaintiff refuses, believing he or she can win more in court, and the plaintiff does succeed, the judge can still refuse to allow the plaintiff the costs which normally are allowed to the successful party. This is done to discourage parties from taking cases to court and clogging the court system, when those cases could have been fairly settled out of court.

DAMAGES

If the plaintiff succeeds, the court must award some damages. **Damages** means money to compensate the plaintiff for loss or injury.

SPECIAL DAMAGES

Special damages are based on an itemized list that could include medical expenses, property damage, loss of employment, loss of future earnings, rehabilitation, and many other possible items for which a fairly accurate cost can be assessed. There is no limit upon the amount of special damages that can be awarded.

GENERAL DAMAGES

General damages comprise a lump sum for compensation for pain, suffering, loss of social amenities, and other things upon which it is difficult to place a specific value. In 1978, the Supreme Court of Canada placed a limit of $100 000 on such awards. However, lower courts soon began adjusting this limit upward to take into account the effect of inflation. There is now some disagreement as to whether the 1978 decision is still good law in Canada, as general damage awards are significantly over the limit the Court imposed.

At one time, there was no legal basis to sue for anything other than financial loss. Grief, emotional upset, and personal hardship were not recoverable. The rule was rooted in a fundamental truism: for some injuries, no amount of money will remedy the damage, and the courts will not award damages for non-monetary injuries.

In the 1970s, most provinces amended their family laws to extend the basis for which damages could be awarded. For example, the Ontario *Family Law Act* allows a spouse, parents, grandparents, children, grandchildren, brothers, and sisters to sue for "loss of guidance, care and companionship that the claimant might reasonably have expected to receive from the person if the injury or death had not occurred." Other provinces have similar laws. Alberta and New Brunswick are the only provinces that allow parents to claim damages for "grief" when children are killed or injured. Alberta limits the award to $3500 but New Brunswick places no limit on the amount parents can recover.

PUNITIVE DAMAGES

A court may award **punitive** or **exemplary damages** when the behaviour of the defendant has been very obnoxious, as the following case illustrates.

URSEL v. JENKINS

British Columbia, 1988

The plaintiff was sued for trespass after he chopped down 20 of his neighbour's trees to increase the amount of sunlight that reached his lot and to improve his view. The plaintiff also believed that the trees he cut down were old and unattractive and might even represent a danger to his house if they should fall in a wind storm. However, the plaintiff had no permission from the defendant to cut the trees. The Court ordered the plaintiff to pay the defendant $5000 for the trespass and $7500 in punitive damages for his "cynical disregard for his neighbour's rights."

The largest punitive damage award in Canadian legal history is a $4.8-million award against the National Bank of Canada for conspiring with another person to defraud a company of its assets. In *Clairborne Industries Ltd. v. National Bank of Canada* (1989) the Ontario Court of Appeal held that "the Canadian banking system demands that each bank be a symbol of public trust."

NOMINAL DAMAGES

The issues of liability and damages are two different matters. Although rare, it is possible for the plaintiff to win the case on the legal issues involved, even though there was no demonstrable harm. In such a case, a court will award a very small sum, called **nominal** or **contemptuous damages**, as the basic rule is that the successful plaintiff must be awarded damages, no matter how small.

DUTY TO MITIGATE

There is a duty upon the plaintiff to **mitigate**, or keep his or her injury to the smallest possible amount. For example, if a person suffered an injury and was told by a doctor to rest, the person could not hold the defendant liable if he or she did not rest and thereby aggravated the injury. In *Janiak v. Ippolito* (1985) the Supreme Court of Canada refused to award damages to a plaintiff who refused to have corrective surgery because of an illogical fear of surgery.

RULE AGAINST DOUBLE RECOVERY

In a very important decision, the Supreme Court of Canada held that an injured person cannot recover damages for loss of earnings when his or her salary has been paid under a contract of employment.

RATYCH v. BLOOMER

Supreme Court of Canada, 1990

The respondent, a police officer, was injured in a motor vehicle accident involving the police car he was driving. He was unable to work for several months but was paid his salary pursuant to the collective agreement with his employer. He did not lose any sick leave credits. It was argued that if the appellant had to pay damages for injuring the officer, the officer would collect twice: he would have his full salary, plus damages. He would not be "compensated for his loss" through the accident, but would profit from it.

The Supreme Court of Canada held that the respondent could not recover from the appellant. An injured person should recover the amount of his or her actual loss. To allow a "double recovery" violates this principle. It follows that where a plaintiff sustains no wage loss because his or her employer is paying the plaintiff's full salary, he or she cannot recover damages.

THIN SKULL RULE

It is a long-established rule of law that a defendant cannot avoid paying damages because the plaintiff had a pre-existing condition that made the injury worse than it would have been if the plaintiff had been healthy. The rule is called the **thin skull rule**, which states that "You must take the victim as you find him or her." In *Graham v. Rourke* (Ontario, 1990) the defendant negligently struck the plaintiff's car from the rear. It was a minor accident, but the plaintiff had a pre-existing condition of spinal deformity and had suffered a whiplash accident in 1984. The plaintiff was awarded $750 000.

DAMAGES FOR EMOTIONAL INJURY

Injury can take the form of an illness resulting from nervous or emotional shock. It must be an actual illness; mere anguish is not enough. Courts are willing to recognize that injury can be inflicted upon the nervous system of a person and that this can cause other complications, even death. The injury may or not have been intentional.

The law does not require each person to have the same amount of intestinal fortitude, only a reasonable amount. The source of the shock cannot be too remote. This means that the relationship between the accident and the resulting injury must be close enough for it to be said that the defendant could reasonably have foreseen that what was being done was going to cause someone nervous shock. In *Hay v. Young* (England, 1943) a woman nearly witnessed a fatal vehicle accident. She heard the collision and saw blood on the street, but did not actually see the accident. She later had a miscarriage and sued the defendant who caused the accident. The Court denied her damages, saying her nervous shock was not foreseeable to the defendant. From this case, and others, a rule developed that a plaintiff could not sue for nervous or emotional injury if the plaintiff did not personally witness the unpleasant cause of the injury. That is, a plaintiff who merely heard about what happened, but was not personally present, could not sue. The rule was aimed at limiting damages to people most directly affected by accidents, not those who might be distraught at hearing the news. Otherwise there could be hundreds of emotionally upset plaintiffs from the news of one accident. However, the rule has not always been applied strictly.

RHODES v. CNR

British Columbia Supreme Court, 1989

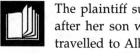

The plaintiff sued the defendant rail company for emotional injury after her son was killed in a train accident in Alberta. The plaintiff travelled to Alberta for a memorial service, but was given the wrong information about the date and time. She wanted to bring her son's remains home, but could not arrange it. She was then told the remains would be shipped to her.

Back in British Columbia, the plaintiff, a divorcée, felt alone and depressed. She received a phone call from Edmonton that her son's remains were ready for shipment. The body had been burned in the accident and she was told she would receive bone fragments only.

A week later, the plaintiff received a plain parcel in the mail, without any indication on the outside of what it was. When she opened the box, she was horrified to find the remains of her son. She suffered from manic depression, insomnia, and suicidal tendencies. The Court awarded her damages even though she did not personally see the tragic accident. The Court held that there was "no particular logic in distinguishing between a nervous shock suffered from actually seeing an accident or attending its aftermath and simply learning about the loss of a loved one from a third party."

The case did not completely break with precedent, because the Court took strong exception to the totally insensitive manner in which the plaintiff was sent an unmarked parcel containing the remains of her son.

ECONOMIC LOSS

Pure economic loss is a term which implies that, while a plaintiff in an action was not directly injured by the defendant, the plaintiff did suffer a loss. He or she may have lost employment, money, or opportunities.

The provision of remedies for economic loss is a later development of law, since the courts traditionally held that the plaintiff could not have foreseen such an injury. A good illustrative case is *Weller v. Foot and Mouth Disease Institute* (England, 1966). The defendant brought a virus to England from Africa to study. The virus was negligently allowed to escape and it infected many cattle in the area, which then had to be destroyed. This incident put the plaintiff, a cattle auctioneer, out of business.

The plaintiff sued the defendant for the loss of income but the Court denied the action because the plaintiff had a duty of care only toward the cattle owners. To accept the plaintiff's claim could have led to many more claims being brought, including claims from consumers who would have to pay higher beef prices.

However, economic loss is growing in acceptance as a valid claim for damages. In particular the courts are accepting the concept of a "relational economic loss," which holds that physical damage to one person's property may have a consequential effect upon another party. For example, if a motorist drives negligently and knocks down a hydro pole, the loss of electricity may shut down an entire industrial park and cause financial loss to the companies and workers who cannot work without power. The motorist could be liable for much of this loss.

In *Seaway Hotels Ltd. v. Gragg and Consumers' Gas* (Ontario, 1969) a gas company employee negligently cut a feeder line of the electric company, thereby cutting off electricity to the plaintiff's hotel. The power could not be restored easily and the hotel suffered a major financial loss because guests checked out and food spoiled. The defendant accepted liability only for the damage to the power line. It denied liability to the hotel. However, the Court awarded damages to the plaintiff, holding that, since the gas company knew of the location of the hydro line, it could have foreseen the damage that would occur if the hotel lost its electricity.

In *Heeney v. Best* (Ontario, 1980) a motorist drove negligently and knocked down a hydro pole, cutting off electricity to the plaintiff's chicken farm. This stopped ventilation fans from working in the plaintiff's barns and thousands of chickens died from the buildup of excessive heat. The defendant was held liable for 75 percent of the plaintiff's loss.

Generally, the courts have refused to award damages for economic loss where:

1. The damage is too remote from the wrongdoer's actions;
2. The wrongdoer could not reasonably have foreseen the result of his or her actions;
3. The victim suffered no personal damage to his or her property; or
4. The loss was purely a contractual problem with a third party.

There are normal risks of living and doing business that one assumes. Every loss or inconvenience in life cannot give rise to an action.

Economic loss is a very complex area of law and court decisions seem almost random. Plaintiffs sometimes suffer serious losses but find that they cannot hold someone else liable. In *Edgeworth Construction Ltd. v. N.D. Lea and Associates Ltd.* (1991) the British Columbia Court of Appeal refused to award damages to the appellant because there was no contractual agreement between the parties. Edgeworth Construction claimed highway plans prepared by Lea and Associates were faulty, resulting in millions of dollars in cost overruns when Edgeworth built the road. Lea had been hired by the provincial government to prepare the plans. The province then hired Edgeworth to build the highway. The Court held: "There must be foreseeability of economic loss being caused to someone in a specific class which is put at risk by the carelessness in question. Reliance must be justifiable and reasonable." The Court concluded that Edgeworth should have protected itself by putting a specific clause in its contract with the provincial government that the plans must be accurate.

CLASS ACTIONS

A **class action** brings together the claims arising from a common complaint among a number of people against the same defendant. The action can be brought by a group of people or by one plaintiff who asks to be allowed to bring the action on behalf of other people having the same complaint. The primary problem in a class action is to prove that every person in the class has the same complaint.

The Rules of Practice of all provinces appear to permit class action suits, but in many provinces it is very difficult to bring a successful class action. British Columbia is unique in that its *Trade Practices Act* allows a class action to be brought on behalf of consumers in the province. In *Chastain v. British Columbia Hydro and Power Authority* (British Columbia, 1973) the plaintiff sued the power authority for return of a security deposit the defendant had collected from him when he first applied for service. The plaintiff showed that the defendant had discriminated by demanding deposits only from people who were regarded as poor credit risks. The Court ordered deposits repaid to more than 20 000 customers.

ENFORCEMENT OF JUDGMENTS

Once a case has been decided, the court judgment (order) can be carried out against the losing party for a period of up to 20 years. The court does not enforce the judgment; this is the responsibility of the plaintiff. The judgment may be collected in various ways, including the seizure of property that is then sold at auction, putting a lien (legal claim) against real property, attaching bank accounts or other assets, or garnishment of wages.

If a debtor refuses to pay a judgment even though he or she has the money, the debtor can be brought back to court and ordered to "show cause" why the judgment has not been paid. It is possible for the judge to fine or jail the debtor for not paying the judgment. A judgment won against a person with no money has little value, since obviously nothing can be collected.

LEGAL FEES

The party who loses a court action must pay court costs. Costs include some of the legal fees for the other side, but not everything that the other party has had to pay. Courts follow a schedule of fees and allow the winner to recover the amount on the schedule. Court costs also include fees paid for filing documents, making transcripts, and other expenses.

A person who believes he or she has been overcharged by a lawyer may refer the matter to the court **Taxing Officer,** who may reduce the fees.

All provinces except Ontario permit a lawyer to take a case on a **contingency** basis. This means that the lawyer will not charge the client any fees, but will keep a percentage of any damages won. However, this practice is not widespread.

REVIEW: POINTS OF LAW

1. Canada's system of law is based upon British common law in all provinces except Quebec. The civil law of Quebec is an adaptation of the French *Code Civil.*
2. Laws passed by the federal or provincial government are called Acts or statutes.
3. Many so-called laws are not laws at all, but are regulations created by boards and commissions that have the force of law.
4. Canada's legal system includes an independent judiciary, free from political interference. Judges are appointed for life, not elected.
5. The rule of precedent requires that judges follow the decisions of higher courts. This provides the legal system with three benefits: uniformity, predictability, and impartiality.
6. The judiciary has the power to examine not just the procedural application of a law but the very substance of the law to determine if it violates the *Charter of Rights and Freedoms.*
7. Any power not specifically assigned in the *Constitution Act, 1867* to the federal government or the provinces reverts to the federal government under the "Peace, Order and Good Government" clause in the Constitution.
8. Under the *Constitution Act, 1867*, the Governor General wields enormous executive power. In reality, major decisions are actually made by the Prime Minister and the federal Cabinet.
9. In a civil case, the burden is upon the plaintiff to prove his or her allegations "on a balance of probabilities."
10. The Supreme Court of Canada has tried to keep general damage awards to $100 000 to avoid "monster" liability awards now prevalent in the United States.

LEGAL BRIEFS

1. People often refer to a lawsuit that claims a sum of money for "pain and suffering." What type of damages would this come under?

2. "Parliament is supreme and may therefore legislate anything it wants. The legislature, within its jurisdiction, may do everything that is not naturally impossible and is restrained by no rule human or divine." Is this a true statement?
3. A superior court judge took a temporary leave of absence from the bench and headed a royal commission to study the problems of native land claims in northern Canada. In the report, the judge wrote a severe criticism of the *Indian Act* and how it has abused the rights of native people. After the report was published, the judge returned to the bench. The first case before him involved a Canadian Indian who had been hunting out of season. What problem does this situation present?
4. H has a legal problem, so he visits the office of a lawyer, N. After describing his problem, H asks N what he thinks will happen. N replies: "If you have described the facts correctly, you will almost certainly be convicted. However, as you have never been in trouble before, I expect the judge will give you a small fine and probation." What basis does N have for making this statement?
5. G and Y were engaged to be married. G was struck by an automobile driven by W and suffered permanent disability and brain damage. Y becomes greatly depressed and emotionally ill. Would Y have a legal case against W?
6. P negligently started a fire in a building adjacent to a theatre. The fire spread to the theatre, and damaged it. However, water from fire hoses caused most of the damage to the theatre. P admits liability for damage to the theatre caused by fire and smoke, but denies liability for water damage. P's problems increase when he learns that 18 employees of the theatre and 12 actors are suing him because they are unemployed. Discuss P's liability and the possible basis for the claims against him.
7. T was fired from his job as a bartender because it was alleged he was giving his friends free drinks. The employer, R, knew that the accusation was not true but wanted to fire T and needed a strong reason. After T's dismissal, customers asked R what had become of T. R told many of these people that T was fired because "He was stealing me blind." T sues R. What damages would be proper in this case?
8. When the F Corporation accidentally allowed chemicals to discharge into a stream, some of L's farm animals became sick and died when they drank the water. F agreed to pay for the loss of the animals but refused to pay for the cost of trucking water to L's farm until the stream was safe again. L then allowed the animals to continue drinking the polluted water and many more became sick and died. Can L hold F liable for the loss of all the animals?

PREMIER
OAKLEY
HARO

C H A P T E R   T W O

TORT LAW

"We live in a society that demands excessive compensation for every loss, pain, and inconvenience. My job is to see that they get it."

Melvin Belli,

civil litigation lawyer

COMMON LAW AND TORTS

For many years, French was the official language of British courts. While only a few French legal terms remain in use in Canadian common law, one survivor is the word **tort**. The root word is *torquere* which is Latin for "to twist." A tort, then, is:

> *wrongful or injurious misconduct committed by the defendant outside of a contractual obligation, redressable by some appropriate legal action brought by the plaintiff.*

Although there are specific statutes that affect tort law, it is primarily a branch of the common law, evolving slowly over centuries of case law. It has been said that there are an infinite number of torts because there are infinite ways for one person to injure another.

A tort must have four basic characteristics. First, it must cause harm. Second, a tort must be recognized by the law as coming within the broad area of actions for which the injured person should be compensated. For example, at one time the law did not recognize nervous suffering as an injury for which a person could be compensated. As the science of psychiatry developed, tort law changed with it, and today, a person can sue for nervous suffering.

Third, to constitute a tort, the actions of the defendant must violate a duty owing to the injured person. It must be shown that the defendant did not have a right to do what was done and that the plaintiff has a right to redress.

Fourth, in order for the plaintiff to commence an action in tort, there must be no specific remedy provided by statute. If there is an established system to deal with the problem, no action lies in tort. Thus, in *Bhadauria v. Seneca College* (Supreme Court of Canada, 1981) it was held that "discrimination" is not a tort because there are specific provincial laws to deal with allegations of discrimination.

Some torts are intentional, others are unintentional. It is generally understood that tort law is not concerned with the intent or motive of the defendant but with the defendant's actions. This is true for most torts, but not all, since some torts contain an element of malice or deliberate intent to injure the plaintiff.

Tort law basically serves four purposes: justice, compensation, appeasement, and deterrence. The plaintiff wants justice done, compensation for a loss, a soothing of hurt feelings, and a warning to the defendant and others not to do the same thing again. Tort law encompasses the doctrine *ubi jus ibi remedium,* which means "Where there is a right, there is a remedy."

Certain types of statutes have reduced the importance of tort law. For example, in all Canadian provinces there is legislation to provide for universal coverage of injured workers, thus prohibiting any private lawsuits.

A wrongful act may be both a tort and a crime. If Green assaults Brown, Green may be prosecuted in criminal court and sued in civil court.

LIABILITY FOR TORTS

Tort law does not apply the same rules of mental capacity as does criminal law. A bad intention does not necessarily make damages actionable and a good intention is not necessarily a defence. Children may commit torts under many circumstances and mentally disturbed people can commit unintentional torts.

A corporation can sue and be sued in its own name because a corporation is regarded as an artificial person with its own legal entity. Principals are liable for the torts committed by their agents in the course of their duties and employers are liable for torts committed by their employees within the scope of employment. In such situations, the injured party would sue both the employer and the employee. Partners are liable for the torts committed by other partners within the scope of the business partnership.

The Crown is liable in tort for actions committed by an employee of the Crown if the tort is committed by the employee while he or she is carrying out official duties. For example, if a federal officer were to commit assault and battery while questioning a suspect, the Crown would be civilly liable for the officer's actions.

INTENTIONAL INTERFERENCE

The common law has long held that individuals should be free to conduct their daily affairs free from threats, injury, or confinement by others. It is a rule that is deeply rooted in our legal system, predating some of the earliest written laws.

ASSAULT AND BATTERY

Although the words *assault* and *battery* are often used interchangeably, they are two distinct torts. **Assault** represents the threat by one person to commit bodily harm to another person, with the reasonable belief by the other person that the wrongdoer has the present ability to carry out the threat.

It is said that "Assault takes place in the mind of the victim." This means that assault occurs if the victim feels mental apprehension, whether or not the aggressor has any intention of carrying out the threat. Thus, if Green points an empty gun at Brown and threatens to shoot Brown, this is assault because Brown does not know that the gun is unloaded and believes that the threat is real.

Battery involves the application of violence against the victim by the aggressor. The violence does not have to be major or cause pain or harm. The slightest touching of a person can be battery, unless it is accidental. Assault and battery are intentional torts.

A form of battery with major legal implications is medical battery. A physician who treats a patient or performs an operation must first obtain the consent of the patient. Consent requires that the patient be fully informed of the nature of the procedure, the risks, and the alternatives. Often a printed form is used for this purpose. However, the form does not excuse negligence, no matter how it is worded. If the patient is unconscious, the doctor may apply procedures necessary to protect life and safety, but no more. Any further treatment must be postponed until the patient can give consent. In a medical battery case, the patient is not complaining about the adequacy of the treatment, but about the fact that it was done at all.

MALETTE v. SHULMAN

Ontario, 1990

The plaintiff was taken to a hospital after an automobile accident that killed her husband. She had abdominal injuries and was vomiting blood. The defendant, the emergency doctor that evening, concluded that the plaintiff was suffering incipient shock cause by blood loss. Immediate treatment was intravenous glucose and a clear volume expander. No blood was given at this time.

A nurse found a card in the plaintiff's purse which stated that the plaintiff, a Jehovah's Witness, declined the transfusion of any blood products and that the cardholder fully realized the implications of this position.

The plaintiff's daughter arrived at the hospital but refused to sign any authorization for a blood transfusion. She confirmed that the card in her mother's purse was current and represented her mother's true wishes. The defendant asked her: "Don't you care if your mother dies? You will be responsible. I am responsible and I will give blood." Blood was transfused. The plaintiff recovered and sued for battery.

The Court noted that it is not battery for a doctor to perform emergency treatment without the consent of a patient who is incapable of giving consent. However, the plaintiff's card clearly withheld consent. The trial judge awarded damages of $20 000 to the plaintiff, saying:

> *The right to refuse treatment is an inherent component of the supremacy of the patient's right over his or her own body and that right to refuse treatment is not premised on an understanding of the risk of refusal. However sacred life may be, fair social comment admits that certain aspects of life are properly held to be more important than life itself. Such proud and honourable motivations are long entrenched in society whether it be for patriotism in war, duty by law enforcement officers, protection of the life of a spouse, death before dishonour, or religious martyrdom. Refusal of medical treatment on religious grounds is such a value.*

The Court of Appeal upheld the decision.

FALSE IMPRISONMENT

Although the *Canadian Charter of Rights and Freedoms* makes no specific mention of "liberty," Canadians enjoy a historic right to remain at liberty. **Liberty**, in its purest sense, means freedom to move at will. The unlawful restraint or confinement of a person constitutes the tort of **false imprisonment.**

If someone has voluntarily consented to be restrained, that person cannot later sue. A partial restraint does not constitute imprisonment. For example, if there are two doors leading out of a room and a person blocks one of them, the alleged victim cannot claim to have been imprisoned when it is obvious that person could have left by the other door.

In *Buck v. The Queen* (Federal Court of Appeal, 1987) two RCMP officers "shook down" the appellant in a shopping mall because "he looked like a punk." The officers handcuffed and searched the youth in front of many shoppers. Finding no drugs on the appellant, the officers released him and told him not to hang around the mall. The Court awarded damages of $2500 for false imprisonment.

DISNEY v. TORONTO TRANSIT COMMISSION

Ontario, 1991

The plaintiff had transferred from one streetcar to another. As he was walking to the back of the car, the driver called to him, asking what kind of pass he had. Disney returned to the front of the car and showed his transfer a second time. When the car approached his stop, the driver refused to open the back door where Disney was waiting to exit. The driver said that the stop was not an official transfer point and therefore Disney could not get off there. The car continued past a second stop and to the TTC barn at the end of the line. Disney lodged a complaint, waiting an hour to see a TTC inspector. He also called the police.

The inspector refused to make any apology and the police declined to make it a police matter. Disney was driven home by the police. He sued for false imprisonment. The Court awarded damages for false imprisonment and emotional upset. The burden was on the defendant to show why the plaintiff had been detained on the streetcar, but the defendant did not call the driver as a witness and offered no evidence.

DEFENCES TO ASSAULT, BATTERY, AND FALSE IMPRISONMENT

A defendant may raise several defences to an action for assault, battery, or false imprisonment. One defence is consent. If the plaintiff consented to the action, there can be no liability upon the defendant. The consent must have been a truly informed consent, which means that the plaintiff fully understood what would take place. Consent obtained by deceit or duress is not true consent.

Another defence is self-defence, which can be raised as a defence whenever a defendant uses force to ward off an attack by the plaintiff upon the defendant or another person. A parent or teacher is authorized by the criminal law to use force upon a child or pupil by way of correction, as long as the force is not excessive. Force may also be used to protect the child from attack.

It is also a defence to show that the touching was unintentional, such as accidental bumping. Provocation is not a defence, but if the court finds that there was provocation, it is likely to reduce the damages.

DEFAMATION OF CHARACTER

An action for defamation offers the injured person legal remedies for injury to reputation. Defaming a person can remove the esteem that other people hold for that person. It may cause personal injury and damage to professional standing. Defamation is not a tort because it hurts self-respect, pride, or feelings, but rather because the person's status in the community has been hurt.

Defamation can be committed by various methods. Generally, tort law tries to divide defamation into two categories, libel and slander. **Libel** includes statements that are printed, written, filmed, or recorded in a permanent manner. **Slander** includes oral statements only.

Libel is far more serious than slander and the amounts of money awarded in libel cases are far greater than in slander cases. The general reason is that libel endures longer than slander and reaches a much larger audience. If it is printed in books, the libel continues as long as the books survive.

SLANDER

To sue for slander, the plaintiff must establish two things: (1) the remarks were made public, and (2) the statements caused harm. A defamatory statement is not slander when it is made by one person to another, in privacy, and in the absence of a third person. The legal requirement is that the slander must escape the privacy of the speaker and listener and reach a third person. The requirement would be met even if the third person was not supposed to hear the words, but did so by accident. For example, if Brown verbally abused Green in what was thought to be a private conversation, it would be slander if another person overheard the words because the walls were thin.

The plaintiff must also show harm. The courts have held that slander must be such that "right-thinking" people in the community might be led to believe it. A suit for slander will fail if it can be shown that no one believed what was said.

Mere name-calling does not qualify as slander. Name-calling is essentially abuse aimed at a person's pride, not at the person's community standing. Much also depends on the tone of voice, the manner of the conversation, and the purpose the speaker had in mind.

Slander may be made by **innuendo**, which is an attempt to defame the person by indirect, subtle, thinly veiled, negative comments. Innuendo may appear harmless on the surface, but the informed listener can infer the intended meaning of the words. For example, if Brown says that Green "should learn to put a straw in his mouth, not his nose," it would be understood by an informed listener that Green is being accused of cocaine use.

In some cases, the nature of the slander is so bad that the plaintiff can succeed without proving harm, because harm would be presumed. Such a statement is referred to as **slander per se** and unquestionably causes injury. The courts have generally recognized as slander per se any statements that a plaintiff commits criminal acts, has a loathsome disease, is professionally dishonest or unfit, or is immoral.

LIBEL

The tort of libel lies in the publication of the defamation in a permanent form. The basic elements of proof are the same as slander, but there are many special rules that may apply.

Although regarded as an intentional tort, libel does not necessarily require that the defendant knowingly set out to injure the plaintiff. If a person publishes what he or she believes to be harmless material and it turns out to be libellous, that person is still responsible. The concept of "intentional" means that the words printed were the words which the defendant intended to be published, even though the intention was not to harm.

Every repetition of a libel is a new libel and every publisher is answerable for publishing the words. One possible exception is where the repetition is so newsworthy that repetition is the "natural and probable consequence" of the original publication. In that case, the original defendant is liable for all of the injury done. For example, when a provincial premier sued the CBC for libel, national newspapers reported the words that the premier claimed were libellous, but only the CBC was the defendant in the case and paid damages. As well, libel cases may be reported in full by law journals.

SWIFT et al. v. *MACLEAN'S* et al.

British Columbia, 1982

Columnist Allan Fotheringham wrote in his magazine column that two Vancouver lawyers were rising in the pecking order of Vancouver law firms and had been "cementing their connections through the lawn tennis circuits and wife-swapping brigades." Fotheringham later apologized and said the column was meant to be humorous. The column did not say that the two plaintiffs or their wives were actually engaged in wife-swapping, but were achieving success in a system in which such a practice existed. The Court awarded damages to the plaintiffs, saying:

> *The defendants clearly admit there is no truth to the allegation, and in fact it is clear from the evidence that both the plaintiffs are happily married with young families and have not wife-swapped nor associated with, or even know, wife-swappers. To insinuate the plaintiffs and their wives were capable of such immorality, or of associating with such people for the purpose of advancing professionally, goes too far and is unacceptable.*

The law does not recognize group defamation; at most, it protects the members of a group as individuals. Each group member must prove that the defamation was aimed at him or her individually. Usually, the group must be small, such as the members of a city council or a sports team. However, in *Alberta Union of Provincial Employees v.* Edmonton Sun (Alberta, 1987) an action was brought by 200 correctional officers and guards against the defendant newspaper, which referred to them as "goons ... a joke ... yo-yo's ... who haven't the brains to be Nazis, the discipline to be jackboots or the mentality to endorse either."

The defendant argued that it was not referring to all the guards, just a few. The Court rejected this defence and awarded damages to all 200 plaintiffs because the words conveyed the meaning that the article was directed at all of them.

The law does not recognize defamation of a deceased person as actionable. Unfortunate as this may be for the reputation of a deceased person who cannot defend his or her name, the basic obstacle is that a deceased person is no longer a "person" and has no legal standing. Relatives of the deceased can bring an action only if their personal reputations also suffer.

DEFENCES AGAINST DEFAMATION ACTIONS

Under the common law, a variety of defences can be raised against a libel or slander action. These include truth, privilege, and fair comment.

TRUTH

The court will not defend the reputation of a person who does not deserve such protection. It is an old legal adage that "The court will not protect the honour of a thief or the virtue of an adulterer." If the defendant can prove that the statements made are true, the plaintiff will fail.

Proving the truthfulness of a statement requires that each and every element be proven. To prove that a person is a thief requires evidence that he or she stole something.

PRIVILEGE

There are situations that allow a person to speak or write without fear of civil action. **Privilege** affords immunity from lawsuit. There are two types of privilege: absolute privilege and qualified privilege.

An example of **absolute privilege** is what is said inside the Parliament and legislative buildings during parliamentary proceedings. It is felt that the free functioning of government must not be limited in any way. However, a member of Parliament does not have absolute privilege outside the House.

The record of judicial proceedings cannot be actionable in a tort suit. All court members and all witnesses are free to speak openly. A lawyer enjoys privilege with a client, as do husband and wife. Their conversations are privileged and cannot be divulged in a defamation suit.

Qualified privilege means that people who, because of the nature of their duties are required to comment about others, may do so without action being brought against them, as long as their comments are fair and not malicious attempts to injure someone. Employers write evaluations of employees and teachers write evaluations of students. These reports can be critical, as long as they are objective.

In *Strutt v. Ahmed and Samuel* (Saskatchewan, 1987) two psychiatrists complained to the Mental Health Association that the plaintiff, the director of the psychology centre, had been negligent in allowing a dangerous, disturbed patient to escape, by overruling the doctors who wanted to commit the patient. The defendants argued that they believed their views were correct, that a serious problem existed, and that the Association had a duty to receive the information. The Court agreed and said the doctors were protected by qualified privilege.

FAIR COMMENT

The most controversial defence to defamation is **fair comment**, the main principles of which are:

1. The comment must be on a matter of public interest.
2. The comment must be based on fact.
3. The comment, although it can include inferences of fact, must be recognizable as comment.
4. The comment must satisfy the following objective test: Could any person honestly express that opinion on the proven facts?
5. Even though the comment satisfies the objective test, the defence can be defeated if the plaintiff was motivated by malice.

The news media have a duty to comment upon matters of public interest. The comments may be sharply critical, as long as they are fair-minded. The Canadian political system encourages citizens to criticize, believing that open discussion is a healthy part of democracy. The same attitude applies to art, literature, drama, and sports. A critic or an ordinary individual may give an honest opinion that is very negative, even though it may have an adverse effect upon others. However, comparisons with odious individuals or organizations should be avoided, as the following case illustrates.

CHRISTIE v. GEIGER AND *EDMONTON SUN*

Alberta, 1986

The plaintiff was the leader of a western separatist group. An article published in the defendant newspaper, written by the defendant Geiger, discussed the group and the media coverage of its activities. The article stated that the members of the media made it appear that Western separatism was widespread when in reality it was very small. The writer used language that was very strident and controversial. Part of the article read:

> So Doug Christie and his group of misfits known collectively as Western Canada Concept (WCC) plan to run a candidate in Olds-Didsbury once a provincial by-election is called. There could not be better news for Canadians who want to rid themselves of this collection of throwbacks.
>
> For close to a year we have seen publications like *Alberta Report* give these losers some credibility; they have actually taken seriously the right-wing rantings of WCC's Christie and West-Fed's Elmer Knutson. They made it appear that Western separatism was fairly widespread—when in reality it is just an Alberta version of the Ku Klux Klan.
>
> If Doug and his WCC slugs attract any votes at all in Olds-Didsbury it will be from the lunatic fringe and perhaps a couple of farmers who have spent too many summer days in the hot Alberta sun. Separation in Alberta was never a mass movement. It just made for good conversation at business luncheons.

At trial the Court found that the defendants had committed libel, in that the statement linked the plaintiff to the racist and anti-Catholic pursuits of the Ku Klux Klan and was neither true nor fair comment upon a fact. The defendants appealed. The Court of Appeal upheld the decision of the lower Court. The defence of truth failed on the basis of evidence at trial that was accepted as showing the plaintiff's ideals were free of racial invective. Hence, the statement could not be true.

The defence of fair comment on fact also failed. The trial judge had not failed to delineate between fact or comment on fact, as evidenced by his comments that fair comment must be based on fact. The onus is on the person raising the defence of fair comment to establish that the underlying facts are true and that the comment is objectively fair. The published statement did not meet this test.

A fair comment may be exaggerated, obstinate, or prejudiced. As long as it is honestly held and based on fact, it is not libel. In the preceding case, the writer attempted to use a metaphor for the purpose of comparison. However, the writer was careless in not making this clear to the reader. The article flatly asserted that the WCC is the Alberta version of the Ku Klux Klan, and the reader would assume that it had the same ideals and policies.

The trial judge should explain to the members of the jury that they should not consider whether they agree with what was written. The proper test is to ask whether a fair-minded person, holding strong views, could have made this comment. If the answer is yes, then the defendant is protected by the defence of fair comment.

Newspapers publish "Letters to the Editor," which are written by people who do not bother to study libel law before attacking individuals and policies that they dislike. The liability of newspapers in this regard is a matter of considerable concern to editors. In *Cherneskey v. Armadale Publishers* (Supreme Court of Canada, 1978) two law students wrote a letter to the editor of the Saskatoon *Star-Phoenix*. The letter accused city alderman Morris Cherneskey of having a racist attitude. Cherneskey sued, but when the case came to trial the two students were not available as witnesses. The newspaper defended the case alone. The editor testified that he thought the letter was wrong, but he printed it because his newspaper wants to represent all points of view. The Supreme Court of Canada held that the newspaper was liable for defamation because there was no evidence before the Court that the two students honestly believed what they wrote.

Concern over the *Cherneskey* case caused the Ontario legislature to amend its *Libel and Slander Act* to protect newspapers. A newspaper may print a letter to the editor if the letter contains views that a person could honestly hold. The newspaper does not have to produce the writer of the letter in court.

INVASION OF PRIVACY

Historically, **invasion of privacy** has had almost no recognition in Canadian law. The problem is that privacy is unknown in the common law and most legislatures have not filled the gap. The problem is typified by the case of *Motherwell v. Motherwell* (Alberta, 1976) in which the Court held that persistent harassment of the plaintiffs by as many as 60 phone calls in one day, over a period of years, was not invasion of privacy. The Court concluded that the problem could be dealt with as a private nuisance but not as invasion of privacy. There are two general areas involving matters of privacy:

1. The government collecting and abusing information about individuals;
2. Individuals invading the privacy of other individuals.

Different statutes have been enacted in the first category but very little exists in the second.

Under the federal *Privacy Act*, any citizen may learn what information the government has in its computer banks about himself or herself. Forms and instructions for making an application for complete information are available at public libraries.

Ontario has two privacy laws. One provides for freedom of information and protection of individual privacy as these pertain to government agencies. The second extends the protection to the employees of municipalities and local boards, including school boards. The law limits the personal information that may be kept on file about an individual and guarantees that the individual can have freedom of access to see what is in his or her file.

The most extensive legislation is the British Columbia *Privacy Act*, which states that violating the privacy of another person by eavesdropping or surveillance is a tort. The Act also states that the "unauthorized use of the name or portrait of another person" for advertising is a tort. Thus, in British Columbia, a person actually owns his or her name and likeness.

There is evidence that the courts are willing to accept invasion of privacy as a tort, although grudgingly. In *Saccone v. Orr* (Ontario, 1981) the Court awarded damages to the plaintiff when the defendant tape-recorded a conversation between them without the plaintiff's knowledge. The tape was later played at a city council meeting and was published in a newspaper. The trial judge held that, although there was no libel involved, it was an invasion of privacy.

OCCUPIERS' LIABILITY

The common law originally held that a person entered another person's land at his or her own risk. Gradually, it developed that the occupier of land did owe a duty of care to people who entered. The duty was based primarily upon negligence in not keeping the premises in a proper state of repair.

Having established that a duty could be owed, the courts then developed rules that tried to classify people into categories, according to their purpose and their lawful right to be on the property. This process of classification has been discontinued in some provinces as unworkable. Every province has a law, similar to the Ontario *Occupiers' Liability Act*, which establishes the duty of the occupier toward people who enter his or her property.

PEOPLE ENTERING BY RIGHT

Some people, including the owner, acquire a right to enter property. The public has a right to enter places that are open to the public. Some public servants, such as mail carriers, enter property in the performance of their duties. Many people enter property by right of contract. For example, a person who buys a ticket to a sporting event enters under a contractual right and has a right not to be injured by hidden dangers. Often such tickets contain words that try to limit the liability of the occupier, but these limitations are sometimes rejected by the courts because the holder of the ticket did not see them or agree to them.

WILSON v. BLUE MOUNTAIN RESORTS

Ontario, 1974

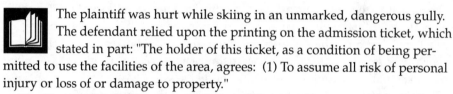

The plaintiff was hurt while skiing in an unmarked, dangerous gully. The defendant relied upon the printing on the admission ticket, which stated in part: "The holder of this ticket, as a condition of being permitted to use the facilities of the area, agrees: (1) To assume all risk of personal injury or loss of or damage to property."

The Court held that the plaintiff did not know that there was such printing on the ticket and that he had not read any such limitation clauses on tickets issued by other ski resorts. The words on the ticket had not been brought to his attention. In such circumstances, the defendant had not contracted out of liability and was liable.

INVITEES

An **invitee** is a person who enters a property for the purpose of conducting business in which the invitee and the occupier have a mutual interest. This category can include a very large number of people such as patients, clients, customers, delivery and service personnel, and many others. The invitee must use the main entrance and has no permission to wander all over the property.

The occupier must use reasonable care to prevent injury from unusual dangers about which he or she knows or ought to know. Ignorance is no defence. The occupier should inspect the property regularly to find dangers before invitees get hurt.

BUEHL v. POLAR STAR ENTERPRISES

Ontario, 1990

Dr. Frederick Buehl and his family rented a room at a fishing lodge operated by the defendant corporation. The building in which they were lodged was still under construction and some features were not yet complete. The room was on the second floor and there was a sliding glass door that was supposed to open onto a balcony, but the balcony had not yet been built. The door opened onto nothing and there was a three-metre drop to a cement patio below.

The defendant's representative told Dr. Buehl about the situation and pointed out that the door was locked. Noting that Dr. and Mrs. Buehl had a small child, he offered them another room. When they declined, he suggested putting furniture in front of the door. The agent was obviously concerned about the child.

It was not the child, but Dr. Buehl, who was killed. He drank to excess and, in what the Court called "a drunken stupor," opened the door and stepped out, falling to his death. The action was brought by his estate.

The Court held the defendant liable, but then held that the deceased was 65 percent responsible for his own death. The burden upon the occupier is to ensure that premises are reasonably safe. An oral warning to a sober person might be adequate, but it had no effect upon a person who later got drunk and did not remember what was said. The Court noted that a physical barricade could have been constructed by the defendant with minimal effort and cost.

GUESTS

People who are invited to enter property as social guests are called **licencees.** The invitation may be extended by the occupier or a member of the occupier's family. The duty of the occupier toward a guest is to warn of unusual dangers of which he or she is aware. The obligation goes no further. Since the obligation is not as great as toward invitees, a plaintiff usually will try to argue that he or she entered the property for a business purpose rather than a social one.

In recent years, the courts have rejected the defence that the occupier was not aware of the danger. An occupier is expected to regularly inspect and maintain the property in good condition. Ignorance of the danger is a defence only where the danger was so concealed that it could not be found by prudent inspection.

SAUVE v. PROVOST

Ontario, 1990

The plaintiff, Eileen Sauve, was visiting her parents, the defendants in the case, at their home. Mrs. Sauve was nine-months pregnant at the time. She left her two young children playing in the yard and went into the kitchen to talk to her mother. She heard one child crying and went through the back door onto a porch. She could not see the child, so she leaned over a porch railing to look around the corner. The railing collapsed, causing the plaintiff to fall 1.5 m to a sidewalk below. The plaintiff instinctively used her hands and arms to break the fall. The fetus was not injured but the plaintiff broke both her wrists and forearms. She sued her parents.

The defence argued that the defendants were not aware of any defect in the railing. However, a painter testified that he had told the defendants eight years earlier that the porch was rotting. The defendants had told him to get some wood and make repairs.

The Court held that the provincial *Occupiers' Liability Act* goes beyond the common law duty to warn of dangers about which the occupier knows. It creates a positive duty to inspect the premises on a regular basis to find dangerous conditions. The trial judge awarded damages to the plaintiff, saying:

> *The occupier has to make the premises reasonably safe. It is no longer sufficient for the occupier to plead ignorance of the facts. Homeowners must be taken to know that wood rots.*

TRESPASSERS

A **trespasser** is a person who enters land without the occupier's knowledge or consent and without any colour of right to be there. The term **colour of right** denotes an honest belief in something that, if it actually existed, would legally justify or excuse some action. A person may trespass intentionally or unintentionally. Once the occupier knows a trespasser is on the property, he or she must take action to remove the trespasser. If no action is taken, the trespasser may become a licencee since he or she has the implied permission of the occupier to remain.

The occupier has no duty to warn trespassers about dangers on the property. The occupier cannot set traps for trespassers, however, and cannot alter the property in such a way that unwary trespassers will be likely to suffer injury. Traditionally, the common law held that a trespasser had no claim against the occupier unless the occupier deliberately inflicted injury upon the trespasser. In the following case, the Supreme Court of Canada stunned the legal profession by radically altering the common law.

VEINOT v. KERR-ADDISON MINES

Supreme Court of Canada, 1974

Veinot was riding a snowmobile at night with another snowmobiler. They came to a wide, well-packed road on which they travelled at moderate speed. Veinot, in the lead, struck a rusty pipe stretched across the road at face height. He suffered serious injury. Both machines had their lights on but the pipe had rusted over the years and was a dull colour that was impossible to see at night.

The pipe was part of a gate built by the defendant company in 1950. The road led to a dynamite shed and the gate was built to prevent unauthorized vehicles from using the road.

A company security officer testified that many snowmobilers used the company property for recreation and that no attempt was made to evict them. There were no signs prohibiting snowmobiling.

The legal arguments centred around Veinot's status. The company argued he was a trespasser. Counsel for Veinot argued that he was a licencee because he had an "implied licence" to be on the road since the company had never objected to the presence of snowmobilers.

The Supreme Court of Canada upheld the lower Court's award of damages to Veinot, but surprised both counsel by ruling that Veinot would succeed even if he was trespassing. The Court said:

> *Even if the appellant was a trespasser, his appeal should succeed. His presence on the ploughed road could reasonably have been anticipated and the respondent owed him a duty to treat him with ordinary humanity.*

The Court adopted the "ordinary humanity" rule from a British case. The Court went on to say that liability would be based upon four factors: (1) the likelihood of injury; (2) the character of the intrusion; (3) the nature of the place; and (4) the occupier's knowledge of the trespasser's presence.

The *Veinot* case troubled occupiers of rural land because the presence of snowmobilers and hunters on their land had never represented a legal problem for them in the past. Such invaders might be a nuisance but the occupier did not expect to be sued if a trespasser was injured. It should be kept in mind that the Supreme Court was saying in the *Veinot* decision that trying to place people who enter property into "categories" is not a good system. The law should provide minimum requirements of safety for all people who enter property.

OCCUPIERS' LIABILITY STATUTES

Alberta, British Columbia, and Ontario have adopted the same basic wording as a British statute to eliminate the classification differences between invitee and licencee. Trespassers are still treated in a special manner. The statutes are not identical, but all require the occupier to "take such care as is reasonable to see that persons entering property are reasonably safe" while they are on the property. The word "reasonable" is used repeatedly in the statutes: reasonable care must be taken to make property reasonably safe.

In response to farmers' concerns, the Ontario law specifically excludes certain people from having any claim upon the occupier, including people who:

1. Willingly assume an identifiable risk;
2. Enter for criminal purposes;
3. Enter rural land for recreation without paying a fee;
4. Trespass where entry is prohibited under the *Trespass to Property Act*.

The wording of the Ontario statute has been interpreted by the Supreme Court of Canada to limit the defences which the occupier may raise.

MALCOLM v. WALDICK

Supreme Court of Canada, 1991

The plaintiff was visiting his sister, the defendant. It was a winter day and the access road and parking area near the defendant's farmhouse were ice-covered. The plaintiff left the house and went to his parked car to get some cigarettes he had purchased for his sister. When he did not return, the defendant went to look for him and found him lying unconscious near his car. He had slipped and fallen on the ice, fracturing his skull.

The plaintiff sued under the *Occupiers' Liability Act*. The parking area is a widening of the laneway with enough space to park three cars. The defendant did not salt or sand this area. The statute requires an occupier to "take such care as in the circumstances of the case is reasonable to see that persons entering the premises are reasonably safe."

The defendant argued that people who live in the country do not salt or sand lanes or parking areas because they are too extensive and rural people are accustomed to living with snow and ice. The defendant also argued that the plaintiff must have been running and injured himself by his careless actions.

The Ontario Court of Appeal held the defendant liable and the case reached the Supreme Court of Canada, which upheld the lower Court. The Court ruled that the statute incorporates the common law doctrine of voluntary assumption of risk. The occupier who knows of a dangerous condition must protect all visitors who enter the property from that risk. The occupier cannot argue that the injured plaintiff voluntarily accepted the risk unless the plaintiff knew of the risk and waived the right to take legal action against the occupier.

The Court held that the statute establishes one standard upon the defendant, not a set of standards that varies with the characteristics of the premises being occupied. The same standard applies to rural occupiers as applies to urban occupiers.

Although the decision specifically involved only the Ontario statute, the statutes of Manitoba, Alberta, and Saskatchewan have very similar wording.

SPECIAL STATUS OF CHILDREN

The problem of trespass by children is a common one. Children do not appreciate dangers or property rights as adults do. Children are curious, adventurous, and brazen at times. They will climb over or squeeze under the most formidable obstacles to reach what they want.

A child can be a trespasser, but society expects adults to make up for children's lack of experience and foresight. As well, some provinces have special sections in their property laws dealing with children. For example, Alberta law requires that if the occupier knows or has reason to know that a child is trespassing, and that there is a danger to that child, the occupier has a duty to see that the child is reasonably safe from that danger.

A special rule of law may change a child trespasser into an implied licencee. The rule is called **allurement** and basically holds that if a child was lured into danger the child is not at fault for the injury he or she suffers. Water is an allurement, so swimming pools must be fenced.

HOULE v. CALGARY and CANADA SAFEWAY

Alberta, 1983

The plaintiff, an eight-year-old boy, climbed over a fence surrounding a power transformer substation owned by the defendant city, situated on the property of the Canada Safeway store, and received severe electrical burns that resulted in the amputation of his left arm below the elbow. The plaintiff had climbed over the fence to retrieve a ball that had gone inside the enclosure.

The substation was old and did not meet the standards of modern installations, although it met the standards in effect when it was built. The transformer was surrounded by a low, wooden fence that was not difficult for children to climb. The plaintiff had been helped over by his older brother. Other children testified about how easy it was to climb over the fence. There were signs on the fence reading: "Danger: High Voltage" and "Danger: 13 200 V." It was agreed that the boy understood the word "Danger" but did not know what a volt was and did not understand the nature of the danger. The plaintiff's mother testified that she had told him not to climb over the fence but had never explained to him what was dangerous.

The provincial statute requires the occupier to take such care as is reasonable if the occupier knows that a child trespasser is on the property. The defendant argued that the child was a trespasser, but the defendant had no knowledge that he was there. The Court held in favour of the plaintiff, saying:

> *Considering the fact that this installation was located in an area where children were bound to play and considering the fact that the structure was such that play objects often entered, the structure was not sufficiently safe and did constitute a hazard in the manner that it was maintained. It is apparent that the structure was too easy to enter.*

PRIVATE AND PUBLIC NUISANCE

Nuisance can be divided into two categories: public nuisance and private nuisance. A **public nuisance** is one that annoys the general public and as such must be dealt with by government authorities. Only Parliament can prohibit a criminal public nuisance that endangers the "lives, safety, or health of the public." If a nuisance is a public nuisance, no private lawsuit by a plaintiff is permissible. A citizen can initiate an action only if it can be demonstrated that the citizen suffered a separate and special damage, distinct from that suffered by the general public.

In *Hickey v. Electric Reduction Co.* (Newfoundland, 1972) a group of fishermen sued the defendant company for polluting Placentia Bay and thereby destroying their livelihood. The case was dismissed because the plaintiffs' damage was not unique from that of other people using the bay. The Court held that the matter was a public nuisance, not a private nuisance.

A **private nuisance** may be committed in one of two ways. The first is conduct by the defendant that results in physical damage to the land of the plaintiff as an indirect consequence of what is done on the land of the defendant. The second is conduct that causes inconvenience to the plaintiff, making it impossible for the plaintiff to enjoy his or her land. The forms of nuisance are infinite and include an assortment of activities and substances, including noise, smell, smoke, water, dirt, dust, chemicals, vibrations, radio transmissions, and so on.

Nuisance complaints centre around land. The plaintiff is entitled to the quiet enjoyment of his or her land and the defendant is entitled to the reasonable use of his or her land. The courts try to mediate between the two entitlements. It is important to realize that it is not correct for a defendant to say, "It's my land. I can do anything I want on it." The common law has long recognized that the occupier of land must make reasonable use of the land. There is no right to annoy others.

CHU v. DAWSON

British Columbia, 1985

The appellants bought a serviced lot from the District of North York. The lot sloped away at the rear extremity, ending at a cliff 70 m high. At the bottom of the cliff were homes belonging to other residents, including the respondents. The appellants levelled their lot by adding fill. They then installed a swimming pool and added more fill.

A heavy rain saturated the fill. This water was joined by water from a storm sewer that backed up and overflowed onto the appellants' lot. Eventually, the earth became so water-logged that the entire bank, composed of fill and part of the cliff, fell upon the homes below. The Court found that the fill constituted a hazard endangering the stability of the cliff, resulting in a mud slide that was an invasion of the neighbours' right of quiet enjoyment of the adjacent lands.

In a nuisance action, the plaintiff does not have to prove negligence or illegality on the part of the defendant. The defendant may be carrying out an activity very carefully and it may be quite legal. It may still be a nuisance.

There are a number of defences that the court may consider. The defendant may show that the land is being used reasonably and that the plaintiff is overly sensitive. If the activity has been going on for a very long time, it is improbable that the court will stop it, unless changed circumstances can be shown. An action specifically sanctioned by law that provides a public good can seldom be stopped by nuisance action. For example, a person who lives next to a train track may not bring an action demanding that no trains run at night.

SCHENCK v. THE QUEEN

Supreme Court of Canada, 1987

Schenck sued the Government of Ontario for the destruction of his peach trees. The trees died because salt spray from an adjacent highway was constantly drifting into Schenck's orchards.

The Supreme Court upheld a decision of the lower courts to award damages to Schenck for nuisance. The Government of Ontario could not prove that the use of salt was necessary for safe highway travel. Evidence at trial indicated that there are non-harmful substances that can be used on highways, but that salt is cheaper.

The plaintiff in a nuisance case may request a number of remedies. The first is an **injunction**, which is a court order directing the defendant to cease and desist from creating the nuisance. The plaintiff may also be awarded damages. If the nuisance continues, the plaintiff may sue again. The payment of damages is not licence to continue the nuisance.

A person adversely affected by a nuisance must attempt to limit the effects of the nuisance. The plaintiff must do everything reasonable to minimize the damage. This action is called **abatement.** For example, if the defendant causes water to flow from the upper floor of a building to a lower floor, the plaintiff must try to protect his or her property from the water to the extent possible. The plaintiff cannot stand idly by and cannot do anything to make the damage worse.

The growth of urban centres into rural areas has caused some legal problems involving farmers. When housing projects are constructed in rural areas, the homeowners discover that the scenic surrounding farms often come with noises and smells. In a New Brunswick decision, a court ordered a pig farmer to spend

$85 000 to store pig manure so the smell of pigs would go no farther than 100 m from his barn. The common law has long recognized the principle of **prescription**, suggesting that if an activity is common to an industry and has gone on for a long time in a certain area, then it is assumed that those in the area accept its presence. It is when new settlements come into existence that the problems begin and the courts have not applied the rule of prescription very firmly. The courts today tend to follow more the principle of "reasonable use."

DAMAGE BY ANIMALS

Society is much less agrarian today than it was 50 years ago. Therefore, the number of cases involving damage caused by horses and cattle is decreasing. At the same time, the number of cases involving pets owned by city dwellers is increasing. It is estimated that nearly 60 000 Canadians suffer severe dog bites every year. Some dogs can exert 200 kg of pressure per square centimetre upon human flesh and bones.

WILD ANIMALS

The law divides animals into one of two categories: wild by nature or domesticated by nature. If a person owns or keeps a wild animal, that person must control the animal to a very high degree and will be held strictly liable if it injures someone. Such animals include lions, tigers, bears, elephants, large monkeys, ferrets, and many others. It is the duty of the owner to prevent any type of injury by the animal, even if the owner believes that the animal is harmless. Injury by an animal may include an attack, fright, or a fall in the process of trying to escape the animal. In an early British case the judge awarded damages to a person frightened by a wild animal, saying, "If a person wakes up and finds an escaped tiger on his bed and suffers a heart attack, it would be nothing to point out that the intentions of the tiger were quite amiable." The owner of a wild animal may escape liability by showing any of the following:

1. Consent of the victim;
2. Contributory negligence by teasing the animal;
3. An act over which the owner had no control, such as a vandal opening a cage door;
4. An act of God, such as a landslide that derails a circus train and releases the animals.

DOMESTICATED ANIMALS

Traditionally, the common law held that "a dog is entitled to the first bite." This rule meant that a dog owner could not be liable for injury caused by a dog until the second time the dog bit someone. The logic of the rule was that, until a dog had bitten the first victim, the dog owner did not know the dog was likely to bite and therefore could not be prepared to prevent it. The rule was called **scienter** which meant that the owner was liable only if he or she had constructive notice or strong reason to believe that the dog was dangerous.

The rule was never uniformly applied and dog owners were often sued the first time their dogs bit people. If a dog had snarled and snapped at people before actually biting someone, this satisfied the court that the dog owner should be liable.

The recent tendency to breed dogs that are perceived to be dangerous has caused some provinces to make laws tougher. Manitoba, Ontario, and Newfoundland have imposed strict liability upon dog owners for any injury caused. The plaintiff need not prove scienter in cases of dog bite. Most provinces have laws that permit the court to order dangerous dogs destroyed.

Injury can also be caused by a playful animal, as the following case illustrates.

PORTER v. JOE

Nova Scotia, 1980

Porter was injured when his motorcycle collided with a black Labrador retriever in a city park. Evidence was that two dogs belonging to Joe were playing in the park in the company of Joe's daughter. The dog did not attack the plaintiff but merely ran in front of his vehicle because it was excited and running about.

The plaintiff introduced evidence that a city by-law prohibited dogs from being in the park unless they were on a leash.

The Court awarded damages to the plaintiff but the damages were reduced by 35 percent for contributory negligence because the plaintiff was driving too fast and was not alert. The by-law was held to be irrelevant to a personal injury claim. The by-law was aimed at regulating the use of the park. It did not support any civil action caused by animals.

ANIMAL TRESPASS

If an owner of cattle, sheep, horses, or other farm animals does not erect and maintain proper fences, the owner can be liable for animal trespass if the animals go onto the property of others. No actual damages need be proven. Animal trespass does not extend to dogs and cats in urban areas. Municipal by-laws usually deal with pets running at large. In rural areas, a dog owner can be liable if the dog trespasses and injures or frightens farm animals. Farmers may shoot dogs if they are on the farmer's land and worrying or attacking livestock. However, the farmer cannot shoot all stray dogs on sight.

Animals that escape control and go onto highways may cause accidents when they are struck by motor vehicles. Most provinces have a *Stray Animals Act*, or similar legislation, that requires that animals not be taken onto any road or highway except in the custody of a person competent to control them. A farmer may be liable if fences and gates are not maintained, allowing animals to wander on roads. Any person finding stray animals on his or her land may take them into custody. The farmer is usually not liable if the animal stampeded or jumped a fence out of fear of lightning or some other occurrence.

NON-TORT COMPENSATION

Under the common law, the terms used to describe employer and employee are "master" and "servant." Modern usage, however, avoids these terms because they imply a different type of relationship.

Toward the middle of the nineteenth century, unions began to acquire legal recognition. Laws were passed to limit child and female labour in factories. Courts began to question the assumption that employers owed their employees nothing in the way of safety. In the next half-century, cases established that, by common law, employers had certain duties toward employees. These duties, which still apply today, generally fell into four categories, which required that employers had to:

1. Hire competent co-workers so that injury would not result from the ignorance of an untrained co-worker;
2. Provide a safe place to work;
3. Maintain a safe system of work;
4. Provide proper safety equipment or ensure that workers provided their own and used it.

Employers also have a responsibility to third parties for the torts of their employees that are committed within the scope of employment. This is a form of vicarious liability, which means to be responsible for the torts of another person. For example, in *Hawes v. Ryczko* (British Columbia, 1988) John Ryczko shot and killed Hawes. Ryczko was the president of Greenridge Holdings, which operated a farm. The defendant and the deceased man had a business contract for the sale of hay. They quarreled over the price and Ryczko killed Hawes, whose family brought an action against Ryczko and Greenridge, arguing that the company was liable for the torts of its president. The Court agreed and ruled that the defendant was acting "within the scope of employment" when he shot the victim. The defendant was personally liable and the corporation was vicariously liable.

The desire to compensate injured workers more quickly, and to reduce the number of court cases, caused the provinces to enact workers' compensation schemes, beginning with Ontario's program in 1914. These plans provide insurance to compensate workers with respect to the injury and financial losses which they may incur as a result of occupational injuries. The plans are compulsory and are paid for by employers. The plans also remove the right to sue and replace it with an administrative system that compensates the injured worker.

Removal of the right to sue was not well received by all workers and their families, who argued that the compensation received under provincial plans was inadequate. The right to sue is a constitutional and common law right which, the complainants argued, could not be taken away. However, in 1989, the Supreme Court of Canada ruled that the provincial compensation plans do not violate the constitutional rights of injured workers and the provinces may reasonably limit the right to sue.

Another form of non-tort compensation is no-fault automobile insurance. Quebec and Ontario have such plans. A person injured in a motor vehicle accident does not sue the other party, but looks to his or her own insurance company for compensation. A private lawsuit is permitted only in cases of death or permanent, disabling injury.

BUSINESS TORTS

The conduct of everyday business is governed by various statutes that apply to the actions of businesses toward the consumer. Few laws exist that govern the actions between businesses themselves. Over the years, the courts have established a number of torts which give rise to legal action by one business against another, outside of a contract between the two.

INDUCING BREACH OF CONTRACT

It is an actionable tort for one party to directly or indirectly interfere with the contractual relationship between two other parties for the purpose of persuading one of those parties to break the contract. This is called **inducing breach of contract**. For example, if Green has a recording contract with Brown Studios, and Gold Records urges Green to break the contract and record for them, Brown Studios has a cause of action against Gold Records.

Perhaps the most dramatic case of inducing breach of contract is the U.S. case of *Pennzoil v. Texaco* (Texas, 1988). The plaintiff had entered into a contract to purchase a small oil company, at a very advantageous price. The defendant, learning of the deal, offered the small company a better price, and at the same time urged the small company to ignore its contract with the plaintiff. The small company did so and the defendant acquired the smaller company. The plaintiff sued and, in one of the longest civil jury cases in history, was awarded billions of dollars in damages. The case was made more controversial by the fact that it was heard by a civil jury that had no training in corporate mergers.

INTIMIDATION

The tort of **intimidation** arises if one party makes threats to cause economic injury to compel another person to do some act that results in a loss to that person. In a few cases, threats of personal violence have been involved.

POULIN v. HARAL et al.

Ontario, 1988

The plaintiff acquired a contract to cut logs on timberland. Loggers who normally worked in the area were angered by this contract, believing that "outsiders and non-union scabs" were stealing their jobs. Approximately 40 loggers went to the plaintiff's campsite and threatened the plaintiff and his workers. Some equipment and vehicles were damaged and the plaintiff was physically assaulted.

The workers refused to continue cutting out of fear for their safety and the plaintiff had to abandon the contract. He sued the lumber workers' union and 24 of its members. The Court awarded the plaintiff $75 000 in damages for harassment and interference in a contract.

In *Central Canada Potash Co. Ltd. v. Attorney General for Saskatchewan* (Supreme Court of Canada, 1975) the government of Saskatchewan entered into an agreement with the government of New Mexico to limit the production of potash because the market was glutted and prices were too low. The appellant company sued on the basis that this was economic interference with its contracts with customers and that there was intimidation because the Attorney General of Saskatchewan had threatened the company with severe penalties for non-compliance.

The Supreme Court of Canada ruled that the agreement was *ultra vires* (beyond the power) of Saskatchewan, but that there was no intimidation. The Court said: "It would be unfortunate if it were to be held that a government official, charged with the enforcement of legislation, could be held to be guilty of intimidation."

INJURY TO BUSINESS RELATIONS

A lawful activity may give rise to a civil action, not because of the nature of the activity but because of the effect. If the motive of the action is wrongful, the fact that the action itself is lawful may not afford a defence.

For example, suppose that Green operates a small food store. Brown, offended by something personal about Green, decides to put him out of business. Brown, a wealthy businessperson, opens a food store across the street and sells food at a low price, at times below cost. Within a short time, Green is bankrupt. It is not unlawful for Brown to open a food store, but Green would still have a cause of action against Brown because he opened a store to injure Green, not to go into the food business. Another avenue open to Green would be to request that Brown be prosecuted under the *Combines Act*. This Act is discussed in Chapter 9.

In *Canadian Tire Co. Ltd. v. Desmond* (Ontario, 1972) the plaintiff sued the defendant for injury to business relations because the defendant was picketing one of its stores with a placard saying that he had purchased a defective product from the plaintiff. The Court held that the defendant could carry out his actions if the picketing was peaceful and the words on the placard were true.

Similar actions have been taken by people who purchased used automobiles that turned out to be "lemons." One individual painted the car yellow and lettered all the defects on the side of the car. He parked the car near the auto dealership where prospective customers would see it. The Ontario Court of Appeal held that the action was lawful if the defendant could prove that each and every one of the complaints made was true.

REVIEW: POINTS OF LAW

1. A tort is a civil wrong, committed by one party against another, that does not arise from a contract.
2. A corporation may sue or be sued in its own name.
3. Assault is the threat to harm another person. Battery is the unlawful touching of another person.
4. There are two types of defamation. Slander is oral defamation while libel is written, printed, or recorded.
5. It is a defence against a libel action to show that the words were a fair comment, based on fact, about a matter of public interest.
6. The occupier of land owes a duty to make the premises reasonably safe for all persons who enter.
7. Although a child can be a trespasser, if the child was lured onto the premises by something that attracted the child, the occupier is liable.
8. A property owner can sue for nuisance if his or her land is invaded by smell, smoke, chemicals, noise, and many other types of offensive substances.
9. The owner of a dangerous animal is under a strict liability not to let that animal injure any person.
10. The Supreme Court of Canada has ruled that non-tort compensation plans, such as workers' compensation, are constitutional.
11. It is an actionable tort to persuade a party to breach a valid contract with another party.
12. Intimidating a person so that the person cannot carry out a contract is an actionable tort.

LEGAL BRIEFS

1. The plaintiff, M, sued the defendant, S, for nuisance. Although their properties were not adjacent to one another, they were in close proximity. Unknown to M, S was a beekeeper. When M installed a swimming pool, the

bees from S's honey operation swarmed to M's property to obtain water. The bees stung every member of M's family, including the family dog. As a result, M could not use his pool at all. S defended the case by saying that he made plenty of water available to his bees and could not be responsible for where his bees flew. Who is correct?

2. Whenever Y played the piano and sang, her downstairs neighbour, J, howled like a dog and banged on pots and pans. J said it was his way of telling Y that her singing was so bad it would hurt any poor animal, including him. Can Y take action against J?
3. Rumours circulated for weeks in a community that two city employees frequently drank alcohol on the job. The mayor made a regular appearance on a radio talk show and a caller asked about the rumours and allegations. The mayor would not answer the question. However, the radio host discussed the allegations with the caller. The mayor then broke into the conversation and said: "Look, I think they have cut that out and the matter has been taken care of." The city employees sued for libel. Liability of the mayor?
4. D received a traffic ticket from a police officer. D thought the officer was not well mannered and decided to write a letter to the chief of police to complain. He penned the following: "The officer was rude, officious to the extreme, with threatening overtones. From the beginning, it was obvious the officer was looking for some physical confrontation with me. A uniform does not give the man the right to act as if he were in the Nazi SS. How long does the public have to endure a moron like this before he is told he may be suited for another type of work?" D shows the letter to you before mailing it. He believes that what he wrote is accurate and has a witness who will support what he wrote. Advise D.
5. The plaintiff, R, sued Q, a publisher, for comments made in a book about wealthy Canadians. The book stated that R was so eccentric that she once ordered a uniform for her chauffeur to match the colour of her swimming pool. R denied the entire story as a complete fabrication. Q argued that the story was incorrect, but that it was based upon a normally reliable source, was not made with malice, and even if incorrect caused no injury. Liability of Q?
6. G went to a ski resort to ski. There was no one present to operate the ski lift and no one to take his money. Finally, an employee started the ski lift but declined payment, saying that he was not allowed to collect money. The employee said that G should pay after he finished skiing. G was injured by the T-bar of the ski lift and sued. The defendant argued that because G had not paid to enter, he had no right to sue. The provincial law denies status to any person who engages in non-paying recreational activities. G insisted that he intended to pay later. Who will succeed?

7. P was injured when he fell from a moving train that belonged to the defendant. The defendant kept a pile of sand near the tracks of a siding for use in winter. There was no fence next to the tracks. Children played in the sand, a situation known to employees of the defendant. P was playing in the sand when a freight train backed slowly along the siding. Another boy, Y, jumped on a car and rode it, then jumped off. P tried to copy this but fell under the car. Both of his legs had to be amputated. The plaintiff argued that the pile of sand was a dangerous allurement for children. The defendant argued that P trespassed when he jumped on the moving train. Liability of the railway company?
8. L, an eight-year-old boy, suffered serious injury when he was struck by a baseball. L was playing on a community playground adjacent to a baseball field that was also owned by the community. The baseball field was quite small and the outfield fence was very low. It was common for strong batters to hit home runs over the fence, with the balls landing in the playground area. The practice was for the outfielder to shout a "Heads up" warning to the children, who would then take evasive action to avoid being hit. L did not hear a warning on the day of injury and was hit in the head by a baseball. Is the community liable?

APPLYING THE LAW

McKAY v. CANADIAN PACIFIC LTD.

Manitoba, 1987

The plaintiff frequently took a shortcut to and from his employment by crossing a railway yard that belonged to the defendant. The yard was not fenced, but it was patrolled by CPR police. There was a pedestrian overpass, but the plaintiff saved five minutes by crossing the yard.

On the day of injury the plaintiff was crossing the yard but was stopped by a train that was moving slowly through the yard at 5 km/h. He could have waited until the train passed, but decided to cross by climbing between the cars. He fell off and was run over. Surgeons were forced to amputate both of his legs.

The plaintiff claimed there had been a breach of the federal *Railway Act*, which requires that railway companies erect a fence to a height of three metres around railway yards, unless the company requested and received an exemption. The railway had not applied for an exemption. There was no other evidence that the defendant had been negligent. The plaintiff was relying exclusively upon the failure of the defendant to erect the required fence.

The Court reviewed the case law and concluded that the defendant had a duty to treat all people who enter the property with a reasonable duty of care to make the premises reasonably safe. At the same time, the plaintiff had a duty to refrain from actions that would cause his own injury. As the plaintiff had not acted reasonably, he was not awarded damages. The Court held:

> *Regardless of how an adult plaintiff comes onto the defendant's property, in darkness, as an invitee, a trespasser, or whatever, whether he crosses a barrier or not, or ignores signs, he proceeds totally at his own risk, and at his own peril, if he chooses to climb onto a moving train in an attempt to cross over to the other side to gain a few minutes' time. If, in these circumstances, he loses his footing and falls beneath the train, then he must be found to have totally assumed the risk to himself and cannot succeed in action against the railroad when, for its part, it has done nothing but operate its train in a totally lawful manner and without negligence. There is no doubt the train posed an obvious danger to the plaintiff and as a thinking adult he must have been aware of the danger. He chose to ignore that danger.*

Questions

1. What duty of care does the occupier owe to a person who trespasses?
2. The defendant was clearly violating a law that required a fence around the yard. Why did the Court give no effect to this point?
3. If the train had been moving at high speed and had struck the plaintiff, who did not see it approaching, do you think this would have altered the decision of the Court?
4. Why did the Court finally rule against the plaintiff?

TAIT v. CKNW

British Columbia, 1982

The plaintiff sued the defendant radio station for broadcasting a story that Tait, a lawyer, had been fined $2000 after pleading guilty to a charge of fraud in the handling of a client's trust funds. The news items was broadcast in Vancouver and the Fraser Valley. It was completely false, telephoned to the station by a prankster or someone who had a grudge against the plaintiff.

When the radio station learned what had happened, it broadcast retractions with every news broadcast for the next two days. It also issued news releases advising the public about the mistake and apologizing for the error.

The issue at trial was whether the radio station had taken sufficient action to reduce the harm to nothing and thereby to render itself immune from any damages. The British Columbia *Libel and Slander Act* provides that a broadcaster may reduce the damages it might otherwise have to pay if it can show: (1) the false broadcast was made without malice; (2) the broadcast was made without gross negligence; (3) that a full apology was broadcast; and (4) the apology was broadcast as soon as possible.

The defendants argued that no damages should be assessed against it because it had been thorough in its apology and that there was no malice. The plaintiff argued that the station was grossly negligent in broadcasting the story without making any effort to check its accuracy. As a minimum, the station could have first asked the plaintiff for comment.

The trial judge concluded that malice was not present in the case. However, the plaintiff was a professional person and the libel was extremely serious to a lawyer. Although retractions had been broadcast, there was no way of ever knowing how many people had heard the first news story, but never heard the retractions. The station was grossly negligent in making the broadcast and damages of $17 500 were awarded to the plaintiff.

Questions

1. On what basis did the Court conclude that the radio station was liable?
2. Why was the story so injurious? Is a lawyer's reputation more valuable than that of an ordinary person?
3. If you were the radio station's counsel, what procedures would you suggest it should adopt to prevent future incidents of this type?
4. The defence of fair comment was not raised in the case. Why not?

PRINCIPLES AND CASES

Case 1: Legal Principle

A comment is not protected if it appears to be an allegation of fact. For the defence to hold, the ordinary unprejudiced reader must take the remarks to be a comment based on fact. Thus if the sting of the words complained of do not appear to be comment at all the defence will fail.

Case Facts

The plaintiffs brought a defamation action against the defendant, the mayor of a small city, for statements he made to the CBC. The plaintiffs owned and operated a trailer park that had not been subject to full taxes for water and other services. The town presented the plaintiffs with a large tax bill, which they refused to pay, saying it was a hidden tax upon the tenants of the trailer park. While the plaintiffs were refusing to pay the tax, they increased the rent of the tenants in the trailer park upon the justification that they would eventually be forced to pay the tax. Some tenants paid the increased rent while others protested.

This state of affairs continued for some time. The plaintiffs refused to pay the tax but were collecting increased rents from tenants. The town finally cut off the park's water supply, which caused an uproar among the tenants. The mayor made the following statement to a radio reporter:

> *It is quite obvious that they have no interest in their tenants. A delinquent taxpayer, the first thing you do is cut off his service. He has fooled the city for years and we have made every effort to resolve this matter. Talk about irresponsibility. I would say that's downright crooked to take money from people given to him for this purpose and not paying it.*

The plaintiffs sued, contending that the mayor's statement was defamatory. The defendant relied upon the defence of fair comment. As well, he argued that the expression "crooked" has several possible meanings, not just one.

Possible Decisions

A The plaintiff will succeed because the words "downright crooked" imply criminal conduct, which is defamation per se and not protected by the defence of fair comment.

B The plaintiff will succeed because the mayor made a false statement of fact, not a fair comment upon fact.

C The defendant will succeed because the words "downright crooked" do not imply criminality but are a colloquialism for improper conduct.

D The defendant will succeed because the facts were correct: taxes were collected but never paid to the city. The comments were fair.

Case 2: Legal Principle

A property owner is entitled to the quiet enjoyment of his or her land. His or her neighbour must make reasonable use of his or her land so as not to create a nuisance.

Case Facts

The plaintiff purchased a condominium apartment in a residential-commercial complex in Vancouver. Before buying, she checked with the owner of the building to make certain that none of the commercial operations in the building would bother her. On the ground floor, there were two restaurants but they did not deep-fry food on the premises.

A year later, one restaurant was sold to a new owner who began cooking more food on the premises. He installed a large exhaust fan which ran 18 hours a day, making a humming noise. The fan pushed food odour outside, directly under the plaintiff's balcony. She was subjected to the oppressive odours of deep-frying fat until 2 a.m. every day. She sought an injunction against the defendant restaurant, which counterargued that its activities were licensed, were legal, and did not violate the condominium by-laws. In addition, the defendant contended that the plaintiff knew she had purchased a suite in a mixed residential-commercial building and must accept the normal problems in such a building. The defendant introduced expert evidence to show that it was operating its facilities in a manner normal and consistent with good restaurant practices.

Possible Decisions

A The plaintiff will succeed because the installation of the fan was a changed circumstance from when she bought her suite.

B The plaintiff will succeed because the smell and noise are an unacceptable interference with her enjoyment of her suite.

C The defendant will succeed because a person who purchases in a residential-commercial neighbourhood must accept the smell and noise.

D The defendant will succeed because the plaintiff knew there were restaurants in the building before she bought her suite.

YOU BE THE JUDGE

1. The plaintiff brought an action against a hospital and the resident anaesthetist. The anaesthetist was responsible for the administration of an anaesthetic to the plaintiff during an operation. The defendant saw the plaintiff for the first time just prior to the commencement of the operation. She had been given Valium to relax her. She said, "Please don't touch my left arm. You'll have nothing but trouble there." Apparently, she had previously had difficulty with attempts to find a vein in her left arm. The defendant's response was, "We know what we're doing." To commence the operation, the defendant administered the anaesthetic in the plaintiff's left arm. She did not protest this. During the operation, the needle slipped out of her arm, causing some of the solution to leak into the tissue of the arm. Normally, the only result of this is that the patient has a sore arm for a day. The plaintiff suffered a very unexpected reaction to the solution in her arm. She brought an action for battery. Who would succeed?

2. The 16-year-old plaintiff was on a right of way on a snowmobile when he stopped next to a tower that belonged to the defendant power company. He noted a guy wire that was loose. He touched it and received a severe electrical shock when the guy wire touched the tower. The power company was not aware of the loose wire. It had a program of making regular checks of its towers and the report of the last check, made eight days earlier, listed no defects of the tower. When asked why he touched the guy wire, the plaintiff said he had no reason. He just impulsively grabbed it. A "High Voltage" sign was on the tower and the plaintiff admitted that he saw it. Who would succeed?

3. The plaintiff was scalded by hot water while using the shower in the defendant's hotel. The plaintiff was on a group tour with other senior citizens. She shared the room with another woman, who used the shower first. This woman told the plaintiff that she had trouble adjusting the water temperature and that it definitely seemed too hot. When the plaintiff used the shower, she felt she had adjusted the temperature to a proper level before standing under the water. One minute later, the water suddenly changed to scalding hot, burning the plaintiff so badly she fell and had to be rescued by her roommate. Evidence showed that the hotel water system had a stuck valve. The pressure system operates to keep an even flow of water when water is turned on elsewhere. When someone on the floor below turned on the cold water, this had the effect of cutting off the cold

water in the shower the plaintiff was using. She received hot water only during that period. The defendant argued that the plaintiff had been warned by her roommate that the shower was not working correctly and should not have used it at all. Who would succeed?

4. The plaintiff sued the defendant restaurant for personal injuries resulting from being struck by a waiter/bouncer. The plaintiff entered the restaurant with three companions and misbehaved. They were intoxicated, noisy, and insulted other patrons. The waiter told the four to move to a table away from all other patrons, but the problems persisted. The waiter finally ordered all four to leave the premises and they indicated they would do so. The waiter stood by the door as the four men filed past. The plaintiff was last in line. He stopped and asked, "Why are you kicking us out? Why did we have to move to another table?" The waiter gave no reply. The plaintiff then uttered an obscenity and the waiter punched him so hard that the plaintiff's cheekbone was broken. He lost the sight of his right eye. The action was against the waiter and against the hotel for the battery allegedly committed by its employee. The hotel denied liability, arguing that the waiter had committed the battery as a result of a personal dispute between the two persons, not within the scope of his employment. The hotel produced a copy of strict rules that prohibited any physical altercations with patrons. Problem patrons were to be dealt with by the police. Counsel for the waiter argued that the plaintiff had brought about his own misfortune by his provocation. It was agreed that if the waiter was not liable, the hotel could not be vicariously liable. Who would succeed?

5. The plaintiff brought an action for slander. She had worked for the defendant for a short period of time as a gold jewellry designer. She was very talented but quit her job because the defendant sexually harassed her. She found employment with a different company. The defendant was very angry because he felt the plaintiff had deserted him. The defendant met the plaintiff's new employer at a convention and the conversation turned to the plaintiff. The defendant said, "Well, I'm glad you have her. I couldn't afford to keep her around any longer." The other employer asked what the defendant meant, and the defendant added: "Have you checked your inventory lately?" The plaintiff was fired from her new job and she sued for wrongful dismissal. It was during this case that she learned why she had been fired. She then brought a second lawsuit against the defendant for slander. The defence argued that nothing in the spoken words was defamatory. The plaintiff argued that there was innuendo in the words that suggested she had stolen gold from her employer. Who would succeed?

SCHOOL BUS

C H A P T E R   T H R E E

TORT LAW–NEGLIGENCE

"The rule that you are to love your neighbour becomes, in law, you must not injure your neighbour."

Lord Atkin,
British judge

NATURE OF NEGLIGENCE

Negligence is difficult to consider as just one tort. There are many variations of negligence and each has its own special rules. As one judge said, "Negligence is difficult to define, but easy to recognize." A general definition might read as follows:

> *Negligence consists of doing, or omitting to do, something that a reasonable person would do or not do under the circumstances; failing to exercise a duty of care toward others where a reasonable person could foresee that a neighbour would be injured.*

Negligence involves a number of elements that a plaintiff must prove in order to show that the defendant should be held liable for the plaintiff's injuries. Negligence is an unintentional tort—that is, a person does not set out to be negligent.

REASONABLE PERSON

Perhaps the most enduring aspect of negligence case law is the constant reference to "the reasonable person." The law considers a reasonable person to be one who is thoughtful, acts only after reflective consideration, carefully contemplates the probable results of any action, and avoids any behaviour that might present a danger to others. However, the law does not expect the reasonable person to be a perfect person, realizing that anyone is capable of judgmental errors. The law does not demand perfection.

ELEMENTS OF PROOF

A negligence case requires that certain elements be proven, including duty of care, required standard of care, proximate cause, and foreseeability. They do not have to be considered in any particular order. Not every case contains all of these elements, but in any given case most of them will be found.

DUTY OF CARE

The plaintiff must show that there existed a **duty of care**, recognized by law, governing the conduct of everyone for the protection of the plaintiff and all others.

The term "duty of care" implies that the defendant is in control of his or her actions or that the defendant has assumed control of an article that, from his or her actions or failure to act, could cause injury to someone else. A person who drives a car has a duty of care to other motorists, passengers, pedestrians, and property.

At one time, the common law greatly restricted the concept of duty of care. The earliest cases held that a duty of care could exist only if there was a contract between the two parties. In *Winterbottom v. Wright* (England, 1842) the driver of a stagecoach was injured when a wheel collapsed. He sued the man who had a contract with the coach company to maintain the coaches. The defendant had obviously been derelict in his maintenance duties but the Court denied the plaintiff's claim because there was no contract between the coach driver and the mechanic. The judge commented that the lawsuit was frivolous, because if such suits were accepted, there would be no end to potential liability.

The *Winterbottom* decision was obviously unjust to people who were injured by everything from runaway rail cars to collapsing buildings. Despite its obvious unfairness, it was not until 90 years later that the situation changed.

DONOGHUE v. STEVENSON

England, 1932

The plaintiff, Donoghue, brought an action against Stevenson, a manufacturer of bottled ginger beer. Donoghue became ill after finding the remains of a decomposed snail in the bottom of a bottle of ginger beer that she had just consumed. The plaintiff contended that there was negligence on the part of Stevenson for not having a system of proper inspection of his bottles.

The defendant argued that Donoghue had no cause of action against him because there was no contract between them. The bottle had been purchased by a friend who had given it to Donoghue. The defendant relied upon the principle established in *Winterbottom* that there is no duty of care except that arising out of contract.

The trial judge summarily dismissed the case and Donoghue appealed. The House of Lords reversed the decision, ruling that Donoghue had a proper cause of action, and ordered the case tried. The case was never actually tried because the parties settled out of court. The significance of the case lay in the decision that the plaintiff did have a proper case to be tried. The majority opinion was delivered by Lord Atkin who wrote:

> *A person who engages in the manufacture of articles of food and drink intended for consumption by the public has a duty of care to those whom he intends to consume his products ... The rule that you are to love your neighbour becomes, in law*

you must not injure your neighbour, and the lawyer's question, "Who is my neighbour?" receives a restricted reply. You must take reasonable care to avoid acts or omissions which you can reasonably foresee would be likely to injure your neighbour. Who then, in law, is my neighbour? The answer seems to be—persons who are so closely and directly affected by my act that I ought reasonably to have them in contemplation as being so affected when I am directing my mind to the acts or omissions which are called in question.

The events of this case might seem trivial but the legal issue was of great importance. The "neighbour principle" would henceforth dominate negligence law and extend everyone's potential liability to previously unknown levels. It is to Lord Atkin that the law owes its "reasonable person" rule.

The duty of care principle is not without limits. There are situations in which a person does not owe the injured party any duty and is therefore not liable for those injuries. In *Craven v. Strand Holidays Canada Ltd.* (Ontario, 1981) the plaintiff sued the defendant for injuries suffered in Colombia. The plaintiff booked a tour with the defendant that included transportation. The bus that took the tourist group from the Bogota airport to the hotel was in poor condition, had bald tires, and was driven over bad roads by a maniacal driver who wrecked the bus and injured the passengers. The trial judge held that the defendant owed the plaintiff a duty of care to arrange safe transportation, even in a foreign country. The Court of Appeal overturned that decision and held that the defendant was not negligent for not personally checking out the bus company. The defendant relied upon recommendations by the Director of Tourism of Colombia.

In principle, the defendant does not owe a greater duty of care to a plaintiff with special needs, such as the elderly and disabled, than to any other person.

STRICKLAND v. CITY OF ST. JOHN'S

Newfoundland, 1982

The plaintiff, Mrs. Strickland, brought an action against the city transportation commission, a bus driver, and a motorist. The plaintiff was nearly blind and carried a special bus pass entitling her to ride the bus free of charge. On the back of the pass was a disclaimer clause which purported to relieve the transportation commission of liability in the event of an accident.

The plaintiff boarded a bus at a bus terminal. It was a dark, rainy night and visibility was poor. She showed her pass to the driver and asked to be let off at a hostel operated by the Canadian National Institute for the Blind. The driver was obviously alerted to the fact that the plaintiff was blind or nearly blind. He told her she was on the wrong bus. He said the bus she wanted was on the opposite side of the terminal parking area.

The plaintiff expressed concern about trying to safely reach the other bus and asked the driver, "Will you look out for me?" He replied that he would. She got off the bus and started to cross three lanes of a roadway when she was struck and injured by a car. The driver of the car said he did not hit the plaintiff—she walked into his car. The Court rejected this testimony because of the nature of the plaintiff's injuries.

The Court considered whether there exists a special duty of care toward blind persons. After reviewing a number of cases, the judge concluded that there is not, but then concluded that Mrs. Strickland was a special case. She safely boarded one bus but was put off by the driver who told her to take another bus. She had to cross a dangerous area that would require special care, even for a sighted person. Although the terminal was lighted, it presented a danger. The driver's words of reassurance to her in the form of saying that he would look out for her made the driver responsible to see that she made the trip safely. The judge said:

> *To instruct a partially blind person that she should undertake such a venture and to assure her that a lookout would be maintained would invite the kind of tragedy that in fact occurred.*

Counsel for the city argued that when the plaintiff left the bus she was no longer a passenger and the city no longer had any duty of care toward her. The Court rejected this argument: as she had not completed her journey, she was still a passenger. A passenger who is transferring to another bus is still the responsibility of the bus company.

Liability was apportioned at 50 percent against the city and its driver and 50 percent against the motorist. The disclaimer clause on the back of the ticket was of no effect because a blind person could not read it. Nor would it have relieved the city of liability in this particular accident.

A recent development in negligence law, and in particular in relation to the principle of duty of care, has been to hold bar owners liable for accidents caused by customers who drink to excess and then cause vehicle accidents later. Equally damaging have been cases where people have drunk too much in a bar, tried to walk home, and been struck by vehicles when they wandered onto highways. The courts have generally held that a bar owner cannot be absolutely certain of a person's condition when the person enters the bar, but the bar owner cannot sell a disproportionate amount of alcohol to a customer and take no responsibility for what that person does after leaving the bar. The bar owner must make a reasonable effort to determine the physical state of the customer. It is also against provincial liquor laws to serve a person more alcohol if that person is already drunk.

HAGUE v. BILLINGS and SHIP 'N SHORE

Ontario, 1989

The defendant, Kevin Billings, consumed an enormous amount of alcohol during a 10-hour period. He and two companions ingested 50 bottles of beer, a bottle of whiskey, and some marijuana as they cruised the back roads of an Ontario community.

At 9 p.m. they went to a tavern called the Oasis. After drinking one beer each, they were ejected because the owner realized they were drunk. The owner did not call the police. The judge criticized this failure to act but did not find the Oasis owner liable.

The trio then went to the Ship 'N Shore Tavern where Billings drank four beers in the next 90 minutes. The waiter testified that he did not notice that Billings was drunk, but the trial judge rejected this evidence as incredible.

After Billings left the tavern, he drove his car across the centre of the highway and crashed head-on into a car coming from the opposite direction. The driver, Jacqueline Hague, was killed and her daughter was injured. The action was brought against Billings and the tavern. The Court held both defendants liable:

> *If tavern owners are allowed to sell intoxicating beverages they must accept as a price of doing business a duty to attempt to keep the highways free of drunk drivers. The Ship 'N Shore continued to supply alcohol to a grossly intoxicated person.*

It is probable that the rule extends to a person who hosts a private party and either serves the guests too much alcohol or exercises no control over the behaviour of the guests, where that control is possible. The promoter of a dangerous sport also has a duty of care toward those who take part in the sport, as the following case shows.

CROCKER v. SUNDANCE NORTHWEST RESORTS

Supreme Court of Canada, 1988

Several days before a "tube race" took place on a ski hill, the appellant signed an application form and paid a $15 fee to enter the race. The appellant did not read the form or know it was anything other than a registration form. In fact, it contained a disclaimer purporting to release the respondent organizer from "all damages sustained ... claims and demands of any nature." Tube racing involves two-person teams racing down a snow-covered hill on inner tubes from large earth-moving machines.

The appellant was highly intoxicated when he appeared for the race. The respondent was also operating a bar at the top of the hill and the appellant bought more drinks there. The appellant's intoxication was obvious because the race starter questioned whether the appellant should race. The starter suggested strongly that Crocker not race, but did not try to stop him. The appellant broke his neck during the race and was left a quadriplegic. The trial judge awarded him 75 percent of his claim but the Court of Appeal ruled that the appellant caused his own injury. Appeal was made to the Supreme Court of Canada, which restored the trial judge's decision, saying that the respondent owed the appellant a duty of care to take all reasonable steps to prevent him from participating in the sport when it was aware that he was visibly intoxicated.

> *While it may be acceptable for a ski resort to allow or encourage sober, able-bodied individuals to participate in a dangerous recreational activity, it is not acceptable for the resort to open its dangerous competitions to persons who are obviously incapacitated.*

The disclaimer on the application form did not protect the respondent because the appellant did not know it was there. When the appellant accepted the risk of the race, he was sober. When he took part in the race, he was drunk. Even if he had known about the disclaimer, he could not be bound by it in his intoxicated state. The issue was not his mental state when he signed the application, but his mental state when he was injured.

LIABILITY OF GOVERNMENT

Although a government is not exempt from negligence suits, the liability of a government depends upon the nature of the supposed negligence. There is a marked difference between malfeasance and nonfeasance. **Malfeasance** means that something was done, but done in a careless or negligent manner. **Nonfeasance** means that something was not done that should have been done. In both situations, a person may suffer injury, but it is more difficult to sue a government for nonfeasance.

For example, in *Just v. British Columbia* (British Columbia, 1989) the appellant was injured and his daughter killed when a large boulder crashed down a hillside onto their stopped car. The suit contended that the respondent government negligently failed to properly maintain the highway. The Department of Highways used a system of visual inspection that was then followed up by close inspection if dangerous rocks were sighted. Each section of highway was checked several times a year.

The trial judge dismissed the case on the ground that the plaintiff had no basis to challenge the government inspection policy, but the Court of Appeal ordered a new trial. The Court held that the province owes a duty of care to inspect and maintain highways.

Government agencies may be exempt from the application of the traditional tort law duty of care if an explicit statutory exemption exists or if the decision arose as a result of a policy decision. Generally, decisions concerning budgetary allotments for departments should be classed as policy decisions. It is open to a plaintiff to attack the system adopted by the government as not being reasonable.

The liability of a government differs from that of an individual. It is first necessary to examine the statute law to see if the law has imposed a duty upon the government to carry out a certain activity or if the law merely authorizes it. If it is merely authorized, the government may decline to do it at all and normally cannot be held liable for nonfeasance. For example, a city government does not have to operate a fire department. If a person's house burns down, he or she cannot sue the city for not having a fire department. However, if the city creates a fire department, the city could be liable if the fire department is totally inadequate or is negligent in not responding to a fire, etc.

If a government decides to undertake an activity, it must do so reasonably. The government must consider its financial resources and make policies. In the case of inspecting for loose rocks along highways, it would be too expensive to hire hundreds of inspectors to check every metre of highway every day. On the other hand, a policy to check for loose rocks every 10 years would be inadequate. The court cannot impose its own policy, it can consider only whether the existing policy is reasonable. In the *Just* case the trial judge failed to consider the reasonableness of the policy at all.

ROTHFIELD v. MANOLAKOS

Supreme Court of Canada, 1989

The respondent property owner, Manolakos, contracted with Gohmann, who in turn subcontracted with Barber, for the construction of a backyard retaining wall. Neither Gohmann nor Barber were engineers, but both claimed to have experience in building such walls. The respondent later learned that a building permit was required and, even though the work had been started, insisted that Barber obtain one.

Barber went to the city building inspector, Phillips, and showed him a rough drawing of the project. Barber did not tell Phillips that the wall was already half-completed, and that backfilling had begun. Phillips issued the permit based on the drawing. When Phillips came to inspect the project, he expected to see only the preliminary work. To his surprise, the wall was 90 percent completed and it was impossible to inspect the work unless all of the backfill was removed again. Phillips took no action.

The wall soon developed cracks and Manolakos called Phillips to inspect the wall again. Phillips ordered the work stopped and waited 20 days, during which the wall did not deteriorate further. Barber was then allowed to finish backfilling. Several months later, the wall collapsed, damaging the property of Rothfield, who lived at the bottom of the hill.

Manolakos sued Gohmann, Barber, and Phillips and the city. Rothfield sued Manolakos and Manolakos took third party proceedings against the other three defendants.

The trial judge first ruled that Manolakos was fully liable to Rothfield. He then ruled that Gohman and Barber would have to reimburse Manolakos for 60 percent of his liability. Phillips and the city would have to reimburse Manolakos 40 percent of his liability. The Supreme Court of Canada varied this liability to 70 percent and 30 percent, respectively.

The city, once it had made the policy decision to inspect building plans and construction, owed a duty of care to all whom it is reasonable to conclude might be injured by the negligent exercise of those powers. This duty was subject to those limitations arising from the statute bearing on the powers of the inspector. It was not unreasonable for the building inspector to accept a rough drawing and not to require plans by an engineer. The city, nevertheless, must at least examine the specifications.

Manolakos was negligent in not giving the inspector timely notice of the project. However, the inspector had the power to order cessation of the work and whatever corrective measures were necessary to enable him to properly inspect the structure.

The preceding case emphasizes that a government often undertakes a certain type of regulatory activity to protect the public. The public relies upon government officials to carry out such regulations, thoroughly and professionally. Once a building inspector approves the completion of a construction project, it is very difficult for any person to challenge that decision in court. Having approved the project, however, the inspector and the city were liable if the inspection was carried out in a negligent manner.

STANDARD OF CARE

Having established that the defendant owed the plaintiff a duty of care, the court must then examine whether or not the *amount* of care required was met. Negligence can be construed as conduct falling below the **standard of care** a reasonable person would provide under the circumstances.

Precise rules cannot be set down about the amount of care required, because far too many possibilities exist. The facts of the case, the professional training and skill of the defendant, and the legal obligation of the defendant vary from case to case.

At the same time, failure of a person to obey every provision of a statute does not impose automatic liability. If your car was struck by a driver who had no driver's permit, you would still have to prove who was at fault. The fact that the driver had no permit, as required by law, may help your case in proving that the driver was not a skilful driver, but you must still prove that he or she did not drive with the standard of care required of all drivers. Medical cases often afford a good basis for the examination of the rule of standard of care. Patients who have had ill effects from treatment are inclined to sue the doctor for **malpractice.** Such suits raise the question of whether the treatment was approved medical practice or was below the quality of treatment the patient had a right to expect. Malpractice cases can be brought against any professional person, including lawyers, architects, and accountants. The difficulty in such cases is trying to determine what is the proper standard.

The first recorded case of malpractice occurred in 1374 when a surgeon treated an injured hand that later had to be amputated. The Court ruled that the doctor was not liable because he had used "the best of his abilities." This *subjective* standard has gradually given way to an *objective* standard. Generally, a physician is expected to act in the same manner as another physician with comparable professional training, standing, and experience. There is no guarantee of a cure and something more than a mere error of judgment must be proven before a physician is liable for negligence.

If a physician has two treatment choices available and chooses the wrong one, the physician is not negligent just because the other choice was better, as long as both choices were reasonable and had a chance of success. Nor is it relevant for another physician to "second-guess" the defendant by testifying that he or she would have made a different choice. It must be shown that the course of treatment taken should not have been taken at all or that the defendant was totally negligent in diagnosing the nature of the problem.

HAINES v. BELLISIMO

Ontario, 1977

From 1971 to the date of his death, Robert Haines was under the care of the defendant psychiatrist, Dr. Bellisimo. The widow of the deceased alleged negligence on the part of the defendant in failing to take steps to prevent the suicide of her husband.

Robert Haines had a history of mental illness that dated back to his university years in the early 1950s. He later secured employment as a high school teacher and was head of the science department at his school. His earlier problems returned, and he quit teaching.

Haines tried to study accounting but could not concentrate. His behaviour was erratic at times, he suffered manic-depressive moods, and would not take the pills prescribed by Dr. Bellisimo. He finally obtained a job as a grounds keeper at a zoo and seemed to improve. He loved animals and felt less stress.

Then, suddenly, he bought a gun and said he was going to go deer hunting. For a man who loved animals to suddenly decide to become a hunter was inexplicable.

His wife was alarmed and called Dr. Bellisimo, who came to the house. Dr. Bellisimo said if Haines did not surrender the gun he would call the police and have them seize it. After a long argument, Haines gave the defendant the gun. He called the doctor the next day and apologized for the gun incident. Two days after this argument, Haines bought another gun and shot himself to death.

The suit alleged that the doctor was negligent in not recognizing that Robert Haines was suicidal and that he should have committed Haines to a hospital for intensive care. Admission would have presented no difficulty for the defendant.

The suit further alleged that a trained psychiatrist would have known that a patient who loved animals would not take up hunting as a sport. Mrs. Haines further argued that the defendant should have given her detailed instructions about what to watch for in the continued care of her husband.

Dr. Bellisimo testified that he was reluctant to involuntarily commit Haines because this would shatter the trust that Haines had in his doctor. He had to weigh protecting the patient's physical being against destroying the patient's progress with his mental illness. The trial judge rejected the action saying:

> *While there, no doubt, was an element of paranoia in the reaction of Mr. Haines to the threat of calling the police, I am not satisfied that the reaction of this man was totally disproportionate to the facts. The experts agree that there was no impairment of his perception of reality and that he was in no way delusional. He had no previous experience with guns and when he first arrived home on the evening of June 28 he reprimanded his wife for disclosing that he had a gun. It may be that he had not unreasonably concluded that it was illegal to have a loaded weapon in the house. In any event, the prospect of having the police come at the request of his therapist may well have had an unsettling effect on a person in a rational frame of mind ... I accept the evidence that Dr. Bellisimo acted reasonably in the belief that his therapeutic relationship, so important to the continued treatment of Mr. Haines, was intact. I do not consider that Dr. Bellisimo was negligent in failing to give Mrs. Haines more instructions than he did; namely, to call him or the resident psychiatrist should any problem arise.*

In *Riebl v. Hughes* (1977) the Supreme Court of Canada held that it is negligence for a doctor to perform a medical procedure upon a patient without first obtaining the **informed consent** of the patient. Prior to this case, lower courts regarded such a procedure as medical battery, but the Supreme Court ruled that this is a misapplication of the term "battery."

To meet the requirement of informed consent, a physician has a duty to disclose four things to a patient before undertaking any treatment or surgery:

1. The nature of the procedure;
2. The material risks of the procedure itself;
3. Any possible side effects and new problems that might arise;
4. Alternatives.

It is only after receiving this information that a patient can make an intelligent decision about what he or she wants done. The physician does not have to describe every slash and cut of an operation, but must explain its basic nature in terms that the patient can understand. The primary issue of informed consent is that a patient, having all the facts, may decide not to have the operation at all. In *Riebl* the Supreme Court summarized the issue as follows:

> *Merely because medical evidence established the reasonableness of a recommended operation does not mean that a reasonable person in the patient's position would necessarily agree to it, if proper disclosure had been made of the risks attendant upon it, balanced by those against it. A reasonable person in the plaintiff's position would, on a balance of probabilities, have opted against the surgery rather than undergoing it at the particular time.*

Once given, consent can be withdrawn. In *Nightingale v. Kaplovitch* (Ontario, 1989) the Court ruled that if a patient screams and demands that the procedure stop, the patient has withdrawn consent. The plaintiff underwent exploratory surgery of the bowel and suffered so much pain he wanted the procedure stopped. The doctor urged the patient to tolerate the discomfort a little longer as the procedure was nearly finished. The defendant continued, and punctured the bowel. The Court concluded that the injury occurred after consent had been withdrawn and held the doctor liable for negligence.

An issue that has caused much discussion is whether a hospital is vicariously liable for the negligence of a doctor. It is generally agreed that a hospital is liable for negligence on the part of any of its employees, including doctors and nurses. However, many doctors are not direct employees of a hospital. They are independent practitioners who have hospital privileges and are regarded as members of the hospital medical staff.

In 1980 the Ontario Court of Appeal dealt with this sticky problem in the case of *Yepremian v. Scarborough General Hospital.* The plaintiff was taken to the emergency department of the defendant hospital where a doctor on staff, although not an employee, assumed responsibility for his care. The internist who was ultimately assigned to him was in a similar position. The physicians were negligent and the trial judge held the hospital vicariously liable. The judge ruled that a patient expects the hospital to control the quality of medical care within the hospital. It is a duty that cannot be delegated. The Ontario Court of Appeal overturned the trial decision. The majority of the Court found that the hospital had met the required standard of care if the hospital:

> *... has picked its medical staff with great care, has checked out the credentials of every applicant, has caused the existing staff to make a recommendation in every individual case, makes no appointment for longer than one year at a time, and reviews the performance of its staff at regular intervals.*

Before the case could reach the Supreme Court of Canada, the defendants settled out of court with the plaintiff. It was rumoured that the defendants paid the plaintiff more money than the trial judge had initially awarded him. The purpose of this settlement was obvious: having won in the Court of Appeal the defendants wanted the decision to stand. The decision is an important one. By a slim majority, the Ontario Court of Appeal established the principle that a hospital is not responsible in law for the negligence of a doctor who is not employed by the hospital.

A unique question of standard of care arose in 1974 in *Tarasoff v. Regents of the University of California*. The issue was the duty of care and standard of care that a doctor owes to people other than his or her patient. A student at the University of California fell in love with a girl who did not return his affection. As a result, the student became depressed and sought psychiatric help. During therapy, the student revealed his intentions to kill the girl. The psychologist contacted the campus police, who temporarily detained the student, but released him when he promised to stay away from the girl. The psychiatrist in charge of the campus clinic ordered that no action be taken to commit the student. The girl was never warned, and the student killed her with a knife. The Supreme Court of California held that a cause of action existed against the therapist, the clinic, and the police. A duty was imposed on the therapist to take action for the protection of others.

Another area of law where the principle of standard of care is very important is in education. Wherever masses of children congregate, running, shouting, and shoving, accidents will happen. And nowhere do children congregate with other children more than at school. Accidents and their resulting injuries are a constant danger at every school.

The law requires parents to send their children to school. What duty of care and what standard of care does the school owe the parents and children? The primary duty is known as the duty of supervision. It was articulated very well in 1893 in a classic English decision, *Williams v. Eady*. In that case a student was injured when a bottle of phosphorus exploded. In his decision, Lord Esher said:

> *The schoolmaster was bound to take such care of his boys as a careful father would take care of his boys, and there could not be a better definition of the duty of a schoolmaster. Then he was bound to take notice of the ordinary nature of young boys, their tendency to do mischievous acts, and their propensity to meddle with anything that came in their way.*

The **careful parent rule** is often cited in Canadian cases, but it does not form the totality of negligence law in school injuries. Studies of accidents in which the teacher or school board were held liable have found four common failures:

1. Failure to instruct;
2. Failure to supervise;
3. Failure to secure;
4. Failure to employ competent teachers.

Some accidents involve one or more of these failures. For example, a student might be hurt because an unskilled substitute teacher did not explain something properly and then did not supervise the student to prevent injury.

If the teacher is found to have been negligent and was acting within the scope of his or her employment at the time of the injury, the school board will be vicariously liable for the negligence of its employee. School boards are also liable if the board has failed to supply adequate protective equipment or knew about a dangerous situation and failed to correct it. In the following case, many of the omissions mentioned were present in a tragic accident.

JAMES v. RIVER EAST SCHOOL DIVISION 9

Manitoba, 1975

Joni James was an 18-year-old student attending Grade 12. She was a good student, in her second year of chemistry. As part of the laboratory requirements an experiment was conducted to find the atomic weight of tin. James and another student were working alone in the laboratory during the noon hour. As senior students they were permitted to work independently. The experiment was conducted in accordance with the instructions found in the lab manual prescribed by the Manitoba Department of Education, verbal instructions received from the teacher the preceding day, and directions written on the blackboard. There was no evidence to suggest that the students had misbehaved in any way. Goggles were available, but were not required. The lab manual recommended them, but did not state that they must be worn.

The experiment involved the placing of one gram of tin in an evaporating dish. To this was added five millilitres of nitric acid. This produces a reddish gas. The reaction is complete when the gas is no longer visible. The residue was a white, pasty mass. The students were to then heat the mass over a Bunsen burner to create a dry residue for weighing. When the material turned powdery, the heat was to be increased to complete the experiment.

The two students were not getting the intended results and wanted to ask the teacher what was wrong, but the teacher was not available. They increased the heat. The mass suddenly bubbled in the centre, then exploded, causing permanent facial injury to the plaintiff. An expert chemist testified that the written instructions were wrong, badly worded, and filled with danger. It was likely that the instructions would cause the students to super-heat the mass and cause it to explode.

The trial judge held the teacher and school board liable on two of the basic failures: failure to instruct and failure to supervise. The manual and written directions were confusing, and the teacher was not available to answer questions. The students were permitted to work without supervision and were not required to wear goggles, which led them to mistakenly believe there was no danger in what they were doing.

The degree of instruction and supervision required varies considerably from case to case. The teacher should first take into consideration the inherent danger of the activity. The teacher should then consider the age, maturity, and experience of the student. For example, a senior student in his or her fourth year of woodworking could use power tools without supervision. A novice should not be allowed to do so. A teacher cannot closely supervise each student individually. As long as the system of supervision is adequate, there is no liability.

In the following case, failure to provide proper equipment was a major factor.

MYERS v. PEEL COUNTY BOARD OF EDUCATION

Supreme Court of Canada, 1981

The case involved an accident suffered by a 15-year-old boy, Myers, while attempting to dismount from the rings in a gymnastic class at his high school. As part of the physical education program, the plaintiff was in the advanced level of gymnastics. On the day of the accident, 40 students were being supervised by one teacher. Myers and a classmate received permission to go into the exercise room to practise. The teacher stayed in the main gymnasium. There was no supervision in the exercise room.

Myers was working on the rings while his classmate acted as his spotter. The spotter is present to break the fall should the gymnast lose his grip or not exercise a manoeuvre correctly. There were slab mats on the floor below the rings. Myers was a very capable gymnist, who had the potential to become an Olympic athlete. However, he lacked the experience and training to perform complicated feats.

Myers told the spotter he was going to do one more manoeuvre, then dismount. The spotter did not hear this and thought Myers was finished. The spotter walked away while Myers continued his workout. He tried a difficult dismount, which he had never done before, and broke his neck when he fell. He became permanently disabled.

The Court reviewed evidence regarding the mats and found that slab mats are thin and hard. The proper mats for gymnastics are crash mats, which were available but were not being used. The Court found that there was no supervision at all. Further, the preparatory training was not adequate: students were attempting dangerous manoeuvres for which they were not trained. The marking system encouraged them to do so because the more difficult the manoeuvre, the higher the marks awarded.

The Court held the teacher and school board to be 80 percent liable. Myers was held to be 20 percent liable for attempting a dangerous manoeuvre that he knew he was not capable of doing safely.

Injuries during sports activities can form the basis of lawsuits. Schools have generally eliminated such dangerous devices as trampolines, but injuries still occur during contact sports such as football and rugby. Lawsuits against coaches have risen dramatically in the past decade. These suits allege everything from failure to properly instruct how to play the game safely to failure to prevent a player from aggravating an injury. In *Robitaille v. Vancouver Hockey Club Ltd.* (British Columbia, 1980) the plaintiff sued his team manager, coach, and team because of permanent injuries that ended his hockey career. The plaintiff suffered a series of injuries and complained about pain in the neck, arm, and shoulder areas. The team doctor reported that he did not think the injuries were serious and that the plaintiff was a "quitter and a slacker." The plaintiff was kept in the line-up.

After another injury, the plaintiff was told by the team doctor to "go home to bed and have a shot of brandy." The result was permanent disability, for which the defendants were ordered to pay the plaintiff $435 000. The Court ruled that the club owed a duty to its players to protect them from sustaining unnecessary injuries.

PROXIMATE CAUSE AND REMOTENESS

There must be a reasonable relationship between the defendant's conduct and the plaintiff's injury. This relationship is called the **proximate cause**. In some cases, the issue is not whether the defendant committed a certain act, but whether this act caused the bad effect upon the plaintiff.

In some cases it is argued that the defendant set in motion a chain of events which led to the injury. For example, suppose that Brown leaves a door open and her dog runs from the house. The dog runs into the path of a car, causing the driver to swerve and strike Green. It is absurd to say that leaving a door open caused Green's injury. It is not illogical to say that leaving the door open started a chain of events that led to Green's injury.

There is a difference between a *chain* of events and a *series* of events. Just because event C follows event B does not mean that B caused C. It might be a coincidence. For liability to exist, it must be clearly proven that B caused C to happen. The courts sometimes apply the **but-for test**, meaning that the injury would not have happened "but for" the defendant's negligence.

MOORE v. FANNING and ROACH

Ontario, 1987

Roach, a police officer, left his keys in his car when he parked it in a parking lot behind police headquarters. He placed the keys under the floor mat on the driver's side, which he said was a common practice because the lot was small and officers had to park in a manner that often blocked other vehicles. Officers coming off duty would move cars that blocked theirs in order to leave the lot.

Roach's car was stolen by Fanning who then drew attention to himself by running red lights. A police car pursued the stolen car, which then sped up. Fanning deliberately sideswiped a police car and then lost control of the stolen vehicle. He crashed into an oncoming car, killing Yvonne Moore and injuring her husband.

Mr. Moore brought an action against Fanning, Roach, the officers who chased the stolen car, and the municipality. The action against Roach was based upon his act of leaving his keys in his car.

The Court held that Roach was not negligent. His act of leaving his keys in his car did not, in itself, cause it to be stolen or to be driven in a criminally dangerous manner by the thief. Roach's conduct was not the proximate cause of the accident. Fanning was held to be 100 percent liable for the accident.

If the court finds that a chain of events is unbroken and not freakish, liability rests upon the person who started the chain. On the other hand, it is a valid defence to show that another act, separate and distinct, entered the chain at some stage and created a new situation. This is called ***novus actus interveniens*** (an intervening act) that breaks the chain of events, so that the cause is too remote from the effect to be considered negligence by the person who started the chain of events. The intervening act must be the act of another person, not an act of nature. There must be another person to whom liability can be shifted.

CHAPMAN v. HEARSE

Australia, 1961

Chapman drove negligently and collided with a car in front of him. That car turned over and the occupants were trapped inside. Chapman lay unconscious on the highway. Another car stopped and the driver Cherry, a physician, got out and went to attend to Chapman. Hearse came along, also driving negligently, and killed Cherry.

Hearse was sued by Cherry's estate and had large damages levied against him. Hearse in turn sued Chapman for starting the entire accident and thereby putting a chain of events into motion. In law, Hearse alleged that Chapman was a joint tortfeasor and liable for some or all of the damages.

The trial judge held that Chapman should pay 25 percent of the damages Hearse was ordered to pay Cherry's estate. Chapman appealed.

Chapman's case centred on the question of whether there was an intervening act. The death of Cherry, in Chapman's view, was caused by an intervening act. It was not caused as a result of his hitting the car in front of him. Chapman admitted liability to the people he hit, but no further. The Appeal Court upheld the decision against Chapman. In its view the two accidents were not separate accidents, but a chain of events which Chapman had started.

The issue of causation is important in cases where an injured person, in turn, commits suicide because of pain and suffering. This is not an uncommon event, arising primarily after automobile accidents. In *Swami v. Lo* (British Columbia, 1980) the plaintiff, Mrs. Swami, sued the defendant for damages arising from the death of her husband. Mr. Swami had been injured in an automobile accident for which Mr. Lo was found to be liable. Mr. Swami languished for 14 months after the accident in great pain and mental depression because of his inability to engage in any physical activity. Finally, he committed suicide, leaving a note that his condition was intolerable. The plaintiff alleged that the defendant "caused" the death of her husband. The defence argued that suicide was an intervening act.

The Court dismissed the action because it was not shown that suicide was the "natural and probable consequence" of the accident. However, in *Wright v. Davidson* (British Columbia, 1989) Mrs. Wright committed suicide after suffering whiplash in an automobile accident. The Court allowed the action against the defendant because the Court was convinced that Mrs. Wright suffered acute mental depression after the accident and that her suicide was "causally linked to the motor vehicle accident."

FORESEEABILITY

People are obliged to exercise care toward those whom they can reasonably foresee might be injured by their acts or omissions. This was the edict laid down in *Donoghue v. Stevenson* in answer to the rhetorical question: Who is my neighbour?

This does not imply that a defendant knew exactly what would happen or who would be the victim, but only that the defendant could have known that the victim belonged to a class of people whose presence was reasonably foreseeable

In *Hay v. Young* (England, 1943) the plaintiff had just alighted from a bus when a speeding motorcyclist passed on the other side of the bus and collided with a car at an intersection. The cyclist was killed. The plaintiff did not see the crash, but she heard it and instantly knew there must have been an accident. The plaintiff later saw blood on the pavement. She was pregnant at the time and became very ill. One month later, she miscarried. She sued the estate of the deceased cyclist. The House of Lords dismissed the case, ruling that the cyclist could not have foreseen that his dangerous riding would have affected the plaintiff in the manner that it did.

RES IPSA LOQUITUR

The burden of proof in a civil case is normally on the plaintiff, the person who alleges some wrongdoing. In a negligence suit, the plaintiff must prove the defendant was negligent, using the basic elements of proof discussed previously in this chapter. However, it is conceivable that an accident might be completely without explanation. In such a case, the plaintiff may try to rely upon the principle of ***res ipsa loquitur*** (the act speaks for itself).

This principle demonstrates the difficulties that may confront the plaintiff. In certain situations, the plaintiff has no way of proving what the defendant was doing or how the injury occurred. In order for a plaintiff to rely upon the principle of *res ipsa loquitur*, the following requirements must be met:

1. The accident must have been of a kind that does not ordinarily happen unless there has been negligence;
2. The defendant must have been in control of the overall situation or in control of the instrument that caused harm;
3. The exact cause of the injury must be unexplained, because once the specific act or omission has been established, there is no longer need for an inference of causal responsibility.

Basically, the plaintiff is arguing that someone was negligent and all fingers point to the defendant. It is the absence of any reasonable, alternative explanation that establishes liability.

This principle does not establish some form of automatic liability upon the defendant. The defendant can succeed by proving that the injury might reasonably have happened without any negligence on his or her part. The defendant can show what actually happened, offer reasonable alternative explanations, or show that the instrument causing injury was no longer under his or her control. The burden of proof then shifts back to the plaintiff and the case is treated as an ordinary case of negligence.

In *Wylie v. RCA* (Newfoundland, 1973) the purchaser of a new television set sued the manufacturer after the set caught fire and destroyed the plaintiff's home. The Court held that the principle of *res ipsa loquitur* put the burden on the defendant to provide a plausible explanation of the fire that would free it from liability. As the cause of the fire was never learned, the defendant could not meet this requirement and damages were awarded to the plaintiff. The case was criticized by many legal writers as imposing a standard of absolute liability upon the manufacturer. In the absence of any statute that established such a standard of liability, it was arguably wrong for the court to create one.

However, contrast this case with *MacLachlan & Mitchell Homes Ltd. v. Frank's Rental* (Alberta, 1981) in which a rental television set caught fire and damaged a home. The Alberta Court of Appeal held that there was no duty upon Frank's Rental to open and inspect sets unless there was evidence of malfunction. In fact, constantly opening them would increase the likelihood of malfunction.

The Court heard expert evidence from the manufacturer that 150 000 television sets of this model had been sold and that no fires had ever been reported. The case did not properly invoke the principle of *res ipsa loquitur* and the case was dismissed.

CONTRIBUTORY NEGLIGENCE

The principle of **contributory negligence** basically means that the plaintiff's claim may be defeated because of his or her own conduct. A plaintiff who fails to act carefully and neglects his or her own safety cannot blame the defendant for injury. At one time under the common law, if the plaintiff was even the slightest bit responsible for his or her own injury, the plaintiff would receive no damages. The harshness of this rule has been reduced by statutes which permit courts to reduce the damages if the plaintiff contributed to the injury, but not to eliminate the damages entirely. To eliminate the damages totally would be tantamount to holding that the defendant was not liable at all.

In many cases the courts apply the rule of "last opportunity," which holds that blame rests chiefly upon the person who had the last chance to avoid the accident.

HAMEL v. CHARTRE

Supreme Court of Canada, 1975

The action was brought by the widow of the deceased man, as a result of her husband's death by electrocution while engaged in the examination of an electric water pump (sump pump) under the floor of the appellant landlord's house. The pump was improperly wired and the floor was wet. When the deceased man touched it, he received the fatal shock.

The lower courts held the landlord to be 50 percent liable, but the Supreme Court dismissed the action completely. The Court held that the deceased had a general knowledge of pumps and of the fact that there was a short circuit. He should have turned off the electricity before touching the pump. He was the author of his own misfortune.

VOLENTI NON FIT INJURIA

The plaintiff cannot sue for damages in tort if the plaintiff has consented to what happened. The Latin expression ***volenti non fit injuria*** means "no wrong is done to one who consents." The principle means that the plaintiff, having freely entered into a relationship with the defendant and knowing that there might be some risk involved, has agreed not to blame the defendant if he or she suffers from that risk. The plaintiff has personally assumed the risk and has clearly absolved the defendant of liability.

The courts have held that the risk must have been recognizable. A person cannot be said to have consented to a risk if the person did not know the risk was there. As well, if a person accepts a specific risk, the person does not accept all risks. For example if the plaintiff paid a fee to enter a sporting event, the ticket will inevitably contain a disclaimer clause by which the defendant tries to absolve itself of liability from injury. A person who attends a baseball game accepts the risk of being hit by a baseball. However, the person does not accept the risk of being hit by a bat thrown by an angry player at an abusive fan. The risk of being in a hockey arena is to be hit by a puck, but not by a hockey stick when a fight breaks out between two players on the way to the dressing room.

McCARTHY v. ROYAL AMERICAN SHOWS INC.

Manitoba, 1967

The plaintiff, a 16-year-old girl who weighed 81 kg, broke her ankle after sliding down a 12-m steel slide at a fun house. She followed the instructions given to her and stopped herself at the bottom by hitting a rubber pad feet first. Her ankle broke upon impact.

The defendants argued that the slide was safe and had been used by 70 000 people without accident. Engineers who testified for the plaintiff demonstrated that the rubber pad at the bottom was too rigid and hard. The Court rejected the defendant's argument that the plaintiff had used the slide at her own risk. The plaintiff could not have consented to a risk that she did not know about.

A worker who is employed in a dangerous job must accept the risks of the job, sometimes called the hazards of the profession. These risk are well known and unavoidable. However, even a person in a dangerous job can sue for damages. In *Hambley v. Shepley* (Ontario, 1967) the Ontario Court of Appeal held that a police officer could recover personal damages from the defendant who smashed into the officer's car at a roadblock. The officer could not get out of the car in time to avoid being hit. While police work contains numerous risks, the officer had not absolved the defendant of liability and had not forfeited personal rights against the defendant.

A person cannot voluntarily accept a risk that the person is incapable of accepting. For example, suppose that Brown wants to borrow a large truck from Green. The truck is difficult to drive and requires training and experience. Brown has none of these qualifications, and Green knows it. Green cannot lend the truck to Brown simply because Brown agrees to accept the risk.

CLYKE v. CLYKE

Nova Scotia, 1987

The suit arose when Nellie Clyke, driving a rented car, slid on a patch of ice and became stuck in a snow-filled ditch. Aubrey and Carl Clyke (not related to Nellie) stopped to lend assistance, as did a third man. Carl took the wheel while Aubrey and the third man pushed. The rear wheels of the car spun, shooting out a large rock that struck and broke Aubrey's leg. Aubrey Clyke sued Nellie Clyke on the ground that it was her negligent driving that resulted in the car going off the road and leading to the injury. The defence argued that the injuries were voluntarily received.

The Court dismissed the case on the ground that there was no causal connection between Nellie Clyke's driving and Aubrey Clyke's broken leg. The plaintiff voluntarily assumed the risk of injury when he agreed to push the car. The Court also noted that the defendant was no longer in control of the instrument that injured the plaintiff. The plaintiff's brother gunned the motor, which caused the injury.

LIABILITY TO RESCUERS

The situation of an injured rescuer raises special problems in negligence law. If the defendant is negligent and endangers a victim, and a rescuer tries to assist the victim and is injured, then the defendant is liable to both the victim and the rescuer. The plaintiff is often referred to as a **forced rescuer**, a person who has no choice but to act.

Mr. Justice Cardozo of the U.S. Supreme Court once wrote:

> *Danger invites rescue. The cry of distress is the summons to relief. The law does not ignore these reactions ... it recognizes them as normal. The wrong that imperils life is a wrong to the victim; it is also wrong to the rescuer.*

MODDEJONGE v. HURON COUNTY BOARD OF EDUCATION

Ontario, 1972

A teacher who took some students on a field trip allowed the students to go swimming in a lake. Two students were carried into deep water by an undertow. Another student, Geraldine Moddejonge, quickly swam to their assistance. She rescued one of of her classmates but drowned trying to save the second girl, who also drowned. Geraldine's parents sued the teacher and the school board. The Court found the defendants liable. In a decision of unusual eloquence, Mr. Justice Pennell concluded:

> *It was argued that the efforts of Geraldine constituted a rash and futile gesture. The rescue of the first girl is sufficient answer that it was not. To Geraldine, duty did not hug the shore of safety. Duty did not give her a choice. She accepted it, and more need not be said. The law will give her actions a sanctuary.*

If the rescuer attempts a hopeless, dangerous rescue, the defendant will not be liable. If the defendant negligently starts a fire that totally engulfs a building, the defendant will not be liable to a rescuer who recklessly enters the building to rescue a victim who is inside.

RULE OF STRICT LIABILITY

In tort law it is difficult to assign liability to a defendant who did not intend harm or act negligently. The notion that there could be "liability without fault" does not fit comfortably within the common law.

The **rule of strict liability** encompasses the belief that the defendant should be liable because he or she undertook an action so inherently dangerous that the defendant was under the most strict duty not to let damage occur. The person who keeps a wild animal may be liable if the animal escapes, even if the person was not personally negligent in allowing the animal to break loose.

More frequently, strict liability pertains to land and the use of land and, currently, to liability of products of defective manufacture. The following case is a famous one.

RYLANDS v. FLETCHER

England, 1868

Fletcher brought an action against Rylands and Horrocks to recover damages for injury to his mine caused by water flowing into it from a reservoir built by the defendants. The declaration alleged negligence on the part of the defendants.

Fletcher, with the permission of Lord Wilton, the landowner, had a working coal mine on Lord Wilton's property. Rylands and Horrocks owned a nearby mill. With Lord Wilton's permission, they constructed a reservoir to supply water to their mill. They hired competent engineers and contractors to construct the reservoir. They did not know that coal had ever been worked under or near the site. When the reservoir was completed and was partially filled with water, one of the old mine shafts collapsed and allowed water to flow into Fletcher's mine. The question was whether the defendants were liable for damages even though there appeared to be no personal negligence in the manner in which the reservoir had been built. The lower court ruled in favour of the defendants and Fletcher appealed to the House of Lords, which found the defendants liable, saying:

> *We think that the true rule of law is that the person who, for his own purposes, brings on his lands and collects there and keeps there anything likely to do mischief if it escapes, must keep it in at his peril, and, if he does not do so, is* prima facie *answerable for all the damage which is the natural consequence of its escape ... The person whose grass or corn is eaten down by the escaping cattle of his neighbour, or whose mine is flooded by the water from his neighbour's reservoir, or whose cellar is invaded by the filth of his neighbour's privy, or whose habitation is made unhealthy by the fumes and noisome vapours of his neighbour's alkali works, is damnified without fault of his own; and it seems but reasonable and just that the neighbour, who has brought something on his property which was not naturally there, harmless to others so long as it was confined to his own property, but which he knows to be mischievous if it gets on his neighbour's, should be obliged to make good the damage which ensues if he does not succeed in confining it to his own property.*

The case of *Rylands* is unique because it does not really follow the ordinary rules of negligence. A basic interpretation of what the Court said would include these elements:

1. The substance causing harm must be inherently mischievous or dangerous;
2. The defendant must have brought it onto his or her land—it was not there naturally;
3. The defendant must have failed to control it by allowing it to escape and cause damages to the plaintiff on his or her land.

In *Schunicht v. Tiede* (Alberta, 1980) the defendant was spraying a herbicide from his airplane to kill weeds in his crop fields. A light wind blew some of the chemical onto 16 ha of Schunict's adjacent lands. Schunict's alfalfa crop was killed by the chemical and he sued Tiede. The Court concluded that the rule of strict liability should apply and held the defendant liable.

CHILDREN'S TORTS

It is very difficult to apply the principles of negligence to children. A child does not have the maturity to grasp concepts such as reasonableness or duty of care. Most of all, the absence of experience causes children to act in a manner that adults consider dangerous and irresponsible. Children learn many things by life's process of trial and error. Most experiments are harmless, but some can have very serious results.

LIABILITY OF THE CHILD

The common law begins with the proposition that children are liable for their torts. It then excludes very young children because they cannot understand what they have done and what proceedings are being taken against them. As well, young children are seldom held liable for intentional torts such as slander because intentional torts require a much more mind-directed intent than unintentional torts such as negligence.

When a person causes damage because of negligence, the normal question asked is, "Were the consequences foreseeable and did the wrongdoer behave as a reasonable person would have behaved?" But, can the same rules be applied to children? They do not have the mental capacity of an adult to think ahead and lack the necessary experience to understand and anticipate possible injury. How much can a child foresee?

Some lawyers have suggested that the "reasonable person" rule must be altered to the "reasonable child" rule. This would not be very successful, because negligence law is complicated enough without creating a new standard.

The courts have generally held that a child is expected to conform to the intelligence and experience of other children of the same age. If a child is unable to understand the nature of an action, negligence cannot be attributed to the child at all. Given some understanding of the risk, the child must display the judgment and behaviour normal for a child with the same characteristics.

McHALE v. WATSON

Australia, 1966

The plaintiff, a girl aged nine, was hit in the eye by a piece of steel welding rod. The rod was thrown by the defendant, a boy of 12. The defendant was playing a game of throwing rods at a fence post. One end of each rod was sharp and he was trying to make them stick into the post. The plaintiff was watching this game and was standing close to the fence post.

A rod bounced off the post and struck the plaintiff in the eye, causing loss of sight in that eye. The plaintiff, through her parents, sued the defendant. The Court had no trouble determining that if the defendant had been an adult, there would be no question of his liability for negligence since any adult could foresee the danger to someone standing near the post. However, the Court considered the case in light of the fact that the defendant was 12. The judge said:

> *Sympathy with the injured girl is inevitable. One might also wish there was a rule that saved all children from harm. But, there is not. Children, like everyone else, must accept as they go about in society the risks from which ordinary care on the part of others will not suffice to save them. One such risk is that boys of twelve will behave as boys of twelve, and that is a risk indeed. The case against the defendant must be dismissed.*

This case, with its refusal to apply adult standards to a child, deserves considerable recognition. It embodies the principle that the standard of care in negligence law rests upon a "sliding scale" which varies according to the age and experience of the defendant. There is no absolute age at which a person becomes capable of negligence. To a certain extent, the courts apply the common phrase, "The child should have known better."

However, if a child is performing an adult act, such as driving a farm machine, the same standard of care is expected from that child as from an adult. If the child is incapable of operating the machine safely, the person who permitted him or her to do so is liable.

PARENTAL LIABILITY FOR CHILDREN'S TORTS

Parents are not automatically liable for their children's torts. The parents may become liable only if they in some way brought about a tort or failed to control their children when they should have been exercising parental control. Children who are destructive may place a greater burden of control upon parents than would be required of parents of ordinary children.

If a suit is brought against a child, an adult must defend it. The adult, usually a parent, acts in a representative capacity and does not incur personal liability. If the parent is also named as a defendant, then the parent represents both defendants.

The behaviour of children cannot be controlled by their parents at all times. Children must have freedom to move about as all human beings do. They cannot be supervised 100 percent of the time. As long as parents do not put dangerous things or ideas into the possession of their children, and do teach them right from wrong, parents are not liable.

In *Strehlke v. Camenzind* (Alberta, 1980) two boys, ages seven and eight, entered a partially built house and set fire to some wood shavings left by carpenters. They thought they had put the fire out with some wet cement, but the building burned down. The Court held that both boys knew it was wrong to play with fire but neither child had sufficient experience in the handling of fire and could not have foreseen that playing with matches might result in a serious fire.

SCHOOL DIVISION OF ASSINIBOINE SOUTH v. HOFFER, HOFFER and GREATER WINNIPEG GAS CO. LTD.

Manitoba, 1971

A 14-year-old boy was having trouble starting the family snowmobile because he did not have enough strength to pull the starting cord with one hand. His father taught him to start the snowmobile by putting the machine on its kickstand, tying the throttle open with string, then pulling the cord with two hands. When the machine started, the boy had to jump on, untie the string , push the machine off the kickstand, and take control of the machine himself.

On the day of the accident, the boy forgot to put the machine on the kickstand, and when he started it, it raced off without him, the throttle wide open. The machine went across a parking lot and into a schoolyard, where it hit a gas riser pipe beside the building. The pipe was broken by the impact and gas seeped into the basement of the building. The gas was ignited by a pilot light and the building was nearly demolished in the explosion that followed.

A suit was brought by the school board against the son, the father, and the gas company. The gas company was held 50 percent liable for not putting a protective covering over the riser pipe. The son and father were each held to be

25 percent liable. Although they could not have foreseen exactly the type of damage that would occur, they could have foreseen that some sort of damage or injury would occur if the son ever lost control of the machine. Permitting a snowmobile to run wild was compared to firing a rifle blindly down a city street. The father was liable because he taught his child to do a dangerous thing.

In *Christie v. Slevinsky* (Alberta, 1981) the plaintiff claimed damages when struck by a dune buggy driven by an 11-year-old. The action was against the parents for allowing the child to either have access to the vehicle or to drive it. The action was dismissed. The parents had prohibited their child from driving the vehicle when alone, and he had done so without permission. The child was too young to understand the consequences of his impulsive act.

AUTOMOBILE NEGLIGENCE

Automobile negligence covers all of the elements of any negligence case, but it is also subject to special rules created by statutes in addition to rules of common law. For example, the liability of a vehicle owner who lends his or her vehicle is imposed by provincial law.

OWNER'S LIABILITY

The owner of a motor vehicle, as well as the driver, is liable for loss suffered by any person by reason of negligence in the operation of the vehicle. The owner can escape liability only by showing that the vehicle was being used by some other person without the owner's consent. The owner would not be liable if the vehicle had been stolen. The owner cannot escape liability by arguing that the vehicle was not used for the purpose for which it was loaned or in the manner it was to be used. For example, if Brown allowed Green to borrow his or her vehicle for a short errand, but Green drove the vehicle a long distance and in a reckless manner, Green still had the vehicle with Brown's consent.

The court will give considerable weight to the issue of whether the person who borrowed the vehicle, having allowed someone else to drive, is still a passenger in the vehicle. The following case illustrates this point.

PAYNE v. DONNER et al.

Saskatchewan, 1981

One of the defendants, Eugene Foy, permitted his daughter to drive his truck. He instructed her to never allow anyone else to drive it. She disobeyed her father's instructions and allowed her boyfriend, Donner, to drive the truck. He struck the plaintiff, who sued Donner and Foy.

The Court held that the owner of the vehicle was liable because the provincial law excuses liability only if the vehicle was taken out of the owner's possession "wrongfully." The Court held that Donner had not wrongfully taken the vehicle from Foy because Foy's daughter had allowed Donner to drive. The instructions given to the daughter did not eliminate liability to third parties.

LIABILITY TO PASSENGERS

A passenger who rides free of charge assumes a foreseeable risk in accepting the ride. This risk is a normal hazard of highway driving. In some provinces, the passenger can sue the driver only if the driver was guilty of **gross negligence.** There is no definition of this term, but it is interpreted to mean "a very great negligence." In Ontario, Quebec, and British Columbia, the passenger may sue the driver for ordinary negligence.

In the following case, the British Columbia Court of Appeal applied the rule of *ex turpi* to an automobile accident.

HALL v. HEBERT

British Columbia, 1991

Hall and Hebert had been drinking heavily. Hebert was driving his automobile, but decided he was too drunk to drive. He then asked Hall if he was capable of driving. Hall said he could, but both men were very drunk. Hall drove the car off a steep embankment and suffered permanent injury. He sued Hebert, arguing that the appellant had a duty to remain sober while driving and should not have allowed a drunk man to drive his car. The trial judge found Hebert 75 percent liable. Hebert appealed.

The Court of Appeal overturned the decision and denied Hall any damages. Under the *ex turpi* principle, a plaintiff will be denied damages if the plaintiff's injuries arose out of his or her own wrongful or immoral act, regardless of the defendant's liability or negligence. The Court said:

> *The* ex turpi *defence will be available wherever the conduct of the plaintiff giving rise to the claim is so tainted with criminality or culpable immorality that, as a matter of public policy, the Court will not assist him to recover. The plaintiff engaged in a kind of conduct that daily wreaks havoc upon the highways of the nation and devastates the lives and futures of innocent victims. People would be outraged if the Court lent its assistance to this drunk driver to recover damages from his drunk passenger.*

CONTRIBUTORY NEGLIGENCE

A person guilty of **contributory negligence** may receive reduced compensation depending upon the extent to which the person contributed to his or her own injuries. In *Yuan v. Farstad* (British Columbia, 1971) the defendant was the sole cause of a vehicle accident that killed Dr. Yuan. However, the damages were reduced by 25 percent because the deceased man was not wearing his seat belt and thereby contributed to his own death. Failure to wear a seat belt will not automatically reduce damages. The court must be convinced that the seat belt, if worn correctly, would have made a difference in the results of the accident.

INEVITABLE ACCIDENT

The defendant can escape liability for an accident if the defendant can show that the accident was inevitable. An **inevitable accident** is one that the party accused of causing the accident could not have prevented by reasonable care and skill. The most common causes of an inevitable accident are mechanical failure, driver failure, and weather conditions.

Mechanical failure means that a driver loses control of a vehicle because of a mechanical malfunction over which the driver has no control. The malfunction must be one that the driver had no warning about or one that could not be detected by ordinary inspection. Thus, driving a vehicle with bad brakes is not a defence, because the driver knew about the problem. If the accident was caused by a sudden failure of the power steering, the defence could succeed.

Driver failure means that an accident occurs because of a physical problem that suddenly seizes the driver. For example, if an accident results because a driver with no known history of heart problems suddenly has a heart attack and cannot control his or her vehicle, the law would consider this to be an inevitable accident. However, a driver with a bad heart who drives despite warnings from his or her doctor and without taking proper medication cannot escape liability.

Road conditions also can cause inevitable accidents. Drivers should reduce speed and drive carefully in bad weather, but some incidents are totally unexpected. If, after a heavy rain, water lies on the roadway in puddles, a vehicle is likely to "plane" when the tires hit the water. This situation is similar to a vehicle "water skiing" across the surface of water. It is impossible to steer in such a situation and courts have held that accidents caused by planing are inevitable.

TELFER v. WRIGHT

Ontario, 1978

Telfer suffered permanent injury when her car was involved in a head-on collision with a vehicle driven by Wright. Wright's car had suddenly crossed the roadway into her lane.

Evidence was led that Wright had blacked out just prior to the accident. The plaintiff verified this, saying that Wright was slumped over the steering wheel as he came toward her vehicle. The evidence was that Wright had suffered dizzy spells before and had felt very dizzy earlier that day. Wright claimed that the feeling had passed, allowing him to drive.

The trial judge accepted the defence of inevitable accident, but the Court of Appeal overturned this decision. The defendant knew he had a medical problem and had felt dizzy just prior to the collision. He was negligent in continuing to drive, knowing that he was not well.

PRODUCT LIABILITY

For many years, the concept of **product liability** was between the buyer and the seller only. When nearly all goods were manufactured locally, this was the only logical relationship. With the development of the industrial age, more and more goods were made in factories and then shipped to local shops where they were sold. If the goods were defective, the consumer was faced with the problem of suing either the manufacturer or the retailer. Originally, British courts ruled that the manufacturer did not owe any duty to the consumer because the two parties did not have a direct business relationship. The manufacturer sold the product to the retailer. The manufacturer did not know who might buy the product and thus there was no contract between the manufacturer and the consumer.

In 1932, in the famous case of *Donoghue v. Stevenson*, the House of Lords in England ruled that a manufacturer owed a duty of care to all people who might buy the defective products they manufactured. The extent of that liability has since been altered by provincial legislation and varies considerably across Canada. Generally, the burden is upon the plaintiff to show that the defendant manufacturer was negligent in the manufacture of the product or in failing to give proper instructions for its safe use. The plaintiff must show that he or she did not misuse or tamper with the product.

MANUFACTURERS' LIABILITY

The manufacturer owes a duty to every person who might reasonably purchase or use the product. The rule of foreseeability applies here. The manufacturer is potentially liable to every foreseeable victim. This could include direct users of the product as well as innocent bystanders. For example, if the XYZ Auto Company manufactures an automobile with defective brakes, the company is potentially liable to the person who buys the automobile, the person's family or other passengers, and other motorists who are struck by the automobile should the brakes fail. The potential liability is very great, and could extend for years to include people who purchase used vehicles.

NICHOLSON v. JOHN DEERE LTD. et al.

Ontario, 1987

The plaintiffs sued the defendant manufacturer and the local dealer for loss of their home to fire. The fire started when one of the plaintiffs was filling the gas tank of a John Deere riding mower. It was an older model and the plaintiffs had purchased it second-hand from the original buyer. The mower had a battery-start system. The battery was very close to the gas tank and, when manufactured, had a special battery cover to keep gas fumes from reaching the battery. Batteries have a small amount of electrical charge around them at all times and this charge can ignite gasoline fumes. The problem was that the battery cover had to be removed to service or replace the battery and consumers tended to leave them removed, even though each cover had a bright sticker, warning against leaving it off. The sticker did not say anything about the danger of gas fumes igniting.

When the plaintiffs purchased the riding mower, no battery cover came with it because the original owner had removed it and had forgotten all about it. Nor did the plaintiffs receive the owner's handbook that came with the mower, which cautioned against removing the cover. The company later redesigned the machine and newer models had the battery located far from the gas tank.

The plaintiffs once took the mower for servicing to their local dealer and the dealer did not tell them about the missing battery cover or give them any warning, even though John Deere Limited had sent bulletins to its dealers that they had received reports of accidental fires.

The fire started when one of the plaintiffs poured gasoline into the tank. A dip-stick that measures the fuel level was lying near the battery and suddenly the battery "arced" and ignited the gasoline. The plaintiffs testified that they had no knowledge about battery arcing.

The Court awarded damages to the plaintiffs. The duty of the manufacturer, who knows that it has sold to the public a dangerous product, is to make every reasonable effort to implement a recall and safety program to correct the defects. The defendant did not put into effect such a program but left matters to chance. The defendants owed a duty not only to the original buyers but also to all potential victims who may have purchased used machines. The dealer was also liable because it saw, first-hand, that the plaintiffs had a mower without a battery cover but never warned them.

The plaintiff must also claim that the defendant was negligent in the design or manufacture of the product. The burden of proof rests upon the plaintiff. The fact that the plaintiff was injured does not, in itself, prove negligence on the part of the manufacturer. Some other party, such as the retailer, may have tampered with the product or a technician may have installed it incorrectly. Or the plaintiff may have misused the product or failed to read the instructions. A manufacturer can be held liable for failure to warn the consumer of potential dangers in a product. Such cases are most often brought against the manufacturers of drugs with potential side effects.

BUCHAN v. ORTHO PHARMACEUTICAL CORP.

Ontario, 1986

The appellant took Ortho-Novum birth control pills, which were manufactured by the respondent drug company and prescribed by the appellant's doctor. The appellant suffered a stroke that resulted in partial paralysis. The trial judge had ruled that the respondent was negligent for failing to properly warn doctors of the risk of stroke and that birth control pill makers have a common law duty to warn consumers, not just physicians.

The respondent had argued that the technical information about drugs is too complex for consumers to read and, since the doctor must prescribe the pills, it is sufficient that the doctor have the information.

The Court of Appeal was split on the question of whether drug manufacturers should warn consumers, but did agree that the manufacturer had not sufficiently warned doctors about prescribing the pills. The company must have had some information that its pills posed a risk for some users, but nothing in the company literature to doctors disclosed this risk. The Court recognized that birth control pills are not exactly the same product as "medicine." Although the following comments were in the form of an *ober dictum* (not part of the Court's actual decision but only added comments) they reflect a subtle warning to drug manufacturers of products that are not related to illness or disease:

> *Whereas with most drugs a doctor is prescribing to prevent or treat a disease, the pill introduces a new element in the doctor-patient relationship because the physician is prescribing for socio-economic reasons a potentially dangerous product to a perfectly healthy patient. And unlike other drugs where patient involvement is minimal, consumer demand for oral contraceptives prompts their use more often than doctors advise. The decision to use the pill is one in which the consumers have made the decision before visiting a doctor to obtain a prescription ... Therefore, information that would help women make informed and intelligent decisions about oral contraceptives would not impose any real burden on drug manufacturers.*

The Court awarded the plaintiff $837 000 in damages.

The plaintiff must prove that the defective product caused his or her injuries and that it was not caused by some other source. For example, if the plaintiff prepared a meal using foods from four sources or manufacturers and all of the food was consumed, if the plaintiff suffered food poisoning it would be difficult for the plaintiff to show which company produced the tainted food. It is not sufficient to argue that it must have been one of the four, so all four are liable. In *Cohen v. Heinz of Canada* (Ontario, 1986) the plaintiff became ill after consuming Heinz ketchup. Maggots were found in the lid of the ketchup bottle. The lawsuit argued that Heinz allowed flies to get into the ketchup at the manufacturing plant. Heinz strongly defended the action and proved that flies and fly eggs cannot live in ketchup during the manufacturing process because it goes into the bottle at a temperature near boiling, immediately after which the bottles are sealed. Further, the maggots were very young, which showed that they entered the bottle after it left the Heinz plant, most likely in the warehouse of the retailer. Someone had opened a bottle, used some of the ketchup, left the lid off for a while, then put it back on the bottle. The Court held that Heinz was not negligent.

SALE OF GOODS ACT

Most provinces have a *Sale of Goods Act* that may contain wording similar to the Ontario statute, which reads in part:

> **Where the buyer expressly or by implication makes known to the seller the particular purpose for which the goods are required so as to show that the buyer relies on the seller's skill or judgment, and the goods are of a description that it is in the course of the seller's business to supply, whether he is the manufacturer or not, there is an implied condition that the goods will be reasonably fit for such purpose, but in the case of a contract for the sale of a specific article under its patent or other trade name there is no implied condition as to its fitness for any particular purpose.**

The main purpose of this section is to discourage sellers from making misleading claims just to sell products. The product must match what it is that the customer says he or she wants. It is important to note that in such a case the buyer is revealing personal lack of knowledge and relying upon the advice of the seller. If the seller gives bad advice and the buyer suffers injury, the seller is liable. If the buyer relies upon personal judgment or just buys a product by its brand name, the seller is not liable.

Recent decisions tend to suggest that the courts have almost completely eliminated the practical effect of the latter part of the section. Retailers have been held liable even though they did not specifically recommend a product. The current view is that there is a "warranty that runs with the goods" and the retailers must take responsibility for what they sell. The retailers profit from the sales and must share the responsibility. When the many products that are manufactured outside Canada are taken into consideration, it is impractical to tell the consumer that he or she must personally sue a foreign company for injury. The law basically holds the retailer liable to the consumer and the retailer may turn around and sue the manufacturer for making the retailer liable.

HOUWELING NURSERIES v. FISONS WESTERN CORP.

British Columbia, 1988

The plaintiff ran a nursery in which it grew plants for sale to retail outlets. In 1983, many of the plants died after they had been planted in a defective potting soil mix supplied by Fisons Western Corporation. Houweling's customers had to be reimbursed for the loss of their plants and many of them transferred their business to other companies, causing the plaintiff long-term injury to its business reputation.

The Court held the defendant liable because it breached the contract through misrepresenting the product as being the same as the mix the plaintiff had used before and for not testing the product before delivering it to the plaintiff. Fisons had breached the implied warranty as to fitness for the purpose for which the goods were required under the British Columbia *Sale of Goods Act*. Damages were assessed at $400 000. The Court did not award damages for injury to the plaintiff's reputation, but only for the amount it directly had to refund to its customers.

The concept of warranty running with the goods can have a long trek. Liability may extend to others in the distribution chain even though they played no part in manufacturing the product but only in applying it. In *Ostash v. Sonnenberg* (British Columbia, 1973) an inspector employed by the provincial government was held liable for failing to detect and rectify the inadequate installation of a gas furnace.

STRICT LIABILITY

Strict liability in cases of product liability means that the consumer can sue the manufacturer and retailer for damages caused by defective products, without having to prove negligence. Saskatchewan, Quebec, and New Brunswick now have such legislation. The logic behind the legislation is that the consumer does not have the financial means to sue large, powerful companies and prove negligence. Nor does the consumer have access to the company plant and records to show how the defendant was negligent. The injured consumer has a *prima facie* case by virtue of the injury. The burden should be upon the manufacturer to show that it was not negligent.

Strict liability places strong demands upon manufacturers to ensure that products are free of defects when they leave the plant. It requires the keeping of extensive records so that the manufacturer can determine in which plant a product was made in order to prevent similar problems from happening again. The law does not make the manufacturer automatically liable. Rather, it shifts the burden of proof to the defendant to show that it was not negligent.

FARRO v. NUTONE ELECTRIC LTD.

Ontario, 1990

Mr. and Mrs. Farro purchased a ceiling fan for their second-floor bathroom. A contractor installed the fan, which soon caught fire and burned a hole in the ceiling. It then fell down and set fire to a plastic toilet seat. The fire then spread throughout the house, causing $60 000 in damage.

Farro sued the contractor and the manufacturer, Nutone. A problem arose when it was learned that the fan had been taken by a fire inspector to a CSA laboratory for examination. The insurance adjuster failed to notify Nutone that the Farros had suffered a fire and were planning to sue the company. The fan was eventually thrown away before Nutone had an opportunity to inspect it.

The trial judge dismissed the case because Nutone had not been given an opportunity to inspect the fan and defend itself. It was possible the contractor had wired the fan incorrectly. The Farros dropped the action against the contractor.

The fan was built in Canada using some parts made in the United States. It was designed to shut off should it overheat. A special one-shot fuse was built into the fan to do this. The plaintiffs argued that the fuse was defective or not installed. Both parties agreed it was not possible to determine what had actually happened.

However, the Ontario Court of Appeal held that Nutone was liable. The Court stressed that the fan is boxed as a complete unit. Installation does not require the contractor to open the fan unit or do anything to the motor. If the fan is installed incorrectly, it either will not operate or will overheat immediately and shut off. No mistake on the part of the contractor should cause a fire unless the contractor opened the fan and tampered with it. The Court said:

> *It is not necessary, and it is generally impossible, for a plaintiff to adduce direct evidence that a defect existed when the manufactured product left the factory. It is mere speculation to suppose that Nutone had been deprived of an opportunity to*

prove that they had properly installed a functioning thermal protective device. The suggestion that the fuse may have failed due to a non-visible, latent defect was pure speculation and should not have been given any weight by the trial judge. To give effect to such a speculative defence would undermine the progressive line of cases which placed liability on the manufacturer of a defective product; this is so even in the case of a latent defect if the manufacturer failed to rebut the onus on it to disprove negligence ... It would be unjust to deprive the Farros of their damages by reason of the failure of the insurance adjuster to notify the respondent of a potential lawsuit.

The Court did not specifically establish strict liability for products in this case. However, it stressed that the burden is upon the seller of a product with sealed units to show what caused damage. The fact that a product is sealed almost totally eliminates the argument that the consumer tampered with the product. In the final analysis, the Court in this case concluded that improper manufacture was the most likely cause of the fire.

ASSESSING DAMAGES

In some cases the nature and extent of the injury is obvious. The plaintiff may recover for personal injury or for direct financial loss. The courts have been extremely reluctant to extend that principle further. In *Rivtow Marine Ltd. v. Washington Iron Works* (Supreme Court of Canada, 1973) the plaintiff rented a crane from the defendant manufacturer. The defendant knew that its cranes had serious defects, but told no one. When a similar crane collapsed elsewhere, killing the operator, the plaintiff took the crane out of service and inspected it. It found dangerous cracks that it had to repair. The plaintiff sued for the cost of repair and for loss of profits while the crane was out of use.

The British Columbia Court of Appeal held that the defendant was liable only for personal injury and damage to other property caused by the article or its use. The Supreme Court of Canada, while allowing some recovery for loss of profits, upheld the denial of liability for the cost of repair.

This case is troubling, to say the least. If the defect had not been detected and the crane had collapsed, all damage caused to property and people would have been recoverable. The plaintiff was being penalized for showing a proper regard for the safety of its workers by not allowing them to work on a dangerous crane.

REVIEW: POINTS OF LAW

1. Negligence consists of doing or omitting to do something that a reasonable person would do or not do where it was foreseeable that someone could be injured.
2. In a negligence case, the plaintiff must show that the defendant owed him or her a duty of care.
3. The defendant can be liable for negligence if the evidence shows that the defendant did not meet the required standard of care.
4. A government can be liable for negligence for not properly carrying out its policies of inspection or maintenance.
5. A doctor is negligent if the doctor does not tell the patient the risks of the procedure, possible side effects, the nature of the procedure, and alternatives.
6. A school teacher owes his or her pupils the standard of care that a prudent parent would show toward his or her own child.
7. If the plaintiff has voluntarily consented to the risk, the defendant is not liable.
8. If the plaintiff has contributed to his or her own injuries, the amount of damages awarded will be reduced.
9. In some cases, the act speaks for itself and the burden is on the defendant to show how the injury might have occurred without negligence by the defendant.
10. If an injured person sues the manufacturer of a defective product, the burden is upon the plaintiff to show that the defendant was negligent in the manufacture of the product or in not printing proper warnings regarding the safe use of the product.

LEGAL BRIEFS

1. The plaintiff, GH, was the widow of TH. She brought an action against the defendant, R, arising from a motor vehicle accident. The parties went to court and it was held that R was 80 percent liable for the accident and TH was 20 percent liable. Two people in R's car were killed in the accident. After the accident, TH underwent a personality change. He then became

manic-depressive and blamed himself totally for the accident. All arguments to the contrary failed, including the fact that the Court had ruled otherwise. TH continually said, "It was all my fault. I could have prevented it." TH committed suicide, leaving a note saying he felt such guilt about the accident that he decided to take his own life. The action alleged that R was liable for the deceased man's suicide. Was TH's death foreseeable?

2. L was visiting the farm of her uncle, B. L was six years old and was playing with B's daughter, age eight. They found a wasps' nest and told B. B poured gasoline on the nest and set fire to it. After it burned out, a few wasps were still visible and the children asked if they should use more gasoline. B said to leave it alone. While B was busy elsewhere, the children obtained more gasoline from an unlocked pump and tried to burn the wasps' nest again. L was severely burned when the gasoline flared and set fire to her clothes. Liability of B?
3. G sued the county government for injuries suffered when his car slid off the road during a winter storm. The Department of Highways supervisor inspected the road early that morning and noted that it was very icy. He decided not to sand or use salt until the wind dropped, because the sand would have blown off the road. Before the sanding truck began its work, G had his accident. There was no statutory requirement of the government to sand the roads, but there was a policy in effect to do so. Liability of the county?
4. N was injured when a 100-kg man landed on top of him. The man was being towed behind a boat, wearing a special para-sail. The recreational activity was operated by W. Evidence was led that the boat did not have the power to pull a person who weighed 100 kg. Shortly after the man was lifted upward his weight caused him to fall and hit N. W argued it had no duty of care toward N as the accident was not foreseeable. Is W correct?
5. H sued the city for damage to his house. An employee of the city was operating a bulldozer and left it for 30 min for a break. The employee lowered the blade to the ground and turned off the ignition, but did not remove the key. It was late at night and he did not expect anyone to be in the area. In the employee's absence, someone started the bulldozer, put it into motion, and then ran away. The driverless machine crashed into H's house. The culprit was never found. The city based its defence upon two things: an intervening act of an unknown person, and the unforeseeability of someone starting the machine. Is the city liable?
6. W transported children, ages three to six, to and from school in a taxi. It was a four-door vehicle. G was one of six children in the car and W saw him playing with the door lock button. He told G to leave it alone. After delivering two more children to their homes, W saw that the button was up again. He made

sure it was down and again told G to leave it alone. Shortly afterward, the door opened and G fell out and suffered injury. Liability of W?

7. C had a ringing sound in her right ear and went to Dr. E for treatment. The problem was annoying but did not impair C's hearing. E said that surgery might correct the problem but did not tell C that the chance of success was less than 10 percent. He told her that it was remotely possible that she might have a stroke after the operation and that she should consider that when making a decision. C had the operation and suffered a stroke that paralyzed her right side. Is E liable?
8. U stored tubes of phostoxin, a poisonous fumigant used to kill insects, in an unlocked storage shed. Some children took some of the tubes. They noted that the tubes had a bad smell so, as a joke, they put some in H's car. H noticed the odour but did not become concerned for three days. Then, he conducted a search of his car and inhaled strong fumes, which made him very ill. U argued that the trespass, theft, and other acts of the children represented an intervening act that relieved U of liability. Who is correct?

APPLYING THE LAW

THORNTON v. BOARD OF SCHOOL TRUSTEES

British Columbia, 1975

Gary Thornton was 15 years of age and nearing completion of a course in gymnastics at his high school. On the day in question Gary and some other students went into an equipment room and obtained a springboard and some foam chunks. The foam chunks were placed around a wrestling mat as a landing area and the boys began doing somersaults. Not satisfied with this activity, the boys then took a box-horse and placed it at the end of the board. They jumped from the box-horse onto the springboard and were attempting complete somersaults onto the mat. The teacher was not observing this activity as he was filling out report cards elsewhere in the gym.

Some of the boys started trying "circus tricks," including double somersaults off the board. They were unsuccessful at these tricks and landed very hard. One boy went to the teacher and reported that he had hurt his arm. The teacher told him to run cold water on it. It turned out that the arm was broken. The teacher then went to look at the landing area and concluded that it was too small. He told the boys to put more mats around the area. He saw, but did not question, the configuration of a springboard and box-horse. He did not ask any of the boys what they had been doing, including the boy who had hurt his arm. Shortly afterward, Gary broke his neck when he landed on the mat. He suffered total paralysis of his four limbs.

The Court held that the configuration was "an attractive trap" and that the teacher and the school board were both liable. The Court then dealt with the issue of contributory negligence. The decision was that Gary had not contributed to his own injury, despite the fact that he obviously had been taking part in dangerous stunts. It was held that Gary did not have the same experience as his instructor and that he could not have recognized that his actions were a grave danger to himself. It followed that he did not realize that he should have asked the teacher for guidance or instructions. Had he been an experienced gymnast, the conclusion might have been different, but he had had less than 20 hours of experience in gymnastics.

Questions

1. What standard of care did the gym teacher owe to the students?
2. How important was it that another boy was injured before Gary was injured and that the teacher saw the configuration of springboard and horse?
3. Why did the Court conclude that Gary did not contribute to his own injuries?
4. What did the expert mean when he called the configuration "an attractive trap"?

HORSLEY et al. v. MacLAREN et al.

Supreme Court of Canada, 1972

The respondent, MacLaren, owned a cabin cruiser named "The Ogopogo." On May 7, 1961, he invited some friends for a cruise on Lake Ontario. The water was choppy and most of the passengers went below. A passenger named Matthews went topside and for no apparent reason fell overboard. MacLaren stopped the boat 15 m away, put it into reverse, and backed toward Matthews in the water. When close to Matthews, MacLaren cut the motor but the rough water immediately separated the boat from the motionless man. Another passenger tried to hook onto Matthews' clothing with a pike but could not do so. Much evidence was given at the trial about this method, which was criticized as an improper way to rescue a person. Experts testified that the proper method is to swing the boat in a circle and come alongside the body, bow first. This method will protect the person in the water from the propeller blades and allow the boat to get right next to the person. MacLaren testified that a rescue could also be done stern first, even if it was not the best method.

A passenger, Horsley, removed some of his clothing and jumped into the lake. He did not tell anyone of his intention before doing so. Another passenger, Jones, also jumped into the lake. She was later rescued, but Horsley died from exposure to the cold water. Matthews' body sank and was never found.

Matthews' family sued MacLaren but did not succeed. There was no negligence on the part of MacLaren in causing Matthews to fall overboard. While the rescue method was not the best, there was also reason to believe that Matthews was dead very shortly after hitting the water. He was motionless all the time he was seen in the lake.

Horsley's family also sued MacLaren, alleging that because of MacLaren's clumsy rescue attempts, Horsley was "forced" to attempt a rescue. MacLaren testified that he would have ordered Horsley not to jump into the lake, but Horsley did not tell him what he was going to do. Horsley did not wear a life jacket and he simply added to the problem by jumping into the water.

The trial judge awarded damages to the appellants. He held that it was MacLaren's inept rescue attempt that compelled Horsley to jump into the water and such negligence was the cause of Horsley's death. The Ontario Court of Appeal reversed this decision and the case was further appealed to the Supreme Court of Canada, which upheld the Ontario Court of Appeal:

> *In the present case a situation of peril was created when Matthews fell overboard, but it was not created by any fault on the part of MacLaren; and before MacLaren can be found to have been in any way responsible for Horsley's death, it must be found that there was such negligence in his method of rescue as to place Matthews in an apparent position of increased danger subsequent to and distinct from the danger to which he had been initially exposed by his accidental fall. In other words, any duty owing to Horsley must stem from the fact that a new situation of peril was created by MacLaren's negligence which induced Horsley to act as he did ... I do not think that the evidence justifies the finding that any fault of his induced Horsley to risk his life as he did.*

Two justices dissented and thought that MacLaren was negligent and that Horsley was a forced rescuer who felt he had to take matters into his own hands because MacLaren was so inept.

Questions

1. Since MacLaren did not cause Matthews to fall overboard, what duty did MacLaren owe to Matthews?
2. Knowing that lake water in May can be so cold that it can kill a human in minutes, did Horsley act reasonably? Why or why not?
3. What is the proper definition of a forced rescuer? Did Horsley fit this definition? Why or why not?
4. The Court concluded that the decision in the Horsley case depended upon the decision in the Matthews case. Why?
5. What led the Court to finally conclude that MacLaren was not liable?

PRINCIPLES AND CASES

Case 1: Legal Principle

A physician must advise a patient of possible side effects and complications of surgery. The explanation must include all material risks, but not every possible side effect.

Case Facts

The plaintiff wanted to have a sterilization operation but did not want anyone other than her husband to know. Her reasons for this were based on her religion and her concern that her parents would be very displeased if they learned of the operation. She discussed the surgery with the defendant doctor and he told her that the operation would be done in such a way that the resultant scar would be minimal and a bikini could be worn afterward, without a scar being visible. The plaintiff did not tell the doctor why she was interested in the scar issue. Nor did she say it was imperative that the scar be small.

The doctor performed the operation called a laparoscopic sterilization, but during the course of the operation, the plaintiff's bowel was perforated. This necessitated a second operation to save her life. The sterilization operation did not normally carry much risk of bowel perforation and the doctor had not told the plaintiff that such a thing might happen.

The plaintiff sued because of the large scar that was the result of the second operation. The Court concluded that the first operation was not done negligently and that the second operation was medically necessary. The only remaining issue was whether the doctor was negligent for not telling the plaintiff about the possibility of a bowel perforation which would require a second operation.

Possible Decisions

A The doctor is liable because he owed the plaintiff a standard of care to ensure that she did not have a large scar.

B The doctor is liable because he failed to disclose a material risk to his patient that might have caused her to not have the operation.

C The doctor is not liable because the chance of a perforation was very slight and not a material risk.

D The doctor is not liable because the plaintiff did not tell him why she was concerned about a scar. Had she done so, he would have discussed the possibility of a second operation.

Case 2: Legal Principle

The manufacturer of a product that has an inherent danger, such as high inflammability, must warn the public of the attendant dangers and to do so in sufficient detail that an ordinary user will fully understand the dangers.

Case Facts

The plaintiff, an engineer, was injured by an explosion that occurred when the vapour from a floor sealer, which he was applying in his recreation room, was ignited by the pilot light of his furnace. The furnace was located in the room next to the recreation room. Although it was summer at the time, the plaintiff had not extinguished the pilot light because he was unaware that leaving it on could create a danger of fire or explosion.

There were three warning labels on the can. The largest label contained an end panel stating the drying time information along with the words: "Caution: Inflammable. Keep away from open flame." Along the side of the panel were the words: "Danger! Harmful if swallowed." A red label with black letters warned: "Keep away from fire, heat and open-flame lights. Do not drop." A third label, rectangular in shape, said: "Caution: Do not use near open flame or while smoking." Evidence was introduced that a competing product had similar labels, with one important difference. Its labels also contained the words: "All furnaces, pilot lights and spark producing switches must be eliminated in the work area."

The defendant's label did not specifically warn against pilot lights. The plaintiff argued that he never thought about the pilot light and did not realize that vapours could travel that far. He felt he was working in an area that was free of open flame. The defendant argued that the plaintiff, an educated engineer, was fully aware that his furnace had an open pilot light. The instructions said to keep away from open flame. The defendant further argued that it was impractical to try to put warnings on a can against every possible form of flames in existence in the world.

Possible Decisions

A The plaintiff is liable because the manufacturer failed to give adequate warning regarding possible dangers.

B The plaintiff is liable because a home-owner cannot be expected to realize how dangerous a product is. The duty is upon the manufacturer to warn of all dangers about which it knows.

C The defendant is not liable because the plaintiff is an engineer and knows how furnaces work and that vapours are inflammable.

D The defendant is not liable because the warning labels on the can are adequate.

YOU BE THE JUDGE

1. The plaintiff went to the defendant doctor to have an abortion. The plaintiff was 16 years of age at the time. The operation was performed, but was not successful. The post-operative report clearly showed no fetal matter had been removed, so the patient was still pregnant. The plaintiff never came back for her checkup. The defendant made no effort to locate the plaintiff and tell her that she was still pregnant. The plaintiff gave birth to twins and sued the doctor for stress and financial support for the two children she did not want. Who would succeed?

2. The defendant police officer investigated an accident and noted that the road surface was very icy. The officer radioed this information to the dispatcher and advised that the city should send a sand truck to the area.

The officer then left the scene and resumed patrol. The plaintiff drove along the same section shortly afterward and suffered injury when he lost control of his vehicle. The city sand truck was not on the scene for another three hours. The plaintiff sued the officer for not remaining at the scene and directing traffic away from the dangerous section until the sand truck arrived. The action alleged that failure to do so was negligence because the officer owed a duty of care to other motorists. Who would succeed?

3. The defendant driver, without negligence, knocked down a traffic sign located in the middle of a gravel strip dividing the eastbound and westbound lanes of a highway. The defendant stopped and removed the debris, except for a metal post which was too securely imbedded. It was now bent over and projected at a right angle toward the eastbound lane. The defendant mentioned the accident to a garage attendant and said he intended to report the accident. The attendant talked the defendant out of it, saying that if the defendant reported the matter, the city would send him a bill for the sign. Later, another driver was killed when he tried to pass another vehicle on the gravel strip, an action contrary to highway traffic law. The deceased was fatally injured when the post, which came through the floor of the car, pierced the deceased's chest. The estate of the deceased sued the defendant. Who would succeed?

4. The plaintiff sued the defendant for injuries suffered while riding the defendant's motorcycle. The plaintiff, 17 years of age, had no experience riding motorcycles. The defendant, 16 years of age, had considerable experience and knew that his powerful machine was dangerous for a novice to ride. The plaintiff persisted in his request and the defendant finally allowed him to ride, saying, "Okay, but don't blame me if you wipe out." The plaintiff said he would take the responsibility. The plaintiff suffered permanent injury when he lost control of the machine. Who would succeed?

5. The plaintiff sued the owner of a restaurant for injuries suffered when she tried to climb out of a cubicle in the washroom. The plaintiff entered the cubicle and locked the door. When she tried to leave, she found that the handle was defective and would not open. She called out for assistance, but no one heard. After waiting 20 minutes, the plaintiff tried to escape by climbing over the top of the cubicle. She fell to the floor and suffered head injuries. The defendant argued that the plaintiff's actions were foolish and that she injured herself. Had she waited where she was, she eventually would have been rescued. Who would succeed?

CARBOLIC SMOKE BALL

WILL POSITIVELY CURE

COUGHS Cured in 1 week	**CATARRH** Cured in 1 to 3 months.	**HOARSENESS** Cured in 12 hours.	**THROAT DEAFNESS** Cured in 1 to 3 months.	**INFLUENZA** Cured in 24 hours.	**CROUP** Relieved in 5 minutes.
COLD IN THE HEAD Cured in 12 hours.	**ASTHMA** Relieved in 10 minutes.	**LOSS OF VOICE** Fully restored.	**SNORING** Cured in 1 week.	**HAY FEVER** Cured in every case.	**WHOOPING COUGH** Relieved the first application.
COLD ON THE CHEST Cured in 12 hours.	**BRONCHITIS** Cured in every case.	**SORE THROAT** Cured in 12 hours.	**SORE EYES** Cured in 2 weeks.	**HEADACHE** Cured in 10 minutes.	**NEURALGIA** Cured in 10 minutes.

As all the Diseases mentioned above proceed from one cause, they can be Cured by this Remedy.

£100 REWARD

Free Trials at our Consulting Rooms.
For Inhalation Only.

WILL BE PAID BY THE

CARBOLIC SMOKE BALL CO.

to any Person who contracts the Increasing Epidemic,

INFLUENZA,

Colds, or any Diseases caused by taking Cold, after having used the **CARBOLIC SMOKE BALL** according to the printed directions supplied with each Ball.

£1000 IS DEPOSITED

with the ALLIANCE BANK, Regent Street, showing our sincerity in the matter.

During the last epidemic of **INFLUENZA** many thousand **CARBOLIC SMOKE BALLS** were sold as preventives against this disease, and in no ascertained case was the disease contracted by those using the **CARBOLIC SMOKE BALL.**

Free Trials at our Consulting Rooms.
For Inhalation Only.

THE CARBOLIC SMOKE BALL,

TESTIMONIALS.

The DUKE OF PORTLAND writes: "I am much obliged for the Carbolic Smoke Ball which you have sent me, and which I find most efficacious."

SIR FREDERICK MILNER, Bart., M.P., writes from Nice, March 7, 1890: "Lady Milner and my children have derived much benefit from the Carbolic Smoke Ball."

Lady MOSTYN writes from Carshalton, Cary Crescent, Torquay, Jan. 10, 1890: "Lady Mostyn believes the Carbolic Smoke Ball to be a certain check and a cure for a cold, and will have great pleasure in recommending it to her friends. Lady Mostyn hopes the Carbolic Smoke Ball will have all the success its merits deserve."

Lady ERSKINE writes from Spratton Hall, Northampton, Jan. 1, 1890: "Lady Erskine is pleased to say that the Carbolic Smoke Ball has given every satisfaction; she considers it a very good invention."

Mrs. GLADSTONE writes: "She finds the Carbolic Smoke Ball has done her a great deal of good."

Madame ADELINA PATTI writes: "Madame Patti has found the Carbolic Smoke Ball very beneficial, and the only thing that would enable her to rest well at night when having a severe cold."

AS PRESCRIBED BY

SIR MORELL MACKENZIE, M.D.,

HAS BEEN SUPPLIED TO

H.I.M. THE GERMAN EMPRESS.

H.R.H. The Duke of Edinburgh, K.G.
H.R.H. The Duke of Connaught, K.G.
The Duke of Fife, K.T.
The Marquis of Salisbury, K.G.
The Duke of Argyll, K.T.
The Duke of Westminster, K.G.
The Duke of Richmond and Gordon, K.G.
The Duke of Manchester.
The Duke of Newcastle.
The Duke of Norfolk.
The Duke of Rutland, K.G.
The Duke of Wellington.
The Marquis of Ripon, K.G.
The Earl of Derby, K.G.
Earl Spencer, K.G.
The Lord Chancellor.
The Lord Chief Justice.
Lord Tennyson.

TESTIMONIALS.

The BISHOP OF LONDON writes: "The Carbolic Smoke Ball has benefited me greatly."

The MARCHIONESS DE SAIN writes from Padworth House, Reading, Jan. 13, 1890: "The Marchioness de Sain has daily used the Smoke Ball since the commencement of the epidemic of Influenza, and has not taken the Influenza, although surrounded by those suffering from it."

Dr. J. RUSSELL HARRIS, M.D., writes from 6, Adam Street, Adelphi, Sept. 24, 1891: "Many obstinate cases of post-nasal catarrh, which have resisted other treatment, have yielded to your Carbolic Smoke Ball."

A. GIBBONS, Esq., Editor of the *Lady's Pictorial*, writes from 172, Strand, W.C., Feb. 14, 1890: "During a recent sharp attack of the prevailing epidemic I had none of the unpleasant and dangerous catarrh and bronchial symptoms. I attribute this entirely to the use of the Carbolic Smoke Ball."

The Rev. Dr. CHICHESTER A. W. READE, LL.D., D.C.L., writes from Banstead Downs, Surrey, May 1890: "My duties in a large public institution have brought me daily, during the recent epidemic of influenza, in close contact with the disease. I have been perfectly free from any symptom by having the Smoke Ball always handy. It has also wonderfully improved my voice for speaking and singing."

The Originals of these Testimonials may be seen at our Consulting Rooms, with hundreds of others.

One CARBOLIC SMOKE BALL will last a family several months, making it the cheapest remedy in the world at the price—10s., post free.

The CARBOLIC SMOKE BALL can be refilled, when empty, at a cost of 5s., post free. Address:

CARBOLIC SMOKE BALL CO., 27, PRINCES ST., HANOVER SQ., LONDON, W.

C H A P T E R   F O U R

CONTRACT LAW–MAKING ENFORCEABLE AGREEMENTS

> *"A verbal contract isn't worth the paper it's printed on."*
>
> Samuel Goldwyn,
> movie producer

CONTRACT AS AGREEMENT

The word **contract** often conjures an image of long documents with tiny print in a strange language. Some contracts are indeed long and seem to contain excessive wording that often repeats itself over and over again. This is not to say that average people cannot read and understand a contract. They *can* read contracts, but often fail to do so because they are in a hurry or assume that they have no choice but to sign the contract as it reads. Contracts are often presented to people in a "take-it-or-leave-it" manner.

A contract has numerous characteristics. Some legal writers refer to a contract as a set of promises. The parties entering into the contract promise to perform certain acts, or refrain from performing them, in exchange for other promises, such as payment. Other scholars see contracts not so much as promises but as a way of enforcing restitution. That is, the contract is the means by which people are compelled to do something.

One aspect of a contract which nearly all writers accept is that a contract is a **voluntary agreement**. It is an agreement by which the parties accept obligations that bind them. A workable definition of a contract is the following:

> *A contract is a legally recognized agreement, voluntarily entered into, that the parties intend to be enforceable at law.*

The phrase "enforceable at law" implies that either of the parties may sue if necessary to require the other to keep the obligation. A contract must be distinguished, then, from a mere social agreement. If two people make an agreement to engage in some social activity, one may not sue the other if the agreement is not kept. In cases where the parties dispute the existence of a contract, a court will look for clear evidence of consent. The rule is ***consensus ad idem*** (mutual agreement on the same subject) and the court will try to determine the existence and nature of the parties' intentions.

In the case of *Forde v. Grant* (Ontario, 1974) the plaintiff lived with the defendant for two years. During this time, the plaintiff made repairs to the defendant's house. When the couple separated, the plaintiff sought payment for the work. The Court ruled that, when the plaintiff did the work, he did it out of personal interest and "just for something to do." There was no expectation, at the time, that the defendant would pay for the work. The Court held that there was no contract and dismissed the plaintiff's claim.

The enforceability of a contract can be described by one of three terms:

1. **Valid**: A contract is valid if it meets all of the legal requirements and can be enforced by either party against the other. It is a contract without major defect.

2. **Void**: A contract is void if it fails to meet the essential requirements. Neither party can enforce such a contract and, in most cases, a court would hold that the contract never existed because it was defective from the start (void *ab initio*).
3. **Voidable**: A contract is voidable if one party is able to escape the terms at his or her option. In other words, there is a defect that one party may use to declare the contract void. If this party does not so choose, the contract remains enforceable.

MAKING AN OFFER

A contract comes into existence when one person, called the **offeror**, proposes a contract that is accepted by another person, called the **offeree**. The language of the offer must be capable of being interpreted as a serious intention to be legally bound. Therefore, words that indicate only a willingness to discuss a contract are not offers. For example, if Brown says to Green, "My car is for sale," Brown has not offered to sell it. The words indicate only an interest in entering into contract negotiations. The basic requirements of an offer are as follows:

1. The offer must be definite. If its terms are imprecise, it cannot be acted upon by the offeree.
2. The offer must be seriously intended. Offers made in anger, as a joke, or hastily thrown out in retort to an insult are not valid offers.
3. The offer must be communicated to the person or the class of people for whom it was intended. If the offer never arrives and the offeree hears about it later, he or she cannot act upon it. If the offer is delivered to the wrong person, it has not been properly communicated to the person who received it by mistake and that person cannot act on it.
4. The offer must be distinguished from an advertisement or an invitation to treat. Advertisements are not offers in the true sense. The law regards them as invitations to the public to inspect merchandise and then offer to buy. Although there are penalties for false advertising, the invitation is still not an offer which the offeree can accept.

An **invitation to treat** is not an offer, but rather a request by one party to another party asking for an offer. If Brown says to Green, "I want to sell my car—make me an offer," this is not an offer in itself. In *Saltzberg v. Hollis Securities Ltd.* (Ontario, 1964) the executor of an estate asked by letter that three parties bid for the entire estate. The letter stated that the property would be sold to the highest bidder. The plaintiff submitted the highest bid but the executor refused to make the sale. The Court held that the letter was not an offer nor a binding promise to accept the highest offer. It was only an invitation to the three parties to bid. The executor could then communicate acceptance, if any, to the highest bidder.

Although advertisements are generally not regarded as offers, there are exceptions to the rule. If an advertisement is worded in such a way that any person meeting stated criteria can make an acceptance, the advertisement may be regarded as a true offer. For example, if an announcement is made that a reward will be paid for the return of lost property, this is an offer that may be accepted by the finder. Perhaps the most famous case involving a dispute about the wording of an advertisement is the following.

CARHILL v. CARBOLIC SMOKE BALL CO.

England, 1893

The defendant company offered to pay a sum of money to any person who caught influenza after using its product, a type of incense, for two weeks. The company claimed that the smoke from the incense would ward off influenza. The plaintiff used the product and contracted influenza but the defendant refused to pay.

The Court noted that the defendant had advertised that it was serious about its claims and had deposited the "prize" money with a bank. This offer was made to the world at large and anyone could claim the money.

The basic defence that the company raised was that a person who was going to use the product for the stipulated time should first notify the company that he or she would like to be enrolled as an official contestant before beginning the test period. Otherwise, any person who contracted influenza could claim to have used the product. However, the advertisement said nothing about such a registration requirement.

The Court ordered the defendant to pay the money. The wording of the offer made it unreasonable to infer that all prospective users of the product would notify the defendant in advance.

After an offer has been made, it can be **revoked** by the offeror, who may notify the offeree that the offer no longer stands. An offer is automatically revoked if the offeror dies before acceptance, a counteroffer is made, or there is no acceptance within the time stipulated or within a reasonable length of time.

ACCEPTING THE OFFER

Once the offer has been made to the offeree, there are certain rules that apply if the offeree wants to accept. It is important that the offer be read carefully to determine if it has a time limit and if it describes the manner of acceptance.

1. The acceptance must be made in the manner and time stipulated in the offer. If no manner is stipulated, the acceptance may be made in any customary manner. If no time is stipulated, the acceptance must be made within a reasonable length of time. What is reasonable depends upon the subject matter of the offer. For example, the reasonable time to accept an offer to sell ice cream in July would be very short.
2. The acceptance must be communicated to the offeror. An offer cannot be worded in such a way that if the offeree says nothing, he or she accepts. For example, if the offer is worded, "If you do not accept the offer within 10 days, we will treat this as an acceptance," the offer is not valid. It is a general rule of law that "silence does not make consent."
3. An acceptance must be unconditional. If the offeree tries to accept the offer and change it at the same time, this is not a valid acceptance.

Once an offer has been accepted, neither the offer nor the acceptance can be revoked. A contract has been formed. Neither party can then try to add to or delete from the agreement. For example, if Brown and Green agree upon the sale of the car, Green cannot then add new terms such as "I want that dent in the door repaired before I take the car."

The time question can be important to both parties. An offer becomes effective when communicated to the offeree. An acceptance becomes effective when mailed, deposited with a telegraph office, faxed, or telephoned to the offeror. The **postal acceptance rule** holds that an acceptance becomes effective when mailed, even though the offeror is not aware that the acceptance has been made. It is wise to use registered mail as proof of the exact time that the letter was mailed. If the offeror wants to revoke the offer, he or she must communicate the revocation to the offeree before the acceptance is mailed. The greater time burden, then, is upon the offeror. The Ontario Court of Appeal has ruled that offers and acceptances may be transmitted by facsimile machine if both parties agree to this method.

RITCHIE BROTHERS AUCTIONEERS v. EVANS TURF FARMS

Ontario, 1990

Gordon Evans registered as a bidder with the plaintiff auctioneer. He signed a contract agreeing to honour all bids he made. He was assigned the number 176 and given a card with that number.

Evans walked around and looked at the farm equipment to be auctioned. He decided there was nothing there he wanted to buy, so he threw the card into a trash can. He did not tell the plaintiff that he was withdrawing from the auction.

On the day of the auction, someone bid $34 000 for a used tractor, using the card 176. Evans was sent a bill and told to pick up the machine. He refused, denying having attended the auction. The plaintiff sold the tractor privately for $20 000, then billed Evans $14 000. There were 2000 people at the auction and the judge concluded that it would be impossible to prove whether Evans had personally made the bid. The issue was whether Evans had accepted liability for the bid when he signed the contract that said he would pay for anything on which he was "the successful bidder." Evans denied he was the bidder.

The Court ruled that Evans could not be held accountable to the plaintiff. The agreement that Evans signed was not the contract in question before the Court. The basic question was whether there had been an offer and acceptance and, if so, who were the parties. There was no evidence that Evans had offered to purchase the tractor.

CONDITIONAL CONTRACTS

A **conditional contract** is generally one that contains a term specifying that the contract can be postponed or cancelled if the condition is not met or fulfilled.

For example, assume that Green offers to purchase a parcel of land from Brown on the condition that Brown drills a well that will produce a good flow of potable water. If Brown does not drill the well, or finds water fouled by sulphur, then the contract is not binding. Finding good water is a condition of the contract. Conditions are often placed in contracts that involve the purchase of real estate. The most common condition is a clause making the sale conditional upon the purchaser obtaining the necessary financing to make the purchase.

An offer of employment may contain a condition that the prospective employee pass certain tests or have certain qualifications. An offer to purchase a used automobile may be conditional upon it passing a mechanical fitness inspection.

Difficulty in interpretation may arise when one party alleges that the condition could have easily been met, but that the other party never tried to satisfy it. For example, if Green offered to buy a house from Brown, on condition of obtaining satisfactory financing, it may be presumed that Green will at least try to arrange the financing. Suppose Green simply decides he does not like the house and never applies to any bank or trust company for the money. Is Green in breach of the contract?

Another issue that might arise is whether one party may waive (not apply) a condition and then demand completion of the contract. For example, let us suppose that Green decides he will buy Brown's land without the well being drilled. Since the condition appears to protect only Green, may he unilaterally waive the condition and demand that Brown complete the sale? Or, must both parties agree to the waiver?

Although the courts are divided on the issue, the majority of decisions have held that one party cannot unilaterally waive a condition in the contract. The party must offer to do so and the other party must accept the waiver. This is true even if it appears that one party is gaining more from the condition than the other. Fine distinctions have been drawn where courts have found that a condition was only an "internal condition" and not a true condition that affected the entire contract. In British Columbia, the confusion has been settled by legislation: the *Law and Equity Act* states that a condition may be waived unilaterally provided it benefited only the party waiving the condition.

As well, courts often distinguish between inability to meet a condition and refusal to try to meet it. In *Rohr v. Tunney* (1982) the Supreme Court of Manitoba ruled that the defendant was in breach of contract for refusing to apply for financing of a real estate deal. The Court held that when parties enter into a contract, they must make a serious effort to meet their obligations. The defendant had refused to apply for financing because the market value of the property he had offered to buy had declined sharply and he was no longer interested in buying it.

STANDARD FORM CONTRACTS

The tendency of companies to prepare and make extensive use of printed, multi-page, standard form contracts causes special problems for the courts. Such contracts are prepared by lawyers who represent one party only. Although they may try to maintain some balance within the agreement, the more probable result is that the contract heavily favours one party over the other. Standard form contracts can be very lengthy and contain legal wording (**legalese**) which the other party might not understand. In many instances, the person does not even attempt to read the contract. The issue then arises as to whether the contract is binding.

As a general rule, people are bound by the printed terms on documents they sign whether they read them or not. They may try to escape the provisions of the printed wording by saying that the print was so small it could not be read, important terms were put in a hidden or obscure place where they would not be read, the document did not appear to be a contract at all, or the contract was so long that no one would have the time to read it.

Faced with the problem of printed contracts, the courts have developed some policies of fairness to assist people who sign contracts without reading them. For example, the courts have generally adopted the rule of **unfair surprise,** which means that very complicated and important terms must be specifically brought to the attention of the other party. The rule implies that the reasonable expectations of the other party as to what the contract states must not be upset or sabotaged by an unfair surprise hidden somewhere in the contract. The following was such a case.

TILDEN RENT-A-CAR v. CLENDENNING

Ontario, 1978

While in Vancouver, Clendenning rented a car from the plaintiff company. The clerk asked Clendenning if he wanted "additional coverage" (insurance) and the defendant said, "Yes." The contract was presented and signed, without being read, in the presence of the clerk. The contract was three pages of small print and Clendenning was in a hurry for a business appointment. He never read the contract, but assumed that he was fully insured for any possible accident, as he had requested maximum insurance and had paid an extra fee.

However, a provision in the contract stated that the customer must not operate the vehicle after consuming alcohol. It did not say after consuming *excessive* alcohol. The contract stated the customer would consume *no* alcohol.

The defendant was involved in a motor vehicle accident while driving the car. He told the investigating officer that he had consumed a modest amount of alcohol but there was no suggestion that he was impaired. The plaintiff, relying upon the terms of the contract, sued for damage to the car.

The Court noted that the contract was very long and that, when people rent cars, they are often in a hurry. In fact, much of the advertising of rental companies stresses that they will put the customer into the driver's seat without protracted delays at airports, etc. In one television advertisement, a famous athlete was shown renting a car at an airport. He ran through the airport, jumped into a convertible, and drove away.

The clerk knew Clendenning was in a hurry and had not read the contract. Since the company was aware that the contract contained important terms, the company was under an obligation to take reasonable measures to draw the customer's attention to the wording that stated that *any* consumption of alcohol would invalidate the insurance. Since the company had failed to do so, the terms were not enforceable against a party who did not know that such words were in the contract.

The *Clendenning* case should not be misunderstood to mean that a person may carelessly sign all contracts without making an effort to read them. The Court only held that, where the nature of the agreement makes it impractical for one party to read it, then the party who prepared the contract has an obligation to point out the key terms. Failure to do so creates an unfair surprise which cannot be used against the other party.

SIMPLE OR PAROL CONTRACTS

A **simple contract** includes any contract not made under seal. It may be in writing, made orally, or made by the implied actions of the parties. Implied actions can included shaking hands, raising one's hand at an auction, or any physical behaviour which leads the other party to assume a contract has been made. The casual nature of simple contracts is the reason they are often called "informal contracts."

Simple contracts are sometimes called **parol contracts**. This is a bit misleading, because the term "parol" really means "oral." Simple contracts are enforceable if they meet all the basic requirements of voluntary agreement. The primary danger of a simple contract that is not in writing, or is not carefully drafted, is that later the two parties might disagree about what the terms were and, unless there are witnesses, it is nearly impossible to enforce the contract.

SPECIALTY OR FORMAL CONTRACTS

A **specialty contract** is a contract under seal. A sealed instrument (document) or deed, is signed and a seal affixed which gives "formality" to it. In early England, the common practice was to drop melted wax onto the document, then impress some letter or design into the wax to indicate the genuineness of the signature. Today, wax is seldom used. The common practice is to paste a red sticker on the contract, then impress an image into the sticker with a special machine. On many contracts, the word "Seal" is printed next to the place where the parties sign. There is usually an **attestation clause** containing words such as "In witness whereof I have hereunto set my hand and seal" printed above where the person signs.

However, despite this formal appearance, some courts have taken the strict view that these may not be proper specialty contracts. In some cases, the seals were on the documents before the parties signed and the courts ruled that the contracts were only simple contracts.

LINTON v. ROYAL BANK OF CANADA

Ontario, 1966

A bank employee, without the knowledge of the plaintiff, placed a seal on a loan guarantee after it had been signed. The guarantee contained an attestation clause and had the word "Seal" in parentheses opposite the space provided for signature.

The Court held that the language of the guarantee indicated that the plaintiff intended from the outset to constitute the guarantee as his formal deed. The bank had not materially altered the guarantee, because pasting a seal on it had not changed the legal consequences of the original document. Because the guarantor had already sealed the document, no further sealing was necessary.

The specialty contract, because of its formal nature, is the more secure form of contract. It extends by many more years the limitations period under which the parties may sue. There are some legal transactions, including mortgages and deeds, that require a specialty contract. Some of the contracts requiring formal preparation are included under the *Statute of Frauds*, which is discussed in the next section.

STATUTE OF FRAUDS

Historians do not agree as to why the *Statute of Frauds* was first passed in England in 1677. Some believe that the law was needed to deal with problems of perjury and deceit. Too many contracts that had been made orally were being challenged by one of the parties, who claimed the other had violated the terms. Without a written contract, the matter fell to the courts to try to determine which party was telling the truth.

Other historians believe that the law merely codified the growing legal practice of putting more and more contracts into writing. Whatever its origins, the *Statute of Frauds* still greatly affects contract law in Canada.

Two very important sections were part of the original statute. Section 17 dealt with the sale of goods, which will be examined in a later chapter. Section 4 pertained to certain types of contracts that required written agreement. The original section read as follows:

> No action shall be brought whereby to charge any executor or administrator upon any special promise to answer damages out of his own estate; or whereby to charge the defendant upon any special promise to answer for the debt, default or miscarriage of another person; or to charge any person upon any agreement made upon consideration of marriage; or upon any contract or sale of lands, tenements, or hereditaments, or any interest in or concerning them; or upon any agreement that is not to be performed within the space of one year from the making thereof; unless the agreement upon which such action shall be brought, or some memorandum or note thereof, shall be in writing and signed by the party to be charged therewith or some other person thereunto by him lawfully authorized.

Every word of this archaic law has been subject to judicial interpretation. That so much of it has survived so long is, in itself, an extraordinary credit to the drafters of the law. The basic thrust of the law is that certain contracts must be in writing or they are not enforceable. In most provinces, the types of contracts include:

- Long-term leases, for periods of longer than three years.
- Contracts for the sale of land or an interest in land, to apply to royalties, rights, and mortgages. This would include such things as mineral rights, oil production royalties, etc.
- A promise by one person to pay the debt or default of another person. This is generally referred to as a guarantee.
- A contract not to be completed within one year of the making. If no specific time period is mentioned, the court will consider whether or not the contract could have been completed within one year of the making.

- A promise by an executor of an estate to pay the debts of the estate out of his or her own pocket. Such a promise must be in writing and the executor must receive some form of consideration for the promise.
- Contracts in consideration of marriage. This would be a contract whereby the parties agreed to the transfer of valuables or the payment of a sum of money if a certain marriage took place. It does not include the actual promise between the man and woman to marry each other.

There have been numerous modifications to the original British law. For example, nearly all provinces have repealed the wording regarding marriage contracts because such contracts are covered in other statutes dealing with family law. British Columbia and Manitoba have repealed the statute completely. Matters regarding specialty contracts are dealt with under other statutes, such as British Columbia's *Law and Equity Act*. Quebec never had a *Statute of Frauds*. Contracts are covered under the Quebec *Code Civil*.

A formal contract does not have to be in a particular form. The law will accept any written document or collection of documents which, taken together, form what is referred to in the statute as a "written memorandum," proving the existence of the agreement. Letters, receipts, telegrams, and even notes have been accepted as proof of the existence of a contract. In some cases the courts have accepted a combination of written documents, oral evidence, and personal action to prove the existence of a contract.

JOHNSON v. NOVA SCOTIA TRUST COMPANY

Nova Scotia, 1974

The appellant, Laura Johnson, claimed possession of a house belonging to a deceased woman. The woman had persuaded Johnson to live with her in 1967 as a companion and had promised that if Johnson was still with her at the time of her death, Johnson would receive the house and furnishings. Several letters and the testimony of a number of witnesses were used as evidence to prove the existence of the agreement between the two women. The deceased had made out a will in her own handwriting and had given it to the appellant along with a copy of the deed, saying, "Now, there, Laura, is your security." Later, the deceased had changed her will without telling Johnson.

The trial judge refused to award the property to Johnson, but the Court of Appeal held that the letters and the handing over of a copy of the deed formed sufficient "written memorandum" within the meaning of the *Statute of Frauds* to form a binding contract. The Court held that it was not an agreement that the deceased woman was free to change later on by changing her will. Johnson received the house and furnishings.

While it is normal practice for both parties to sign a contract, this is not always required. It is a long-established principle of law that a plaintiff who has not signed a contract can sue a defendant who has signed it.

The case law surrounding the *Statute of Frauds* is immense, and the possible variations unlimited. For example, in the case of *Shaver v. Hamilton Corp. Creameries Ltd.* (Ontario, 1936) the plaintiff orally agreed to sell milk from a herd of Guernsey cows, for a stated price, in return for shares of the defendant corporation. The contract was not within the statute because the plaintiff might sell the cows within one year, might have no milk to sell, or might die. If no time limit is mentioned in the contract, the court must try to determine if the contract could have been performed within one year.

Guarantees are commonly used in business and result in many legal disputes. The practice of one person promising to pay the debt of another person is fraught with many legal pitfalls. It is a complex area of law because of many other potential problems, including the ignorance of the person giving the guarantee as to the true nature of the agreement. Defendants have successfully argued that they gave guarantees without knowing what they signed. The defences of mistake, misrepresentation, undue influence, duress, and fraud have all been raised at one time or another. Notwithstanding all these other potential problems, a person giving a guarantee must do so in writing, in unambiguous terms, and without conditions.

One of the problems that can arise from a rigorous application of the *Statute of Frauds* is that the statute itself can be misused to defraud someone. For example, assume that Green orally agreed to build a garage on Brown's land. Green buys the materials and does the work, then asks for payment. Brown refuses to pay anything because the contract was not in writing. Brown is correct that the contract should have been in writing, but to allow him to use the *Statute of Frauds* in this manner means Green will be cheated by the law, not protected by it. Brown has used the statute to obtain a free garage. The courts decided quite early after the passage of the statute that they would not allow it to be abused in this manner and create injustices. Although the statute says nothing about "equity" or "part performance" the courts took the position that one party could not stand by while the other party acted to his or her own detriment. Thus, the remedy of part performance was invented by the courts.

DOCTRINE OF PART PERFORMANCE

The doctrine of **part performance** means that the *Statute of Frauds* does not apply where there has been performance or part performance of an oral contract or where otherwise the result would be a fraud or injustice. The actions of the party claiming part performance must be consistent with the contract alleged and must prove the existence of the contract.

In the British case of *Wakeham v. MacKenzie* (1968) the plaintiff orally agreed with the defendant that she would become the defendant's housekeeper if he left his house to her in his will. She gave up her apartment and cared for the defendant for two years. He did not leave his house to her, so she sued his estate. The Court awarded her the house, saying that her actions were explicable by reference only to some contract and her version was consistent with the contract she alleged. Thus, the Court found part performance.

The *Wakeham* case suggests obvious dangers. Although the plaintiff's claim was consistent with a contract, it was also consistent with other possible explanations. Conceivably, the deceased offered her only a half-interest in the house. Or he may have promised that, after his house was sold upon his death, she would be paid some amount of money. The Court was very generous in accepting the truth of what the plaintiff claimed, considering there was no other evidence.

BAY TOWER HOMES v. ST. ANDREW'S LAND CORP.

Ontario, 1990

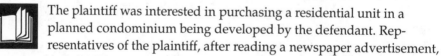

The plaintiff was interested in purchasing a residential unit in a planned condominium being developed by the defendant. Representatives of the plaintiff, after reading a newspaper advertisement, went to the defendant's business office and saw the artist's drawings of the building. They were interested in the penthouse unit and were told the price was $1.3 million. Although the sales representative did not have so much as a floor plan of the penthouse, the plaintiff's representatives said they would buy it. They were told they must submit three cheques totalling $195 000 as a deposit. They wrote the cheques and left, understanding they would be asked to sign a formal offer form later. A few days later they received a telephone call from the president of the defendant company who said: "We inadvertently sold you the penthouse." The defendant tore the plaintiff's cheques into pieces and mailed them back.

The plaintiff argued that it had a binding contract by virtue of part performance of the contract. However, the Court disagreed that the matter had been taken out of the *Statute of Frauds*. The judge held that there was no enforceable contract. There was no signed memorandum, no contract under seal, nothing that specifically said the plaintiff had purchased the penthouse or any other unit. The judge ruled that a newspaper article and three uncashed cheques do not satisfy the "formalities of the statute."

The doctrine of part performance is normally applied to contracts for the sale or purchase of land, but it can be applied to other types of cases. Part performance is a rule that obliges one party to a contract to pay for work that may be only partially completed by the other party, even in the absence of a proper, written contract. In other words, the defendant may not stand by and allow the plaintiff to perform part of the contract and then refuse to fulfil his or her part by raising a "technical defence" that the contract was not in proper form. In such a situation it would really amount to fraud to permit the defendant to abuse the *Statute of Frauds* in this manner.

STEWARD et al. v. GASKIN et al.

New Brunswick, 1970

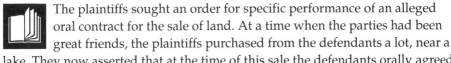

The plaintiffs sought an order for specific performance of an alleged oral contract for the sale of land. At a time when the parties had been great friends, the plaintiffs purchased from the defendants a lot, near a lake. They now asserted that at the time of this sale the defendants orally agreed to sell them the shore lot between the plaintiffs' land and the lake if the defendants were able to buy it from a third party. The defendants were able to buy the lot but then refused to sell it to the plaintiffs. As a result, the plaintiffs did not have access to the lake at all.

The plaintiffs argued that they had partly performed their part of the bargain by purchasing the first lot and then purchasing a boat. They had also started to bulldoze a road to the lake through some trees, but had done so without the permission of the defendants.

The Court held that this was not part performance. The purchase of a boat, on the expectation that there would be access to the water, had nothing to do with the purchase of the second lot. The purchase of the first lot was an independent contract. The action was dismissed.

QUANTUM MERUIT AND UNJUST ENRICHMENT

When a person expressly requests another person to perform a service without specifying any remuneration, but with an understanding that the service is to be paid for, there is an implied promise to pay ***quantum meruit***, which means "whatever amount the person deserves." A claim under this rule requires that the work has been done and that the person doing the work believed he or she would be paid.

KENNEDY v. DOYLE

Ontario, 1976

The plaintiff cared for her father from 1966 until his death in 1972. She never asked him for payment and he never offered any. However, the daughter had an expectation that she would inherit her father's estate upon his death. When she did not receive it, she sued the estate.

The Court held that the daughter could recover her actual out-of-pocket expenses, but nothing further. When a person performs services for a stranger without an agreement as to compensation, the law implies that reasonable compensation is to be paid. However, between father and daughter, that presumption does not operate; the services were presumed to be gratuitous. For there to be liability for compensation, an express or implied contract must be found. On the evidence, neither existed and therefore only the portion of the plaintiff's claim for expenses was allowed.

A more difficult situation may arise if the plaintiff does something that unintentionally gives the defendant a benefit.

RUABON STEAMSHIP CO. v. LONDON ASSURANCE

England, 1900

The appellant steamship company owned a ship that was due to go into dry dock for inspection and repair. At this time, its insurance company would inspect the ship and assess the insurance premium for the next year. All of this procedure would be done at the expense of the steamship company.

Shortly before the ship was to enter dry dock, it was rammed and damaged by the negligence of another ship's captain. The London Assurance Company, as insurer for the second ship, was required to pay the damages. The ship was brought in for repair and, while in dry dock, also had its regular insurance inspection. This resulted in the appellant having the inspection done at no cost to itself. The respondent insurance company, having paid the claim, sued for repayment of part of the money—an amount equal to what the appellant would have paid for the inspection.

The lower courts ordered the money repaid, but the House of Lords dismissed the action. The cost to London Assurance had not been increased at all by what happened. They were obliged to pay for the ship's repair and that is what they paid, nothing more. The fact that the shipowner obtained some secondary benefit did not compel the shipowner to reimburse the insurance company. The judges disputed the idea that there exists "some principle of justice that a man ought not to get an advantage unless he pays for it."

To argue that the defendant has received an **unjust enrichment**, the plaintiff must establish three things:

1. The defendant was enriched;
2. There was a corresponding deprivation or cost to the plaintiff;
3. The absence of any just reason for the enrichment.

If the person is paid money that should not have been paid and the mistake is identified, the law generally requires that the money be repaid. For example, if, because of a computer error, a taxpayer receives an income tax return that is too large, the taxpayer must refund the money to the government. There can be exceptions to this rule, however, as illustrated by the following case.

BACHE v. BORINS

Ontario, 1986

The defendant went to the plaintiff stockbrokers and presented them with a certificate for 1000 shares of Washington Natural Gas Company of West Virginia. She asked what the shares were worth. The account executive could not find the stock listed, so he asked the manager, who said that Washington Natural Gas of Delaware had changed its name to Washington Natural Gas of West Virginia. In fact, the two companies were completely different and had no relationship with each other. Washington Natural Gas of Delaware was worth $15 per share. It would later be learned that Washington Natural Gas of West Virginia was worthless. The broker sold the stock for the defendant and she was paid $15 000, less commission.

Four months later, the plaintiff discovered the error and demanded that the money be repaid. However, the defendant had spent $10 000, which was not recoverable.

The Court held that the plaintiff had waited too long and could recover only $5000. The judge ruled:

> *The law appears well established that money paid under a mistake of fact may be recovered, however careless the party paying may have been in failing to use due diligence to enquire into the facts. Nor is the payor prevented by law from collecting once the money was spent.*

However, the judge found that Bache had taken too long to detect the mistake and notify Borins before she spent the money. Therefore, it was no longer recoverable.

In the *Bache* case, the judge appears to have created something that might be called "unjust solution" to offset the principle of unjust enrichment. The defendant was lured into reckless spending by the mistake of the plaintiff. To repay the money she would have to work long and hard to correct the plaintiff's error.

PAROL EVIDENCE RULE

The **parol evidence rule** is that if the language of a written contract is clear and unambiguous, then parol (oral) evidence may not be admitted to alter, vary, or interpret the words used in the writing. If the court is faced with two different versions of the contract, one in writing and one oral, then the court must accept the written contract as the true agreement. To allow oral evidence to take priority would serve to undermine the importance of putting agreements in writing.

The rule is not absolutely rigid in its application. In some situations, to apply it would create an injustice. The most notable exception to the rule is where one party wants to show that the contract was obtained by fraud, misrepresentation, or mistake. In such circumstances the party does not want to vary the agreement but rather have a court nullify it at common law. For this reason, some legal writers argue that fraud is not a true exception to the rule at all, because it does not affect the terms of the contract but attacks the entire agreement.

Courts have allowed oral evidence to explain incomplete documents, explain the meaning of controversial terms, and ascertain the true intention of the parties. The court may also accept oral evidence to show that the written contract is not the entire contract. There may be a second, collateral agreement that should be made part of the overall contract.

CODERRE v. CODERRE

Alberta, 1975

The defendant husband, after 27 years of marriage, left the matrimonial home, which was registered in his name, to live with another woman. The wife and the couple's three children remained in the home. The wife petitioned for a divorce and the initial decree (decree *nisi*) was granted.

On the way home from court, the husband was alleged to have agreed orally to let the wife have a one-half interest in the house. This claim was not included in the settlement agreement worked out by the lawyers. The wife later sued, claiming this was a clerical error.

The suit was dismissed. The Court would not alter a written agreement unless the applicant could prove beyond a reasonable doubt that the written agreement was not the complete agreement and that there was a term which both had intended to conclude. The plaintiff was unable to prove to the satisfaction of the Court that the husband had made the promise she claimed.

As people are not generally aware of the existence or importance of the parol evidence rule, there are situations under which people are victimized by oral promises. For this reason, some provinces have inserted provisions in specific statutes relaxing the rule. For example, under the Ontario *Business Practices Act*, which is discussed in a later chapter, a court may ignore the parol evidence rule if "the consumer is not reasonably able to protect his interests because of ... physical infirmity, ignorance, illiteracy, inability to understand the language of an agreement, or similar factors." Alberta, British Columbia, and Saskatchewan have similar legislation.

PRIVITY OF CONTRACT

The idea of being **privy** to a contract refers to being a party to the agreement, with rights and obligations. The common law distinguishes between those who are actually involved in a contract and those who claim rights under a contract, even though they are not parties to it. For example, if Brown signs a contract with Green under which Brown promises to convey property to Black, Brown and Green are the parties to the contract. Black is not a party to it. The **privity rule** applies only to Brown and Green. If Brown does not convey the land as promised, Black cannot personally sue upon a contract to which he is not a party.

The basic reason for the rule is obvious. Black has not given Brown anything for the promise and, as far as Black is concerned, it is a gratuitous promise to make a gift. A person who is not a direct party to a contract has neither rights nor obligation under it. Black will have to persuade Green to enforce the contract on his behalf.

The privity rule works in reverse as well. Brown and Green cannot sign a contract that compels Black to perform an obligation. Two people cannot contract to impose a duty upon some third person who is not a party to the contract at all.

There are exceptions to the rule. If it can be shown that one of the parties to the contract is really acting as an agent for the third party, the agreement might be enforceable. As well, contracts under seal could be enforced because consideration is not relevant. Cases involving estates have often been held to be outside the normal rule. For example, if Mr. Green contracted with the ABC Life Insurance Company to pay the proceeds of an insurance policy to Green's widow, the contract could be enforced by Mrs. Green even though she was not a party to the contract.

GREENWOOD SHOPPING PLAZA LTD. v. BEATTIE

Supreme Court of Canada, 1980

The owner of a shopping mall (the lessor) entered into a lease with a business (the lessee) for the use of premises in the mall. The lease contained a clause which said that if there was any loss caused by the acts of the lessee, the lessor would not grant subrogation rights to the insurance company with which the lessor was insured against loss by fire. **Subrogation** means the right to sue for loss caused by someone else. In insurance contracts it means that if G causes damages to the insured premises of D, the insurance company will pay D for the loss. The insurance company will then sue G. The lease stated that this would not be done.

A fire was started by the negligent acts of employees of the lessee. The insurance company agreed that it could not sue the lessee directly. However, the company sued the employees personally for the damage. The insurance company took the position that nothing in the lease prevented them from suing individuals, only the company. The employees argued that they were protected by the lease as well. They argued that their employer was their agent when it signed the lease.

The Supreme Court of Canada ruled in favour of the insurance company. It held that the lease did not protect the employees. There was no evidence that the employer was their agent in signing the lease. They were not parties to the lease and the privity rule allowed them to be sued directly.

A person cannot seek protection in the wording of a receipt or guarantee if the person is not a direct party to the agreement. This was the decision of the Court in the following case.

MULLER MARTINI CANADA v. KUEHNE AND NAGEL LTD.

Ontario, 1991

The applicant brought a motion for leave to argue a special case. The applicant had stored 14 machines in one of the respondent's warehouses. The warehouse receipt clearly stated that merchandise was not insured by the respondent. The applicant had not arranged for insurance. The receipt also stated that the warehouseman's responsibility was reasonable care and diligence required by law, but that liability was limited to $40 per package. One of the applicant's machines was dropped by two of the respondent's employees, who were being supervised by a third employee. The machine had been damaged and could not be repaired. The loss was $54 000.

The applicant sued the respondent company and the three employees. The question for the Court was whether the employees could rely upon the limitation of liability clause in the warehouse receipt as a defence. The Court held that there was no privity of contract between the employees and the applicant. The contract had been between the applicant and the respondent company only. Exceptions to the privity of contract rule are agency, trust, assignment, or statute. The evidence did not suggest that the respondent had been acting as agent or trustee for the employees. Accordingly, the employees could not look to the limitation of liability clause in the contract between the applicant and respondent as a defence to the applicant's claim. The term "warehouseman" did not clearly refer to the employees. The respondent could have included its employees under the limitation clause, but had not done so.

COMPETENCE TO CONTRACT

A basic principle of law is that a contract cannot be enforced against a person not mentally competent to enter into it. As well, in some situations, a contract may be set aside simply because of a basic inequity of enforcing it against a person who really did not have true freedom to contract.

Those generally having special status include minors, intoxicated people, mentally impaired people, native people on reserves, and limited companies.

MINORS

People are legally classed as **minors**, or infants, until they reach a certain age, upon which they "attain their majority" and become adults. The legal age is determined by each province, and differs across Canada.

Age of Majority	Provinces
18	Alberta, Manitoba, Ontario, Prince Edward Island, Quebec, Saskatchewan
19	British Columbia, New Brunswick, Newfoundland Nova Scotia, Northwest Territories, Yukon Territory

To protect minors from their lack of knowledge and experience, the law has generally held that contracts entered into by minors are voidable by the minors. The mechanism of voidability permits minors to contract with adults but permits the minors to cancel their contracts without penalty in most cases. The adults, however, are usually bound to their contracts with minors to the same extent that they are with adults.

The most important exception to the rule is that of **necessaries of life**. A minor may contract to obtain necessaries that are within the minor's station in life (living standard). In any action against a minor, the burden is upon the plaintiff to show that the goods supplied were suitable to the **station in life** of the minor and also that the minor did not have the necessaries at the time of sale. Necessaries have been recognized by the courts to include food, clothing, shelter, medical care, education, tools to earn a living, and transportation to work.

When a court examines a minor-adult contract it is relevant to determine how the contract has affected the minor. The following basic rules apply:

1. A contract detrimental to the minor's interest is void from the outset and neither party can sue the other. The parties may recover any money paid.
2. If a minor has performed work under a contract that is void because it is detrimental to the minor's interests, the minor should be paid a fair value for the labour and materials provided.
3. Those contracts that are for necessaries of life are looked upon as valid and binding upon the minor if the contract is for the minor's benefit.

A minor can cancel any contract, including a contract for necessaries, if the minor has never received any benefit under the contract.

TORONTO MARLBORO HOCKEY CLUB v. TONELLI

Ontario, 1977

Sixteen-year-old John Tonelli signed a two-year contract to play hockey with the Toronto Marlboros. The following year, this contract was replaced by a new three-year contract, with a fourth year at the club's option. The contract provided that if Tonelli obtained a contract with a professional hockey team, he would pay the Marlboros 20 percent of his gross earnings for each of his first three years. In return for this promise, Tonelli would receive a salary, coaching, and the chance to play in the Junior A League. The contract could be terminated at the club's discretion.

When Tonelli turned 18, he repudiated his existing contract and signed a new contract with the Houston Aeros under which he would be paid $320 000 over the next three years. The Marlboros brought an action against Tonelli for breach of contract. The plaintiffs sought 20 percent of Tonelli's salary, or $64 000.

The Ontario Court of Appeal held that the Marlboros' contract had been unfairly weighted in favour of the club. It had not been freely negotiated between the parties but had really been offered to the defendant on a take-it-or-leave-it basis. In effect, the clubs in the league had the young players over a barrel, which created an unequal bargaining position. If the players did not sign the standard contract that all the teams used, the player would be frozen out of hockey.

The plaintiffs argued that the overall scheme of bringing young players into hockey was a fair one. The fortunate players who were signed by professional clubs were expected to share the wealth with other players who were less successful.

The Court was not persuaded that the overall plan was the issue. The Court said: "The question is whether this contract at the time it was made was beneficial to this player having regard to its terms and the circumstances surrounding its execution." The Court held that the contract was so unfair that it could not be enforced against Tonelli.

The years 16 to 18 (or 19) are awkward years in the legal sense. In most provinces, parents may legally stop supporting a child at the age of 16 if the child has withdrawn from parental control. However, the child cannot fully contract for several more years. In this interim period, there are problems determining if the parent must support the child at all.

A parent is liable for necessaries that a child, living at home, charges to the parent's credit if the parent is not providing the necessaries. A parent must also pay for necessaries for a child under the age of 16 who is not living with the parent. A parent is not liable for a child's debts for non-necessaries unless the parent has guaranteed them in writing or has somehow indicated to the creditor that the parent will pay the debts on a continuing basis. Thus, if a minor joins a record club, the parent cannot be required to make the regular payments just because of the parental relationship. In *Torrens v. Torrens* (Ontario, 1991) a father was permitted to stop paying child support under a divorce agreement for his 19-year-old son who had inherited $23 000 from his grandfather. The Court held that when a young person has his or her own financial resources, the parent is relieved of the support obligation.

If a minor signs a contract while under age but then reaches the age of majority, the question arises as to whether the contract can now be enforced. The law tries to distinguish between two types of contracts:

- **Contracts affording one-time benefits**: The contract may have afforded the minor a benefit on one occasion only. In such a case, the law requires that the minor specifically ratify (legally confirm) the contract in writing after becoming an adult.
- **Contracts affording continuous benefits**: The contract may have afforded the minor a continuous benefit, such as a car bought on the instalment basis. In this case the law requires that the minor specifically repudiate the contract after becoming an adult. If the minor says nothing or continues to

use the item and make payments, then the law interprets the minor's actions as having ratified the contract.

INTOXICATED PEOPLE

People who enter into contracts while they are intoxicated can later repudiate the contracts if they can prove that (1) they were truly impaired to the point where their mental processes were not operating properly, (2) the other parties to the contracts knew or ought to have known of their condition, and (3) they sought to repudiate the contracts within a reasonable time.

If a person does not act promptly after recovering from the impairment, it will be assumed that the person is content with the contract. The person must also return as many benefits obtained under the contract as possible, in an attempt to return the parties to their original position.

LANDRY v. TAKIFF

New Brunswick, 1979

The plaintiff, an elderly man, conveyed a half interest in a woodlot to the defendant. The defendant paid for the half interest. A few months later, the old man conveyed the other half to the defendant. The plaintiff was in a state of drunkenness at the time of the second conveyance and received no money or payment for the second conveyance. He permitted a number of months to go by before trying to rescind the contract.

The Court held that the plaintiff could not have the second conveyance set aside, because he failed to act promptly when he became aware of the circumstances that entitled him to avoid the agreement.

The mere consumption of alcohol itself is not enough to set aside a contract. The plaintiff must show that alcohol rendered him or her incapable of sound judgment. If the alcohol serves only to make the plaintiff excited or somewhat adventurous in business dealings, this is not enough to later repudiate the contract. As well, the other party must be aware that the plaintiff was impaired by alcohol.

MENTALLY IMPAIRED PEOPLE

A person's mental impairment may be caused by a variety of factors, including disease of the mind, senility, or stroke. Someone suffering from mental impairment is liable for contracts made for necessaries that have been received, but is not liable for any other contracts.

In recent years, the extended life expectancy of Canadians has created a class of people who are not truly mentally impaired but who are not fully able to represent their own interests. This class is primarily composed of the aged and the handicapped. There are no special common law rules relating to the contractual capacity of people who are sane, but who have a diminished capacity because their mental competence is starting to decline with age. Elderly people are often the target of dishonest business schemes.

This inequality of bargaining power has led to the enactment of a number of special laws designed to protect those who are most often victimized. In Ontario, the *Business Practices Act* identifies unfair business practices and also allows people to cancel contracts if they were unable to understand the contract by reason of ignorance, infirmity, or illiteracy. People may also cancel contracts if they were overcharged or did not receive substantial benefit. Alberta, British Columbia, and Newfoundland have very similar legislation.

Even in the absence of special legislation, the courts have been protective of people who were unable to fully protect their interests. Defences such as misrepresentation and mistake have been given generous latitude.

NATIVE PEOPLE ON RESERVES

Native people on reserves are wards of the Crown and occupy a special status. They cannot enter into contracts, except for necessaries, and their land and chattel property cannot be pledged as collateral or seized for non-payment of any debt. This law also creates problems for native people by denying them full capacity to contract. For example, banks are reluctant to lend to native people because they cannot pledge property as collateral for the loans.

LIMITED COMPANIES

The law recognizes organizations as "artificial people" who may contract. Groups of individuals can acquire an identity as a single person. However, there are restrictions upon the power of a corporation to contract, depending upon the type of corporation created.

The Crown is a corporation at common law and has capacity to enter into contracts. There is a federal Crown and provincial Crowns. Each has the power to contract in those areas it controls under the *Constitution Act, 1867*. The legislation that creates Crown agencies also empowers those agencies to enter into contracts within the scope of the enabling legislation. Any contract outside that power is void.

COMMUNITY ECONOMIC DEV. FUND v. MAXWELL et al.

Manitoba, 1990

The Manitoba Communities Economic Development Fund loaned $150 000 to Canadian Pickles Company Ltd., a family business located in the town of Stoney Mountain. The loan was personally guaranteed by Robert O'Donnell, who owned 51 percent of the company. Rudy Maxwell, the corporate secretary, owned 25 percent of the company. He also guaranteed the loan.

The legislation which created the Fund stated that loans were to be made to "encourage economic development in remote and isolated communities." Stoney Mountain is not a remote or isolated community and the loan should not have been made. The company used the loan to pay off other creditors, and then soon after went broke. The Fund sued the two guarantors personally.

The Manitoba Court of Appeal ruled that the loan could not be collected from either O'Donnell or Maxwell because the loan was illegal and the Fund had no statutory power to make it.

Unincorporated associations do not have the power to contract unless they are not specifically recognized by statute. Chief among these are private clubs and religious societies. In *Canada Morning News Co. v. Thompson* (1930) the issue was whether an unincorporated society could enter into a lease. The Supreme Court of Canada held that it could not become a tenant and that the person who signed the lease was personally liable for it.

Trade unions and labour unions at one time had no recognition under the common law. It is only under specific legislation that they have been given legal recognition, provided the union has been properly certified.

A limited company or corporation may be considered an artificial person that may enter into contracts in its own name. The charter of the company identifies the nature and scope of the business that the company will conduct. All other contracts are unlawful. Usually, the secretary-treasurer of the company is the official designated to sign contracts. When a company incorporates, it acquires a corporate seal which should be affixed to specialty contracts.

REVIEW: POINTS OF LAW

1. A contract is a voluntary agreement which the parties intend to be enforceable at law.
2. A simple contract may be oral, written, or implied but is not under seal.
3. A specialty contract is a contract under seal.
4. Under the *Statute of Frauds,* certain contracts must be in writing to be enforceable.
5. A contract that would not be enforceable under the *Statute of Frauds* may be enforceable if it has been partly performed.
6. Under the rule of *quantum meruit* a person may be entitled to payment for services performed, even in the absence of a formal contract.
7. To be valid, an offer must be definite, serious, and communicated to the other party.
8. In most instances, newspaper advertisements are not offers, they are invitations to the public to make offers.
9. To be valid, acceptance of an offer must be made within the time stipulated or within a reasonable length of time.
10. The attempt to accept an offer and change it at the same time creates a counteroffer.
11. Under the parol evidence rule, oral evidence cannot be admitted to contradict the clear, unambiguous terms of a written contract.
12. The use of standard form contracts has caused the courts to adopt countermeasures to protect parties from unfair surprises in printed contracts.
13. A minor is generally not liable on a contract except for necessaries of life.
14. A minor can enforce a contract against an adult.

LEGAL BRIEFS

1. The G Corporation offered to sell lumber to the B Stores at the price of $400 per thousand metres. The offer was sent by facsimile machine. It read: "Offer good till noon tomorrow." B Stores accepted the offer at 10 a.m. the next day and sent the acceptance by facsimile machine. It was not received until 2:30 p.m. because an employee of G had accidentally turned off its fax machine. Is there a contract?
2. State yes or no to indicate whether the following contracts must be in writing in order to be enforceable:
   a) A personal loan of $250 between friends.
   b) A mortgage on a house.
   c) An agreement to rent an apartment for an indefinite period.
   d) A contract for the sale of a small strip of land for $1.
   e) A promise by a grandparent to pay for the wedding of a granddaughter.
3. M signed a contract with the E dance studio for dance lessons. The contract was for 20 years of dance lessons and M prepaid for the entire package. At the time M signed the contract, she was 78 years of age. Is this a valid agreement?
4. The W Corporation had a major contract with the Y Company. When the Y Company broke the contract, the employees of W were faced with layoffs. They urged their employer to sue Y in order to enforce the contract. The employer refused, citing legal costs as a reason. The employees banded together and wanted to sue Y directly. Can they do so?
5. L rented a parcel of land to H for several years. H indicated that he wanted to buy it and L said he would sell it to him for $15 000. H asked for one year's time to raise the money and L promised not to sell it to anyone else. H made major improvements on the land. Six months later, L was committed to a mental hospital because of brain damage due to alcoholism. L's affairs were taken over by his son, N. Six months later, H approached N with $15 000 to complete the purchase. N retorted: "A crummy fifteen thousand for that land? You must be joking!" Must N sell H the land?
6. F owned a used car that was in very good mechanical condition. The paint was a bit faded, but there was no rust. R sideswiped F's car. R's insurance company paid to have the body repaired. The company then said it would also pay to have the damaged side painted. F objected to this, saying: "You can't paint one side of a car. It will look stupid. One side will be dull and faded; the other side bright and shiny. You have to paint the whole car." The insurance company replied, "Why should you get a free paint job out of this? That's unjust enrichment." Who is right?

7. U and T were neighbours. Their land adjoined at a low spot, which was under water much of the time. U dug a drainage ditch to carry away the water and used a large, commercial pump to pump the standing water from the land. The process drained T's land at the same time, thereby greatly increasing the value of the land. U sent T a bill for half the work. T refused to pay, saying, "This was your idea, not mine." Must T pay?
8. C offered to purchase from S a hotel, restaurant, and bar complex. The offer was conditional upon "satisfactory audit of financial records of the business." The offer was good for two months. C's accountants began their work four weeks later. In the meantime, S received a better offer from V for the business. Thereafter, S refused to let the accountants see the business records and they could not complete the audit. When the two months had passed, S advised C that the offer had expired and he was going to sell the business to V. C brought an action to compel S to carry out the terms of their agreement. Who would succeed?

APPLYING THE LAW

DYCK v. MANITOBA SNOWMOBILE ASSOCIATION

Manitoba, 1982

To compete in a snowmobile race sanctioned by the defendant association, the plaintiff signed an entry form containing a general release of all claims against the association and its agent, officials, and representatives. At the end of the race, the official starter moved onto the track, where he was struck by the plaintiff's snowmobile. The snowmobile then struck the track wall, causing serious injury to the plaintiff. The plaintiff sued the starter and the association for damages for personal injuries.

The biggest issue in the case was the fact that there was no contract between the plaintiff and the starter. The plaintiff had not absolved the starter of liability by signing the general release form. The plaintiff further argued that the starter was an employee of the association, so the association should be liable by virtue of vicarious liability.

The Court dismissed the plaintiff's action. There was no privity of contract between the plaintiff and the starter but, in obtaining the release, the association acted as the starter's agent. The starter fell within the exception to the privity rule and was protected from liability. The purpose of having the plaintiff sign the release was to prevent liability for exactly the type of accident that occurred.

Questions

1. What is the privity of contract rule and how does it operate?
2. Why did the Court conclude that the starter was not liable?
3. What relationship did the Court say existed between the starter and the association?
4. If a driver refused to sign the entry form, he or she would not have been allowed to race. Was this not a take-it-or-leave-it situation, which the courts have often refused to recognize?
5. The plaintiff was clearly injured because of the starter's negligence. Why, then, did the Court not hold either the starter or the association liable?

DOMINION HOME IMPROVEMENTS LTD. v. KNUUDE

Ontario, 1986

The plaintiff was a company that sold home improvements. The defendant was an 83-year-old widow who had signed a contract with the plaintiff for aluminum siding and other work. The defendant was hard of hearing and partly blind.

The defendant first noticed the salesman standing outside her window, looking at her house. He told her that she needed new windows. She said that he was mistaken, since the house was recently constructed. He then suggested aluminum siding. He pushed his way into her house and began talking about various home improvements. The defendant said she did not need any work done. The only thing wrong with the house was a wet wall because the roof leaked. The salesman said the work he recommended would correct that. When the salesman learned that the defendant lived alone, he became very intimidating and aggressive. He refused to leave the house when the defendant ordered him to go and yelled at the defendant, "You treat me like dirt! Why don't you scream?"

The defendant signed a contract for repairs she did not need. She did not read the contract. Her explanation was that she signed the contract because, "I knew I wouldn't get him out of the house until I signed that paper." The defendant signed a cheque for $300 as a down payment. The salesman left four hours after he had arrived. The defendant stopped payment on the cheque the next morning.

Workmen arrived the next afternoon to start work and the defendant ordered them away. Shortly afterward, the salesman returned with his assistant. This time, rather than being abusive, he was in despair, saying that he had been up all night cutting material for the job. At trial, it was determined that this was a total lie. The defendant testified that the salesman seemed "broken-hearted." The defendant finally relented and said the work could go forward.

The work was completed, but the damp wall was not fixed. The defendant believed the workers had actually made the situation worse. She called the president of the company who arrived within an hour. His first words were, "You have a nice house. I think I'll put a lien on it." At this point, the defendant refused to make any further payment and the company sued.

Expert witnesses testified that the work was not necessary and was overpriced. They also testified that the work done would not fix the wet wall problem. There was no concensus upon whether or not the work had made the wet wall problem worse, although the experts suspected this was the case. The trial judge made no ruling on this particular issue.

The trial judge found the entire transaction was unfair and dishonest. The salesman had falsely led the defendant to believe he would correct the problem of the wet wall, had refused to leave her house until she signed a contract, had failed to read the contract to her, and had played upon her sympathy by saying he had spent an entire night preparing materials.

The judge refused to award the plaintiff any of the costs of the work done. The judge said it was not a proper case of *quantum meruit* because the plaintiff should not be compensated for its own fraudulent conduct. The plaintiff was ordered to refund the $300 down payment and to pay all court costs.

Questions

1. Was it significant that the defendant was an elderly widow who lived alone? Why or why not?
2. What importance did the judge place upon the fact that the salesman had lied when he said he had spent all night preparing the materials?
3. The defendant had not read the contract before signing it. What interpretation did the judge place upon that fact?
4. The plaintiff was obviously out of pocket a considerable amount for the work done. Why did the judge not require the defendant to pay anything for this work?

PRINCIPLES AND CASES

Case 1: Legal Principle

Parol evidence cannot be received to add to, vary, or contradict a written agreement. As an exception to the rule, oral evidence may be received to show that no contract has yet become effective.

Case Facts

The Roses Aluminum Company was indebted to the Hickman Company for $16 000. The credit manager of Hickman called in the president of Roses Aluminum, Harry Rose, to talk about his company's past due account. Rose asked her to "hold off" any legal proceedings because he was going to sell a trailer he owned for $6000 and would then pay this money to Hickman. He said he would personally guarantee the debts of his company. The credit manager then typed a statement which Rose signed. It read:

> *Sirs: This letter is to personally guarantee payment in full plus accumulated interest charges at one and one-half percent per month to cover the account of Roses Aluminum, all charges up to and including February 1979 to be paid in full by May 31, 1979.* *(Harry Rose)*

When the $6000 was not paid, the credit manager called the Rose residence. Mrs. Rose said that the trailer had been sold but she was keeping the money because the trailer had been her property. The Hickman Company then sued Roses Aluminum and Harry Rose personally. The aluminum company had no real assets, so the plaintiff knew it had to get a personal judgment against Harry Rose to recover any of its money.

The most important issue in the case was the guarantee that Harry Rose had signed. Counsel for Rose argued that the document was defective because Rose had received no consideration for signing it, and it was not under seal.

Counsel for Hickman wanted to put the credit manager on the stand to testify about the circumstances under which Harry Rose signed the paper. It is important to remember that nothing in the paper said anything about Hickman "holding off" a lawsuit as Rose requested. The plaintiff's lawyer wanted the credit manager to be allowed to give oral evidence about the negotiations that led to the signing. Counsel for Rose argued that this was not acceptable because it would violate the parol evidence rule.

Possible Decisions

A The evidence of the credit manager is admissible because the parol evidence rule does not apply to this case at all.

B The evidence of the credit manager is admissible because it does not add to, contradict, or vary the written agreement.

C The evidence of the credit manager is inadmissible because its real purpose is to orally insert additional terms that should have been typed into the contract.

D The evidence of the credit manager is inadmissible because it is an attempt to insert a crucial missing term—that Rose did not receive any consideration for his promise and therefore the contract should have been under seal.

Case 2: Legal Principle

A person who inserts a condition in a contract must make a reasonable effort, in good faith, to satisfy that condition.

Case Facts

The defendant entered into a contract with the plaintiff for the sale of his farm. Under the provincial law at the time, if a married man sold real property his wife also had to sign a document by which she would "bar her dower" (give up dower rights) to the property. A condition in the contract said that the agreement would be null and void if the spouse would not bar her dower.

The defendant notified the plaintiff that he was unable to persuade his wife, from whom he was separated, to bar her dower. Accordingly, he regarded the agreement as terminated. The plaintiff's lawyer contacted the defendant's wife and asked what inducement she required in order to sign the papers. The lawyer was surprised to learn that the defendant's wife knew nothing about the matter and had never been asked to bar her dower. The plaintiff sued to compel the defendant to proceed with the sale.

Possible Decisions

A The plaintiff will succeed because the defendant was trying to use a condition of the contract to repudiate the contract at will.

B The plaintiff will succeed because the condition in the contract was of minor importance to the overall agreement.

C The defendant will succeed because the condition in the contract is clear and unequivocal and says nothing about "reasonable effort" or anything similar.

D The defendant will succeed because, if a condition of a contract is to be waived, both parties must agree to it.

YOU BE THE JUDGE

1. St. Denis entered into an agreement of purchase and sale with a man named Labelle. Labelle took possession of the land and house, then contracted with Nicholson to make home improvements to include aluminum and rock siding. Labelle's bank gave him a good credit rating, so Nicholson proceeded with the work. Nicholson was under the impression that Labelle owned the house, which was not true. He was only buying it on an instalment plan through a purchase and sale contract. After the work was finished, Labelle made three payments to Nicholson and then defaulted. He also stopped making his house payments to St. Denis, who then brought an action to have Labelle evicted. Labelle disappeared and St. Denis recovered the house. It was then that he learned about the improvements that had been made. Nicholson demanded that St. Denis make the remaining payments. When St. Denis refused, Nicholson sued, saying that St. Denis should not receive the unjust enrichment of all the home improvements at no cost. St. Denis counterargued that he did not request the work done on his house and that he knew nothing about it. Had Nicholson taken the time to check the title at the land registry office, he would have learned that Labelle did not own the house. Who would succeed?

2. The plaintiff sued the defendant company for breach of contract. The plaintiff read a promotion package about the defendant's company and was interested in buying a franchise. The franchise was for a popcorn outlet that operated in shopping malls. The plaintiff met with a representative of the defendant and discussed the details. When they finished the conversation, they shook hands and the defendant's representative said, "You've got a deal." The plaintiff paid $45 000 for the franchise and was sent a written contract. However, some of the terms in the written contract were different from those that had been discussed. He asked for clarification, but did not receive an answer. His money was repaid to him and the franchise was sold to someone else. The plaintiff initially demanded specific performance of

the contract, but later changed the suit to a suit for damages. The defendant argued that there was no contract because the plaintiff refused to sign the written contract. Who would succeed?

3. The plaintiff, a minor, sued the defendant for part of the proceeds of a winning lottery ticket. The plaintiff, who was 16 years of age when the case arose, was a religious boy who believed in various "saints" and "spirits" that guided him. It was known that he particularly favoured "St. Eleggua." It is important to the case to note that the Catholic Church does not recognize any such guardian named St. Eleggua. There is a "St. Eligius" who was immortalized on television as "St. Elsewhere." The defendant, a 38-year-old welfare mother of three, knew that the plaintiff was religious. She gave him four dollars and told him to buy four lottery tickets for her. Her instructions to him were to ask St. Eleggua to pick the winning numbers. She then said, "If I win, I'll give you half the money." The plaintiff picked a winning ticket that paid $2.8 million. However, the defendant refused to share any of the money with the plaintiff. He argued that they had an oral contract under which he was to use his "special relationship with a saint" to pick a winning ticket. Having met his end of the bargain, the defendant owed him half the money. The defendant counterargued that there is no such saint as St. Eleggua and therefore a non-existent saint could not help the plaintiff pick a winning ticket. It was pure luck that she won and the plaintiff had nothing to do with it. As a second argument, the defendant argued that the lottery prize was to be paid out over a 10-year period. Under the *Statute of Frauds,* any contract not to be completed within one year must be in writing. The defendant could not pay the plaintiff within one year and therefore her oral promise was void. Who would succeed?

4. The plaintiff bought a condominium unit from the defendant. When the plaintiff was viewing the unit, she specifically asked the real estate agent about the soundproofing because she was easily awakened by noises. The real estate agent said that the soundproofing in the building was "maximum." The agent further stated that "You couldn't hear your neighbours if they operated a bowling alley." The plaintiff bought the unit and soon discovered that the walls were quite thin. She sued for breach of contract and rescission of her purchase agreement. Her case was based primarily upon what the real estate agent told her. The defendants, the condominium corporation, argued that the real estate agent had no authority to make such statements. Although the soundproofing was good, the agent had overstated the quality of it. The defendants argued that the contract of purchase was silent on the matter of soundproofing and that the

oral statements made by the real estate agent were barred by virtue of the parol evidence rule. Who would succeed?

5. The plaintiff operated a company that provided services to farmers by use of a fleet of airplanes and helicopters. The plaintiff sprayed fields with various substances, ranging from fertilizer to pesticides. The defendant was a farmer who was a regular customer of the plaintiff. The defendant's neighbour contracted with the plaintiff to spray 30 acres of fields with a solution of malathion and soap to eradicate a troublesome insect invasion. The pilot became disoriented and sprayed the defendant's fields by mistake. The plaintiff advised the defendant of the error and requested payment for the work saying, "In view of the widespread problem of the insect invasion, it was inevitable that you would have to have your fields sprayed. As we have already performed this service for you, we request that you tender payment accordingly." The defendant refused to pay anything, saying he had not contracted for any spraying. The plaintiff sued, arguing unjust enrichment if the defendant obtained a free spraying because of the plaintiff's navigational error. The defendant argued that the plaintiff must bear the cost of his own mistake. Who would succeed?

6. The plaintiff sued for possession of a house promised to him by the defendant. The plaintiff and his wife lived in the old house and paid a very low rent to the defendant, who was his wife's aunt. The oral agreement was that the plaintiff would remodel the house at his expense and the defendant would either give or will the house to her niece. When the plaintiff's wife died, the defendant had a sudden change of attitude and said she would sell the house. She offered the plaintiff the first opportunity to buy it. The plaintiff argued that the rule of unjust enrichment should be applied to the case. He had greatly increased the value of the house at his own expense and was entitled to the property. The defendant argued that she had promised the house to her niece only. She had not promised anything to the plaintiff. As the niece was deceased, any oral agreement was now void. Who would succeed?

99

C H A P T E R F I V E

CONTRACT LAW– ESSENTIALS OF A VALID CONTRACT

"The large print giveth and the small print taketh away."

Bishop Fulton Sheen, upon signing a TV contract

GENUINE CONSENT

A contract may be void or voidable if the parties did not give their **genuine consent** to it. If the parties lacked legal capacity to contract, there can be no genuine consent. This applies to minors and certain other people, as was discussed in the previous chapter.

In addition, situations may arise that allow one party to seek to avoid the contract because consent was obtained by mistake, *non est factum*, (ignorance of the facts), duress, undue influence, illegality, or misrepresentation.

MISTAKE

Sometimes what appears to be a valid contract is the product of a mistake by one or both parties. Two opposing principles seem to be at work. On the one hand, agreements must be kept—contracts have a sanctity that must be respected. On the other hand, the common law has long allowed relief to a party where it would be unjust to make that party carry out an agreement that is not at all what it was supposed to be.

The law does not protect parties from their own ignorance or carelessness. One cannot claim that a bad bargain was a mistake when what is really meant is that the contract was unwise. For example, if someone agrees to purchase a tract of land for an exorbitant price, thinking it will increase further in value, this is not a mistake in the legal sense. It is simply lack of good business judgment.

A **mistake** refers to a misunderstanding about the subject matter of a contract. If the two parties both make the same mistake as to the existence of the subject matter of the contract, this is called a **common mistake**. For example, if Brown bought a ship from Green, but neither was aware that the ship had sunk the day before, they are both making the same mistake and the contract is void from the start.

A contract is also void if the two parties are making two different mistakes, but neither is aware of any misunderstanding. This is called a **mutual mistake**. For example, suppose Brown has two cottages for sale. Green views a cottage on the north shore of the lake and offers to buy it. The offer refers to "Lot 333," which actually describes the lot located on the south shore of the lake. Brown accepts the offer without knowing that Green was looking at a different lot when he made the offer. A mutual mistake is made and the contract is void.

With regard to clerical errors, the law holds that one party cannot be allowed to profit from an obvious clerical error on the part of the other. If Green receives an offer or other document from Brown that contains an obvious clerical error that gives Green a great advantage, Green cannot accept it and bind Brown to a disastrous contract. An obvious error is referred to as a **palpable error,** meaning that it was immediately recognized as an error. However, if the error is small and the other party had no reason to believe that there was an error involved, he or she may accept it and the contract is valid.

In situations where a mistake is made in a written document and both parties overlook it, the court may correct the document under the principle of **rectification**. The contract is the relationship between the parties. The written agreement is merely evidence of that agreement. If the written document does not represent what the parties intended, and both parties agree on this point, a court may rectify the error.

The parties may make either a mistake of law or a mistake of fact. A **mistake of law** would occur in a situation where the parties thought it was lawful to enter into the agreement. An illegal contract is void.

The more frequent occurrence is **mistake of fact**. These cases take many forms, but the most significant cases have developed in the area of contract tendering. The following case is the leading one on this point.

ONTARIO WATER RESOURCES COMMISSION v. RON ENGINEERING

Supreme Court of Canada, 1982

In July 1972, Ron Engineering submitted the lowest of several bids on an Ontario Water Resources Commission contract and, as required, submitted a certified cheque for $150 000 with the bid as a deposit of good faith. Such deposits are returned either at the completion of the contract or if the bid is rejected. The company's bid was $2 748 000, which was the lowest of eight bids. It was $632 000 below the closest bid.

When the bids were opened and read aloud, Ron Engineering's representative was alarmed by the gap between the two lowest bids. A hasty telephone call to the company headquarters alerted the president that there must be an error in the calculations. One hour after its bid was accepted, Ron Engineering sent a telegram to the Commission stating that the bid was $750 000 less than it should have been because of an error caused by the rush in compiling the final figures. The company sought to show how the error had been made and to withdraw its erroneous bid. The Commission would not accept the withdrawal and Ron Engineering sued to recover its deposit, arguing that because its bid contained a mistake, it could not be accepted and no contract existed.

The Supreme Court of Canada, hearing an appeal from the Supreme Court of Ontario, ruled that the deposit would not be refunded. The defence of mistake must be such that the mistake is so obvious that it would have to be apparent immediately to the other party at the time that the bid was submitted and not at some later time after a demonstration of error. There was no mistake, since the company had done exactly what it had intended to do: submit a firm bid in the required form.

The Court construed the case as having two distinct contracts. The first came into existence when the tender was submitted. This was the tender that Ron Engineering *intended* to submit. There was no mistake in this contract. The second contract came into existence when the tender was accepted. There was no palpable error. The tender documents contained terms that allowed for any party to "forfeit" if it did not wish to carry out the contract. The parties were now bound by this clause. Ron Engineering could either do the work for the price it offered, or it could forfeit its deposit.

While it is possible to sympathize with Ron Engineering in the preceding case, it should be kept in mind that the rules must be rigid or companies could submit last-minute bids (a practice called "bid shopping") that they really do not intend to honour, just hoping to obtain generous contracts.

In the case of *Northern Construction v. Gloge Heating* (Alberta, 1984) the plaintiff was a general contractor who bid on a contract. The bid contained calculations given to the general contractor by the subcontractors who would do some of the work. A subcontractor made a mathematical error that caused the general contractor to enter a bid 10 percent lower than it should have been. The general contractor tried to withdraw its bid, but the Alberta Court of Queen's Bench refused to allow withdrawal. The Court held that the bid was an "irrevocable option."

NON EST FACTUM (its not what I thought it was)

If a person has entered into a contract in ignorance of its true character, that person may raise the common law defence of ***non est factum*** which means "it is not my deed." To be successful the defendant must show:

1. Absence of intention;
2. Absence of carelessness;
3. An instrument that is fundamentally different from the one the party believed he or she was signing.

This defence originally applied only to people who could not read or write. If an illiterate person signed a document that was misrepresented to him or her, then the signature was not valid. However, the defence was never intended to apply to educated people and particularly not to those with business skills. However, the complexity of business transactions and legal forms has caused courts to extend the rule to any person who misunderstood what he or she signed. The defence does not protect a person who was careless and did not make a reasonable effort to understand what was signed.

MARVCO COLOUR RESEARCH LTD. v. HARRIS

Supreme Court of Canada, 1982

The mortgagors, Mr. and Mrs. Harris, executed a mortgage on their home in favour of the mortgagee, Marvco Research. The mortgage was to secure the indebtedness of the man with whom their daughter was cohabiting. The man misrepresented to the couple that the mortgage was merely a correction of an existing mortgage of the man and the daughter. Mr. and Mrs. Harris did not read the papers they were asked to sign although they were literate and reasonably familiar with mortgages. When the debt was not paid, the mortgagee brought an action for foreclosure. The respondents pleaded *non est factum.*

The trial judge dismissed the action against the respondents and the Court of Appeal agreed. Appeal was taken to the Supreme Court of Canada, which ruled in favour of the mortgagee. The respondents were negligent in failing to read the document before they signed it. They were barred by their negligence from pleading *non est factum.* As between innocent parties, the court must take into account that the mortgagee was completely innocent of any wrongdoing. It had not deceived the respondents in any way.

Although the defence of *non est factum* was originally established to protect illiterate people, it does not necessarily do so if they can understand what they are signing. In *Jenkins v. Strickland* (Newfoundland, 1990) Mr. and Mrs. Strickland agreed to buy a house. For tax reasons, it would be in her name only. The transaction was explained to her by a real estate agent and her husband. Mrs. Strickland could not read nor write, but she understood what was involved. The couple could not arrange financing and decided not to buy the house. Mrs. Strickland thought all they had to do was to tell the vendor they changed their minds. However, the contract did not allow for cancellation and the vendor sued. The Court rejected the defence of *non est factum* even though Mrs. Strickland could not read. The Court held that there was no evidence that she was unable to understand what the contract said if it had been read to her.

In *Royal Bank v. Wood* (British Columbia, 1989) an elderly couple signed a bank loan guarantee for their daughter. The daughter borrowed the money to speculate in a risky stock venture. The bank loans officer knew the loan was risky. He also knew the elderly couple did not understand English, but made no attempt to explain anything to them. The stock venture collapsed and the bank tried to collect from the couple. The Court held that the defendants did not have to pay the money as they did not know what they were signing.

The decision in *Wood* differs from the *Marvco* case because in the *Wood* case there was no innocent third party. The bank officer knew the loan was very risky and was only seeking to find a person foolish enough to guarantee it. The Court ruled that a lender cannot obtain a guarantee on a loan that is almost certain to go into default and fail to adequately warn the guarantor.

DURESS

If people enter contracts because of actual or threatened violence against themselves or members of their families, the contracts can later be avoided. Compelling a person to enter a contract by threats of harm, criminal prosecution, or libel is called **duress.** As soon as the person is free of the duress, that person must declare the contract void. If the person says nothing after escaping the duress, the contract becomes binding.

Ordinary business pressure is not duress. If a person is driven to a certain contract because of financial pressures, the person cannot claim duress, as long as the business pressure applied was lawful.

Another form of duress is **economic duress**. It may take various forms, including the threat to break a contract without justification, to cause the other party financial injury. In the case of *North Ocean Shipping v. Hyundai Construction Ltd.* (England, 1978) the defendant company was contracted to build a ship for the plaintiff. The defendant knew that the plaintiff desperately needed this ship to meet shipping contracts it had signed with its customers. The defendant demanded more money for the project and threatened not to complete construction unless it was paid. The plaintiff agreed to pay the extra sum, then sued to get it back. The Court ordered the money repaid because the defendant had used its knowledge of the economic circumstances of the plaintiff to compel the plaintiff to agree to something it otherwise would not have agreed to do. The trial judge called it "extortion, pure and simple."

GRAHAM v. VOTH BROS. CONSTRUCTION

British Columbia, 1974

The plaintiff entered into a trucking contract with the defendant. When the work was completed, the defendant alleged that the loads were short and, knowing the plaintiff was in financial trouble, refused to pay anything unless the plaintiff reduced the charges. The plaintiff, unable to pay his subcontractors and facing bankruptcy, complied with the demand and sent amended invoices, which the defendant paid. The plaintiff then sued for the balance, which he believed was properly owed.

The Court allowed the action. The defendant had deliberately created the inequality of bargaining power by wrongfully withholding the sum not in dispute, with knowledge that its action was putting severe financial pressure on the plaintiff.

In *CIBC v. Boudreau* (New Brunswick, 1982) the defendant was sued for non-payment of a note that she had co-signed with her son. She testified that she signed because her son often beat her and she was afraid that if she did not sign he "would get back at me." The Court held in favour of the bank because basic fear of her son was not duress and the bank did not know anything about the situation. Ordinarily, the defence of duress can be successful only when the other party to the contract has been the cause of the duress or had constructive notice of it.

UNDUE INFLUENCE

A contract may be voidable because the consent of one of the parties was obtained under circumstances that rendered the party "morally unable" to resist the will of the other. This is called **undue influence**. The law recognizes that some people exert influence over other people because of a family, business, or personal connection. A trusted advisor can generally tell a person what decisions to make. Undue influence lies in having the person make contracts that are not to his or her betterment, but to the betterment of the advisor.

Contracts involving undue influence are voidable at the option of the person so influenced. While the burden of proving undue influence is on the person who alleges it, there are some situations where the relationship is so close that the court will presume that some degree of influence most likely exists. Such relationships include husband and wife, parent and child, guardian and ward, lawyer and client, doctor and patient, and religious leader and adherent. The plaintiff must then establish that the influence was undue.

Charges of undue influence are often made when wills are probated and the relatives find that an unusual settlement has been made in favour of one person—particularly if that person spent much time with the deceased during the last few years of the deceased's life.

Lawyers, bankers, and accountants, who should reasonably suspect that a client is making unwise decisions because the client is under the influence of someone else, must refuse to carry out instructions which are against the client's interest. Otherwise, they may be personally liable, as the next case illustrates.

ST. MARS v. BELL

British Columbia, 1990

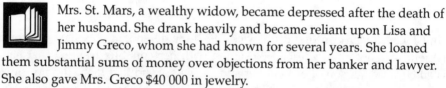

Mrs. St. Mars, a wealthy widow, became depressed after the death of her husband. She drank heavily and became reliant upon Lisa and Jimmy Greco, whom she had known for several years. She loaned them substantial sums of money over objections from her banker and lawyer. She also gave Mrs. Greco $40 000 in jewelry.

St. Mars discussed her problems with her children and agreed to hand over all of her affairs to her eldest son. A formal trust deed was signed to this effect.

Jimmy Greco went to his lawyer, David Bell, to contest the trust deed. Bell insisted that a hearing be held to determine the mental fitness of St. Mars. A psychiatrist prepared a report saying that St. Mars was an alcoholic. Bell persuaded the psychiatrist to remove this statement from the report.

The Court, unaware of the drinking problem, set aside the trust deed. Within a short time, St. Mars signed her house over to the Grecos. Bell handled the transaction. When St. Mars no longer had any money, she went to Bell to complain about her situation and, rather astonishingly, he said he would sue the Grecos on her behalf. He did, but won a hollow judgment because the Grecos had left Canada with all of the money. St. Mars then sued Bell. The basis of the lawsuit was that St. Mars was under the influence of the Grecos, who were robbing her. Bell knew, or ought to have known, that this activity was taking place. He was acting for two clients: one was a predator who was robbing the other.

The Court held Bell personally liable and awarded St. Mars $490 000 in damages against the lawyer.

One of the most prudent actions that any professional person can take where there is doubt about the existence of undue influence is to insist that the client obtain **independent legal advice**. The importance of this was demonstrated in the case of *Bank of Montreal v. Hancock* (Ontario, 1982). In that case the wife was left with her divorced husband's bad debts. The bank loaned the money to the husband on a promissory note and with generous overdraft privileges. He suggested to his wife that the chequing account be made a joint account for convenience. The wife also guaranteed her husband's note for $27 000. She was not aware of this guarantee or that her husband was in debt. The husband then deserted his wife and the bank sued her.

The Ontario Supreme Court held that the wife did not have to pay the money. The judge held: "At the very least, the bank should have satisfied itself that the customer was independently advised. Had she had the advantage of legal advice, no lawyer would have advised her to assume such a liability."

The rule of independent legal advice is very imprecise and there are court decisions on both sides of the issue. The rule first began during a time, under the common law, when a wife could not be held liable for her husband's debts. The major reason was the total absence of the wife's signing authority. Only the husband could be found liable upon a contract. This rigid rule has been abolished, but the courts have been slow to effect a change of attitude. There is still a presumption that a married woman is inexperienced in business matters and subject to undue influence from her husband. Recently, the courts have added a belief that elderly people are subject to undue influence from their children or financial advisors. In neither situation should it be presumed that the guarantor is incompetent, but precautions should always be taken.

As a minimum, the following guidelines should be followed whenever one person is guaranteeing the indebtedness of another person. The person guaranteeing a debt should know the full extent of indebtedness, the extent of liability (one-time or continuing liability), the true purpose of the agreement, the likelihood of the debtor defaulting, and the penalty for late payment or non-payment. The lender should satisfy himself or herself that the guarantor is signing something that, in the personal absence of the debtor, would be advisable and that the person is capable of understanding the transaction and the consequences that would follow upon default.

The lender should also question the intelligence and experience of the person who is guaranteeing the debt. All discussion should take place in private, without the debtor being present to exert influence upon the guarantor. If there appears to be even the slightest hint of confusion or reluctance, the loan should not be made. One cannot rule out the psychological effect of a lawsuit by a large bank against an elderly widow to collect on a note that she signed without any apparent benefit to herself.

MISREPRESENTATION

A contract can be rendered voidable by **misrepresentation**, which is a false statement of material facts that induces the offeree to sign a contract. It is generally assumed to have been made accidentally, without intention to deceive. The falsehood must pertain to material facts, not to some small detail. As well, material facts differ from opinion. A salesperson is expected to be enthusiastic about his or her product and will naturally describe it in positive terms. Such expressions as "high quality, durable, and sturdy" are not material facts. They are opinions, generally referred to as **puffing**.

Misrepresentation applies to all contracts, not to just the sale of goods. It is an interesting aspect of law that also comes under tort law. It gives the injured party two possible ways to attack the contract.

SULEK and SULEK v. CAIRNS HOMES LTD.

Alberta, 1986

The defendant planned to build two high-quality condominiums on two adjacent lots. The plaintiffs were interested in buying a unit in the first building and were shown plans for another unit in the second building. They were told that the prices in the second building would be higher than in the first, but that units in both buildings would have a high resale value because the two buildings represented a "prestigious project." Nothing in the purchase agreement said anything about a second building.

After the first building had been finished, the economy went into a recession and the defendant cancelled the second building. The land was sold to another company, which built 88 multi-family, low-income townhouses on the land. The plaintiffs sued for rescission of the contract or damages on the grounds of misrepresentation. Expert evidence suggested that the market value of their unit had dropped dramatically.

The Court ruled in favour of the defendant, saying:

> *For an oral representation made during the course of contractual negotiations to form part of the contract, there must have been an intention to warrant the truth of the fact asserted. In this case, there was no evidence to support the plaintiff's contention that the statement concerning the intended project on the second lot was a term of the sales agreement or that it was a collateral agreement. It was not even mentioned in the executed sales agreement. There was no evidence that the statement was made just to induce the plaintiffs to buy the condominium.*

An extreme form of misrepresentation is **fraud**, which is also an offence under criminal law and a tort. Fraud differs from misrepresentation in that it is an intentional, deliberate misstatement of facts, while misrepresentation may be accidental. Fraud renders a contract void and the injured party may sue for the return of money paid and additional damages. Misrepresentation only renders a contract voidable: the injured party may sue to get his or her money back, but may not sue for damages.

It has also been held to be fraud if one person makes a reckless statement of facts in order to persuade another person to enter a contract. A **reckless statement** generally implies that the speaker made statements of material fact without knowing if they were true or false. In the following case, the issue of printed brochures was examined by the Court.

JARVIS v. SWAN TOURS LTD.

England, 1969

Jarvis decided to take a holiday in Switzerland. In a brochure issued by the defendants, a travel agency, he read an advertisement for a tour to Morlialp, Switzerland. The advertisement stated:

> House Party Centre with special resident host ... Morlialp is a wonderful resort on a sunny plateau ... Up there you will find yourself in the midst of beautiful alpine scenery, which in winter becomes a wonderland of sun, snow and ice with a wide variety of fine ski-runs, a skating rink and an exhilarating toboggan run ... Why did we choose the Hotel Krone? ... Mainly because of the Gemuetlichkeit and friendly welcome you will receive from Herr and Frau Weible ... Mr. Weible, the charming owner, speaks English ... All the arrangements are included in the price of your holiday ... Welcome party on arrival. Afternoon tea and cake for 7 days. Swiss Dinner by candlelight. Yodeler evening. Chali farewell party in the Alphutte Bar.

The plaintiff booked a 15-day holiday. During the first week, there were only 12 guests in the hotel. During the second week, he was the only guest. The host could not speak English. The yodeler was a man from the village who came in working clothes and sang four short songs. The skiing was terrible and the luscious Swiss cakes he was looking forward to turned out to be potato chips.

The Court awarded the plaintiff a refund of his money and damages because his vacation was ruined. The brochure he was given was a clear and flagrant abuse of the facts, made either with a reckless disregard for the truth or exaggerated to induce the plaintiff to buy the vacation package.

COLLATERAL CONTRACTS

The interpretation of a contract may be complicated by the argument that there exists some additional agreement or contract between the parties, affecting the meaning and scope of the first contract. That is, one of the parties alleges that the contract before the court is not the total agreement. This second agreement is referred to as a **collateral contract** and must meet the same requirements as any contract. It must be definite and supported by consideration.

In most cases involving a claim of a collateral contract, the second contract takes the form of an oral promise or a printed book, brochure, or promotional advertisement. Ordinarily, these items are not viewed as contracts. However, if they are worded in very strong language and distributed as part of the sales process, they can be viewed as contracts.

In the case of *Hallmark Pool Corporation v. Storey* (New Brunswick, 1983) the respondent purchased a swimming pool from a dealership that sold pools manufactured by the appellant. He was impressed by a warranty that said the pool would last 15 years. The respondent did not actually receive a warranty, but was given an advertisement which displayed the warranty inside the cover. The warranty looked like a formal, legal document.

The pool was installed incorrectly by the dealer and deteriorated. The appellant pool company tried to rely upon small print in the warranty that absolved the manufacturer of liability if the dealer did not install the pool correctly. The print had to be read with a magnifying glass. The appellant also argued that a warranty is not a collateral contract.

The Court held in favour of the respondent, saying that the document the respondent received gave obvious and clear statements that the pool would last 15 years. The Court would give no recognition to words that had to be read with a magnifying glass

In the following case, a piece of promotional literature was also joined with oral promises. Thus, the Court was confronted with a written contract and two potential, collateral contracts.

MURRAY v. SPERRY RAND CORPORATION

Ontario, 1980

The plaintiff, a farmer, wanted to purchase a new forage harvester, a machine that simultaneously cuts and chops hay. From a representative of the defendant company, the plaintiff obtained a brochure that stated in part:

You will fine chop forage to 3/16 of an inch (1.4 cm) ... season after season! ... You will harvest over 45 tons (40.5 t) per hour with ease.

Representatives from the defendant company also visited the plaintiff's farm and gave him assurances that the harvester would perform as described in the brochure and that it was ideally suited for his kind of farming.

Murray bought the machine but it never performed well. The defendant and local dealer made adjustments, replaced parts, and did everything possible but the machine would not do what was described in the brochure. As a result, Murray suffered delays and financial losses. He eventually went out of business.

The Court held that the dealer and manufacturer were liable and that the disclaimer clause was ineffective. The dealer was liable because it was partly as a result of the dealer's oral statements that Murray had bought the machine. The Court further held that the defendant had published its sales brochure in an obvious attempt to induce sales. The statements in the brochure were not mere representations designed to boost the image of the product. They were sales tools. The effect of such statements was that anyone reading the brochure would reasonably conclude that the manufacturer and the dealer were specifically promising that the described performance would be the actual performance of the machine. The brochure and oral statements formed collateral contracts.

Many cases involving collateral contracts involve three-party situations. For example, suppose Green Paint Company makes strong claims about a certain paint. Brown Corporation decides to use the paint on a major project. Brown Corporation hires Gold Painters to do the work and specifically states in the contract that Green's paint must be used. Gold uses the paint and it falls off in a year. What liability rests upon Green or Gold? If the scenario is changed, the decision may change. Suppose Brown hires Gold but does not specify the paint to be used. Gold relies upon Green's claims of quality and decides to use Green's paint. When it falls off, who is liable? Finally, suppose Green made no specific claims but Gold has used the paint before and tells Brown that it is the best. Brown accepts Gold's advice. Who is liable?

The case law is decidedly firm regarding the liability of a manufacturer. Manufacturers benefit through the sale of their products. There is no necessity for the claims to be made directly to the end user, as long as it can be traced back to the manufacturer. As far as a dealer or contractor, liability rests upon such a person if the decision to use the product was that of the dealer or contractor. In the first hypothetical case, the painter did not give advice or make the decision. It used the paint that Brown specified. Therefore, the quarrel is between Brown and Green only. In the other situations, both Gold and Green could be liable to Brown.

CONSIDERATION IN CONTRACTS

A contract is a business venture and the law assumes that the purpose for entering into any contract is to exchange values in some manner. The value that each party exchanges in the contract is called **consideration** and a contract generally cannot be enforced without some consideration being given by both parties. The court would hold that a contract without consideration is really a promise to do something free of charge and is thus a gift that is not legally enforceable. This rule does not apply to contracts under seal, which require no consideration. The court would presume that, even though two parties to a contract under seal do not mention consideration, they must have seriously intended to make the contract, otherwise they would not have made it formally. Simple contracts, then, require consideration to prove that the two parties were serious.

By definition, consideration consists in some right, interest, profit, or benefit accruing to the one party or some forbearance, detriment, or loss given or undertaken by the other.

As a rule, people cannot enforce promises to pay them to do things that they are already required to do. A police officer cannot charge a citizen a fee for protection. The officer is already bound to protect the citizen.

DEGEOSBRIAND v. RADFORD

Saskatchewan, 1989

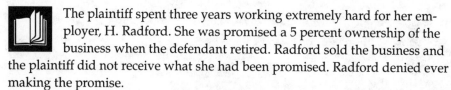

The plaintiff spent three years working extremely hard for her employer, H. Radford. She was promised a 5 percent ownership of the business when the defendant retired. Radford sold the business and the plaintiff did not receive what she had been promised. Radford denied ever making the promise.

The trial judge ruled that Radford had made the promise, but that it was not enforceable because there was no consideration given for it. The plaintiff did not work hard just because she had been promised a share of the business. The promise was made after the employer-employee relationship was already in existence and was not made to induce the plaintiff to work overtime or put in long hours. She was already doing that. The promise was a gratuitous promise of a bonus for good work, which Radford could either honour or ignore, at his discretion. It was not owed to the plaintiff. The judge said:

> *The defendant may owe some moral obligation to the plaintiff. However, I am not satisfied the obligation arises from a contract between them.*

The Court of Appeal upheld the trial judge's decision, saying that the defendant made a "bare promise, with no consideration received by him from the plaintiff."

Consideration may take many forms, such as cash, property, labour, forbearance, and so on. The important thing is that consideration must be something that can be expressed in terms of dollars. It cannot consist of intangible things such as affection, loyalty, etc. **Forbearance** is a form of consideration that consists of giving up a legal right in return for payment. A common example is when a person agrees to give up the right to sue in return for the payment of a sum of money.

ADEQUACY OF CONSIDERATION

A person may use poor judgment in entering a contract and realize later that the consideration received is very small in comparison to what has been given to the other party. Unless fraud or misrepresentation can be proved, or the contract can be set aside on other grounds, the court will uphold the contract. The law does not require that each party receive equal consideration. The position of the court is summed up in a rule of law that states: "The court will not make bargains."

The danger of a long-term contract is that advantageous terms may become unsatisfactory over the years. Unless there is a clause in the contract requiring a review of the terms, there may be very bad results.

RE *UPPER CHURCHILL WATER RIGHTS REVERSION ACT*

Supreme Court of Canada, 1984

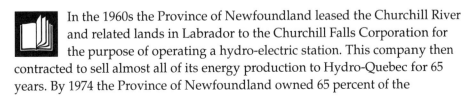

In the 1960s the Province of Newfoundland leased the Churchill River and related lands in Labrador to the Churchill Falls Corporation for the purpose of operating a hydro-electric station. This company then contracted to sell almost all of its energy production to Hydro-Quebec for 65 years. By 1974 the Province of Newfoundland owned 65 percent of the company's common shares. At the time the contract was signed, the price of electricity was quite low and the terms seemed fair to both parties. However, the price of electricity soared and Newfoundland found itself selling electricity for a tiny fraction of its potential value. Hydro-Quebec actually was reselling most of the electricity to the State of New York for a huge profit. Newfoundland wanted to escape the contract.

The Province of Newfoundland passed the *Upper Churchill Water Rights Reversion Act, 1980,* which in effect repealed the Churchill Falls Corporation's lease. It also expropriated the company's interest in the hydro-electric facility. This would have the effect of breaking the contract with Hydro-Quebec, because the Churchill Falls Corporation no longer had any electricity to sell. It was argued that Newfoundland required the electricity for its own development.

Although the case contained many issues, some of them constitutional, there was still a basic contract at the core of the dispute. The Supreme Court of Canada held that the provincial statute was *ultra vires* (beyond the power) of the Newfoundland government because it was a "colourable attempt to derogate from the rights of Hydro-Quebec." This was beyond Newfoundland's territorial powers because the rights so attacked are situated in Quebec and beyond the jurisdiction of Newfoundland. Clearly, Newfoundland had entered into an agreement for which it was receiving inadequate consideration, but could not unilaterally break the agreement.

PROMISES OF GIFTS

A promise by one person to make a gift to another is treated as a **gratuitous promise**, lacking consideration and therefore not legally enforceable. A special problem may arise with regard to a promise by someone to give money to a charitable organization.

At first glance, this would appear to be the offer of a gift and, therefore, not capable of creating a contractual obligation. Canadian courts have established guidelines by which such a promise may be an enforceable one:

1. If the charity has ordered building materials, hired contractors, and made other legal commitments on the basis of the pledge, the charity may in turn require the donor to pay the money promised. The charity has entered into legal obligations upon the good faith that the donor will live up to his or her promise.

2. Since others have also pledged money, each donor must oblige the other donors by honouring his or her pledge. If some donors fail to fulfil their obligations, they undermine the entire project to the detriment of others.

3. Because a charity performs good services for the entire community, all donors benefit and receive consideration, indirectly, for their gifts.

An easy way to avoid the consideration argument is to have pledges made under seal. **Charitable donations are enforceable only if the money is used for the purpose for which it was solicited in the first place. It cannot be diverted to some other use.**

PAST AND FUTURE CONSIDERATION

A promise to do something in return for benefits already received is in effect a gift and not enforceable. For example, assume that Brown saves Green's child from drowning. Green is so grateful, he offers Brown a job with his company. When Brown arrives at the company offices, he learns that Green has changed his mind. Brown cannot demand the job as a matter of contractual right. The promise of the job was made after the good deed, not in exchange for it. This is called **past consideration** and will not support a contract.

A promise to do something in the future in return for benefits immediately received or to be received in the future results in **future consideration** and creates a valid contract. For example, if Green agrees to perform labour for Brown, but Brown has no money at the time, Green may perform the labour with the understanding that he will be paid in the future. Although it could be argued that there was no exchange of consideration because Brown had no money, the agreement is still binding because it is reasonable to believe that Brown intended to pay at the time the agreement was made.

RE GROSCH

Alberta, 1945

The administrator of an estate sought payment for services rendered to the estate. An agreement had been made between the two daughters of the deceased man, who were the beneficiaries of their father's will, and their uncle, who was the administrator and trustee of the estate, to pay the uncle for services that he had performed for them under the will while they were infants. The will appointed the uncle as the trustee but did not provide that he would receive any payment for this service, although he had been told by the deceased man that he would be paid.

When his nieces became adults and were about to inherit the money, he asked them about payment. He said it was unfair that he had done so much work for years without any compensation. They agreed and said that as soon as they received their inheritance they would each pay him part of the proceeds. Neither woman paid their uncle anything and he brought an action to determine if he was entitled to the money.

The Court held that the promises made by his nieces were unenforceable because they were made after the services were performed. The services were not rendered at their request and their uncle could have refused to accept the responsibility of administering the estate. Having done so voluntarily, he cannot later insist upon payment. The Court rejected the argument that the principle of *quantum meruit* could be applied to the case. This principle can be applied only when there is a clear, unequivocal agreement that payment will be made. The promise supposedly made by the deceased man could not be confirmed. The nieces made their promises after the work was done. Therefore, their promises were for past consideration and were not enforceable.

COMPROMISE WITH CREDITORS

If a debtor is unable to pay his or her creditors in full, but agrees to pay part of the debt in return for complete cancellation of the debt, the issue then arises as to whether the creditors may later demand the rest of the money. The case law tends to support the belief that the creditors may demand the rest of the money, notwithstanding the agreement, because they received no consideration for forgiveness of part of the debt. Several provinces have specific legislation allowing for this procedure. Also, a federal statute, the *Companies' Creditors Arrangement Act*, establishes a process under which a company can seek protection from its creditors while trying to make fundamental changes. In *Ultracare Management v. Gammon* (Ontario, 1990) the operators of six nursing homes were given six months to reorganize their business operation and sell some of the assets. The companies owed banks and other creditors $22 million. The companies were permitted to continue operation while they prepared a new business plan, which would have to be presented to the Court.

It is also possible to make the promise binding by establishing an entirely new agreement, with a different form of payment, which replaces the previous agreement. This is generally called a **novation** and allows for payment of a smaller amount than the original debt.

CONTRACT LEGALITY

If a contract is entered into that violates the law, the contract is void. The court cannot enforce a contract that is contrary to the law, or the court itself would be breaking the law. Generally, the entire contract is void: parts of it cannot be saved, because the entire agreement is said to be "tainted with illegality."

A contract may be legal when signed, but a change in the law may later make it illegal. If this happens, the contract is rendered void and the parties must stop carrying it out. They may try to seek a settlement from each other under the *Frustrated Contracts Act*, which prevails in most provinces. An example of a frustrated contract might be a contract under which Green hires Brown to renovate an old building. The local government declares the building as a "heritage building" and will not allow the changes. The contract is at an end, even though neither Green nor Brown has breached it.

UNLICENSED WORK

If an unlicensed person enters into a work contract involving his or her unauthorized status, that contract is illegal and void and the person is not entitled to sue for payment. If both parties knew the work was unlicensed, then neither party may bring an action. In *Bognar v. Borg* (Ontario, 1990) the plaintiffs hired the defendants to build a house, making an advance payment of $45 000. The house was not built on time, so the plaintiffs bought another house and sued to recover their advance payment. They then learned that the defendants were not licensed builders under the provincial *New Home Warranties Act*. The judge held that the contract was illegal, but that the plaintiffs were innocent of wrongdoing. He ordered the money repaid.

ILLEGAL INTEREST

When a person borrows money or buys something on credit, the person is charged an additional sum of money called **interest**. Charging a rate of interest that is too high is called **usury**. Usury will render a contract void and, if interest is charged in excess of 60 percent a year, it is also a criminal offence.

If the method of calculating the interest is so vaguely worded that the debtor does not realize how high the interest is, the contract may be set aside as **unconscionable**. All provinces have laws requiring the lender to show the rate of interest being charged on a loan or instalment purchase.

RESTRAINT OF TRADE

Attempts to restrict the free flow of trade are generally illegal, although some restraints are imposed upon business by the government to ensure an orderly market system. The federal *Competition Act* contains various provisions that attempt to prevent such actions as price fixing, monopolies, or excessive domination of an industry.

A common form of agreement that partially limits free enterprise is a **non-competition agreement**. When people join companies as employees, they may be required to sign contracts containing a condition that, if they quit their jobs with their present employers, they will not go to work for their employers' competitors, or set up their own competing businesses within a certain period of time or distance. The reason for such contracts is to prevent former employees from using inside information to undercut their previous employers.

Any restraints imposed must be reasonable to both the employees and the public. The public cannot be denied a needed service because of a private agreement. In trying to determine reasonableness, the court must consider the extent of the restriction, the availability of such services to the community, and the duration of the restriction.

BAKER et al. v. LINTOFF

Alberta, 1981

A physician contracted with his partners not to compete within 25 miles of the city of Medicine Hat for two years after voluntarily leaving the partnership. Evidence showed that the partnership constituted almost 60 percent of the medical practice in the area. In an action for a court order to enforce the agreement, the plaintiffs argued that the restriction was a reasonable one when considering the training, experience, and exposure to the public that a new doctor receives by being a partner in a large medical clinic.

The Court held that the contract was reasonable between the parties, but it was contrary to the public interest, because it unduly restricted the access of the public to the defendant's medical services. The Court noted that there are two tests to be applied to such a contract. The first is the test of reasonableness between the parties. The second is that the contract must not seriously deprive the public of a choice of services. Patients who did not like the other doctors in the partnership should have the choice of another doctor.

CONTRACTS CONTRARY TO PUBLIC POLICY

A contract that has the purpose of defeating public justice, policy, and morality is illegal and void. The meaning of **public policy** is generally expressed as "that which is in the best interest of the public." For example, a contract to commit a crime would be void, as would a contract to use the powers of a political office for personal gain.

The basic rule against immoral conduct covers a wide area of contract law and tort law. Generally, a plaintiff cannot come before the court seeking damages against the defendant when the plaintiff suffered the injury because of his or her own illegal or immoral conduct. The principle of *ex turpi* is a long-established rule that a person cannot voluntarily take part in illegal or immoral acts and then sue the other party for an alleged injury.

In *Tannock v. Bromley* (British Columbia, 1979) the plaintiff tried to recover fees and gifts he had given to an unlicensed hypnotherapist. He knew the therapist had no licence, but felt that her treatments made his arthritis better. He also was personally attracted to the woman. The Court ordered the gifts returned, but not the fees. The payment of fees to an unlicensed medical practitioner is an illegal contract.

In *Norberg v. Wynrib* (British Columbia, 1990) the plaintiff obtained narcotics from a doctor in return for sexual services. Her civil action against him was dismissed because her alleged injury arose from her own immoral conduct.

GAMBLING AGREEMENTS

For many years, almost every form of gambling was illegal and gambling debts were not enforceable in court. However, the advent of government-run and government-licensed lotteries, horse racing, and other forms of gambling has changed the rule considerably.

A person who purchases a ticket for a licensed lottery may sue for the prize that he or she has properly won. The results of promotional contests are also enforceable if the contestant has met the requirements of the contest.

There are still many forms of illegal gambling, however, and a person engaging in illegal gambling cannot use court action to collect winnings or recover loses. In *MacLean v. Orologopoulos* (Ontario, 1990) the plaintiff sued for repayment of a loan that he alleged was to help the defendant to pay for his wedding expenses. The evidence showed that the loan was for the purpose of a pyramid scheme (similar to a chain letter), which is illegal under the *Criminal Code of Canada*. The suit was dismissed.

REVIEW: POINTS OF LAW

1. If the parties to a contract make the same mistake as to the existence or nature of the subject matter of the contract, the contract is void.
2. A party to a contract cannot take advantage of a palpable (obvious) clerical error to the disadvantage of the other party.
3. If a party makes a mathematical error in submitting a bid for a contract, it is bound by its bid unless the error was immediately apparent.
4. A contract made under duress is voidable. Ordinary business pressure is not duress.
5. If the consent of one of the parties to a contract was obtained under circumstances that rendered that party morally unable to resist the will of the other party, the contract is voidable because of undue influence.
6. Misrepresentation is a false statement of material facts that induces a party to enter into a contract. Misrepresentation renders a contract voidable.
7. Under the defence of *non est factum* a party can escape the terms of a contract if he or she can show that the contract is something totally different from what the party believed it to be.
8. A contract must demonstrate an exchange of consideration (something of value) by each party to be enforceable.
9. A contract under seal does not require consideration.
10. Consideration must take the form of something tangible, such as cash, property, labour, or forbearance.

LEGAL BRIEFS

1. T worked for the Y Advertising Corporation for two years. He worked long hours and was very successful. He was then given the task of obtaining the prestigious account of a large food corporation. W, his immediate supervisor, told T that, if he landed the account, he would be made a

partner in the firm. T worked 18 hours a day for six months and landed the account. When the promised partnership never materialized, T asked W when it would be forthcoming. The supervisor replied, "Soon." Two weeks later, W took a job with another firm. When T approached the senior partner about a partnership, he was told "That's ridiculous." What rights, if any, has T against W or the company?

2. D made a purchase of office equipment. When the bill arrived, D noted that it had been added incorrectly. He had been charged $1000 less than the correct amount. D paid the amount stated on the bill and received a notation in return that read: "Account paid in full." Two months later the equipment company found the error and billed D for $1000. Must D pay?
3. P hired S as a computer consultant to modernize its computer systems. S suggested that P purchase a software program from the M Corporation. When told the price, P balked. He then offered S an increase of 50 percent in his fee if S would copy illegally the software from another client and install it in P's system. P would save 90 percent of the cost this way. S carried out the work, but P would not pay the bonus. Advise S as to his position.
4. W, a small construction contractor, was hired to build a road for a forest company. He rented more equipment for the job, but was then told he would have to extend the road two more kilometres at his own expense. When he refused, the forest company foreman told W that he would cancel the entire contract. The printed contract allowed for cancellation without notice and without reason. W, faced with rental bills and wages owed to his employees, did the extra work. He then billed the company for the additional work. Will W receive the money?
5. Q and B were friends for many years. Q purchased two building lots on a lake. He built a house on one lot and told B that he was "holding" the other lot for him. B did not have the money to buy the lot at the time, but Q said he would wait and that he would sell the lot to B for the same price he originally paid for it. Five years later, B had enough money to buy the lot and build a house. Q advised that he would sell the lot to B, but for double the original price. Q explained that lakefront lots had soared in price and he would be "silly" to sell the lot for half of its present value. What rights, if any, has B?
6. L was a recent widow who had a very limited knowledge of business matters. One day her bank manager asked her to come to the bank and sign "some estate papers." L thought the papers pertained to transferring all of the savings and chequing accounts to her name only. Indeed, some of the documents were for that purpose. However, among the papers was a document which made L liable for her deceased husband's debts. She signed them without reading them. Will L have to pay these debts?

7. C asked K for the loan of $5000 to purchase narcotics. C said he would make a "buy" of narcotics and be able to resell them on the street for $25 000. He promised K a return of $10 000 in one month, an enormous profit. K loaned C the money, but was repaid nothing. What action, if any, can K take to recover his money?
8. N had an affair with E, an investment banker. E told N that he could invest her money successfully, so N gave E $200 000. E promised that the money would be invested in secure stocks and bonds, but he actually invested it in two companies which he personally owned. The companies went bankrupt and the romance soon broke up. N sued E personally for return of her money. Will N succeed?

APPLYING THE LAW

BATTISON AND SONS v. MAUTI

Ontario, 1989

The plaintiff entered into an oral contract with the defendant to reconstruct part of the defendant's residence that had been damaged by fire. The contract price was for $43 000. Of that amount, $20 000 had been paid on account. The plaintiff believed the work was almost completed, but the defendant refused to pay the balance because he was dissatisfied with the quality of the work and felt that the plaintiff stopped short of completing repairs to one wall. It was apparent that the two parties had totally different points of view about the amount of work that was to be done.

The plaintiff applied to have a lien placed on the house for unpaid work. A lien is a claim to secure priority of payment for services rendered or materials supplied in the construction or repair of a building. At this time, it was learned that the plaintiff was not a properly registered or licensed builder in the city of Toronto. A city by-law required every builder and renovator to be licensed. The same by-law required a written contract for every building renovation on a specific form called "Appendix A." The form also contained a warranty as to workmanship and a payment schedule. A copy of the contract form was to be give to the building owner.

The purpose of the by-law was to protect citizens from unscrupulous building renovators who induced homeowners to orally contract for work based on low oral estimates, only to present the homeowner with an inflated final bill containing extras that were never discussed.

The plaintiff acknowledged that it was not registered, but argued that it must be paid the fair amount of work actually done under the common law rule of *quantum meruit*. Otherwise, the defendant would receive the unjust enrichment of a nearly free renovation. The Court held that the imposition of a written contract requirement was consistent with the city's right to govern a particular trade. The oral contract was illegal and unenforceable. The action was dismissed.

Questions

1. According to the Court, what was the purpose of the by-law?
2. The decision suggests that the defendant received a $43 000 job at a cost of $20 000. Why did the Court not agree that this was unjust enrichment?
3. What message would this case send to other unlicensed builders and renovators?

BANK OF MONTREAL v. WINTER and FARDY

Newfoundland, 1981

The plaintiff bank brought an action against the co-signers of an overdue loan to a company. Judgment had been entered against Winter, but he died, so the action was brought against Fardy, an employee. Fardy raised the defences of undue influence and *non est factum*.

Some time previous to the signing of the agreement in question, Fardy had been told that he would be promoted to secretary-treasurer of the company. Winter then presented him with a stack of papers which he said were related to the new job. Fardy's signature was needed in order to transfer authority to him to sign legal papers on behalf of the company. Fardy had been an employee for 20 years and trusted Winter. He did not read the papers before he signed them. He said he was still in a state of euphoria over his promotion and would not have offended Winter by questioning the legitimacy of what he was signing. He also thought the papers had been checked over by the company lawyer.

One of the papers in the stack was a guarantee for a very large loan that had been made to the company two years earlier. Fardy had no knowledge of its presence. Winter did not leave the papers with him to read, but stood over his desk waiting for him to sign them. Winter had explained that the company lawyer wanted them back "in a rush."

The Newfoundland Supreme Court dismissed all of the defendant's arguments and held that his negligence in not reading what he had signed was no defence. The bank had no duty to ensure that the defendant had received independent legal advice. The Court found no evidence of undue influence. The defendant was an educated man who took no steps to safeguard his interests. He could not expect others to do so for him. Fardy was liable for the loan.

Questions

1. What is the defence of *non est factum*? Why did it not work successfully in this case?
2. What is the defence of undue influence? Why did it not work here?
3. What is the general rule about a person who does not read a contract before signing it?
4. In this case, the controversial paper was placed in a stack of other papers. This would obviously have the effect of concealing it from the signer's attention. Why did the Court give this no weight?

PRINCIPLES AND CASES

Case 1: Legal Principle

An error in judgment, or a failure to foresee all the possible consequences of a certain action, do not constitute the defence of mistake.

Case Facts

The defendant leased six pieces of heavy equipment from the plaintiff. When the lease was signed, the defendant believed he would need the equipment for six months and he leased it for that period of time. The defendant had a contract with the provincial government to construct a new section of roadway. The equipment was delivered at the time and place stated in the lease. However, the contract with the government was abruptly cancelled, leaving the defendant with equipment he did not need. He asked the plaintiff to pick it up and cancel the lease. The plaintiff refused to do so. The equipment sat unused for six months, after which the plaintiff sued for payment.

The defendant argued that the contract had become frustrated by the sudden cancellation of the highway project and that the lease should have been terminated. There was no clause in the lease allowing for either party to terminate early.

Possible Decisions

A The defendant is liable because the agreement was ironclad. He leased the equipment for six months with no cancellation clause.

B The defendant is liable because the plaintiff would not be able to lease the equipment to someone else on short notice.

C The defendant is not liable because the contract was frustrated by the act of a third party, which was unforeseeable.

D The defendant is not liable because the defence of mistake applies. Both parties mistakenly believed in the existence of the contract with the provincial government.

Case 2: Legal Principle

A building contract has an implied condition that the work will suit the purpose intended. An oral agreement may constitute a collateral contract that runs with the primary contract.

Case Facts

The plaintiff, owner of a boathouse, claimed damages against the defendant contractor for faulty installation of a roof that blew off. The foundation and walls had been constructed by another contractor and, when the defendant was called in, numerous things were found to be wrong that would make it difficult to install a roof. The boathouse was situated in an area prone to sudden, violent storms.

After discussing the problems, the plaintiff told the defendant to install the roof. The defendant repeated his concerns but the plaintiff replied, "Just do your best." The work was completed according to the written contract. There was nothing in the contract regarding the problems of making the roof stay in place. Two months later, a storm blew the entire roof away.

Possible Decisions

A The defendant is liable because, if the roof could not be installed in such a way that it was certain to stay in place, the defendant should have refused to do the work.

B The defendant is liable because there would be an implied guarantee that the roof would stay on in any weather condition, no matter how fierce.

C The defendant is not liable because the plaintiff assumed the risk by telling the defendant to do his best. This created a collateral contract.

D The defendant is not liable because no one can ensure that a roof will stay on during a storm.

YOU BE THE JUDGE

1. The plaintiff brought an action against the defendant for damages because of large cost over-runs it incurred on a contract. The plaintiff had bid on a contract to construct a power line for the defendant hydro authority. The description of the project was incomplete in that it failed to advise bidders that the land over which the line must be built was strewn with logs, stumps, boulders, and debris. The company that won the contract would have to spend a great deal of money just clearing the land, because the right of way was impassable. The hydro authority knew about the problem and constructed its contract in a very careful way, so as to bind the company that did the work to complete it without demanding extra payment. The plaintiff argued this was misrepresentation. The defendant counterargued that the plaintiff could have sent a representative to check over the land before making its bid. Who would succeed?

2. In 1933, a wealthy man died in the city of Toronto. He had no close relatives to inherit his fortune, so he bequeathed his entire estate to "The woman who has the most children in the 10-year period immediately following my death." The purpose of this unusual will was never known. However, it was a disastrous time for such a "stork derby" to take place. Canada was in the midst of the Great Depression. Many families could not provide for their children. To encourage women to have as many children as possible in the midst of poverty was seen by some as a cruel joke. The Government of Ontario went to court asking that this will be declared void as "contrary to public policy and morals." Is the will valid?

3. The plaintiff brought an action for rescission of a land purchase. The plaintiff bought from the defendant a house situated on a large lot. The house sat 30 m from the highway, and was accessed by a paved driveway lined with mature, elegant shade trees. Eight months after the completion of the purchase, the municipality upgraded the highway that ran past the house from a two-lane highway to a four-lane highway. The construction effectively chopped 15 m from the plaintiff's lot and required the removal of most of the shade trees. The property was radically altered by this work. In addition, the noise of traffic was substantially increased by the closeness of the paved road to the house. The defendant admittedly had received advance notice about the highway project before selling the house and did not tell the plaintiff. The defendant argued that the plaintiff could have checked at the municipal offices and learned about the project and that there was no duty upon him to inform the plaintiff. Who would succeed?

4. The plaintiff bank tried to enforce a loan guarantee against the defendant, a farmer's wife. The bank's lending officer visited the farm while the woman's husband was on a business trip and demanded that she guarantee a loan made for a barn which her husband was having built. When she asked what would happen if she did not sign the papers, the bank officer replied, "Then, I'll shut the boys down." The defendant signed the papers because she did not want the workers to stop construction; the barn was very much needed for the farm operation. The loan went into default and the bank sued the defendant personally. The defence argued that the guarantee had been obtained by duress. The bank's position was that business pressure is not duress. Who would succeed?

5. The plaintiff accountant acted for the defendant in a tax case. The plaintiff prepared deceptive tax information to allow the defendant to avoid taxes. He was promised a $5000 fee for this service. When he was not paid, he sued for the money. Who would succeed?

6. The defendant and her husband owed a bank a large sum of money on a loan. The husband disappeared but the bank said it would not hold the defendant liable on the loan if she helped them find her husband. She made a very honest effort to find her husband, but could not do so. The bank then tried to collect from the defendant, but she argued that she did not have to pay because the bank said it would excuse her from the loan if she would *try* to find her husband. The bank did not say that she *must* find him to escape the loan. Who would succeed?

NOTICE
West Edmonton Mall Ltd. shall not be responsible for any injury, loss or damage howsoever caused which may occur to or be suffered by any person on or using these premises.
PULL

C H A P T E R   S I X

ENDING THE AGREEMENT– SPECIAL CONTRACTS

"The person who said the customer is always right was never in this business."

Robert Hutchings,
department store president

PERFORMANCE OF A CONTRACT

Generally, the parties to an agreement are required to perform in accordance with the express terms of the agreement. These obligations must be carried out exactly as stated. Anything less may result in legal action by the other party.

Although a contract may contain implied terms as well as specific terms, it is unwise to rely upon such hidden terms too much. For example, in *Trask Well Company v. Kinley* (Nova Scotia, 1948) the plaintiff agreed to drill a well on the defendant's land to an unspecified depth. The only stipulation was that the water must flow at a rate of 12 gallons (55 l) per minute. The plaintiff did so, but the water was salty and the defendant refused to pay. The contract said nothing about the quality of water, only the quantity, and the Court required the defendant to pay. The plaintiff had performed exactly what the contract required.

SUBSTANTIAL PERFORMANCE

Although a contract must be performed exactly, a trivial deviation from the terms of the contract will not amount to a breach. There is a general rule of law of ***de minimis***, which means that trifling matters can be ignored. It is a somewhat dangerous doctrine because it implies that a contract is performed if there has been **substantial performance**. This means that the basic nature of the agreement has been completed and only small details remain unfinished or require correction. A party who argues that there has not been substantial performance must show one or more of the following:

1. He or she received no benefit at all;
2. The work done was different from the work contracted to be done;
3. The other party abandoned the contract before completion.

LALONDE v. COLEMAN

Manitoba, 1990

Winnipeg boxer "Golden Boy" Donnie Lalonde entered into a management contract with promoter and agent John Coleman. Under the contract, the manager was to receive 30 percent of Lalonde's boxing purses. The boxer was later guaranteed $6 million for his fight against Sugar Ray Leonard and Coleman wanted $1.8 million.

However, Lalonde had long been unhappy with Coleman's poor performance. Coleman was supposed to promote at least 10 good matches. If Coleman did not promote a match, he was still entitled to 30 percent of the purse. Lalonde fought several matches but received no money. It became apparent that Coleman was in financial trouble when his offices were in a mortgage foreclosure.

Fed up, Lalonde went to another manager. With proper management, Lalonde got better fights and bigger purses, including a Las Vegas fight against Leonard. After this fight, Coleman sued in Nevada for 30 percent of the purse. Lalonde brought a separate action in Manitoba to have their contract declared void.

The Court declared the contract void, holding that the magnitude of Coleman's inability to carry out his duties was so great that it entitled Lalonde to treat their contract as at an end. There was a total breach of contract. Coleman's non-performance, due to his financial problems and bad relationship with the Manitoba Boxing Commission, meant that Lalonde received absolutely no benefit from the agreement. The result was something totally different from what the parties must have contemplated and Lalonde was free to walk away from the contract.

If there has been substantial performance, the party who did the work may demand payment as required in the contract, less the value of the work not done or the work needing correction.

TENDER

If a party to a contract is required to make a payment of money, there must be an unqualified proffering of the exact sum required. Even a certified cheque is not proper tender unless the contract allows it. However, if the other party does not object to the form of the tender, he or she is understood to have accepted it.

TIME FOR PERFORMANCE

A carefully drafted contract will be clear and concise regarding the particular time when it is to be performed. If there is no time stated, then the court has a difficult task trying to determine what the parties intended or what is reasonable. Some contracts contain the phrase "Time shall be of the essence in this agreement." The generally understood meaning of this phrase is that the parties should attempt to complete it as soon as possible and that undue delays are a breach of the agreement.

DEPENDENCY OF PERFORMANCE

In some contracts, the nature of the contract is such that one party must fulfil his or her requirement before the other party must perform. Although both parties have exchanged consideration under the contract, performance by one party may be dependent upon satisfactory performance by the other.

For example, suppose that Brown agrees to buy a business from Green upon the satisfactory submission of complete accounting and financial statements of the business. Green submits incomplete statements and Brown refuses to conclude the agreement. The failure of Green to perform absolves Brown of his legal obligation.

What is involved in such contracts is a **condition precedent**, which establishes the order in which the parties must perform. If the first party does not fulfil his or her requirement, the second party is relieved of any obligation. However, the second party must be prepared to prove that he or she was ready, willing, and able to perform as promised.

A party always has the right to waive a condition precedent, but if the party does so it cannot be reinstated later. Generally, the party that has agreed to perform first cannot cancel a contract because of his or her own non-performance.

GREAVES v. ROBBINS

Ontario, 1981

The plaintiff sued the defendant for specific performance of a contract for the sale of an antique car. The contract was conditional upon the defendant providing the plaintiff with a certificate from a recognized collectors' club that the automobile was authentic and that it had no substitute or replacement parts.

The defendant later received a better offer, so he failed to provide the plaintiff with the certificate. He then notified the plaintiff that the contract was at an end. The plaintiff replied that he would waive the condition that a certificate be provided and buy the car as is. The defendant refused to accept the waiver.

The Court ordered the car to be sold to the plaintiff and that the certificate, if available, be provided to the plaintiff as well. The condition precedent protected the buyer, not the seller. The seller could not avoid his contractual obligation by deliberately refusing to carry out a term which he could easily have performed.

BREACH OF CONTRACT

When one party to a contract fails to carry out his or her obligation, this party is said to be in **breach of contract.** The refusal may be express or implied and, when it occurs, creates new rights for the injured party. That party may bring an action for the damages suffered as a result of the breach. Usually, the injured party may also consider the contract at an end and refuse to carry out his or her obligations.

FUNDAMENTAL BREACH

As was previously mentioned, a minor defect in the performance of a contract is not breach of contract. There must be a fundamental breach that goes to the heart of the contract. A **fundamental breach** occurs when the event resulting from the failure by one party to perform has the effect of depriving the other party of the benefit that it was supposed to receive.The distinction between a fundamental breach and the breach of a condition or small detail depends upon the facts of each case. For example, a defect in a new vehicle would not be a fundamental breach if it could be repaired and if the vehicle could still be operated with the defect. If, however, the defect was so major that the vehicle was useless, it would be a fundamental breach.

In *Keks v. Esquire Pleasure Tours* (Manitoba, 1974) the plaintiff successfully sued the defendant travel agent after his vacation to Hawaii was so badly planned that it was more a nightmare than a joy. The plaintiff paid for accommodation with kitchen facilities and took his housekeeper-cook with him. There was no kitchen and the plaintiff ended up paying an extra $1936 for a hotel room and meals for the housekeeper.

BREACH OF IMPLIED TERM

The alleged breach of contract does not necessarily have to pertain to a specific term of the contract. Breach of contract can arise where one of the parties violated an **implied or unwritten term** of the agreement.

IVO v. HALABURA

Saskatchewan, 1990

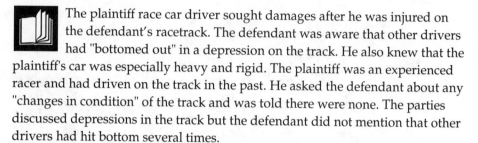

The plaintiff race car driver sought damages after he was injured on the defendant's racetrack. The defendant was aware that other drivers had "bottomed out" in a depression on the track. He also knew that the plaintiff's car was especially heavy and rigid. The plaintiff was an experienced racer and had driven on the track in the past. He asked the defendant about any "changes in condition" of the track and was told there were none. The parties discussed depressions in the track but the defendant did not mention that other drivers had hit bottom several times.

The plaintiff drove some test laps around the track at a slow speed, without difficulty. However, during an actual race, at 155 miles (250 km) per hour, the defendant bottomed with considerable force and broke two vertebrae. He sued the defendant for breach of contract and tort.

The Court held for the plaintiff. The defendant was liable in both contract and tort. The defendant had failed to repair the track and had failed to tell the plaintiff about the danger. The defendant had breached an implied term of their contract that he would inform the defendant of dangerous track conditions. The doctrine of *volenti non fit injuria* did not apply in a case where one party knew of danger and did not advise the other.

REMEDIES FOR BREACH OF CONTRACT

The injured party has a number of remedies to consider. The first, and most common, remedy is to sue for **monetary damages**. The failure of one party to perform as required will often cause the other party financial loss, for which that party is entitled to compensation. Although it is a difficult task, the court tries to put the injured party in the same position as if the contract had been performed.

GEOPHYSICAL SYSTEMS v. SEISMOGRAPH SERVICES CORP.

U.S. District Court, 1990

The plaintiff, GSC, sued the defendant, SSC, for breach of contract. The defendant had been hired to write computer software according to specifications in a contract. At this time, computer companies regarded contracts as formalities. They were often vaguely and poorly worded.

GSC alleged that it suffered a loss because the seismic data processing software written by SSC failed to work as promised on GSC's Digital Equipment computers. None of the software requirements were met and data interpretation applications did not work.

Because of its inability to process the data used in the seismic mapping of underground oil deposits, GSC suffered financial loss and filed for bankruptcy. The suit alleged that the defendant knew that it did not have the technical skills to write such a complex program, but entered into the contract anyway. The evidence was that SSC did not know how to write the program GSC wanted, but believed that its software experts could "develop their expertise" as they went along. That is, they would learn as they wrote the program and that it would eventually be successful. Counsel for the plaintiff described this notion as "winging it."

The Court awarded damages of $48 million. The evidence did not show fraud, but did show incompetence. The defendant knew the plaintiff would suffer serious financial harm if the program did not work.

Another possible remedy is an **injunction**, which is a court order requiring that a person either perform an act or stop doing an illegal act. An injunction has many possible uses, but as it pertains to contract law, it is generally used to prevent a person from entering into a contract with one employer while that person still has a valid contract with another employer. Professional athletes who break their contracts with one club may find that they cannot play for another club because their legitimate employer has obtained an injunction prohibiting them from doing so.

Even though the injured party may demand damages from the other party, the injured party still has a duty to **mitigate** the loss suffered. This means that the injured party must take every reasonable step to limit the loss. For example, suppose that Brown has a contract to sell perishable food to Green. Green refuses to take delivery. If Brown simply lets the food rot, when it was clearly possible to sell it to someone else, Brown will not recover the full loss.

IMPOSSIBILITY OF PERFORMANCE

The fact that a party finds a contract very difficult to carry out does not excuse the party from it. Each party must anticipate possible problems, such as late deliveries, strikes, etc., and provide for them in the contract. However, there are certain situations that are generally held to be beyond anyone's control and, therefore, render a contract impossible to perform. Some examples would be:

1. The subject matter has been destroyed. A contract to buy a building would be declared void if the building burned down.
2. Illness makes the performance of a personal service impossible. An actor is not in breach of contract for failure to appear on stage if the actor has a serious illness.
3. A change in the law makes the contract illegal. A change in a zoning by-law could stop the construction of a type of building.

When personal services are involved, if a person has contracted to do a job based on personal skill, that person cannot send someone else to do the job. If Green pays a substantial fee to have a photographic portrait taken by Brown, a famous photographer, Brown cannot have his assistant do the work. There is no substitute for the personal touch of an artist.

In some situations, a frustrating event may be grounds to end a contract. The principle of **frustration** differs only slightly from impossibility in that it usually arises because of outside interference. This interference might not render performance impossible, but it could make the performance quite useless.

One of the older cases on record, *Krell v. Henry* (England, 1905) illustrates this point. The plaintiff rented an apartment from the defendant from which to watch the coronation parade of Edward VII. A small down payment was made on the rental. The king became ill and the parade was cancelled. The plaintiff wanted the deposit refunded; the defendant countersued for the balance owed. The contract was not impossible, the plaintiff could still rent the apartment. However, the purpose of the rental agreement had been interfered with by unforeseen events. The Court held that the contract was frustrated. Most provinces have a *Frustrated Contracts Act* which provides for an orderly cancellation of the contract and the settlement of monetary disputes. Generally, any prepayment or deposit must be returned, but both parties are permitted to claim for expenses they incurred.

In *Vancouver Milling and Grain Co. v. C.C. Ranch Company* (Supreme Court of Canada, 1924) the appellant ordered a large shipment of wheat from the respondent. The contract said nothing about the method of shipment, but it was common knowledge that the only possible method was by Canadian Pacific Railway. CPR had a shortage of rail cars and the wheat was not delivered. The Court held that the promise to deliver the wheat was conditional upon rail cars being available, even though the contract did not state this. The principle of *lex non cogit impossibilia* (the law does not compel the impossible) was applicable to this case. The respondent had wheat ready and the shortage of cars was not attributable to any fault of the respondent.

BANKRUPTCY OR RECEIVERSHIP

Obligations under a contract may be ended by **bankruptcy,** or **receivership**, a legal process by which a party places all financial affairs into the hands of a trustee. A person can go into bankruptcy in two ways. One is to voluntarily declare bankruptcy. The other is to be forced into bankruptcy by a creditor.

The purpose of the *Bankruptcy Act* is to provide relief for the honest, but overcommitted, debtor. The essence of the bankruptcy process is to give up all remaining assets in exchange for having debts wiped out.

The law requires the debtor to make an application for bankruptcy through a federal government official called the Official Receiver. The application will outline all debts and other information. If the application is accepted, the Receiver appoints a trustee to handle the affairs of the company and complete the bankruptcy process. In practice, the debtor can go to a trustee first. The trustee will then handle the application

Bankruptcy trustees are licensed by the federal government to handle the winding up of the business. They are usually accountants, but some are lawyers. The trustee will call a meeting of the person's creditors and allow them to make arguments as to how the assets should be liquidated. The trustee may also meet with employees to discuss their termination.

The law stipulates the order in which creditors must be paid. The order is to pay the secured creditors, then the preferred creditors, and finally the unsecured creditors. A secured creditor is one who has a legal, registered claim upon the assets of the bankrupt company or person. No creditor is guaranteed payment. If the debtor has no assets, all creditors will suffer loss. Assets that are subject to security interest, such as land mortgages, bonds, chattel mortgages, or conditional sales agreements, rank highest. If any assets remain, they are normally paid to the preferred creditors in the following order:

1. Costs of administration of bankruptcy;
2. Expenses of the trustee;
3. Court costs;
4. Wages, salaries, or commissions of employees for the three-month period preceding bankruptcy;
5. Municipal taxes;
6. Rent for the three-month period preceding bankruptcy;

7. Indebtedness under federal or provincial laws, including money owed under the *Workers' Compensation Act*, *Unemployment Insurance Act*, *Income Tax Act*, or other claims of the Crown.

The unsecured creditors, being at the bottom of the list, share in any balance remaining. This amount is usually prorated. For example, a creditor may receive 10 cents on the dollar because the assets remaining represent one-tenth of the debt owed.

Until a bankrupt person is discharged by the court, he or she is not released from debts. Any earnings received by the debtor before the discharge is granted will be applied to the debts. A person who is an **undischarged bankrupt** must not engage in business without telling the other party of this status.

Revenue Canada has priority over any unsecured creditor. Unlike other creditors, Revenue Canada does not have to sue a taxpayer and obtain a judgment before it can take steps to collect taxes owing. The assessment of taxes has the effect of a judgment. In *Wright v. A.G. Canada* (Federal Court, 1989) it was held that the Crown has priority over a deserted wife and other creditors. Wright abandoned his medical practice, family, and creditors. The Court held that Wright's unpaid taxes ranked above other obligations, including $100 000 in arrears on support payments to his ex-wife.

Whether Revenue Canada can take priority over a secured creditor is a very controversial issue. The basic problem is that the statute is silent on this issue. In *Wright*, the Court concluded that taxes must be paid first, but most courts have ruled that the tax collector ranks after secured creditors. However, in *Royal Bank v. Saskatchewan Power* (Saskatchewan, 1990) the Court held that Revenue Canada may recover unpaid taxes ahead of a secured creditor. The Court declined to follow several other cases where it was held that Revenue Canada did not have a prior claim on assets. Thus, the issue is far from settled.

Bankruptcy does not absolve the individual of every liability. Certain personal obligations remain, even though an individual or company has been discharged by bankruptcy. Future obligations, such as support payments to former spouses, may remain intact. In *R. v. Fitzgibbon* (Supreme Court of Canada, 1990) it was held that a discharged bankrupt is not freed from the obligation to pay compensation ordered by a criminal court under the *Criminal Code of Canada*. The Court held that an ex-lawyer, who defrauded his clients, must pay the Law Society the $330 000 that the Society was required to pay out on his behalf. The compensation order was made when the lawyer was convicted of fraud. The Court held that the important concept of compensation for victims cannot be thwarted by the simple act of the criminal declaring bankruptcy.

A person who seeks to deceive the bankruptcy trustee and creditors by transferring money or property to third persons will find that these transfers can be declared void under the *Fraudulent Conveyances Act* which exists in most provinces. Under this Act, the court can set aside any conveyance which was intended to "defeat, hinder, delay, or defraud creditors." In *Toronto-Dominion Bank v. Miller* (Ontario, 1991) a bankrupt dentist gave large sums of money to charities at a time when he was unable to meet his mortgage payments and other debts. These gifts were often in excess of $15 000 per month. The Court ordered the dentist to stop the practice and ordered the charities to repay the funds, holding that "debts must be paid before gifts can be made."

In *Panamericana de Bienes Y Servicios S.A. v. Northern Badger Oil and Gas Ltd.* (Alberta, 1991) the Alberta Court of Appeal held that environmental laws take priority over secured creditors. When Badger Oil went bankrupt, the trustee reported that it would cost $200 000 to cap its old wells and generally meet environmental standards. The Court ruled that this obligation ranked ahead of a $1.3-million secured debenture held by a Panamanian bank.

ASSIGNMENT OF CONTRACT

The parties to a contract may want to transfer rights or obligations to other parties. This is referred to as **assignment of contract** and the most common form deals with the right to collect money. If a store sells goods on credit, it usually assigns the right to monthly payments to a financial institution such as a finance company. The finance company pays the store and then collects from the debtor.

An assignment must be in writing and must be given for valid consideration. The debtor must be notified that the assignment has been made, but there is no requirement to obtain the debtor's permission. The assignment cannot, in any way, increase the burden on the debtor or change the basic agreement by adding new terms.

While it is easy to assign a right under a contract, it is quite the reverse with regard to obligations. A person cannot assign certain obligations at all, including the payment of a debt or the performance of a personal skill.

If a party is required to perform a certain act that does not require special or personal skills, the work may be assigned. For example, if Brown is obliged to deliver a carload of lumber to Green, but assigns the duty to Amber, Green must accept the lumber, provided it is of the same grade and quality as stated in the contract. A general contractor may sign a contract with a buyer for the construction of a house, then subcontract with the plumber, electrician, and mason for the work. This is a normal, business procedure and is not in violation of the contract terms. The general contractor remains liable for the quality of the work done by the subcontractors. The buyer must make payments to the general contractor, who in turn pays the subcontractors.

If the contract calls for the performance of a personal skill, it cannot be assigned. The substitution of a third party in a contract for one of the original parties may also take the form of a **novation**. By this process, a totally new contract is substituted for the original one. Generally, the following rules apply:

1. The new debtor must assume the complete liability of the original party;
2. The creditor must accept the change;
3. The creditor must absolve the old debtor of any liability.

THE LAW OF BAILMENTS

People often have reason to leave personal property in the care or custody of some other person. A common example is taking a car for a repair. Transactions of this kind are called **bailments**. The person who owns and delivers the property is the **bailor** and the person who receives the property is the **bailee**. A bailment consists of delivery of personal property to another person on the understanding that the property is to be returned at a specified time or when a certain purpose has been fulfiled. It is clear that the parties do not intend that title to the property should change hands. Thus, a bailment is very distinct from a sale.

A person entrusted with the property of another is expected to take care of it. However, the extent of care and liability differ, depending upon whether the person is paid to take care of the property (**bailment for reward**) or is doing it for nothing (**gratuitous bailment**).

GRATUITOUS BAILMENTS

A bailment is gratuitous if one of the parties receives some benefit or service for free. Depending upon who receives the benefit, the bailment is either exclusive for the bailor or for the bailee. If Brown is going away on a holiday and asks Green to care for her dog, Brown is a bailor who is receiving a free benefit because Green is performing a service without fee.

As an opposite example, if Green's lawn mower breaks down and he borrows Brown's lawn mower, Green is the bailee who is receiving free use of the machine. In both examples, property is temporarily in the hands of another person, but for different reasons. Even though there might not be a written contract, a gratuitous bailment requires a certain level of responsibility on the part of the bailee. If a bailment is for the benefit of the bailor only, then the bailee is required to take only such a degree of care of the property as an ordinary, prudent person would take of his or her own property. If the property is lost, stolen, or damaged while it is in the bailee's hands, the bailee is not liable unless the loss occurred through the serious negligence of the bailee or because the bailee ignored the instructions given by the bailor.

If the bailment is for the exclusive benefit of the bailee, the rule changes. The obligation of a borrower of property is that the bailee must use the article only for the purpose for which it was loaned. The bailee must take the utmost degree of care of the article and is liable for any damage caused by carelessness. The bailee is not liable for ordinary wear and tear just from using the property.

CALLFAS v. HUMPHREY

Ontario, 1985

Callfas offered Humphrey the use of her stereo because she was moving in with her boyfriend, who already had a very good stereo. The plaintiff made it clear that she wanted the equipment cared for and that she eventually would want it back. She insisted that the defendant have insurance coverage. The defendant replied that she had tenant's insurance, but was not aware that it covered the building only, not her contents.

A thief broke in and stole the stereo. The insurance company refused to pay and the plaintiff sued. The defendant denied personal liability but the Court held the defendant liable. The fact that the defendant misunderstood the extent of her insurance coverage did not relieve her of liability. Damage did not occur through uninsurable acts. The defendant was duty-bound to make certain her insurance was adequate. She was required to return the set in good condition or compensate the plaintiff for the loss.

BAILMENTS FOR REWARD

Most bailments involve the exchange of consideration between the two parties. This is called a **bailment for reward**. If the two parties enter into a specific contract, then the terms of that contract will apply. If there is no written contract, some general rules apply, depending upon what the bailee is to do with the goods.

RENTING PROPERTY

When personal property is rented, the owner of the goods is the bailor and the person renting the goods is the bailee. An example would be a person who rents an automobile from a leasing company. Each party has duties and obligations.

The bailor's responsibilities include making certain that the goods being rented out are fit and safe for the work for which they are rented. There is an implied warranty on the part of the bailor to be liable for damages or injuries that result from defects of which the bailor ought to have been aware. Therefore, if the rented automobile is mechanically unsafe, the bailor is liable for any injuries that result. In *Frontair Ltée v. Michaud* (New Brunswick, 1983) the defendant, a student in the plaintiff's flying school, rented an airplane for solo flying practice. Even though the weather was clear, the defendant became lost and made a forced landing. The plaintiff successfully sued for the damage to the plane. The only possible explanation for the crash was that the defendant had been inattentive and had not demonstrated the degree of care of a reasonable person.

REPAIRING PROPERTY

If a person takes property to another person for repair, a bailment exists. The bailor has two obligations: to pay the price agreed upon, or a reasonable price, and to pay for the extent of work agreed upon. If the bailee does more than the contract calls for, the bailor does not have to pay the extra cost unless he or she has consented to having the work done.

When the bailor takes an item for repair, the bailor must be specific as to what is to be done. If the item is left just for repair, then the bailee may assume that the bailor wants all necessary repairs done. If a bailor signs a blank work order authorizing repairs, then the bailor must pay for everything that is done.

If the bailor wants to limit either the amount of work done or the cost, then the bailor must specifically instruct the bailee that the work is to be so limited. The simplest way is to limit the dollar cost. Words such as "Repair authorized to a limit of $200" written on the work order will serve as protection against a larger repair bill. For major repairs, it is wise to obtain a complete estimate before authorizing the work. The bailee may charge a reasonable fee for preparing the estimate.

Responding to complaints about padded automobile repair bills, Ontario enacted a law requiring a detailed work order for all motor vehicle repairs. If no written estimate is given to the bailor in advance, the bailor does not have to pay the bill.

The bailee has the duty of doing the repairs agreed upon in a skilful and diligent manner, taking ordinary care of the property. In the event of damage, the onus of proving absence of negligence is upon the bailee. Many repair shops have posted signs and contract terms with such words as: "Items left at owner's risk." These signs do not absolve the bailee of all liability. They are advising the bailor that the bailee is not an insurer of the goods. Thus, if the building burns down and the bailor's goods are destroyed by a fire that is not caused by the negligence of the bailee, the bailee is not required to compensate the bailor for the loss. However, the courts have held that if the bailor does not see the sign or does not read the words in the contract, he or she is not bound by them.

PUNCH v. SAVOY'S

Ontario, 1986

The bailor, Ms. Punch, had given her $11 000 ring to the bailee, Savoy's Jewelers, a local firm, for repair. Unknown to Punch, Savoy's did not make repairs. It sent rings to Toronto for repairs by another company, Walker Jewelry. The practice was to send rings by registered mail, showing a value of $100. Although this seemed risky, the jewellers had never lost any jewellery in the mail in 25 years. In this case, when the repair was complete, a postal strike was in progress, so Walker was not able to return the ring by mail. Without consulting Savoy's, Walker sent the ring by CN Rapidex, a courier system. The CN driver who picked up the ring was inexperienced and accepted the package, even though there was a company policy against accepting anything valued over $300. The true value was marked on the package. The CN office manager did not notice the mistake. The ring was shipped, but disappeared. Punch sued Savoy's, Walker, and CN.

The form that Walker signed when it handed the ring over to CN contained conditions limiting the liability of the carrier to $50 for "loss or damage through negligence or otherwise." Savoy's did not know what Walker was doing.

The Court held all three bailees liable, and then held that CN must reimburse the two jewellers. Savoy's could not be bound by the disclaimer clause in CN's contract because Savoy's had never seen it and did not know CN had the ring. Walker had ignored CN's limitation as to the value CN would accept and had also failed to insure the shipment. Neither Walker nor Savoy's had the plaintiff's permission to ship her ring anywhere without insurance. CN was liable for the loss of the ring, even though it was unaware of the plaintiff as the true owner. The disclaimer clause did not specifically exclude loss by theft by one of the carrier's employees, which is the only plausible explanation of what happened to the ring.

Unless there is an agreement to the contrary, the bailor must pay the bailee before the bailee returns the goods. This is because the law gives an unpaid bailee a lien on the goods. Ultimately, the bailee has the right to sell the goods to satisfy the claim. Once the bailee releases the goods, the right of lien is lost and cannot be recovered. For example, if a garage releases a car to the owner without being paid, the garage cannot later repossess the car for non-payment. In British Columbia, Alberta, Saskatchewan, and Manitoba, a lien may be placed on a vehicle after it has been released if the garage has the owner's written acknowledgment of the indebtedness.

STORING PROPERTY

Bailees who store goods for a fee are in the business of running a warehouse and such people are subject to the following general rules:

1. They must use reasonable diligence and care in looking after the goods that are stored. The onus is upon them to prove that loss was not due to their negligence.
2. If they accept items for storage that require special facilities, such as cold storage, they are obligated to provide those facilities or accept liability for loss.

In *Davidson v. Three Spruces Realty Ltd.* (British Columbia, 1977) the plaintiffs rented bulk storage space from the defendant in which to store possessions and valuables. At the time of the rental, both plaintiffs signed a standard contract that they did not read; a limitation of liability clause was not drawn to their attention. They were assured of the absolute safety of their valuables and were informed that the valuables need not be insured. In fact, the defendant took no precautions for the safety of the items stored. The vaults were broken into by robbers and valuable coins were stolen from the plaintiffs. The Court held in favour of the plaintiffs. The defendant was negligent in not taking reasonable precautions for the safety of the stored items and could not rely on the limitation clause because the negligence was a fundamental breach of the contract.

Numerous cases have arisen regarding damage to vehicles in parking lots or the theft of contents from parked vehicles. The case law is long and complex, varying with the circumstances of each case. In general, the parking lot owner is merely renting space to the vehicle owner or driver. The lot owner does not insure the vehicles and does not guarantee that nothing will happen to them. Most lots are not guarded in any way. Thus, the disclaimer found on parking tickets and on signs that the vehicle is left at the owner's risk is generally correct. Valuable items should be locked in the trunk, out of sight.

However, some parking lots require vehicle owners to leave the keys with the attendant. These lots are small and vehicles are packed in tightly, requiring the attendant to move vehicles to let others go in and out. In these cases, the normal disclaimer of not being responsible does not operate. In the case of *Heffron v. Imperial Parking* (British Columbia, 1974) the plaintiff left his vehicle with a parking lot attendant and, upon handing over the keys, told the attendant there were valuables in the car and to keep a close eye on it. The attendant said he would, but the valuables were stolen. The Court held that a bailment for reward had been established and the defendant would have to pay for the stolen goods.

TRANSPORTING PROPERTY

People who transport goods are called **carriers**. There are two types of carriers, private and common.

A **private carrier** is one who occasionally transports goods for other people and is paid for the service, but does not make it a regular business in a public way. This gives the private carrier the right to accept or reject either the customer or the type of goods to be carried. A private carrier is liable for any loss caused by negligence of its employees.

Companies or people who hold themselves out to the public as being in the business of transporting goods are called **common carriers**. A common carrier does not have the right to pick and choose either its customers or the type of goods to be carried, unless the goods require special facilities which the carrier does not have. A common carrier is an insurer of the goods during their transportation and is liable for loss or damage occurring in the course of shipment, even though the carrier may not be guilty of any negligence. However, a common carrier is not liable if the goods are destroyed by an act of nature, by the Queen's enemies (e.g., during a war), or by defects in the goods themselves.

Carriers issue tickets when goods are shipped and the terms of the shipping agreement are printed on the tickets. In some cases the carrier's liability is limited in some manner, usually by the mass or the number of items. For example, items lost by an air carrier may be limited by the terms of the Warsaw Convention, which is an international treaty covering air travel to many of the countries of the world.

In *Frederickson v. Via Rail* (Ontario, 1988) the plaintiff checked two pieces of luggage with the defendant when she boarded a train in Montreal. She paid $1 to a clerk at the time. The luggage vanished and Via Rail offered to pay $100, which was the maximum required under the terms printed on the luggage claim tags. The plaintiff argued that she had valuables in the luggage worth much more and that the payment of $1 created a separate bailment without limits. The Court disagreed and held that Via Rail was only liable to the amount of $100. The plaintiff had not declared any extra value at the time the luggage was checked. Accordingly, the terms on the tickets applied.

HOTELS, MOTELS, AND INNS

People who operate hotels, motels, and inns are bailees for reward. Hotel keepers are people who hold themselves out to the public as being ready to provide lodging and accommodation to travellers and to accept the travellers' luggage as well. Hotel keepers must accept any fit and orderly person as a guest, provided there is a vacancy. They do not have to accept pets or other animals and can limit the number of people in a room.

As a bailee, the hotel keeper's liability is similar to that of a common carrier. Thus, the hotel keeper is an insurer of the goods which guests bring into the hotel. However, the hotel keeper may avoid liability by showing that loss or damage is due to the guests' own negligence. Liability may extend to insuring guests' cars if they are parked on hotel property, but it does not extend to the contents of the cars.

The liability of the hotel keeper has been limited by provincial statute. Most provinces have laws that limit the liability of the hotel keeper if a notice to this effect is posted in the room. For example, in Ontario, no hotel keeper is liable to make good to a guest a sum of more than $40 except where the goods or property have been stolen or damaged through the willful act, default, or neglect of the hotel keeper or his or her employees. Liability also rests upon the hotel keeper if the goods were deposited for safekeeping with the hotel keeper. In Newfoundland, the liability is $150. In Alberta, the room must be locked and the key left at the desk or there is no liability upon the hotel.

INSURANCE CONTRACTS

The concept of insurance has its roots in antiquity. The first authenticated instances of insurance have been identified in Italy, dating back to the thirteenth century, where a form of maritime insurance existed. Insurance is a pooling of funds by a group of people who want to reduce the risk of a single, disastrous accident. Early sailing ships either returned loaded with valuable spices and goods, or they did not return at all. The profits from the returned ships had to pay for the loss of missing vessels. The crew members were not insured.

A **contract of insurance** in the broadest sense of the term may be defined as a contract whereby one person, called the **insurer**, undertakes, in return for the agreed payment of a premium, to pay another person, called the **insured**, a sum of money on the happening of a specified event. Insurance contracts contemplate the existence of a potential accident or loss. The event is called the subject matter of the insurance and, to obtain insurance, the insured must have an **insurable interest** in the subject matter. As a simple example, Green may insure his or her own house against the risk of fire, but Green cannot obtain fire insurance on Brown's house. A person cannot obtain insurance unless the person stands to benefit by the continued existence of the subject matter or suffer loss if the subject matter is destroyed.

TYPES OF INSURANCE

The most common types of insurance include liability insurance, property insurance, automobile insurance, and life insurance. Under a policy of **liability insurance** the insurer agrees to indemnify the insured against certain liabilities to which the insured may be exposed. For example, a magazine publisher will carry libel insurance to pay for any judgment against the publisher by someone who was defamed in the magazine.

Property insurance protects real property against fire, acts of nature, and injury to people on the property.

Life insurance is an undertaking by the insurer to pay insurance money upon the death of the insured. To obtain a life insurance policy, the policyholder must demonstrate an insurable interest in the life of the insured. A person may insure his or her own life and may also insure the life of another person whose continued existence represents a benefit to the policy holder. For example, spouses may insure each other's lives, and many business partners do the same thing. If one partner dies, the other collects the insurance money, which will enable him or her to buy out the deceased partner's share of the business from the deceased's estate. Employers may insure employees. Some companies identify key personnel as crucial to the company success and maintain large insurance policies upon those employees.

Automobile insurance provides a variety of coverages on the vehicle itself, for bodily injury, and third party liability. Ontario and Quebec have established a **no-fault system**, under which a driver who suffers injury or vehicle damage looks to his or her own insurance company for compensation. An injured person may sue the other driver only in cases of death or permanent serious injury. The vast majority of insurance claims are made without resort to the courts.

PRINCIPLE OF UBERRIMAE FIDEI

A contract of insurance is treated by the court as a contract of ***uberrimae fidei,*** which means the contract is one that involves the "utmost good faith." The applicant for insurance must disclose all information requested by the insurer to enable the insurer to decide if it should accept the risk and what premium to charge. The failure on the part of the applicant to be truthful may allow the insurer to refuse to pay should loss occur.

For example, a person who obtains automobile insurance from a company that offers a special rate for people who never consume alcohol would not be covered if he or she were involved in an accident while impaired. Most life insurance policies will not pay any death benefits if the insured commits suicide within two years of acquiring the policy. This is to prevent people who have already decided to commit suicide from buying life insurance just prior to taking their own lives.

PERRON v. L'INDUSTRIELLE COMPAGNIE D'ASSURANCE SUR LA VIE

Quebec, 1987

Gilles Perron acquired a life insurance policy from the defendant company, claiming that he was a non-smoker. After his death, the insurance company learned that people had seen Mr. Perron smoke cigars in the year before he took out the policy. Tobacco was not a factor in his death, as he died in a car accident, but the company refused to pay the death benefits and Perron's widow sued. She did not testify, so the Court was unable to learn whether Gilles Perron smoked after he bought the policy as well.

The Court held that the insurance company did not have to pay the benefits of the policy because Gilles Perron had acquired the insurance by making a false declaration. Even though he did not die of a lung disease or other health problem related to smoking, he had acquired a policy with lower premiums by being dishonest with the insurance company.

BURDEN OF PROOF

It is a fundamental principle of insurance law that the burden of proof rests with the insured to establish a right to recover under the terms of a policy. The insurer may add further restrictions in the policy.

SHAKUR v. PILOT INSURANCE CO.

Ontario, 1991

Mrs. Shakur claimed she was mugged after leaving a bank and robbed of $66 000 worth of jewellery. The alleged thief was never caught. She admitted that some of the jewellery had been brought illegally into Canada. The insurance company became suspicious when it learned that Mrs. Shakur had been in the bank vault for just one minute—not enough time to take jewels from a safe deposit box. No one saw the robbery and there was no reason for a thief to believe she was carrying valuables. The trial judge ruled that the insurance company must prove that Shakur was perpetrating a fraud against the company.

The Court of Appeal overturned the trial judge's ruling and said that the insured person must prove, on a balance of probabilities, that a loss actually occurred. The Court also ruled that the company could not automatically refuse to pay the insurance on the illegal jewellery, even though Canada Customs would have confiscated such items if they had been detected. However, it was not unlawful for Mrs. Shakur to keep and insure the jewellery once it was in Canada. A new trial was ordered on the issue of whether there actually had been a robbery.

WRONGFUL ACTS BY THE INSURED

It is a principle of insurance law that the insured cannot profit from his or her own wrongful acts. To allow a person to profit from a criminal or wrongful act would reward the wrongdoer, scandalize the court, and bring justice into disrepute.

For example, Peter Demeter was convicted in 1973 of the murder of his wife. In 1983, he sued three life insurance companies who held policies on his deceased wife. Demeter was really seeking, in a civil court, a rehearing of the murder charge against him, claiming he had new evidence. The Court dismissed the suit on the ground that Demeter could not collect the death benefit when he had murdered the insured person.

Although the rule against rewarding wrongdoers seems reasonable and sound, complications can arise when one person commits a wrongful act which also causes financial loss to another. In *Higgins v. Orion Insurance* (Ontario, 1981) the plaintiff sued the defendant insurance company for the proceeds under a fire insurance policy. The plaintiff's business partner had burned down their business and was convicted of arson. The defendant refused to pay any benefit.

Although Higgins was totally innocent of the arson and lost his entire investment, the Court held that there was no way he could be reimbursed under the policy. It was issued to the partnership as a single entity, so the criminal action of one partner deprived both partners of any rights to the insurance benefits.

KOLTA et al. v. STATE FARM CASUALTY CO.

Ontario, 1981

The insured threatened people with a shotgun after an argument. When the police arrived, the insured retreated into his house and refused to come out. He permitted his wife and children to leave but would not respond to police demands that he surrender.

The police fired tear gas cannisters into the house, which set the house on fire. The police entered to both arrest and rescue the insured. They found him sitting in a daze in the basement.

The house was destroyed and the insured and his wife filed a claim. The insurance company refused to pay anything. The insured withdrew his claim, accepting that his criminal act had caused the loss. However, the wife continued her claim for 50 percent of the loss.

The action was dismissed. The fire was a result of a criminal act by the insured. His wife, being a joint insured, was affected by her husband's acts. Where all the insured people have a joint interest, a loss caused by one of them affects the claim of all of them.

REVIEW: POINTS OF LAW

1. A party meets his or her obligation under a contract if the contract is substantially performed.
2. Some contracts contain the wording "Time shall be of the essence," which means that it must be carried out promptly or it is void.
3. A contract may be written in such a way that one party must perform his or her obligation before the other party will perform. Such a requirement is called a condition precedent.
4. A minor defect in performance of a contract obligation is not breach of contract. There must be a fundamental breach.
5. If one party breaches a contract, the other party must mitigate (minimize) the damages as much as possible.
6. A contract may be ended it if proves to be impossible to perform it. The rule is that the law does not compel the impossible.
7. Contract obligations may be terminated by bankruptcy.
8. Rights under a contract may be readily assigned to another party. Obligations cannot be assigned without agreement of the other party to the contract.
9. The obligation to perform a personal skill under a contract cannot be assigned.
10. Under a gratuitous bailment, a person who borrows property must take the utmost care of it.
11. A person who rents goods to others must make certain that the rental item is safe to use.
12. A person who repairs items must take reasonable care of the item, but is not an insurer of it.

LEGAL BRIEFS

1. P, a printer, telephoned Q and requested a new part for a printing press. P asked Q to rush the order and Q promised to do so. The part was delivered three days later, during which time P was unable to print many of its orders. P sued Q for breach of contract. Is Q liable?

2. L purchased a new car from H Autos. The new car had a problem with the steering system, so L returned it to the dealer. She needed a vehicle, so H Autos gave her a "loaner" in the form of a used car that had just been traded in. While driving the loaner vehicle, L had a major accident because the car had worn-out brakes. Liability of H?
3. E had a contract to sell gold jewellery to S. E intended to purchase the gold to make the jewellery from South Africa. However, the Government of Canada imposed trade sanctions against South Africa and E was unable to import the gold. He could purchase gold on the European market, but at a much higher cost. E advised S that he was cancelling the contract. Can E do so?
4. D bought a motor home from N. He paid $1000 down and intended to pay the remainder when he picked up the vehicle. Two days later, N was put into bankruptcy by creditors and its entire inventory of motor homes was towed away. Will D recover his money?
5. C purchased a used sports car from B. The car appeared to be in very good condition. No specific warranty was given with the car, although it had a certificate of mechanical fitness. B did not tell C that the car had been used in racing. Two weeks after purchasing the car, the engine blew up. What rights has C against B?
6. K took his car to Y to be painted. After it was painted, K was notified to come and pick up the car. K said he would not be able to pick it up for two or three days because of a job commitment. Having no indoor parking space, Y parked the car outside and locked it. Parts were stolen from the car. Liability of Y?
7. R bought a new tractor from M. The contract called for delivery not later than August 1. Payment was to be in four instalments over the next year. R fully expected to pay for the tractor from the proceeds of his harvest and M knew this. When the tractor arrived from the manufacturer, M refused to deliver it, saying, "I hear you're having financial problems. I want full payment in cash." What rights has R?

APPLYING THE LAW

SCOTT v. WAWANESE INSURANCE

British Columbia, 1986

The adult plaintiffs held a fire insurance policy on their family home with the defendant insurance company. The named insured were the two adults. However, another clause in the policy defined the "Insured" as including not merely the named insured, but the "relatives of either, and any other person under the age of 21 in the care of an Insured."

The policy also excluded coverage for the "wilful acts" of the Insured. In this clause, the word "Insured" included persons under 21 years of age in the care of the named Insured.The plaintiffs' 15-year-old son was emotionally unstable and sometimes engaged in destructive acts to get even with his parents when they disciplined him. The son deliberately set fire to the house and the building burned down. The defendants refused to pay the insurance, arguing that the policy excluded willful damage caused by their son. The plaintiffs argued that they were the only named insured people on the policy. Further, they argued that they were entitled to the benefits of the policy if criminal acts were committed by a third person.

The Court held in favour of the defendants. The clause defining "Insured" was not ambiguous. It clearly included all people living in the residence under the age of 21 years. Because the son would benefit from the continued existence of his parents' property, their interests were not separate or distinct from his.

Questions

1. What is the basic rule regarding a person who commits a wrongful act benefiting from that act by receiving insurance?
2. The child was emotionally unstable and committed destructive acts. Was that relevant in this case? Why or why not?
3. Parents are generally required to provide shelter for their children until the age of 16. Therefore, the parents could not bar their son from the house except to have him placed in an institution. Did the Court take this into consideration? Why or why not?
4. The son did not pay insurance premiums. Why was he considered to be an insured person under the policy?

BESSER v. HOLIDAY CHEVROLET

Manitoba, 1989

The plaintiff, an automobile mechanic, was hired by the defendant on the condition that he supply his own tools. The plaintiff was assigned to a "stall" and was able to lock up his tools each night. The plaintiff suffered an injury and missed a considerable period of work. The defendant terminated the employment contract and hired another mechanic. The plaintiff's tools were removed from the stall and placed in an area to which the public had access. When the plaintiff was discharged from the hospital, he came back to pick up his tools. Nearly all of them were missing.

As a term of employment, the plaintiff had been told that he must buy insurance for his own tools. The plaintiff had not done so. The plaintiff argued that the defendant was a gratuitous bailee and was liable for the lost tools. The defendant argued that he accepted no responsibility for the tools.

The Court held in favour of the plaintiff. The defendant had a duty to deal with the plaintiff's property in the same manner it would have dealt with its own property under the circumstances. The failure of the plaintiff to insure the tools did not have any bearing on whether the defendant was a bailee. Knowing the plaintiff was unable to return immediately for his tools, the defendant had a duty to provide reasonable security for them.

Questions

1. What duty of care rests upon a gratuitous bailee?
2. Was the employer a bailee when it said it accepted no responsibility for tools when it hired the plaintiff?
3. The plaintiff failed to insure his tools as required. What did the Court say about this issue?
4. If the defendant had asked your advice before it removed the plaintiff's tools from the stall, what advice would you have given him?

PRINCIPLES AND CASES

Case 1: Legal Principle

The burden is on the bailee to show that it has taken reasonable care of the property entrusted to him or her.

Case Facts

The plaintiff took a diamond brooch to the defendant for an appraisal in 1973. She was given a numbered claim check and was mailed an appraisal. Seven years later, she returned and presented the claim check, but the brooch could not be found. The plaintiff brought an action for damages.

The plaintiff argued that there was no time limitation printed on the claim check. Nothing in the contractual relationship discharged the bailee from its duty to safeguard the jewel. The plaintiff had not moved from her address during the entire time the defendant had the brooch, and if he had contacted her, she would have claimed it sooner.

The defendant argued that the contract contained an implied condition that the bailor would return within a reasonable time. The bailee had mailed the appraisal and it was reasonable to expect the bailor to take action in the near future.

Possible Decisions

A The defendant is liable because it did not limit its liability in any way.

B The defendant is liable because it did not take reasonable care of the brooch.

C The defendant is not liable because it mailed the appraisal form as promised.

D The defendant is not liable because the plaintiff did not return within a reasonable time.

Case 2: Legal Principle

Where a person is believed to have suffered an "accidental death" the burden is on the insurer to show that it was not accidental.

Case Facts

A woman attended a going-away party for a co-worker. Her husband was unable to attend, but urged his wife to go to the party. During the evening she drank only two bottles of beer. However, at approximately 1 a.m., the guests organized a "Big Name Table," which was the name given to a table where distinguished guests were urged to consume all the liquor remaining. Three or four bottles of liquor were brought to the table and approximately six people took part. The process was to take a drink from a bottle and pass it to the next person, continuing until all the bottles were empty. The deceased woman took part in the event for 30 minutes, when one of the other participants told her to stop or she would be sick. She was clearly intoxicated at this time.

A friend drove the woman to her home, but could not wake her up. She was pronounced dead on arrival at a hospital. The cause of death was alcohol poisoning. The insurance company paid the basic proceeds of an insurance policy but refused to pay the extra proceeds under a section entitled "Bodily Injury." The policy read in part:

> *Bodily injury caused by an accident occurring while the policy is in force ... and resulting directly and independently of all other causes in loss covered by this policy.*

The insurance company took the position that there was no accident because the deceased had voluntarily ingested the alcohol that killed her. The action was brought by her husband, who argued that his wife had little experience with alcohol and would not have known the danger of drinking so much.

Possible Decisions

A The insurance company must pay, because the deceased woman did not appreciate the danger of alcohol and, therefore, her death was an accidental, bodily injury.

B The insurance company must pay because there is no evidence that the victim intended to harm herself.

C The insurance company does not have to pay because the deceased woman killed herself.

D The insurance company does not have to pay because the deceased woman was grossly negligent and should not benefit from her own negligence.

YOU BE THE JUDGE

1. The plaintiff parked his car in a parking lot owned by the defendant. While it was parked there, it was damaged. At the time the car was parked, a ticket was issued that stated in large letters: "We are not responsible for theft or damage of cars or contents, however caused." In addition, there were four large signs at different places in the parking lot with the same words. The plaintiff denied seeing the words on the ticket or the signs. He testified that he was in a hurry and paid no attention to these matters. Who would succeed?

2. The deceased held two insurance policies with the defendant company. The company refused to pay the accidental death, double-indemnity benefit

because the company believed that the deceased committed suicide. The deceased liked to work on cars and often made repairs to his own. He was found in his locked garage, lying on the floor behind his car. The hood of the car was up, the car doors and trunk were shut, the ignition key was in the "on" position, but the engine was not running. The deceased was neatly dressed. There were no tools near his body, and he was lying on an old quilt. Death was caused by inhaling fumes from the exhaust. The insurance company argued that the deceased was having marital and job problems and killed himself. His widow testified that her husband was an impulsive tinkerer who would pursue any problems with his cars without changing to work clothes. Who would succeed?

3. The plaintiff offered to look after a dog belonging to the defendant while the defendant was on vacation. The defendant said the dog was gentle and very well behaved. However, in the absence of its owner, the dog became nervous and upset. One afternoon, while the plaintiff was outside, the dog was left alone. It chewed and tore the covering of much of the plaintiff's furniture. The defendant refused to pay for the damage. Who would succeed?

4. The plaintiff, vice-president of a television company, was issued an accident policy by the defendant insurance company. It provided coverage for total and irrecoverable loss of speech. The plaintiff suffered injury in an auto accident and was left with a damaged larynx and limited motion in his true vocal folds. He could no longer work as a broadcaster and could only whisper in a person's ear to be heard. The plaintiff argued that he had suffered a total loss of speech. The defendant insurance company argued that the plaintiff could still speak, even though it was just a whisper. Therefore, he suffered only a partial loss. Who would succeed?

5. The defendant company agreed to construct a horse barn for the plaintiff. The work was to be completed within five months. The defendant was unable to start the work for three months because of unusually heavy rains that turned the site into a sea of mud. The plaintiff sued for breach of contract. Who would succeed?

6. The plaintiff union entered into a three year contract with its employer, a coal mining company, to pay the miners at a rate "per car." Shortly after signing the agreement, the company replaced its existing coal cars with new cars, which were 20 percent larger. The union demanded a new pay scale, but the company refused. Who would succeed?

C H A P T E R   S E V E N

BUSINESS ETHICS

> *"Let's make those calls and sell this junk. Remember, the elderly and disabled are particularly vulnerable."*
>
> Charles Keating, indicted president of Lincoln Savings & Loan, in memorandum to sales staff

SETTING ETHICAL STANDARDS

Technology has reduced the role of the individual in our society, but many situations still exist that can generally be classed as positions of trust. Society's values have become more difficult to enforce in a rapid-moving economy characterized by many impersonal transactions rather than face-to-face negotiation. One of the characteristics of business that is placed under constant strain is that of ethics.

> *Ethics in a business context means more than just remaining within the law. Everything that is legal is not necessarily ethical. The business that hopes to earn the trust of the public must aim for a higher standard than just compliance with the letter of the law. It is important to have a clear appreciation of society's values, of which the law is only an imperfect reflection.* **William Mulholland, Chairman of the Bank of Montreal, in a speech at Queen's University, 1989.**

In a business context, the term **ethics** can be defined as "the standards governing the conduct of the members of a profession; a set of moral principles and values."

The age of technology can also be called the age of information. The explosive growth of data has built-in problems, including the theft or abuse of confidential data. Prior to World War II, United States Naval Intelligence cracked the Japanese radio code. When told of this development, the Secretary of the Navy ordered the intelligence discarded, saying: "Gentlemen do not read each other's mail." Today, many people do indeed read each other's mail and sometimes take advantage of it. The courts have been faced with the difficult task of trying to determine what protection information should receive. Virtue may be its own reward, but dishonesty may pay more. Nearly half of the 1000 Columbia University alumni surveyed by two business school professors say that as executives, they have been rewarded for taking action on the job that they considered to be unethical. In addition, one in three reported that refusing to take unethical action resulted in penalties ranging from demotion to dismissal.

FIDUCIARY DUTY

The area of law generally called **fiduciary duty** is, in the opinion of many lawyers, exploding. The non-exhaustive list of fiduciaries grows by leaps and bounds.

The word fiduciary generally means "relating to or proceeding from trust or confidence." Fiduciary law is based on the principle of utmost good faith—*uberrima fides*—and operates where one party places trust in another who consents to act in accordance with that trust. Strictly speaking, fiduciary law is not tort law nor contract law. It has special characteristics of its own, originating in the historic principle of equity. The principle of equity embraces the concept that there is a trustee who must account for his or her actions and indemnify the client for any benefit the trustee improperly obtained or for any loss the client suffered.

To illustrate how such a relationship might arise, let us consider the following hypothetical situation. Mr. Green, a retired civil servant, lives on a small farm that he inherited from his father. He has a modest pension that is adequate for his basic needs. The farm is free and clear of debt. Mr. Green also has a small investment account with the ABC Investment Company. His investments are income-oriented, very low-risk types of stocks and bonds. Mr. Green's account is taken over by a new account executive who immediately urges Mr. Green to invest heavily in a biotechnology company that is developing a new strain of disease-resistant grain. The stock trades over-the-counter, pays no dividends, and has been publicly traded for only two months. With the image of sudden riches dancing before his eyes, Mr. Green approaches his banker and wants to mortgage his farm. He tells the banker that he will invest the money in the hot new stock suggested by his broker. The loan is made, the stock is purchased, the stock price collapses, and Mr. Green loses all his money. The bank tries to take Mr. Green's farm to repay the loan. What fiduciary duties did the broker and banker have toward Mr. Green? Will he lose his home? A basic definition of fiduciary duty was put forward by Ontario Justice J. Gautdreau:

> *A fiduciary duty will occur where a person undertakes, either expressly or by implication to act in relation to a matter in the interests of another ... and is entrusted with a power to effect such interest. The other person relies on or is otherwise dependent on this undertaking, and as a result, is in a position of vulnerability to the exercise of such power; and the first person knows, or should know, of such reliance and vulnerability.*

LIABILITY FOR BAD ADVICE

It is increasingly common for those who give advice to others to find themselves embroiled in legal disputes when the advice proves to be faulty. Whether the defendant was paid for the advice is not, in itself, a crucial factor. The most important issue is whether the defendant knew, or ought to have known, that the advice would be trusted or relied upon.

For many years, the law held that free advice created no liability because there was no contract. Liability could never extend to third parties who were not being directly advised. The courts also felt reluctant to impose what might be a restriction upon free speech. Unfortunately, defendants who were not being paid for their advice were often very careless in the use of language. This situation was radically changed by the decision of the British House of Lords in the following case.

HEDLEY BYRNE & CO. LTD. v. HELLER & PARTNERS LTD.

House of Lords, 1964

The plaintiffs, Hedley Byrne & Co. Ltd., were a firm of advertising agents. Having placed several orders for television time and advertising space in newspapers on behalf of a client, Easipower Ltd., on credit terms, they took the routine precaution of making a credit-worthiness check of their client. The plaintiffs asked their bank, the National Bank, to make inquiries concerning the financial position of Easipower. The National Bank learned that the defendants, Heller & Partners Ltd., were handling the banking matters of Easipower and sent them a letter asking whether Easipower was a good credit risk for a contract worth £9000. The defendants replied that Easipower would be able to pay that amount. Several months later, the National Bank wrote to the defendants and asked whether Easipower would be a good credit risk for an annual advertising contract worth £100 000. The defendants replied: "Easipower Limited is a respectably constituted company ... good for its normal business requirements." The defendants did mention that £100 000 was a very large sum. The letter included the caution: "Your figures are larger than we are accustomed to see." The defendants then concluded their letter with the following disclaimer: "For your private use and without responsibility on the part of the bank or its officials."

The National Bank passed this information to the plaintiffs, who then placed orders for advertising time and space on behalf of Easipower. Easipower went into bankruptcy and the plaintiffs lost £17 000 on the contracts. They sued the defendants, alleging that the defendants' replies were made negligently and that such negligence created a false impression of Easipower's credit.

The trial judge found that the defendants were negligent, but that they owed no duty of care to the plaintiffs. That is, the defendants did not know who was asking for the information. The defendants had no way of knowing whether credit would be extended or how much. There was no direct, contractual relationship between the two parties. The Court of Appeal upheld the trial judge's decision and also noted that it would be unreasonable to impose on a banker the type of obligation that the plaintiffs argued existed. To do so would prevent bankers from ever giving credit ratings and would injure the business of solid, reputable clients. The plaintiffs appealed to the House of Lords.

The House of Lords upheld the decision of the lower courts, but on a very narrow basis. Most importantly, the Court held that the defendants did owe a fiduciary duty to the plaintiffs to give sound advice. Speaking for the majority, Lord Reid said:

> *It is said that the respondents did not know the precise purpose of the inquiries and did not even know whether National Bank wanted the information for its own use or for the use of a customer: they knew nothing of the appellants. I would reject that argument. They knew that the inquiry was in connection with an advertising contract, and it was at least probable that the information was wanted by the advertising contractors. It seems to me quite immaterial that they did not know who these contractors were: there is no suggestion of any specialty which could have influenced them in deciding whether to give information or in what form to give it. I shall treat this as if it were a case where a negligent misrepresentation is made directly to the person seeking information, opinion or advice and I shall not attempt to decide what kind of degree of proximity is necessary before there can be a duty owed by the defendant to the plaintiff.*

However, the Court then ruled that the disclaimer clause that the defendants had made part of their letter protected them from liability. The Court concluded: "A man cannot be said voluntarily to be undertaking a responsibility if at the very moment when he is said to be accepting it he declares that in fact he is not."

The importance of the *Hedley Byrne* case is quite obvious. Since that decision, the courts have adopted the basic principle that someone can be legally responsible for advice which he or she gives, even when that advice was given without payment. Liability can extend to an unknown, third party who will likely act upon the information. However, the presence of a clear, unequivocal disclaimer clause will have a strong bearing on the case.

It is important to stress that liability will be imposed only for inaccurate advice that is given out negligently and not for all advice that is wrong. If the advisor takes reasonable care to ensure that the statements are correct, then no liability can be imposed. Good advice does not mean perfect advice.

In general, liability will be based upon a consideration of the following questions:

1. Was the advice given in response to a specific request?
2. Was it clear to the advisor and the seeker of the advice that it would be relied upon?
3. Was the advice given within the advisor's area of expertise?
4. Was there a valid disclaimer by the advisor that he or she accepted no responsibility for any losses that might occur?
5. Was the advice given professionally and not on a social occasion?
6. Were the plaintiff and defendant (advisor) in a special relationship, a relationship of close proximity, with one another?

Although the rules established in *Hedley Byrne* might seem to be fairly straightforward, in actual practice they are difficult to apply. Let us consider some Canadian cases involving faulty advice.

HAIG v. BAMFORD et al.

Supreme Court of Canada, 1977

The Scholler Furniture Company embarked upon an expansion of its business with the help of the Saskatchewan Economic Development Corporation [SEDCO]. Scholler further obtained a promise from SEDCO of another $20 000 in the future. Defendant accountants, R. L. Bamford & Company, were hired to prepare financial statements for Scholler. They were aware that the company was interested in using the statements to find other, private investors. The plaintiff, Haig, was contacted by SEDCO and advised that Scholler might be a good investment for him. The audited financial statements were shown to Haig and he invested $20 000 in the company. Shortly afterward, Scholler went into bankruptcy. Haig learned that the financial statements he had seen contained an error. A $28 000 prepayment that the company had received had not been put on the balance sheet as a liability. Rather, it had been put through as direct revenue, exaggerating the income of the company and not reflecting its true obligations. As a result, the sales, profits, and capital of the company had been overstated. In reality, the company had been in a loss position for its initial year.

The trial judge made the finding that the defendant accountants owed a duty of care to Haig and were therefore liable to him for the damages that their negligence caused. The Saskatchewan Court of Appeal reversed the trial judge's decision, holding that the accountants owed no duty to Haig, because when the statements were prepared, Haig was not yet involved in any business discussions with Scholler. Haig appealed to the Supreme Court of Canada.

The Supreme Court of Canada, after reviewing both the British and U.S. authorities, held that the defendants were liable. Mr. Justice Dickson, writing for the majority, drew upon the basic guidelines established in *Hedley Byrne* and also noted that the accountants knew that Scholler was looking for investors. Mr. Justice Dickson concluded:

> *In summary, Haig placed justifiable reliance upon a financial statement which the accountants stated presented fairly the financial position of the company as at 31st March 1965. The accountants prepared such statements for reward in the course of their professional duties. The statements were for benefit and guidance in a business transaction, the nature of which was known to the accountants. The accountants were aware that the company intended to supply the statements to members of a very limited class. Haig was a member of that class. It is true the accountants did not know his name but, as I have indicated earlier, I do not think that is of importance. I can see no good reason for distinguishing between the case in which a defendant accountant delivers information directly to the plaintiff at the request of his employer and the case in which the information is handed to the employer who, to the knowledge of the accountant, passes it to members of a limited class in furtherance of a transaction the nature of which is known to the accountant. I would accordingly hold that the accountants owed Haig a duty to use reasonable care in the preparation of the accounts.*

The Supreme Court's decision embraced the view that a duty of care is owed not only to those who employ the person, but to a broader class of people whom it is known will receive and rely upon the report. The duty of care exists even if the exact identity of the potential investor is not yet known.

It would be incorrect to assume from the decision in *Haig* that accountants and other professionals are liable to an infinite number of people for every error made. For example, if an accountant prepared a routine financial statement which was then used, without the accountant's knowledge, to induce investors, the accountant would most likely escape liability.

Several legal scholars have expressed the opinion that liability should be limited to "foreseeable plaintiffs." This is not a universally accepted concept.

The matter of accuracy is not the only possible ground of liability. Having established liability for bad advice, the next question for the courts to deal with, in the course of logical progression, is whether liability could be based upon a failure to advise at all. Can a defendant be held liable for failure to give advice which was owing, even though it was not specifically requested? The courts have held that, in many situations, there is a duty to warn. This principle was firmly demonstrated in the famous "exotic cows" case that follows.

HAYWARD v. BANK OF NOVA SCOTIA

Ontario, 1984

Hayward, the plaintiff, had transacted her banking business with the defendant bank for more than 40 years. She was approached by a man named Poland, also a customer of the bank. Poland had borrowed money from the bank to invest in the breeding of exotic cattle in Europe. The scheme involved artificial insemination of ordinary cows from prize bulls, to produce a new strain of superior animals. The bank manager, W. Dunnell, processed several loan applications from other customers who wanted to invest in the cattle business. However, the bank's head office became worried about these loans as it was of the growing opinion that the exotic cattle business was very risky. Dunnell was ordered to obtain maximum security for any future loans and to acquire additional security for many of the outstanding loans.

Dunnell was aware that Poland needed more money. The cattle broker was behind in his payments to the bank and was canvassing the area for new investors. The plaintiff was one of the people whom Poland approached with the idea that she buy some exotic cattle for $30 000. Although the plaintiff had grown up on a farm, she know nothing about the exotic cattle business. The plaintiff went to Dunnell to ask his advice. Dunnell disputed that he was specifically asked his opinion, but the Court held that this was not an important issue. The scenario was that of a widow in her sixties who was considering jeopardizing her financial security by mortgaging her home, to invest the money in a dangerous venture. She was well known to Dunnell and it is reasonable that she wanted, and needed, his advice.

The loan was approved. At the time of signing for the loan, the plaintiff was accompanied by her son and daughter-in-law, who testified that the banker made positive statements assuring financial success. Dunnell denied making such statements. The plaintiff took out a second loan for two more animals, at $16 000 each. The exotic cattle business went bankrupt and Poland abruptly left town. The plaintiff made attempts to learn what had happened to her money, but she was unable to locate the cattle she had supposedly bought. She could not repay the loans, and sued the bank. The action was based on two grounds: (1) The bank owed the plaintiff a fiduciary duty to warn her against the investment; and (2) the bank manager had made false or negligent misstatements to induce her to enter into the loan. The trial judge ruled in favour of the plaintiff, saying:

I do not accept the argument that the plaintiff had independently reached a decision when she consulted Dunnell ... Given Dunnell's disposition in this matter, I find that the advice was forthcoming in any event. Dunnell possessed a substantial amount of knowledge about this business and was in a position to give the plaintiff an accurate picture. He chose not to do so but instead encouraged the plaintiff. The facts establish the existence of a fiduciary relationship between the two parties. The defendant's breach of the duty is just short of flagrant. In light of my decision on the issue of breach of fiduciary duty, it is unnecessary for me to canvass the alternative ground of negligent misrepresentation.

This decision, along with numerous other, similar cases, established a general rule that financial institutions and other lenders are under a positive duty to warn their unsophisticated clients of business risks. The duty to warn is an active duty and does not depend upon the client asking for advice.

Stockbrokers and other investment counsellors also have a fiduciary duty to advise their clients about the wisdom and safety of certain types of investments. The investment industry is guided by the "Know your client" rule. This rule means that the investment advisor must have detailed knowledge of his or her client's financial position and investment objectives. For example, a young investor with a substantial income could reasonably take greater risks with the possibility of greater rewards. A retired person with a fixed, limited income should not take those risks. Therefore, an investment counsellor must not only advise clients what to buy, but also must advise what not to buy.

In the case of *Ryder v. Osler, Wills, Bickle Ltd.* (Ontario, 1989), an elderly widow sued the defendant stockbrokers for the loss of nearly $300 000 from her investment account. The plaintiff had signed a form giving her broker "discretionary control" over her money. The broker made a series of bad investments which were totally inappropriate for the client, and did so without the knowledge or authority of the company. The Ontario High Court of Justice held the broker and investment company liable because the client was unsophisticated and unaware of all the transactions that were taking place. The company was liable for failure to supervise what the broker was doing.

Not every investor who loses money can blame someone else and recover it. In the case of *Maghun v. Richardson Securities* (Ontario,1989), the plaintiffs lost $34 000 trading sugar futures in the commodities market, which is risky and speculative. However, the trial judge concluded that the broker had "fully and completely" explained the risks of this highly leveraged type of speculation and had thereby met his fiduciary duty. Counsel for the defendants had successfully argued: "When they were making money, they knew what they were doing, but when they started to lose money, we are to believe that they suddenly didn't know what they were doing."

In an often-cited, unusual case that seems to run directly counter to the rules laid down in *Hedley Byrne*, a government official escaped liability despite making misleading statements.

FOSTER ADVERTISING v. KEENBERG

Manitoba, 1987

When rumours spread that a racetrack, called Assiniboine Downs, was in financial trouble, the owners, the Gobuty family, sought to reassure creditors that nothing was wrong. The owners contacted the Manitoba Horse Racing Commission chairman, Ronald Keenberg, for help. Keenberg, a government appointee, was a family friend and a devotee of horse racing. He called a news conference to discuss the situation. Prior to the news conference, he was advised by the accountants that the racetrack had lost $1 million in 1981 and had serious cash flow problems. Despite these warnings, Keenberg told those present at the news conference, "An investigation has not disclosed any reason why the track will not operate in a totally normal fashion. We met with the auditors of the racetrack owners to ask questions, review their work, and give us an overview of the situation. We do not have any concern that racing will be other than normal."

A representative of the accounting firm was present at the news conference and would later testify he was astonished at what Keenberg said. Keenberg's assistant was also present and testified that he could not believe his ears and could not understand why Keenberg ignored the financial information given to him.

Another person present at the conference was a representative for Foster Advertising. Based upon Keenberg's reassuring speech, the agency extended $80 000 in credit in the form of advertising to the racetrack. The racetrack soon went bankrupt and the agency was never paid. It sued Keenberg personally. Keenberg argued that he had only made a speech to "bolster confidence" in the racetrack. The trial judge disagreed and said that Keenberg had given false guarantees upon which the plaintiff had relied. The defendant's official position carried great weight with those people who went to the press conference to ascertain the financial state of the racetrack.

However, the Manitoba Court of Appeal reversed the trial judge's decision and held that Keenberg was not liable. The Court held:

> *It is an elementary principle of our tort law that damage caused by negligent conduct is actionable only if the actor owed a duty of care to the injured party. There was no special relationship between the plaintiff and the defendant.*

It is unclear why the Court in this case did not apply the rules laid down in *Hedley Byrne* and other cases. Indeed, the Court applied only the general rules of negligence rather than those of fiduciary law. The Court concluded that by simply giving a little "pep talk," Keenberg was stating no guarantees whatsoever regarding the accuracy of his words. However, in view of the fact that he said he had specifically examined the financial records and then made a false statement regarding what those records showed, the decision is both troubling and suspect.

In an important professional negligence decision for lawyers, the Supreme Court of Canada held a Quebec notary liable for bad advice on a real estate deal, even though he was following the accepted legal practice at the time. In *Roberge v. Bolduc* (1991), the Court held that "The fact that a professional has followed the practice of his or her peers may be strong evidence of reasonable and diligent conduct, but it is not determinative. If the practice is not in accordance with the general standards of liability, i.e., that one must act in a reasonable manner, then the professional who adheres to such a practice can be found liable." The defendant had advised his client not to close a real estate transaction because the title was defective. It turned out that the title was not defective and the client was held liable for breach of contract.

DISCLAIMER CLAUSES

Accountants, investment counsellors, and other advisors routinely mark their publications with disclaimers such as the following: "Factual material is obtained from sources believed to be reliable, but the publisher is not responsible for any errors or omissions contained herein." Although the disclaimer was an important part of the decision in *Hedley Byrne*, it should not be assumed that such words can excuse all negligence or totally circumvent potential liability. Like many aspects of contract law, the courts are not prepared to allow defendants to excuse themselves from all liability by the routine process of denying liability generally. Courts have used numerous methods to disregard disclaimers. The primary questions that must be decided is why the disclaimer was included and whether the plaintiff saw it. A disclaimer that had the purpose of placing a specific limitation upon liability may protect the defendant. Whether or not the plaintiff was aware of it must be determined on a case-by-case basis. It is sufficient to say that disclaimers do not represent a blanket protection.

One of the perplexing problems involving disclaimers is the frequent necessity of people to rely totally upon information that contains a disclaimer saying that the information should not be relied upon. A good example of the problem can be found in the business practice of tendering for contracts.

For example, let us assume that the City of Gotham wants to construct a new sewer line. It hires, and pays, the engineering firm of Busy Bee Associates to prepare detailed geological surveys and drawings for the project. Busy Bee submits its report with a disclaimer denying liability for errors. Six construction companies bid on the project, relying totally upon Busy Bee's report. Herein lies the heart of the problem: the construction companies must rely upon the report because it is too time-consuming and expensive to hire their own engineers to compile the same information. The construction companies must ignore the disclaimer and trust the report. In fairness to the engineer and municipality, disclaimer clauses must be given some validity or contractors could bid low and then demand more payment for cost overruns.

In the U.S. case of *Texas Tunneling Co. v. Chattanooga* (Tennessee, 1962) an expert witness summarized the problem very well when he said: "Contractors are gamblers. They accept risks and absorb losses."

Let us assume that Northern Lights Construction wins the contract and begins work. It discovers that the engineering report is inaccurate and that the project will cost much more money than expected. Can Northern sue Gotham City or Busy Bee? Can Northern refuse to do the work? Is the disclaimer clause an absolute defence for either the city or the engineering firm?

The courts have had difficulty with such cases, but have tended to uphold the validity of the disclaimer clauses. In *Carman Construction v. CPR* (Supreme Court of Canada, 1982) the Court upheld a disclaimer clause because the information was given honestly, without intent to defraud. The appellant's president had an oral conversation with an official of CPR about a rock-removal project. The official guessed that "about 7000 cubic feet" of rock would have to be removed. The appellant used that estimate in its bid. The project actually involved more than 11 000 cubic feet of rock. The contract, however, contained a disclaimer saying that the construction company could not rely upon "any information made available to it by CPR or its employees." The Court held that Carman knew it could not rely upon the respondent's estimates. If Carman did so, it did so at its own risk.

In the following case, the Court upheld the disclaimer clause and noted that the engineering firm did not owe a duty of care to the construction firm.

EDGEWORTH CONSTRUCTION v. LEA AND ASSOCIATES

British Columbia, 1990

Lea prepared an engineering study for the British Columbia Department of Highways for a 19-km stretch of highway. Edgeworth won the contract and commenced work. The project cost much more than expected because of errors and omissions in Lea's report. Edgeworth complained to the department and was awarded an additional $18 million. However, this sum would not be enough to cover the cost overruns, so Edgeworth sued Lea for another $21 million.

The trial judge held that Lea did not owe Edgeworth a duty of care. The report also contained a clear disclaimer clause stating that companies bidding on the contract were to use their own engineering studies. If Edgeworth had any claim at all, it was against the department. It had accepted $18 million in adjustments and could not bring a further claim against the engineering company.

ABUSE OF CONFIDENTIAL INFORMATION

In this age of information, some legal writers have referred to information as the "new capital of industry." As the rate of progress and change accelerates, the need to keep design, marketing, and customer information secret becomes more important. This information, once locked in drawers and filing cabinets, is now transmitted electronically from computer to computer. Computers themselves must be kept locked and secret access words used to prevent unauthorized reading.

Computers are protected to some extent by the criminal law. It is an offence to obtain, fraudulently and without colour of right, a "computer service." This generally prohibits tapping into someone's computer to run programs and obtain free use of software. It is also considered criminal mischief to destroy or alter data or interfere with the lawful use of data. A hacker who either plants a "virus" in a system or enters a databank to alter or erase information commits a criminal offence.

More importantly, what is the nature of information itself? Can it be "stolen" in the criminal sense of the word? In *R. v. Stewart* (Supreme Court of Canada, 1988) the Court held that a person cannot be convicted of theft or fraud because he or she acquired confidential information by dishonest means, such as bribery. Information is not "property." A person can enjoy confidential information but cannot own it in the same sense he or she owns tangible goods. The Court stressed that it is too difficult to determine what is confidential information.

The decision in *Stewart* was the subject of much comment by writers and speakers at legal conventions. Many felt that the Court failed to grasp the crucial value that information plays in present-day business practices. However, in light of this ruling and in the absence of any new amendments to the *Criminal Code of Canada*, it is clear that criminal charges cannot be brought against a person for just copying or obtaining information. Anyone engaged in overt industrial espionage could be convicted of fraud because he or she would sell trade secrets or designs to someone who could then cause economic loss for the original owner of the information. Nor does the decision mean that there are no civil remedies. Indeed, the Supreme Court strongly suggested that civil remedies were best suited to deal with most cases.

A common concern of companies is that former employees will go into business in direct competition and use confidential client lists and information to build their own businesses. Recent decisions suggest that such practices will be prohibited.

SYLVESTER INSURANCE LTD. v. BOVAIR AND NELSON

Ontario, 1988

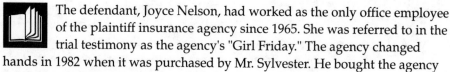

The defendant, Joyce Nelson, had worked as the only office employee of the plaintiff insurance agency since 1965. She was referred to in the trial testimony as the agency's "Girl Friday." The agency changed hands in 1982 when it was purchased by Mr. Sylvester. He bought the agency because it had an established client base.

The defendant had an "encyclopedic knowledge" of all operations of the agency. She knew all the clients and their insurance policies. There was no evidence that she had actually photocopied agency records, but it was a reasonable inference that she had done so. The defendant did not get along with the new owner and quit her job.

She acquired a licence as an insurance broker, and then joined the Bovair Insurance Agency. She actively pursued the plaintiff's clients and urged them to switch their business. She mailed out 150 letters soliciting business before the plaintiff learned what was happening. He sought an injunction against further soliciting and sued for damages.

The Court held in favour of the plaintiff. The defendant had a fiduciary duty with the original owner of the insurance agency which she joined in 1965 not to misuse confidential information. That duty continued with the new owner. Nelson could no more use the information for her own gain than she could have given or sold the information to a competing agency. The Court issued the injunction and Nelson was ordered to pay $18 000 in damages to the plaintiff, which represented the premiums earned by her new employer.

The decision in *Sylvester* is especially significant in view of the fact that there was no written contract which specifically prohibited a former employee from using confidential information. The type of situation raised in the case is not unusual. To a certain extent there is a running argument between the employee and the employer. To whom does the client belong? An employee who first located a client and brought the client's business to the company feels that the client is his or her personal client. As well, if an employee changes firms, clients often follow the employee to the new firm because of a personal relationship of trust. Seldom will a contract or a court ruling prohibit the client from making an independent decision to do so, but it does prohibit the former employee from actively soliciting the business of former clients.

In *Vertlieb Anderson v. Nelford* (British Columbia, 1989), the defendant, a junior lawyer in the plaintiff's law firm, decided to go into practice by himself. When he left the firm of Vertlieb Anderson, he took 17 current case files with him. Before announcing his decision, the defendant had contacted these clients and asked them to sign an authorization to have their files transferred to the defendant's new practice. All had done so. The trial judge held that the defendant had breached a trust owed to his former employer and, regardless of whether he saw himself as an employee or independent contractor, he owed a duty of good faith to his firm. The clients were not "his" in any sense of the word.

Although information cannot be possessed in the same sense as property, its potential value can extend into billions of dollars. If it cannot be stolen, it can be abused, and such abuse may be grounds for a civil action.

One of the most famous, and high-stakes, civil actions involved confidential information about a gold deposit.

LAC MINERALS v. CORONA RESOURCES

Supreme Court of Canada, 1989

Corona was interested in buying property in Hemlo, Ontario. It had excellent geological information suggesting that the property was very valuable because of potential gold deposits. Corona approached Lac, a much larger company, to discuss the possibility of a partnership. Corona had in mind a joint venture to develop the property, because Corona lacked the financial resources to take on the project alone. Corona gave its geological information to Lac. After analysing the information, Lac proceeded to buy the property for itself, cutting Corona out of the deal entirely.

The Supreme Court of Canada upheld lower court decisions that ordered Lac to transfer ownership of the property to Corona. The estimated value of the land, and the mine that Lac had established, was $1 billion. The 5-0 ruling was complex because the five justices wrote four separate opinions. Three of the justices rejected the argument that there had been a breach of fiduciary duty. However, the common ground of all the opinions was that there had been an "actionable breach of trust." Any person sharing information with someone else has a right to have that information protected. Although there was no written agreement between Corona and Lac regarding possible misuse of information, the Court ruled that a trust exists when one party realizes that the information received is confidential and potentially valuable. That party must safeguard the information and prevent its abuse by third parties. Further, if the party receiving the information uses or abuses it for its own profit, to the detriment of the other, this breach of trust is actionable. Mr. Justice La Forest expressed the requirement as follows:

> *It is beyond argument that Corona was vulnerable to Lac. By acquiring the land as a result of the information received from Corona, Lac detrimentally affected Corona's interests ... All power and discretion means in this context is the ability to cause harm. Clearly that is present in this case ... There is no reason to clutter normal business practice by requiring a contract. It is simply not the case that business and accepted morality are mutually exclusive domains.*

In hindsight, it would have been a good idea for Corona and Lac to first enter into a written agreement about the information. However, the mining industry generally works upon a "club" system, in which senior officers of mining companies frequently share information and trust each other not to abuse this trust.

The ruling is important because it places a protective net around confidential information which is essential for the conduct of ordinary business. It also establishes a clear warning to parties who are asked if they want to see information. Parties must be very careful about accepting information because of the potential legal consequences that will flow from using any of the information. For example, if Company R is considering a project and Company W is working on something similar, it would be dangerous for Company R to look at what Company W has developed. If the project went forward, Company R could be accused of stealing or abusing Company W's ideas and information.

In *Tree Savers International Ltd. v. Savoy* (Alberta, 1991), the Court awarded $1.3 million in damages against two ex-managers who left their employment with the plaintiff and started their own company. The two defendants took with them technical information about oil well tools and confidential client lists. The trial judge held that the defendants had sought to benefit themselves, not to harm the plaintiff. However, they knew or ought to have known that they would hurt the plaintiff's business and there was no burden upon the plaintiff to show that the defendants deliberately set out to injure its business. As a general rule, an employee may take with him the *knowledge* that he or she acquired from previous employment. The employee may not take *information*.

NON-COMPETITION AGREEMENTS

Many employers, concerned about the possibility of former employees or associates becoming future competitors, require employees to sign contracts containing **non-competition clauses**. The practice is also commonplace when one person buys a business from another person. One of the most valuable assets of a business is goodwill, which means the established reputation of the business and the solid client base. If the former owner immediately opens a new, competing business in the same locality, the value of the goodwill is greatly reduced.

Non-competition clauses are not always enforceable. The court will carefully consider the reasonableness of the restrictions created. For example, if three dentists are in practice together and have a contract that states if any one of them leaves the practice, he or she "will not practise dentistry anywhere in the Dominion of Canada," the clause would be unenforceable because it is unreasonable.

A non-competition clause usually states that the parties agree not to pursue former clients of the business, establish a new business within a certain radius of the present business, and not utilize any technology or innovations developed in the present business. Where, for example, four researchers with a large computing firm developed an innovative software program, they were in breach of their non-competition clause when they quit their jobs and started a new company that marketed basically the same software. Their contracts said they were not to do so for two years after terminating their employment.

MISASI v. GUZZO

Ontario, 1987

The defendant, Vincenzo Guzzo, was in a partnership with the plaintiff, Misasi. Together, they operated a produce business. Guzzo sold his interest in the business to Misasi and agreed in writing not to start a competing business within five miles of the old business. Shortly afterward, a produce business called DeVille Produce Limited was opened in the town of DeVille, which was four miles from the old business. The operator of this business was Amedeo Guzzo, the 19-year-old son of Vincenzo Guzzo. The business was started with an infusion of interest-free loans from Vincenzo and from a friend and associate of the Guzzo family. Vincenzo Guzzo was seen to be actively involved in the daily operation of this new business, although he was not an employee of the business nor an owner. Misasi sued Vincenzo and Amedeo Guzzo. The issue, of course, was whether the two defendants were conspiring to thwart the terms of the non-competition clause by pretending that Amedeo was operating an independent business.

The trial judge held in favour of the plaintiff, saying:

> *The entire set-up was a sham designed to permit the father to contribute to the carrying on of the DeVille produce business and to evade his legal obligations not to compete with the plaintiff. Not only has Vincenzo Guzzo violated the covenant not to compete, but he has used a devious and dishonourable facade to camouflage the real situation. His violation of his agreement was deliberate, calculated and deceitful.*

The Court held the father liable for breach of contract and the son liable for tort for intentionally interfering with the contractual obligations in the clause. Damages were assessed at $60 000.

PROFESSIONAL INCOMPETENCE

When a person represents himself or herself to prospective employers as having certain professional skills and experience, the person has a duty to demonstrate those skills. The requirement is the same whether the person is an employee or an independent contractor.

Negligence or incompetence can result in serious financial loss to the employer. In many cases, the person is simply discharged and attempts are made to find someone better suited for the task. However, the employer does have the option of taking legal action against the employee. For example, in *Dominion Manufacturing v. O'Gorman* (Ontario, 1989), the defendant was hired to be the company controller. It was an implied term of the contract that he possess skill and competence. The defendant made a mess of the company's books and failed to make tax instalment payments, resulting in fines for late payment. The plaintiff fired O'Gorman, then successfully sued him for the cost of the fines and the cost of hiring an independent consultant to straighten up the mess.

The issue of damages can be somewhat difficult. Some courts have taken the position that the defendant cannot be liable for damage or loss caused by the intervention or actions of a third person. Further to this, it has been generally held that the defendant is not an insurer of the plaintiff's property. However, in the following case, the Court took a much tougher line, extending the duty of care to all foreseeable risks.

MacNEIL v. VILLAGE LOCKSMITH LTD.

Ontario, 1987

The plaintiff hired the defendant company to install security devices on his home, including the installation of a deadbolt lock on his front door. The plaintiff and his family went on vacation and returned to find their home broken into and $11 500 worth of goods stolen. Evidence showed that the locksmith had improperly installed the front door lock, rendering the lock almost useless. Most of the weakness occurred when the installer ignored a gap in the house frame behind the bolt. Although it was not the task of the locksmith to personally fill in this gap, he did not warn the plaintiff about the serious weakness that it represented, so that the plaintiff could have hired someone to repair the door frame. The company installer testified that he did not warn the plaintiff about the gap because in his experience such warnings were futile, because customers never acted upon the advice. The trial judge held in favour of the plaintiff, saying:

> *I find that there was a duty upon the defendant to exercise care in the installation of the system. I also find that there was a breach of that duty in the installation, at least without a warning to the plaintiff of its inadequacy and his acceptance of the risk.*

In *Hamather et al. v. Gregory et al.* (Ontario, 1989) a group of investors who lost money after investing in a restaurant successfully sued their accountant. The accountant was hired to assess the financial status of the restaurant. He studied financial reports and talked to the restaurant owner. The unaudited financial reports contained glaring and obvious discrepancies. The defendant accountant advised the investors that they could invest in the business "with some risk attached." The trial judge held that the accountant had failed to use "the skill and diligence which a reasonably competent accountant or auditor would exercise" and ordered him to compensate the plaintiffs for their losses.

The obligation of a person to exercise due care will have been discharged if the person has acted in accordance with the general and approved practice of his or her profession. (In an action against a person for professional incompetence, it is not enough to say that he or she has made an error of judgment or has shown ignorance of some important fact. The standard is that the person has demonstrated that he or she is reasonably competent and diligent. To be sued, the professional person must be guilty of misconduct, fraudulent proceeding, gross negligence, or gross ignorance.)

VICARIOUS LIABILITY

If professional liability is established against an employee, the question which then arises is whether liability can also be attached to someone else, usually an employer. The imputed responsibility of one person for the acts of another person is referred to as **vicarious liability**. (The law may hold the second defendant responsible for the acts of the first, even though the second defendant was not guilty of any personal wrongdoing. To a great extent, vicarious liability imposes a form of strict liability upon the second defendant.)

Potential liability may be found in the wording of a contract. In *Newfoundland Telephone v. Memorial University* (Newfoundland, 1983) the plaintiff sued the defendant for damage to its telephone equipment caused when a student at the university negligently started a fire. The contract between the parties stated that the university would "indemnify the company for any damage caused by the abuse or negligence of the customer, its agents, servants, employees, invitees, licensees, or trespassers." The Court ruled that the university was responsible for damage caused by students at the university.

(It should be stressed that an employer is not automatically liable for every improper action that an employee may take. The improper action must normally be job-related and, in most instances, be an action that directly or indirectly benefited the employer. The action complained of must also be one which the employer owed a reasonable duty to have supervised.) It is no defence for the employer to argue that he or she did not know what was taking place. The employer will be liable if the court is satisfied that the employer could reasonably have known what was occurring.

MAYERS v. PALMER AND SMITH

British Columbia, 1989

Palmer was a senior salesman for Smith Paper, a packaging company, and had copied the account cards from Mayers, his former employer. When Palmer left the employ of Mayers and went to work for Smith Paper, he used the confidential information to steal Mayers' customer accounts, and quickly established an excellent sales record with his new employer. The Court confirmed the trial judge's decision to award damages against Smith Paper as well as against Palmer. The Court held that an employer has a duty to check that employees who change jobs are not using confidential information from an earlier contract of employment.

The duty to supervise is a very strict duty, applied with consistency by all the courts in Canada. Where there is a fiduciary duty, the requirement is almost absolute. Rarely can an employer escape liability because the employer was ignorant of the facts. In *Baker v. Midlana Doherty* (Ontario, 1987), a stockbroker speculated recklessly with a client's stock account and caused enormous losses. The client had no personal knowledge of investments and had relied on the broker for advice and decisions. The company had initially solicited the client's business with a printed brochure stating that it was a full-service company with highly trained, competent investment counsellors. However, the company had no policy of supervising what its brokers were doing. The trial judge held the company liable saying: "Midland was negligent in the conduct of its business. It cannot urge its reliability and skill in the good times and then turn its back in the bad."

It is possible for a defendant to be liable because he or she gave a strong recommendation or a personal seal of approval toward the employment of another defendant. The troubling aspect of such cases revolves around the common practice of people giving recommendations and endorsements of business associates and clients, not thinking that any potential liability could be attached to a recommendation. Business thrives on a word-of-mouth network of recommendations and positive opinions about others.

RONCATO v. CAVERLY

Ontario, 1991

The plaintiff, Roncato, owned a truck repair business. For many years, the company books were kept by a part-time bookkeeper. The records were simple, but accurate. Caverly, the defendant, who was the plaintiff's accountant, urged Roncato to computerize his system. When the plaintiff decided to do so, the bookkeeper quit because he knew nothing about computers. The defendant suggested that the plaintiff hire a Mrs. Cox, the wife of a client, saying that she was "experienced and competent."

The plaintiff hired Mrs. Cox without interviewing her, relying upon the defendant's advice. After Mrs. Cox assumed her duties, nothing went right. She could not prepare the simplest financial statements and could not tell the plaintiff anything about his financial status. The plaintiff tried to discuss the problem with the defendant, but Caverly replied that it takes time to get the "bugs" out of a new computerized accounting system. He told the plaintiff: "She's doing a wonderful job." In fact, the defendant had no idea what Mrs. Cox was doing because he never visited the premises to see what was going on and never offered to step in and try to sort matters out.

The plaintiff eventually fired Mrs. Cox and hired an auditor to straighten out the books. The auditor reported that the records were a chaotic mess, but that it appeared that Mrs. Cox had either stolen or lost a large sum of the company's money. The company went bankrupt and the plaintiff sued the defendant for $500 000, alleging negligent misrepresentation and negligent performance of his advisory duties. The defendant argued that he had no duty to supervise the plaintiff's bookkeeper and that he had only suggested that Mrs. Cox be considered as a possible employee. He had not guaranteed her work.

The trial judge held that the defendant was 10 percent responsible for the plaintiff's loss. The judge ruled that Caverly knew that Roncato would have been greatly affected by Caverly's recommendation and that Caverly had a duty to ensure that his advice was carefully given.

The Court of Appeal overturned the trial judge's decision, saying that the judge had made errors because he was trying to do justice to the case but ignored the real issue. The issue was whether Caverly's negligence was an effective or proximate cause of the failure of the company and the losses that flowed from that failure. The Court held that it was not. The amount of money actually stolen was much smaller than alleged, and therefore could not have caused the company to fail. Mrs. Cox was convicted of theft and repaid $4000. More importantly, Caverly had not caused the loss. The Court said:

The evidence failed to establish a nexus between the negligent misrepresentations that the judge found and the loss to the company and its shareholders. Recovery in negligent misrepresentation cases is confined to situations where the economic loss resulted from detrimental reliance upon negligent misstatements to a known recipient for a specific purpose. There is very little evidence that Mrs. Cox's incompetence or dishonesty caused the losses which befell the company.

The decision in *Roncato* establishes an important distinction between friendly advice given casually and advice which the advisor knows will be acted upon and could cause economic loss. There are still unanswered questions. If Brown asks Green to recommend a financial advisor and Green recommends Black, saying, "She's excellent," is Green liable if Black makes bad investments for Brown? It was a gratuitous recommendation without any guarantee. Other than a friendship possibly gone sour, what fiduciary duty does a person have who nominates an advisor to another person? The *Roncato* decision suggests that the person asking for the advice must still use his or her own judgment about whether to actually use that person's services.

The extent to which vicarious liability can be extended was greatly increased in the following case.

CANADIAN DREDGE AND DOCK COMPANY LTD. v. R.

Supreme Court of Canada, 1985

Four corporations appealed their conviction for conspiracy to defraud, contrary to the *Criminal Code*. The several counts in the indictment related to dredging contracts between public authorities. The bids were alleged to have been tendered on a collusive basis, with the low bidders including in their costs compensation to be paid to the high bidders. Each company had a manager who submitted the bids. The managers kept "score sheets" by which they paid each other after dividing the contracts among themselves. Criminal liability was denied on the ground that these managers were acting for their own benefit or contrary to instructions and hence outside the scope of their employment. Several companies also challenged the existence of any theory of corporate criminal liability for what is clearly a *mens rea* offence—an offence that requires criminal intent.

The Supreme Court of Canada upheld the convictions of the corporations. Although the criminal law has long resisted the civil law concept of vicarious liability, there is corporate criminal responsibility for an offence committed by the corporation's **directing mind** where the act was done by the directing force of the company within the sector of the corporation operation assigned to him.

The *Canadian Dredge* case is important because (1) it imposed criminal responsibility upon the corporation even though it was unaware of the actions of its manager, and (2) it imposed criminal responsibility upon one person (the corporation) for the acts of an employee. The inference to be drawn is that it is the duty of an employer to closely supervise the activities of key employees who might be called the "directing minds" of the corporation.

CONTRACT, FIDUCIARY DUTY, OR TORT?

If Green contracts with Brown to perform a service, and performs it in a negligent manner, should Brown sue for breach of contract, negligence, or breach of fiduciary duty? There are conflicting opinions in Canada as to whether the plaintiff can sue on all three grounds or whether the plaintiff must confine his or her action to one. If we add to the problem the possibility that the contract contains a disclaimer clause limiting the liability of the defendant, the difficulties increase further.

In the *Hedley Byrne* case, Lord Devlin, who wrote the decision, spoke of a relationship "equivalent to a contract" in which "but for the absence of consideration there would be a contract." This concept was strongly criticized by many legal writers, who rejected the idea that the parties could "almost have a contract" or that a tort action could be based upon something so vague as "equivalent to contract." The criticism is understandable. The sanctity of tort law cannot be invaded by the law of contract, or vice versa. The two areas of law are quite different and the various tests of liability are very distinct. It is not prudent to throw them both into a pot and produce some sort of legal stew.

Canadian cases fall on every side of the controversy. Starting with those that take the view that the action can be based only on breach of contract, let us first consider the concern of the courts. Some judges worry that letting negligence make inroads into contract law will destroy the concept of contract itself. This concern was greatest when it was realized that contractors might be liable for breaches of care years after the work had been completed. The courts have long held that if a person undertakes an obligation by contract, then the contract alone expresses the extent of that obligation.

In Royal Bank v. Clark (Ontario, 1978), it was held that a lawyer's liability to his client for professional negligence is based on breach of the terms of his engagement, the liability being contractual in nature. The Court took the view that there is no such thing as "negligent breach of contract" because this produces a totally confusing concept. In *Nunes Diamonds Ltd. v. Dominion Electric* (1972), the Supreme Court of Canada held that "the basis of tort liability considered in *Hedley Byrne* is inapplicable to any case where the relationship between the parties is strictly governed by the contract, unless the negligence relied upon can properly be considered as an independent tort unconnected with the performance of the contract."

If the contract itself contains a clause limiting liability, then the court will take a dim view of attempts by the plaintiff to get around the disclaimer by alleging tort. The law of negligence cannot be used to give a remedy to a person for breach of contract where the defendant was absolved of liability under the contract. Parties are free to contract out of liability. However, there are cases that support a contrary opinion.

A strong case advancing the position that breach of contract, negligence, and breach of fiduciary duty can co-exist is *Canadian Western Natural Gas v. Pathfinder Surveys Ltd.* (Alberta, 1980). The Alberta Court of Appeal held that the plaintiff could found his claim upon breach of contract and negligence. The defendant surveyor was to mark the route for a pipeline and failed to stake out tangent lines. The pipelayers followed the stakes as they were placed and then realized that they could not possibly make the sharp turns the stakes suggested. The gas company had to fill in trenches, remove pipe already in place, and redesign the entire line. The company sued the surveyor for breach of contract. The surveyor argued that the company was guilty of contributory negligence in not detecting the problem sooner. Thus, it was necessary to consider both the issues of negligence and contributory negligence in the case. The Court held that the surveyor had breached its contract, but the Court also agreed that the gas company was partly liable for contributory negligence—thus approving the concept of breach of contract and negligence being together.

It is difficult to bring together the differing views. However, two general conclusions can be drawn:

1. A party who suffers damage from the negligent performance of a contract may sue for negligence as well as breach of contract. If the defendant was in a position of trust, then an action for breach of fiduciary duty could be added. However, the law of negligence cannot be used to give a remedy for a breach of contract where the defendant is clearly absolved of liability

under the contract; that is, negligence cannot impose liability when the contract clearly states that there is no liability.

2. If the negligence action arises independently of the contract and the action would succeed even if there was no contract at all, then the action may be based exclusively upon negligence.

In the following case, the Court was faced with a situation in which there was a contract but there was no specific term in the contract that had been breached.

MARYON INTERNATIONAL v. N.B. TELEPHONE

New Brunswick, 1982

The telephone company hired Maryon to construct a large transmission tower. After it was completed, cracks appeared in the concrete and the telephone company hired an independent consultant to study the problem. The consultant reported that the tower was not safe and would require expensive reworking. The telephone company sued the contractor for breach of contract.

The Court found that the poorly drafted contract contained no specific clause in which the contractor guaranteed that no cracks would appear. However, it was apparent that the cracks resulted from poor workmanship and improper mixing and pouring of concrete. The Court held that the contractor was liable for negligence. The silence of the contract regarding the type of problem that occurred did not deprive the telephone company of its tort action.

PROFESSIONAL ETHICS AND MISCONDUCT

Every profession and business association has basic rules of ethics and conduct. Some rules are established by law, some by governing bodies such as a Law Society, and some are simply understood or presumed as ethical. An investment counsellor knows, or ought to know, what is unethical or illegal. Misuse of insider information, stock manipulation, and churning of customer accounts to generate excess commissions are condemned by statute and trading rules alike.

Violation can result in loss of licence and criminal conviction.

There are strict rules regarding behaviour in the medical profession. For example, psychiatrists and psychotherapists are strictly required to remain objective and detached. The transference problem often develops as part of the course of therapy. Where a physician uses this to develop a social or sexual relationship with a patient, a breach of ethics exists that will result in disciplinary proceedings against the physician by his or her regulatory body.

Lawyers are officers of the Court and are required to uphold the highest standards of ethical and lawful conduct. A lawyer cannot engage in deceptive or dishonest behaviour and continue to practise law. In the case of *R. v. Sweezey* (Ontario, 1988) a lawyer advised a client that the client could be evasive under oath and tell half-truths, pretending that he could not remember important facts. The lawyer was convicted under the *Criminal Code of Canada* for dissuading a witness from giving evidence. The penalty was 18 months in jail and disbarment. The trial judge recognized that the penalty was harsh, but noted: "Behaviour of this kind in a professional trained in the law is all the more offensive because it defeats the very course of justice he has sworn to uphold."

The obligation to refrain from personal misconduct is not the full extent of professional ethics. In many instances there is also a duty to report misconduct by others. The requirement to report produces a very difficult conflict. On the one hand, a person owes a duty to his or her profession and to the public. On the other hand, it is distasteful to take an action that may result in a colleague or friend being barred from the profession. The following case illustrates the extent of the duty to report.

LAW SOCIETY OF UPPER CANADA v. GNAT et al.

Ontario, 1990

Five senior partners of the Lang Michener law firm were found guilty of professional misconduct for failing to report allegations of impropriety and possible illegal action by a former partner. Solicitor Martin Pilzmaker was found guilty by a panel of the Law Society for giving unethical and possibly illegal advice to immigrants applying for landed immigrant status. The other partners knew of Mr. Pilzmaker's activities but took no action. The panel ruled that the partners failed in their duty to report serious allegations of professional misconduct. The panel concluded:

> *When the respondents became aware of circumstances which at least raised serious questions and suspicions about Pilzmaker's professional conduct, they had an overriding duty to do something about it pursuant to their obligation to*

members of the public to protect it from the consequences of professional misconduct and to the profession to maintain its integrity and reputation with the public.

Where a person directly violates the laws or rules regarding his or her profession, there is seldom any controversy as to whether or not the person should be barred from the profession. The relationship between the misconduct and the penalty is very direct and extreme. A lawyer who steals money from his or her trust account can expect nothing short of expulsion from the profession. A doctor who sexually assaults a patient under the pretext of conducting an examination will lose his or her medical licence.

However, more difficult questions arise when the misconduct is not directly related to the practice of the profession, but bring the profession itself into disrepute.

QURESHI v. PROVINCIAL MEDICAL BOARD

Nova Scotia, 1982

The appellant, Dr. Qureshi, was accused of cheating the provincial medical plan by excess or false billing. The appellant had seen a dozen patients at home in 1976. By September of 1981, that number had risen to 4050. The Court held that the statistics alone proved that the doctor was engaged in false billing. The trial judge said:

> *Retrospective judgment based on statistical analysis by persons without firsthand knowledge is sufficient to meet the standard of proof required in a professional discipline case. The statistics show an extreme change within the doctor's practice and in comparison with other doctors in the area which are too coincidental in its timing in relation to his financial problems.*

However, the most difficult problem proved to be the question of revoking the doctor's licence to practise. There was no evidence that he was not a good doctor. Counsel for the appellant argued that no matter what dispute existed between the doctor and the government, this was not grounds to deny him the right to continue practising medicine.

The Court disagreed and ruled that improper billing practices showed that the doctor had a criminal mind and had used the system to take advantage of his profession to earn income well above the average income of the general citizens of Canada. The Court distinguished conduct that is equally reprehensible for anyone, such as a traffic offence, from conduct that "tends to bring disgrace on the profession which he practises."

The Court concluded that the doctor's behaviour "casts a net over the profession as a whole and detracts from and reflects on the perception of the profession by the public generally." The doctor's name was struck from the Medical Register.

In a similar, controversial case in Ontario, a lawyer was disbarred in 1990 for improper billing of the Ontario Legal Aid Plan. The lawyer, Harry Kopyto, billed the plan for 400 phone calls that were not made, for court appearances on Sundays, and for working on a case more than 24 hours in a single day. The investigation concluded that Kopyto had falsely billed the Plan for more than $600 000 in three years. In his defence, Kopyto argued that he had actually done the work on the legal aid cases but had no time for exact and precise record-keeping. He had just estimated the time and expense spent on the cases. He signed an agreement that he had been guilty of misconduct by his negligence, but denied over-billing the system. However, the Law Society of Upper Canada disbarred Kopyto, saying that the lawyer had acted dishonestly and undermined the integrity of the profession and the legal aid system.

Again, the argument put forward by counsel for Kopyto was that any problems he had with the government should be treated separate and distinct from his abilities as a lawyer. Whatever penalties were assessed should not include disbarment. However, that argument was rejected along the basic lines of bringing the profession into disrepute. Kopyto's errors and omissions were related to his practice of law and to his standing as a lawyer.

The logical progression of the problem of misconduct then moves to behaviour that is totally removed from work or profession. The question that arises is whether a person can be disciplined for purely personal misconduct. Certain professions and jobs in our society carry the mantle of prestige and distinction. Although personal misconduct should not have any relationship to job performance, the case law suggests that there is a code of conduct for many people which requires the highest morality and ethics.

In *Flewwelling v. Public Service Relations Board* (Federal Court of Appeal, 1986) a federal fisheries officer was dismissed from his job when he was convicted of a narcotics offence. The Court upheld his firing, holding that there is an "implied code of conduct" for federal employees. Personal misconduct is incompatible and inconsistent with the duty to enforce the law.

In the *Flewwelling* case, the Court took note of a decision of the Supreme Court of Canada in the case of *Fraser v. Public Service Relations Board* (1982) in which the Court held that a civil servant was properly fired from his job for criticizing the federal government's plan to convert to the metric system. The Court ruled that freedom of expression did not extend to a civil servant criticizing government policy. The same rule could easily be applied to the private sector. A person working for the XYZ Corporation could not vocally criticize the company's policies and products and keep his or her job.

REVIEW: POINTS OF LAW

1. Where one party places trust in another who consents to act in accordance with that trust, a fiduciary duty may exist.
2. Violation of a fiduciary duty may give rise to a civil action. A written agreement is not required to support that action.
3. A person may be liable for faulty advice if he or she knew another person would be likely to act upon that advice. Liability may extend to third persons unknown at the time to the advisor.
4. In some situations, an advisor has the duty to warn an unsophisticated client or investor against a risky course of action.
5. If a party receives confidential information and uses or abuses that information, the party may be liable for breach of trust.
6. Information can be abused, but it cannot be stolen in the criminal sense of the word.
7. A person cannot use client information from a previous employer to benefit himself or herself in a new position of employment.
8. An employer may be liable for the misconduct or incompetence of an employee in carrying out a fiduciary duty.
9. A professional person who violates the rules or ethics of his or her profession will be expelled from that profession. The person may also be expelled for personal misconduct of a nature that brings the entire profession into disrepute.

LEGAL BRIEFS

1. W approaches P and asks him for a letter of recommendation for a job. P hardly knows W and has no knowledge of W's qualifications. Advise P.
2. F, a police officer, becomes a partner with H in an "escort service." F is aware that the persons employed in this service sometimes sell sexual services. Does F have a conflict?
3. J mailed the manuscript for a novel to the M Publishing Co. The manuscript was returned with a card saying, "We cannot accept unsolicited manuscripts." J is puzzled by this action. What reasons would publishers have for refusing to read manuscripts which are just mailed to them?
4. G was employed by the ABC Investment Corporation as a stockbroker (called an account executive). G quit this job and accepted a position with a competing firm. Before changing employment, G made photocopies of the trading records of all the large investors with the corporation, including clients who dealt with other account executives. After starting his new job, G began to actively solicit the business of these individuals. They were surprised that G had detailed knowledge of their investments and had prepared detailed plans under which the investors could supposedly improve their portfolios. What action, if any, can the ABC Corporation take in this situation?
5. R was a self-employed investment counsellor. He was hired by W to locate and arrange for the financing of a major real estate project. R introduced W to L, telling W that L was a "big-time player" who would be able to invest millions of dollars. A fictitious loan paper was drawn up, and W paid a fee to both R and L. It turned out that L had a criminal record and no money. He disappeared with W's money. Can W sue R?
6. V was hired by Q to build an office building. The plans for the building were drawn by C, an architect, but the contract between V and Q made no specific mention of these plans. When the project was approximately one-quarter completed, V began to find the plans very difficult to follow. V consulted the building inspector and they agreed that the building foundation was not adequate to support the structure. The work that had been completed would have to be torn down. Q refused to pay any more money to V, saying they had a contract and V had to complete the building at the agreed price. V argued that it was not his fault the plans were defective. C went bankrupt. Who will pay for the added cost?
7. B attended a seminar sponsored by the H Investment Company. B received a prospectus and a glowing description of a new company with a new product. The new stock issue was underwritten by H. B invested $20 000 in

the new company, which never produced the new product. Money invested had been embezzled by the president of the new company. It was later revealed that the president had a criminal record for fraud, something which was known to H but withheld from investors. However, the prospectus contained a disclaimer that the shares of the new company were speculative and contained a high degree of risk. H said it was protected by the disclaimer. What rights has B?

8. E was an account executive with a large investment company. One of her best clients was D, a woman 70 years of age. When D's husband died, D inherited a large investment portfolio of secure investments. However, she began reading various investment newsletters and frequently called E with "hot tips" she received from dubious sources. D began trading heavily in penny stocks and risky technology companies. E frequently tried to steer D away from these risky investments, to no avail. When she lost money, D did not seem to care. She told E that she was "just having a little fun." E also noticed that D was wearing the latest fashions and gold jewellery. She also purchased a sports car. D would telephone E three times a day and ask, "What's hot? What's everyone doing in the market today?" In a period of four years, D lost $230 000 in bad investments. When D died, the executor of her estate sued E and her employer for failure of fiduciary duty to properly advise D about these bad investments. Must these losses be repaid?

APPLYING THE LAW

LAPENSEE v. COUVILLON AND OTTAWA DAY NURSERY INC.

Ontario, 1986

Rachel Lapensee, injured in a day care centre when she was 15 months old, was awarded $247 000 in damages by the Court. Rachel's mother had applied to the Ottawa Day Nursery Inc. for day care assistance. The company referred her to the home of Mrs. Couvillon. Mrs. Couvillon was officially approved as a day care provider by the corporation, a non-profit corporation that arranged individual child care services in Ottawa private homes.

Mrs. Lapensee visited the home of Mrs. Couvillon and was satisfied that Rachel would receive good care. Each day, Mrs. Couvillon watched over her own child, Rachel, and one other child. On the day of the injury, Mrs. Couvillon suddenly became ill. She urgently needed to use the bathroom on the second floor. Fearing the children might hurt themselves if left downstairs alone, she took them upstairs, put them into a bedroom, and told them to stay there. She then rushed into the bathroom.

Moments later, she heard a loud noise, followed by her own child's crying. She came out to see what had happened and found Rachel lying motionless at the bottom of the stairs. There was no protective gate across the stairs because normally the children were not on the second floor. Rachel suffered permanent brain damage. Mrs. Lapensee sued Mrs. Couvillon and the corporation that had recommended her.

The Court held both defendants liable. Mrs. Couvillon was liable because she failed to provide the required standard of care of a prudent and careful parent. The absence of a child gate on the stairs had greatly increased the foreseeable risk of harm. When Mrs. Couvillon became ill, she could have taken the children into the bathroom with her. The risk was foreseeable and the visible danger was significant.

The liability of the corporation was more difficult to determine. The corporation argued that it exercised no control over how Mrs. Couvillon operated her day care service and therefore could not be vicariously liable. Mrs. Couvillon was not an employee of the corporation. Its responsibility was only to make referrals as a service to parents who were then to visit the home and make their own decision as to whether they wanted to leave their children there. The corporation's procedure was to check the home for cleanliness, a good atmosphere, and a general reputation for quality care, based on the opinions of other parents. It had no supervisory authority over the day care operators other than to remove their names from the approved list. It did not assume any responsibility beyond that.

The Court ruled that the corporation was vicariously liable for Rachel's injuries. The corporation was established as a non-profit organization under a provincial law that authorized municipalities to make agreements with individuals for the provision of home day care. The Ottawa-Carleton region paid the corporation funds to help defray the cost of its operations. The corporation had directed Mrs. Lapensee to Mrs. Couvillon after Mrs. Lapensee approached the corporation for assistance. As well, Mrs. Lapensee paid her day care fees to the corporation, which, in turn, paid Mrs. Couvillon.

The corporation regularly inspected all of its homes to ensure that good levels of service were being maintained. Although Mrs. Couvillon was not a direct employee of the corporation, there was a business relationship. The corporation had influence and authority over the way Mrs. Couvillon operated her business. The trial judge concluded:

> *The corporation actually exercised a significant measure of control over how the day care services are provided as well as the more obvious, and undenied, control over when and where, and by whom, they are provided.*

Questions

1. There are numerous referral services in communities, for doctors, health specialists, day care, and many other purposes. Generally, what would be the basic liability of a referral service?
2. The corporation did not employ Mrs. Couvillon. Nor did the corporation have any authority to direct her day-to-day methods. In the view of the corporation, it was doing nothing more than giving a "rating" to Mrs. Couvillon, much like writers give four-star ratings to hotels and restaurants. Why did the Court reject the corporation's argument that it was not responsible for Mrs. Couvillon's negligence?
3. In any home, on any given day, a parent could be suddenly stricken with an incapacitating illness that would render him or her temporarily unable to supervise small children. Normally, this would not be seen as negligence. Why, then, was Mrs. Couvillon liable?
4. If you were the legal counsel for the corporation, what possible changes would you make to try to limit future liability?
5. Do you agree with the decision in this case? Why or why not?

ENGEL v. JANZEN

British Columbia, 1989

The plaintiffs had arranged a working holiday, as missionaries, in Hawaii for two months. The plaintiff husband went to his insurance agent, the defendant in the case, and discussed his auto insurance under the government-run plan. He explained that he would not be driving his car for two months and asked for advice. The defendant said the plaintiff might as well cancel the insurance for two months and use the money for the vacation.

The defendant forgot to point out to the plaintiff that, under his insurance policy, he and his wife also had under-insured motorist protection. This part of the policy would pay the plaintiffs for injuries if they were hit by an uninsured or under-insured motorist.

Relying on the defendant's advice, the plaintiffs cancelled all of their auto insurance. While in Hawaii, the plaintiffs were struck by a drunk, uninsured driver. Had they kept their own insurance policy they would have been fully protected. They sued the defendant agent for not pointing out to them that cancelling their policy would leave them at risk even though they were not driving their own car.

The defendant argued that she had no duty to offer such advice because the conversation was focused exclusively on the need for coverage of the plaintiff's own vehicle, not extraneous matters.

The Court held for the plaintiffs, ruling that an insurance agent has a duty to a client to keep him or her fully informed of all risks when the client buys insurance, and that the same duty exists when the client is considering cancelling insurance. The plaintiff husband had asked for advice about the wisdom of cancelling. He was justified in assuming that the defendant had correctly advised him, based on her skill and knowledge, that there was no benefit in maintaining the policy. In fact, there was a major benefit and there was an added risk to cancelling, which should have been brought to his attention. Although the plaintiffs might very well have cancelled the policy anyway, and taken their chances, they were entitled to have all the information before making a decision.

Questions

1. Upon what basis was the defendant liable? What duty was not met?
2. Does an insurance agent represent the client, the insurance company, or both? If the agent represents the insurance company, how can the agent also represent the client?
3. Under-insured motorist coverage is not the basic part of any automobile policy. It is a rider or attachment that is merely optional. Why would there be a duty upon the defendant to discuss such an insignificant part of the overall policy?
4. If you were legal counsel for an insurance agency, what advice would you give your clients regarding the situation in which one of its clients is considering the cancellation of insurance?

PRINCIPLES AND CASES

Case 1: Legal Principle

A lender has a fiduciary duty to an unsophisticated borrower to explain the risks of an investment decision and to warn against an unwise or unsuitable investment.

Case Facts

Edna was a 67-year-old widow who owned a small, unmortgaged house. She had a basic government pension and $30 000 in a credit union. She knew nothing about investments and relied on the credit union to invest her money in guaranteed income investments. Her son, Earl, applied for a loan of $6000 from the credit union to start a food catering business. He had quit school after Grade 8 and had no business experience.

The credit union asked Edna to guarantee the loan, expressing great confidence in Earl. Earl was the apple of Edna's eye and she doted on him. She was not advised to obtain independent legal advice, but was clearly told that if Earl got into financial problems, she would have to cover the loan. She said she understood this, but was sure that Earl knew what he was doing. In the following year, Earl applied for a second loan of $7500 and again Edna guaranteed the loan. There was no further discussion about the risks.

Within six months, Earl had obtained a third loan for $16 000. He was also in arrears on the first two loans. He was writing cheques that he could not cover and asked his mother for an urgent guarantee of another $2000. Edna was visiting her daughter, Ruth, at her daughter's cottage at the time. An official of the credit union brought the papers to the cottage for signature. The papers were actually a consolidation of all of the existing loans.

This was the first time that Ruth had heard anything about Earl's dealings. She expressed interest and concern and wanted to read the papers, but the credit union official said he was not authorized to discuss Earl's business with Ruth. Edna did not have her reading glasses but signed the papers, saying she was sure that if anything was wrong Earl would be honest with her. The credit union official did not tell her that the credit union had already concluded that Earl was a financial disaster and that it would soon have to proceed against him and call upon Edna to make good the loans.

The credit union pulled the plug five weeks later. Earl was $27 000 in arrears, basically wiping out Edna's savings. At trial, Edna admitted that she understood she was responsible for Earl's loans, but that she never believed that she was undertaking any risk because the credit union had always expressed great confidence in Earl's business ventures. She was not told he was in default on the first two loans when she signed the third set of papers.

Possible Decisions

A Edna is liable for the loans because she understood the basic nature of a financial guarantee and accepted the risk. She did not ask the credit union officials for advice.

B Edna is liable for the loans because at no time was there any deception or misrepresentation made to her about what she was doing, and she never expressed any interest in knowing the true state of Earl's loans.

C Edna is not liable because she was too naive and unsophisticated to enter into such agreements without proper advice.

D Edna is not liable because her close relationship with her son affected her decision-making abilities.

Case 2: Legal Principle

A bank or accounting firm may be liable for failure to detect or warn about accounting discrepancies of which the bank was aware.

Case Facts

The defendant bank made a $40 000 loan to a furniture company. The loan went into default and the bank examiners went over the company books and tried to put them in order. They found many discrepancies, among which was the practice of putting through orders as immediate sales. This practice is called "pre-billing" and is not proper accounting practice because orders can be cancelled at any time and cannot be counted as sales until the money is received or credit arranged. Pre-billing overstates the revenue of the business. The amount of pre-billing was in excess of $200 000, which caused the bank examiners to suspect that fraud might be involved.

The bank did not tell anyone what it discovered. An accounting firm was appointed as the bankruptcy trustee by the court and began its own audit. The bank was the major creditor of the company but had no meetings with the trustee to discuss what it knew.

The audit had scarcely begun when Hodges, an employee of the company, came forward and said that he wanted to take the company over and try to keep it going. Hodges offered to inject cash and employ the previous manager on the payroll to temporarily maintain operations. The trustee pointed out that it would take two or three weeks to complete the audit, but Hodges wanted to keep the operation going so that employees would not be laid off, creditors frightened away, and customers lost. The trustee agreed to this and stopped the audit. The bank was advised that Hodges was buying the business and would assume responsibility for the loan.

Hodges invested $150 000 and resumed operation. He hired his own accounting firm to try to get matters under control. He was soon told the ugly facts. It was quickly apparent that the pre-billing problem had caused Hodges to throw good money after bad. He blamed the trustee. The trustee defended itself by saying that, at Hodges' request, it had never finished its audit. The trustee talked to the bank examiners, who admitted that they had found the pre-billing problem but had said nothing because "It's none of our business. It's your business to find out these things. You're the bankruptcy trustee. We're just a creditor."

The business went bankrupt again and Hodges sued the trustee and the bank for misrepresentation, negligence, and failure to comply with a fiduciary duty to advise him of the true financial condition of the business.

Possible Decisions

A The trustee is liable because it had a duty to complete its work and get all the facts before agreeing to the investment plan that Hodges suggested.

B The bank is liable because it deliberately concealed what it knew in order to let Hodges invest cash in the business. This action protected the bank's loan at Hodges' expense.

C The trustee and the bank are both liable for the reasons given in **A** and **B**.

D Neither the bank nor the trustee is liable. The bank owed no duty to either the trustee or Hodges. The trustee was unaware of the problem. If Hodges was prepared to buy the business before the trustee completed its audit, that was his decision and no fault of the trustee.

YOU BE THE JUDGE

1. The defendant was sued by his former employer for breach of a fiduciary duty. The defendant had been employed by the plaintiff company for 18 years as an investment counsellor and mutual fund sales representative. He had a regular clientele of nearly 500 people. When he resigned and accepted

employment with a competing firm, he told his former office manager that he would eventually solicit business from his clients. The manager made no reply to this statement. The defendant argued that initially he had not actively solicited business from his former clients. Rather, he relied upon placing advertisements in the newspaper, announcing his change of employers. He felt that his clients would come to him and that he would not have to pursue their business. However, several weeks after making the move, he sent letters to all his former clients that said, "It seems that most of my clients have been assigned to junior or rookie representatives" and urged these clients to contact him "if you have concerns about your investments." Counsel for the defendant further argued that the *Charter of Rights and Freedoms* guarantee of freedom of expression permitted the defendant to solicit freely. The plaintiff's action was for return of all company records, an injunction against further soliciting of its clients, and damages. Who would succeed?

2. The plaintiff purchased shares of a private company that was operated by the defendant. The plaintiff claimed he had been induced to buy the stock by the defendant's representations that the shares were a good investment. As an added inducement, the defendant said that the stock would be traded on a public stock exchange in the near future, and that this would greatly add to its appeal. The plaintiff was a farmer with no knowledge of the stock market. He did not know what the company produced and relied totally upon what the defendant had told him. The defendant argued that he had applied for a public listing. He honestly believed that his company had great prospects and that what he had told the plaintiff was true. He felt he was doing him a big favour by letting him in on "the ground floor." The defendant further argued that he had made no statements guaranteeing anything he said, but had just been enthusiastic about positive events that he felt would actually take place. The stock was never listed and was eventually struck from the stock register. The plaintiff sued the defendant to recover his lost investment. Who would succeed?

3. The defendant, a marine surveyor, was approached by a friend and asked to prepare a marine survey regarding the condition of his boat. The friend stated that he was applying for a bank loan and that the boat would be the security for the loan. The defendant gave the boat a very quick examination and prepared a survey stating that the boat was in good condition. He pointed out that the boat required some deck repairs but that these would not be difficult to make. At trial, the defendant admitted that he had done a very cursory inspection because he was not terribly concerned about a bank

securing its loans. The survey form contained a printed disclaimer on the back that the defendant undertook no liability for his report and that it was based upon visual observation only, meaning that the boat had not been taken into dry dock. The owner of the boat had deceived the surveyor about his intentions. He was actually in negotiations with the plaintiff, who was considering purchasing the boat. The plaintiff had specified that the sale was contingent upon a satisfactory marine survey. The plaintiff had agreed to pay half the cost of the survey. When he read the survey, he did not read the disclaimer printed on the reverse side. Relying upon the survey report that the boat was basically sound, he purchased it. In fact, the boat was in an advanced state of rot and was not seaworthy. The plaintiff sued the defendant surveyor. The surveyor was not aware that the owner intended to sell the boat or that the sale was contingent upon the survey being satisfactory. He argued that the plaintiff could have contacted him personally to discuss the survey's statement before purchasing the boat. He would have pointed out that he made a visual inspection only, for the purposes of a bank loan, and that he was not in a position to make any comment about the hull of the boat unless it was taken into dry dock. The plaintiff took the position that a marine surveyor has a professional duty to prepare reports in a factual and honest manner at all times and not to make misleading statements as a favour to a friend. Who would succeed?

4. The plaintiffs owned a store in a small shopping mall. They were interested in buying the entire mall as an investment. They employed the defendant real estate agent to try to make the purchase, indicating that they would pay as much as $1 million for the property. However, the owners of the mall refused to sell. Three years later, the owners of the mall contacted the defendant and told him they were now interested in selling. The defendant knew that the plaintiffs had not abandoned their hopes of buying the property. The defendant incorporated a small, numbered company and bought the property for $900 000. He then turned around and told the plaintiffs that the mall could be purchased for $1.1 million. The defendant acted for the plaintiffs as their agent in the transaction. The plaintiffs did not know that they were purchasing the mall from the defendant's company. When the deal was completed, the defendant had a profit of $200 000 and a real estate commission. The plaintiffs sued to recover these two amounts. They argued that there had been a breach of fiduciary duty. The defendant argued that he had broken no laws and had done what the plaintiffs wanted—arranged the purchase of the mall. Who would succeed?

5. The defendant, a stock promoter, was chairman of a corporation. She urged numerous investors to buy stock in her company, which she described in glowing terms. One investor, the plaintiff in the case, became concerned about his investment and asked for a personal meeting with the defendant. At this meeting, the defendant told the plaintiff that everything was going very well and that he should keep his stock and perhaps buy more. She told him that major contracts had been signed with large companies to market her company's products. In fact, the defendant had been selling her own shares on the market. Shortly after the meeting, she sold more than 100 000 shares of her stock, all the while telling the plaintiff to buy more. The plaintiff learned the truth when the stock dropped to just a few cents a share. He sued the defendant, who argued that she was under no obligation to provide the plaintiff with any information but did so as a favour. What she did with her own personal stock portfolio was no concern of the plaintiff. Who would succeed?

6. The plaintiff was suspended from her teaching job when it was learned that she had entered a nude photograph of herself in a contest. The photograph was featured in a magazine. The plaintiff said she had entered the contest both as a joke and as a means of building her own self-confidence. There was nothing illegal about her actions, but her school board suspended her because her conduct constituted professional wrongdoing and did not present her as a proper role model to her students. The plaintiff argued that her personal life had nothing to do with her professional duties. Who would succeed?

7. The plaintiff had been accused of a criminal offence when he engaged the services of the defendant, a criminal lawyer. The plaintiff told the defendant that he had an alibi, which he believed was very solid. However, the lawyer told him that it would not be necessary to call alibi witnesses because he was going to get the case dismissed on a "technicality." The plaintiff trusted that the defendant knew what he was doing. On the day of the trial, the judge quickly rejected the technical defence argument and the case proceeded. Without his alibi witnesses, the plaintiff was convicted of a criminal offence. He received a light sentence, but was very upset that he now had a criminal record. He sued the defendant for his gross mishandling of the case. The defendant argued that a lawyer cannot be sued by his client just because he loses a case. To allow such actions would open a floodgate of suits. Who would succeed?

Cooper
Cooper

C H A P T E R   E I G H T

SALE OF GOODS

"In the selling game, you'd better learn the difference between genius and stupidity. Genius has limits."

Ronald Falvo,
sales manager of heavy equipment company

NATURE OF A SALE

Throughout much of history, the process of buying and selling goods was a relatively simple matter. The buyer and seller bargained face to face. The buyer examined the goods and haggled over the price. The seller gave no guarantees regarding the quality of the goods. There were no showrooms or catalogues. The price varied according to the bargaining skills of the two participants. It was assumed that the seller was trying to get the better of the buyer and vice versa.

Sellers used subtle methods to deceive buyers. For example, much trading was done in square marketplaces under the protection of overhanging awnings. Dishonest merchants would display their wares on the side of the square that was in shadow most of the day. Honest vendors could be found in sunlit stalls. The "dark side of the marketplace" was a literal term, not merely an expression. The only rule was the rule of *caveat emptor* (buyer beware). A bad bargain was binding—and a good lesson for the future.

"Buyer beware" is not really the law of sale today. There are now implied conditions as to quality and fitness of goods, and there is no duty on a buyer to examine goods in order for the conditions to be effective. The seller does not have to point out flaws in his or her goods, but the seller cannot hide the defects. The statute law has also altered the relationship between buyer and seller. These statutes will be discussed in Chapter 9, "Consumer Protection."

Although it may appear obvious, it is necessary to make certain that a transaction is truly a sale. For example, under the Ontario *Sale of Goods Act*, a **sale** is defined as "a contract whereby the seller transfers or agrees to transfer the property in goods to the buyer for a money consideration called the price." There are two different types of sale agreements within this definition. The first is a sale because the transfer of ownership of the goods takes place immediately. The second type is a contract by which the transfer will take place later, subject to some condition. The second contract is an **agreement to sell**. It is a contract, but it is not yet a sale. Such an agreement becomes a sale when the time elapses or the conditions are fulfilled.

The effect of the difference between the two types of sale agreements is quite important. For example, if title to the goods passes immediately, as under a sale, then the risk of loss also passes to the buyer immediately. Another distinction arises if there is a breach of contract. If the buyer has acquired title, then the buyer may demand specific performance of the sale, e.g., delivery of the goods. If the contract is only an agreement to sell, the buyer cannot demand specific performance but may sue only for breach of contract.

As the name implies, the *Sale of Goods Act* applies only to the sale of "goods." It does not apply to the sale of land or to labour contracts. The word "goods" includes all chattel property, but the wording of the Act also includes all "emblements, industrial growing crops and things attached to or forming part of the land which are agreed to be severed before sale or under the sale of land." Crops growing on the land, such as wheat, are considered goods. However, things growing naturally on the land, such as trees, are not goods under the statute. Buildings attached to the land are not goods, but the statute recognizes that buildings may be detached as part of the sale agreement and sold as goods.

There are many unanswered questions in the wording of the statute. For example, many companies sell topsoil, gravel, sand, and other components of the land. Are these items goods? In *Saskatoon Sand & Gravel v. Steve* (Saskatchewan, 1973) the defendant gave the plaintiff permission to dig and remove gravel from the defendant's land. The plaintiff stockpiled it on the defendant's land rather than removing it. The case revolved around the basic argument of who owned the gravel. The Court held that it was not a contract for the sale of goods. If something is to be manufactured and then attached to the land, is this a chattel or part of the land? An example might be a tombstone.

A sale differs from a barter or trade, which is merely an exchange of goods. If both money and goods are involved, it becomes difficult to decide whether the agreement is a barter or sale. The deciding factor is whether the major part of the contract involves money. If only a small amount of money is involved in relation to the value of goods being exchanged, the agreement is a barter, not a sale. None of the specific statutes pertaining to the sale of goods applies to barters.

Also excluded from the sale of goods law are contracts of labour. If a person is hired to paint a house and is to provide the paint, the contract is really a contract of hire, not the purchase of the paint used. In such cases, the court must examine the basic nature of the agreement. If the service is to manufacture a chattel, the contract may be regarded as a sale of goods. In the unusual case of *Salo v. Anglo Packing Company* (British Columbia, 1929) fishermen were contracted to catch fish and sell them to the defendant packing company. Even though the defendant had some limited control over the fishermen, the Court concluded that the contract was a contract for the sale of fish, not a contract of employment.

There are several different types of sales, including an absolute sale and a conditional sale. An **absolute sale** is a sale that is final upon the completion of the transaction. Ownership or title passes immediately from the seller to the buyer. If the terms of the sale agreement call for payment to be made at a later date, this does not affect title. Title still passes when the contract is made.

A **conditional sale** does not give immediate ownership to the buyer, although the buyer immediately acquires the use of the goods. Title does not pass until the buyer fulfils some condition in the contract, usually the making of full payment.

A **bill of sale** is a document used to protect the buyer who has bought goods but left them temporarily with the seller. The bill of sale is proof of the transfer of title to the buyer.

SALE OF GOODS ACT

Each province except Quebec has a statute similar to the British statute known as the *Sale of Goods Act*. Quebec law contains some provisions regarding the sale of goods. The British law was first enacted in 1893 and was an attempt to combine many widely scattered concepts about the law and to solve some persistent problems involving the sale of goods. The bill that was enacted was an excellent one, and it was adopted in Canada and other countries that relied upon the common law system.

With the basic safeguards of the *Statute of Frauds* in mind, the drafters of the *Sale of Goods Act* made a similar decision that certain contracts of sale must be in writing. It was decided that a monetary limit would be the basis of the requirement. Each province has a limit, above which a sale of goods requires a written contract. The amount differs from province to province, ranging from $30 to $50. Alberta and Newfoundland place the amount at $50; in Ontario it is $40.

The basic requirement of these provincial laws is that an unwritten contract for the sale of goods with a value above the prescribed limit is not enforceable by court action. Having laid down the basic requirement, the law then recognizes exceptions to the rule. A sale is binding, even if not in writing, if any one of the following conditions is met:

1. The buyer accepts all or part of the goods and receives them;
2. The buyer gives "something in earnest" to bind the contract;
3. The buyer makes a partial payment;
4. Some note or memorandum is made in writing and is signed by the buyer or the buyer's agent.

To analyse these requirements briefly, the basic rule is that a sale that exceeds a certain amount of money must be in writing. An exception is made if the buyer actually receives all or part of the goods. The act of receiving the goods confirms the serious intent of the buyer.

An exception is also made if the buyer gives the seller something "in earnest," which means something of value to hold until payment is made. For example, if Brown wants to buy Green's boat, but has no money at the time, Brown can conclude the sale by giving his watch to Green. The authorities differ on the exact meaning of "earnest." The most accepted belief is that the object given in earnest must be given outright, by the buyer to the seller, with no expectation that it will be returned. In many situations, the object is returned if the money is eventually paid. The object (the watch, in our example) is "held hostage" until the buyer returns. To avoid dispute, the parties should discuss what will happen if the buyer does not come back, or does not come back within an agreed-upon time. It is important to understand that neither party can change his or her mind at this point. The agreement has been made.

An exception is made if the buyer makes a partial payment. The buyer should obtain a receipt as proof of payment and the receipt should include all the details of the sale.

Lastly, an exception is made if a written memorandum is prepared. A written memorandum can be any paper or collection of papers, notes, letters, etc., that prove a contract of sale was made. The written memorandum need not be in any particular form. All that is necessary is that a written document or set of documents clearly indicates the parties' intention to enter into a contract, and explains the terms agreed upon.

DEFINITION OF "GOODS"

The meaning of the word **goods** varies according to the statute that is being applied. In some consumer protection legislation, the term includes labour to make goods. In other statutes, it does not. The confusion arises when under one statute the item is not considered goods and therefore is not subject to any implied warranty as to fitness. At the same time, the requirement to have a sale of goods that exceeds a specified amount of money may not apply if the contract is one of labour.

FUTURE GOODS

If the goods that form the basis of the contract already exist, there is no confusion about their nature and transfer of title. Such goods are called **existing goods**. Perhaps more complex are contracts involving goods which do not yet exist. They have to be manufactured or grown. These are called **future goods.**

A contract for the sale of future goods cannot be called a sale; it is only an agreement to sell. There is nothing unusual about selling goods that do not yet exist; it is a common commercial practice. The difficult arguments arise as to when title passes to the buyer. Some courts have held that title passes as soon as the goods come into existence. Other courts have required that delivery take place before title passes. The difference is an important one. For example, if the goods are destroyed after being produced but before being delivered, will the buyer or the seller suffer the loss? If the goods come into existence but the seller refuses to deliver, can the buyer demand delivery by claiming that he or she now has title to the goods?

In *Olds Products Co. v. Montana Mustard Seed Co.* (Saskatchewan, 1973) the seller agreed to sell mustard seed to the buyer. The seed was to be grown in the future. When the seed was harvested, the seller refused to complete the sale. The buyer sought an injunction to prevent the seller from selling the seed to someone else, claiming that the seed belonged to the buyer. The Court refused the injunction and held that the buyer did not own the seed. The buyer could sue only for breach of contract.

SPECIFIC, ASCERTAINED, AND UNASCERTAINED GOODS

The *Sale of Goods Act* of most provinces distinguishes between specific and unascertained goods. **Specific goods** are defined in the Ontario statute as "goods identified and agreed upon at the time a contract of sale is made." Specific goods are ones that are clearly the only goods to be sold to the buyer. They can be readily identified as the buyer's goods and no substitutions can be made. They are unique in some manner, such as a serial number or identification mark. If the goods have been custom-made or specifically altered to the buyer's specifications, they are specific. Another way to make them specific is to segregate them from all others.

The Act does not contain any definition of **ascertained goods**. However, since the Act defines unascertained goods, it is reasonable that such a thing as ascertained goods exist. Further, they are not exactly the same as specific goods. Goods become ascertained when they can be identified in accordance with the agreement after the time when a contract of sale was made. For example, if a buyer purchased bags of cattle feed and the bags were specifically marked for delivery to the buyer along with a completed invoice, it would be correct to say the goods were ascertained. There was some way of looking at them and matching them to the buyer. However, it would still be possible to substitute other bags of the same feed if necessary. As with specified goods, title to the goods passes when the goods become ascertained.

Unascertained goods are goods that are not unique in any manner and have not been specifically set aside for the buyer. There is no way of identifying them as belonging to a specific buyer. It is possible for goods to start as unascertained, become ascertained, and eventually become specific.

HAYES BROS. BUICK-OPEL v. CANADA PERMANENT TRUST

New Brunswick, 1976

Various car dealers ordered vehicles from Bricklin Canada. Few cars were completed before Bricklin went into bankruptcy. The plaintiff had ordered seven cars, which had been built. The invoices had been prepared, including serial numbers. The defendant trustee-in-bankruptcy refused to deliver the cars. The question was whether title to the cars had passed to the plaintiff.

The Court held that the plaintiff was entitled to the vehicles. They were specific goods, clearly appropriated to the buyer. Title had passed to the plaintiff.

The importance of determining whether goods are specific, ascertained, or unascertained is obvious. In the case of specific and ascertained goods, title passes immediately, as does the risk. The goods must be insured. The buyer has a right to specific performance of the contract and may demand delivery.

DELIVERABLE STATE

The requirement that the goods be specific is not the only requirement. The goods must also be in a deliverable state. The goods are in a deliverable state when they are such that the buyer would be bound to take delivery of them under the terms of the contract.

Thus, if something further must be done to the goods, title will not pass. For example, if Brown agrees to buy a used car from Green Motors on the condition that Green will repaint the car, title does not pass until the car is painted and Brown can take possession of it. Title does not pass even if the purchase price has been partly or completely paid.

McDILL v. HILLSON

Manitoba, 1920

McDill agreed to buy some furniture from Hillson. The furniture was scratched and required polishing before it could be delivered. This could not be done immediately because the plant that would do the polishing had a labour dispute. McDill paid the full purchase price and Hillson agreed to deliver the furniture as soon as possible.

Before the work was done, the furniture was destroyed in a fire. McDill sued for the return of the purchase money, but Hillson refused and claimed that title and risk had passed to McDill when payment was made.

The Manitoba Court of Appeal found that the furniture had not been in a deliverable state when the contract had been made and that the agreement was that title would pass when the furniture was in a deliverable state and McDill notified. McDill was entitled to the return of the money.

The performance of required acts to make goods deliverable is a condition precedent to the passing of the property. For example, in this case, if Hillson did not do the polishing or did not do it properly, McDill could refuse to complete the agreement. The most important issue in such cases is the risk issue. If the seller is to deliver the goods to the buyer, the buyer assumes the risk the moment the goods are ready for shipment and the buyer is notified that they are deliverable. For example, suppose in the McDill case that the furniture is polished and McDill notified. McDill replies to Hillson that he is ready to receive the furniture. Hillson arranges shipment with the Reliable Trucking Company. While it is being loaded on a truck, several items of furniture are damaged by Reliable's employees and McDill refuses to accept them. McDill has no right to reject the goods, because title had already passed to him. All McDill can do is sue Reliable for damaging his goods.

ACCEPTANCE OF GOODS

The buyer has a duty to receive and accept the goods if they fulfil the terms of the contract. The buyer must inspect the goods as soon as is reasonably possible after delivery. Refusal to accept or failure to accept may be a breach of contract. The fact that the buyer receives the goods and is in possession of them is not acceptance. At this point, the buyer is a bailee of the goods and must take reasonable care of them. The buyer may be liable if the goods are damaged or stolen. For title to pass to the buyer, the buyer must do one of three things:

1. Signify his or her approval to the seller;
2. Perform some other act adopting the transaction;
3. Retain the goods without giving notice of rejection beyond the time fixed to return them.

A contract may specifically state that the goods are delivered "on approval." The contract should be clear as to how much time the buyer has to make a decision and whether the buyer must accept or reject all of the goods. If the goods are damaged while the buyer is examining them, the buyer can still return them but the seller can sue for the damage.

If the buyer is careless in his or her inspection or delays too long, the buyer cannot complain of a lack of opportunity to examine. If the buyer says nothing after a reasonable time, makes use of the goods, or resells them, acceptance is implied.

If the seller conceals a defect that a buyer cannot be expected to find in the course of a reasonable inspection, the buyer may later cancel the contract even though the buyer initially accepted the goods.

STAIMAN STEEL LTD. v. FRANKI CANADA LTD.

Ontario, 1985

Franki Canada, a construction corporation, ordered steel reinforcing bars from Staiman Steel Ltd., to be shipped to Edmonton. The general manager for Franki became concerned when he noted that Staiman consistently shipped more than the quantities ordered. He ordered five entire shipments returned to Staiman because they were not required. He kept six shipments, which arrived approximately two weeks apart. He sent a telegram to Staiman saying: "With these quantities returned and cancelled our shipments accepted against this purchase order total 520 tons, not 400 tons. This is well in excess of our planned purchases of bars from your firm."

The next day, the manager sent samples of the bars to be tested for quality. He found that they were not of the grade he had ordered. The company lawyer wrote to Staiman saying that all of the bars were being returned. Staiman refused to accept this and sued for payment for the six shipments initially accepted.

The Court held that Franki had accepted the bars and must pay. A buyer is deemed to have accepted goods from a seller when the buyer intimates to the seller that he or she accepts them or does not reject them within a reasonable time. There was ample time for Franki to inspect the first two shipments, which had arrived several weeks before the telegram was sent. By its silence, and then by saying in the telegram that the bars had been "accepted," Franki had accepted the goods and must pay for them.

PAYMENT FOR GOODS

Unless there is some other agreement, it is assumed that the buyer will pay when the goods are picked up or delivered. If no price is specified, it is presumed that the buyer will pay the current catalogue price or a fair market price for the goods. There is nothing to prevent the two parties from arranging a plan for a delayed payment, such as 30 days after the sale was made. This does not affect any of the other terms of the contract.

The normal method of payment is by cash. However, a buyer may pay by cheque or some other negotiable instrument if this is agreed to by the seller.

The buyer may also pay by instalment. It is important to distinguish between a true instalment payment and a deposit. If the part payment is an instalment, paid according to an instalment schedule, it will be returned if the goods are not accepted. If it is a deposit, it is a matter of contract between the parties as to what happens if the sale is not completed. In the absence of an agreement, the deposit may be forfeited if the buyer does not carry out his or her obligation.

RISK OF LOSS

Unless otherwise agreed, the goods remain at the seller's risk until the property is transferred to the buyer, at which time the goods are at the buyer's risk. Therefore, it is important to know at what point title passes. This is especially important when goods are transported over great distances. If delivery of the goods is delayed because of the fault of either the buyer or seller, then risk lies with whichever party is at fault, regardless of who would ordinarily bear the risk of loss.

Risk is a character of property, not of possession. The parties may agree to some different allocation of the risk in the contract. The element of risk is why the seller must give the buyer notice that the goods are in a deliverable state so that the buyer may acquire insurance.

An **f.o.b.** (free on board) contract places a duty on the seller to put the goods, free of charge, aboard a ship. The goods remain the seller's property and the seller's risk until they are placed on board. Risk then passes to the buyer. Today, the term applies to all methods of transportation, not just ships. A **c.i.f.** (cost, insurance, freight) contract places a duty on the seller to ship the goods, pay the freight, and insure the goods. Risk passes to the buyer when they are delivered.

In *Beaver Specialty Ltd. v. Bain Ltd.* (Supreme Court of Canada, 1970) the seller sold walnut pieces to the buyer. The seller shipped the goods by rail from Vancouver to the buyer in Toronto under a contract that stipulated "f.o.b. Toronto." It was held that the seller was liable when the walnuts were damaged in transit by water and freezing. There was a presumption that title would pass when the goods reached Toronto, in good condition, and the buyer had examined and accepted them. Because the goods were in proper condition when shipped, the seller's action was against the railroad company. However, if the contract had not stipulated that the goods were sold "f.o.b. the buyer's place of business," the risk would have been upon the buyer once the goods were shipped. As well, if the buyer has not been notified that the goods have been shipped, the risk remains upon the seller. The seller is also liable if the seller does not ship the goods in the manner agreed upon in the contract. For example, if the seller shipped frozen goods by ordinary rail car, thereby allowing them to thaw and deteriorate, the seller would be liable.

PERISHING OF GOODS

The possibility that the goods have perished either before or after a contract of sale has been made was anticipated by the drafters of the initial legislation. This is not surprising, particularly in view of the rate of loss on the high seas. The statute uses the word "perished" to distinguish between goods that have been lost and goods that never existed. The statute states that when there is a contract for the sale of specific goods and the goods have perished at the time when the contract is made, the contract is void. The contract must obviously have been entered into by the parties without knowing the goods no longer existed. If the goods have been sold and are then destroyed without any fault on the part of the seller or buyer, before the risk has passed to the buyer, the contract is void. If the goods are lost because of the negligence or fault of either party, that party will be liable to the other.

The rule applies only to specific goods. The purpose of the law is to release both parties from a contract that becomes pointless. As the specific goods no longer exist, they cannot be sold. However, if the goods are unascertained, the contract is still valid because other goods could be substituted for those that have been lost.

The concept of perished goods is not easily applied in some cases. For example, it is unclear if goods "perish" when they are stolen. There is no certainty that the goods no longer exist. They might be recovered from the thief. Also, if only part of the goods perish, it is unclear if the buyer has to accept what remains.

A final point of confusion is whether goods perish if they deteriorate. That is, must they deteriorate 100 percent to be truly perished? In the British case of *Horn v. Minister of Foods* (1948) the contract was for the sale of potatoes. The seller stored the potatoes with care, but they developed a blight and began to rot. The buyer refused to accept them, saying they had perished. The buyer tried to equate the word "perish" with the word "deteriorate." The Court disagreed and ruled that the potatoes were still potatoes, despite their deterioration. However, the ruling was lessened in its importance when the Court held that risk had already passed to the buyer, so the definition of the word "perish" was not the true issue in the case.

CONDITIONS AND WARRANTIES

If a contract contains a condition, the condition must be fulfilled or the entire contract can be rejected. A **condition** is an essential part of the contract, and failure to complete a condition is considered a major breach of contract. If Brown agrees to buy a machine from Green, on the condition that the machine be equipped with special safety features, this condition is part of the contract. If the machine arrives without the safety equipment, Brown can refuse to accept it. Failure to meet the condition can thus mean failure of the entire contract.

A **warranty** is not an essential part of the contract. In most cases, the warranty is a separate document and not part of the sale contract at all. The Ontario *Sale of Goods Act* defines a warranty as follows:

> Warranty means an agreement with reference to goods that are the subject of a contract of sale but collateral to the main purpose of such contract, the breach of which gives rise to a claim for damages, but not a right to reject the goods and treat the contract as repudiated.

Failure to live up to a warranty does not allow the buyer to repudiate the contract. The warranty is not the same as a condition within the contract. The warranty is a separate agreement that runs along with the sale contract. The buyer may bring an action to try to force the seller to live up to the warranty, but this is often difficult since many warranties are vague.

The word **guarantee** does not have much legal recognition, but it must be assumed to mean basically the same thing as a warranty.

Conditions may be expressly identified in the contract or they may be expressly excluded by the contract. Under the *Sale of Goods Act*, some conditions are also implied. Implied conditions relate to the seller's right to sell the goods, the correspondence of the goods with the description of them, the fitness of the goods for the purpose for which they were bought, the merchantability of the goods, the correspondence of the goods with the samples, the opportunity to compare the bulk with the sample, and the merchantability of the goods.

SELLER'S TITLE

When a person sells goods, an implied condition is given that the seller owns the goods and has a lawful right to sell them. If this turns out to be incorrect, the buyer can cancel the contract and sue for damages.

For example, the buyer may have been sold stolen goods. Should the true owner recover the property, the buyer may bring an action against the seller. The rule does not apply to stolen money as part of an honest business transaction. Goods purchased on the instalment plan do not belong to the person who bought them until the final payment is made. Therefore, this person cannot resell the goods to a third person without the consent of the original seller.

A person, such as an auctioneer, may act as the agent for the seller. The buyer obtains good title, provided the seller had good title. An auctioneer can be held personally liable by the buyer if the title to the goods turns out to be defective.

SALE BY DESCRIPTION

Where goods are sold by sample or catalogue description, such goods must match the sample or description when delivered. If they do not, the buyer may refuse to accept them and cancel the contract. On the other hand, if the buyer receives and uses the goods, knowing that they are not correct, the contract cannot later be cancelled on the grounds that the goods do not match the description. If the buyer was unaware that he or she had been deceived, the contract can still be avoided. In *Brousseau v. Lewis Motors* (Ontario, 1974) the plaintiff purchased a 1971 Cortina from the defendant. The car she received was actually a 1970 Cortina. The defendant said it was just following directions from the Ford Motor Company that 1970 models had been "redesignated" as 1971 models because no changes had been made in the design of the car. The plaintiff was awarded damages in Small Claims Court.

A question often arises regarding quality. If the parties have specified the quality of standard of goods in the contract, this is part of the description of the goods and an express condition of the contract.

BAKKER v. BOWNESS AUTO PARTS CO. LTD.

Alberta, 1976

The plaintiff ordered a supply of ethanol-ethylene-glycol antifreeze. The seller delivered a fluid that contained so little ethylene-glycol that it could not be properly be called antifreeze. The Court held that this was a sale by description—the name identified the type of fluid to be delivered. The fluid delivered was not what was ordered and the buyer had the right to refuse to accept it.

If the contract does not specify quality, standard, or content, then the buyer cannot refuse to accept the goods because they do not match the description. The buyer may try to avoid the contract under other conditions, such as fitness of goods or merchantable quality. If the contract is simply for "lumber," then poor-quality lumber meets the description as well as high-quality lumber does. Only if the lumber is so defective as to be useless can it be said that it does not match the description, because lumber that cannot be used at all is not truly lumber. The test is ultimately whether the buyer could reasonably refuse to accept the goods on the ground that their failure to correspond with what was said about them makes them goods of a totally different kind from those the buyer agreed to purchase. The obvious lesson for buyers is to be very precise in the description of goods ordered, including quality and specifications.

FITNESS OF GOODS

Often the buyer does not know the product and must rely on the skill and judgment of the seller. Under these circumstances, two conditions must be met: (1) the buyer must make known, expressly or by implication, to the seller the particular purpose for which the goods are required, and (2) the seller must be in the kind of business that supplies the goods that the buyer wants. Only then is there an implied condition that the goods will be reasonably fit for such purpose. Thus, if the buyer explains to the seller what the buyer wants to accomplish with the goods, the seller must provide the buyer with the proper article for the task. The sale of used goods falls under the rule if the seller is in the business of selling used goods. In *Green v. Holiday Chevrolet-Oldsmobile Ltd.* (Manitoba, 1975), the Court held that, in the absence of contractual terms limiting implied conditions, a used car must be roadworthy and reasonably fit for use. The defendant sold the plaintiff a used car while deliberately concealing the fact that the car had been used for racing.

The *Sale of Goods Act* does not apply to contracts of labour or service. However, if the contract is for a service that produces goods, the statute can be applied.

In *Lakelse Dairy Products Ltd. v. General Dairy Machinery and Supply Ltd.* (British Columbia, 1970), the plaintiff bought from the defendant a tanker for the transportation of milk for sale to the public and made known to the seller the purpose for which the tanker was to be used. The tanker was defective, causing the milk to become contaminated. The plaintiff lost the milk and customers. The Court held that the contract contained an implied condition of fitness for the intended purpose and awarded damages to the plaintiff.

MERCHANTABLE QUALITY

It is implied that the quality of the goods that are delivered will match the price and the manner in which the goods were described to the seller. This normally means that the goods will function adequately for normal purposes. The meaning of the expression **merchantable quality** has been the subject of much debate. Early court decisions held that the phrase refers to a wholesaler or retailer buying goods for the purpose of reselling them, not for immediate use. This view gave strong weight to the word "merchantable" as referring to a merchant. Some courts have suggested that goods must be "legally saleable" in order to properly be called merchantable. However, recent decisions have applied the term to any sale, stressing the word "quality." The goods must be both useable and saleable. In *Georgetown Seafoods Ltd. v. Usen Fisheries Ltd.* (P.E.I., 1977) the buyer purchased fish for processing from the seller. They were found to be unfit for processing. The Court held that they were not of merchantable quality. However, in *Demuynck v. Bittner* (Alberta, 1977), the buyer purchased barley seed for sowing. The seed did not germinate well, resulting in a smaller crop than expected. The Court held that the seeds were of merchantable quality, although a poor quality.

These cases suggest that goods are not of merchantable quality only if there is a total, or near-total, failure of quality. Poor or lower quality does not make goods totally unsaleable. The buyer may have other remedies under the contract, but cannot succeed under this particular heading.

SALE OF GOODS DISCLAIMERS

A sale of goods contract is frequently entered into by means of a printed contract form. These forms often contain wording that is vague and confusing to the buyer, who sometimes does not bother to read the contract at all. Failure to do so is at the buyer's own peril.

There is a duty on the buyer to read and understand a contract. The buyer is bound to a contract as long as he or she knows its general nature—that it pertains to a sale. The buyer does not have to read or understand each and every word. Terms printed on the back of a contract are usually binding if the front contains a notation mentioning that there are additional terms on the back. These additional terms often include disclaimers. A **disclaimer** is a provision which, in effect, states, "I never promised you ... " We have already seen that the *Sale of Goods Act* contains implied conditions and warranties. Disclaimer clauses often try to nullify these same conditions and warranties. The problem for the court is to determine whether such an action is permissible. If the statute law states that something must be, can the parties write their own agreement and say otherwise? A typical disclaimer clause reads as follows:

> **There are no conditions, express or implied, statutory or otherwise, other than those contained in this written agreement.**

Because nearly all printed contract forms are prepared by the seller, if the courts accepted such disclaimers, the effect would be to totally nullify the *Sale of Goods Act*. The courts have been generally unwilling to accept such a procedure. By way of comparison, the court would not recognize a contract that began by stating: "The *Sale of Goods Act* does not apply to this contract."

This does not mean that two parties can never agree upon terms that would set aside the normal effect of the statute. This is particularly true in the sale of used goods.

Many cases come before the court in which the printed contract states that there are no conditions or warranties, and yet the seller orally made such promises. The buyer is caught by the parol evidence rule, which prevents a buyer from adding to, varying from, or contradicting the clear, unambiguous terms of a written or printed contract. The buyer's problem is this: (1) the salesperson makes verbal representations beyond what is contained in the contract, but (2) the buyer signs a contract agreeing that the salesperson made no such representations.

Does the disclaimer clause work or not? That is, does it succeed in destroying the buyer's statutory protection? Does it defeat any argument that the buyer may raise that the seller made promises that were not kept? The answer seems to lie in the nature of the agreement itself and how strongly worded the disclaimer is. Because the disclaimer clause is usually written by the seller, the courts will generally give the benefit of doubt to the buyer if there is any ambiguity regarding the wording of the clause.

In the case of *Karsales Ltd. v. Wallis* (England, 1956), Lord Denning tried to put the problem into perspective. He wrote:

> *A disclaimer clause purporting to deprive a purchaser of the protection and reliance in the* Sale of Goods Act *can have no validity if it is asserted*

> *unilaterally by the seller, but can only come about through agreement. As a rule, when the purchaser signs the contract, the formal requirements are met. However, that should not conclude the question, for in order to enforce the agreement against the purchaser, the seller must show that the consideration which has been promised has been received by the buyer. If the agreement asserts that no promise has been made, the argument becomes circular. We must first find a promise, then demonstrate that it was not kept. If the disclaimer clause insists there was no promise, it could be argued that the purchaser has not received any consideration and no binding obligation exists.*

The immediate objection to Lord Denning's approach was that it limited the freedom to contract. A disclaimer clause cannot just be ignored. It must be read as part of the overall agreement. The court must look at the price, description of the goods sold, delivery date, etc., as indicating that certain promises were given by the seller, with resulting expectations by the purchaser. Therefore, a disclaimer clause must not totally restrict the realization of such expectations. The seller cannot completely disclaim to fulfil his or her obligation, or there is no contract at all. At the same time, if the seller has clearly indicated what he or she is not promising, there is no reason for the court to create those promises.

In *Karsales*, Lord Denning recognized the importance of "fundamental breach." If the buyer receives something so different from what he or she was entitled to receive, the seller has breached the contract totally and it does not matter whether there was a disclaimer clause or not. However, fundamental breach can be misapplied and taken out of context.

KEEFE v. FORT

Nova Scotia, 1978

The plaintiff, Keefe, answered a local newspaper advertisement offering for sale a used Alpha Romeo car. The plaintiff arranged to see the car at the home of the defendant. He test-drove the car, noted several small defects, but was given accurate answers by the defendant.

The plaintiff returned several days later with an Alpha Romeo mechanic and the two men spent two hours in the garage looking at the car. The defendant offered to let the plaintiff take the car to a garage and make a thorough study of it, but Keefe did not take him up on the offer.

The plaintiff bought the car, but found that it burned oil. He took the car to have the oil changed and the mechanic removed the oil pan. He found a bolt in the oil pan, which indicated that new bearings were needed. After driving a total of 400 km, the plaintiff learned that there was damage to the engine block that would cost $2200 to repair. The plaintiff sued the defendant, alleging fundamental breach of the contract. The trial judge held for the defendant and the case went to the Court of Appeal, which upheld the trial judge's decision. The Court dismissed the action against the defendant, saying:

> *In the case before us, the parties acted upon a verbal agreement and there were no exclusion clauses. The trial judge on this particular aspect said: "The contract in my view was that the buyer was purchasing a used car and the seller was selling a used car, and that there was no fundamental breach and that the doctrine of* caveat emptor *applies, that the burden is on the plaintiff to prove on a balance of probabilities his case. This has not been done." The doctrine of fundamental breach was never intended to be applied to situations where the parties had received substantially what they had bargained for. In recent history, the term "fundamental breach" has taken on a meaning of its own, which in its application tends to mystify rather than clarify the true meaning of the concept. In my opinion, it means nothing more or less than the type of breach which entitles the innocent party to treat it as repudiation and to rescind the contract.*

The pendulum swung even farther in favour of recognizing disclaimer clauses in the following case.

PHOTO PRODUCTION LTD. v. SECURICOR LTD.

England, 1980

Securicor, the defendant, was hired by the plaintiff to provide security for the plaintiff's factory. An employee of the defendant, sent to perform the defendant's contractual obligations, deliberately set fire to the factory, destroying it. When sued by the plaintiff, the defendant relied upon an exemption clause in the contract. The clause absolved the defendant of liability for the acts of its employees. The defendant was successful at trial, but the Court of Appeal allowed the plaintiff's action and did not accept the disclaimer clause. Two reasons were given for this. First, the clause appeared to absolve the defendant of negligence, but not for the deliberate acts of its employees. Second, a fundamental breach of contract had occurred. The contract was to provide protection for the factory. Securicor had not protected the factory; its employee had destroyed it. Such a fundamental breach completely destroyed the contract, making the disclaimer clause void.

However, the House of Lords reversed the Court of Appeal's decision and upheld the disclaimer clause. The clause was clear in that it covered the circumstances of the case. More importantly, there was no rule of law by which breach of contract rendered disclaimer clauses void. Parties could agree to modify or alter the terms of a contract as they wished.

> *In commercial contracts negotiated between businessmen capable of looking after their own interests and of deciding how risks inherent in the performance of various kinds of contract can be most economically borne, it is wrong to place a strained construction on words in an exclusion clause which are clear and fairly susceptible of one meaning only.*

Although the exclusion clause in the contract was totally out of place in terms of what the defendant was supposedly selling to the plaintiff, the Court concluded that, if the parties want to make absurd contractual arrangements, they may do so.

To this must be added another problem. There is a difference between a clause that restricts liability and a clause that accepts liability but seeks to limit it. Exclusion and limitation are not the same thing. Clauses of limitation are not regarded by the courts with the same hostility as clauses of exclusion. They must be related to other terms in the contract, in particular to the risk to which the defendant may be exposed. Thus, where a disclaimer clause tries to limit the extent of the warranty given, it may be enforceable. If the disclaimer clause tries to free the seller of all responsibility, the court may take the view that there is no contract at all since the seller gives the buyer no consideration. In *Brown v. Woywada* (Manitoba, 1974) the plaintiff bought a 19-year-old tractor from the defendant for $450. The contract contained a clause saying that no warranties were given with the machine, which was totally defective. The Court held that the plaintiff received what he purchased—an old machine with no warranty.

Concern about disclaimer clauses caused British Columbia, Ontario, Manitoba, and Nova Scotia to pass legislation declaring void any term of a contract that seeks to avoid the implied conditions and warranties under provincial law. Saskatchewan, New Brunswick, and Quebec go further and make the manufacturer and retailer jointly liable for any breach of an implied warranty or condition. The Alberta *Farm Implements Act* declares void any clause under which the seller of farm equipment tries to deny liability for any consequential damages arising from the malfunction of the equipment.

There is no rule of law that automatically nullifies an exclusion clause where there has been a fundamental breach. The question of whether there has been a fundamental breach or whether an exclusionary clause is applicable to such a breach is to be determined by a true construction of the entire contract.

GAFCO ENTERPRISES v. SCHOFIELD

Alberta, 1983

The respondent, Schofield, purchased from the appellant, Gafco Enterprises, a 1980 Volkswagen Scirocco with an odometer reading of 12 723 km. The car was equipped with a turbocharger and the seller told the purchaser that it was a good car. Schofield bought the car without test-driving it and without having a mechanic inspect it.

After driving it for only 12 km, the car gave evidence of problems. When Schofield returned it to the seller the next day, he was advised that the car had a serious engine problem that would require expensive repairs. Schofield sought to cancel the contract and to have his down payment refunded.

The contract stated that the car was sold "as is," without any warranty, and that the purchaser waived the provisions of the *Sale of Goods Act* with respect to any implied conditions or warranties. Schofield argued that there had been a total failure of consideration and that the disclaimer clause could not be a defence to the seller. The trial judge agreed with Schofield and ordered the contract rescinded. Gafco Enterprises appealed and the Court of Appeal held that the contract was binding.

> *In determining what the parties contemplated when the contract was made, the court must first construe the entire contract, including any clause which purports to qualify the obligations of one party ... The approach of the House of Lords in* Photo Production *was approved and adopted by the Supreme Court of Canada in* Beaufort Realties v. Chomedey Aluminum *(1980). I am of the view that the learned trial judge erred in his approach to this case. While there may have been some doubt in the past, it is now clear that there is no substantive rule of law that nullifies an exclusionary clause where there has been a fundamental breach. The question of whether there has been a fundamental breach or whether an exclusionary clause is applicable to such a breach is to be determined according to a true construction of the entire contract, including any exemption clauses contained therein. Within the limits that exemption clauses should not be construed so as to deprive one party's stipulation of all contractual force, they must be given effect where their meaning is plain. The defects in the Scirocco do not amount to a breach going to the root of the contract. They are repairable, albeit at some expense.*

REMEDIES OF THE UNPAID SELLER

If the seller is not paid for the goods sold to the buyer, the seller is given certain remedies under the *Sale of Goods Act*. The seller must act to protect his or her interests, but must do so in a manner that does not create liability for some other reason. For example, some contracts call for delayed payment. If the buyer's credit rating suddenly dropped, the seller would still be on shaky grounds to refuse to deliver.

REFUSE TO DELIVER

If the goods are sold but not paid for, the seller may refuse to turn them over to the buyer until paid. In doing this, the seller is essentially exercising a right of lien (the right to hold property as security) over the goods.

In *Jankins v. Corona Motors* (Ontario, 1968) the plaintiff, Jankins, signed a contract for the purchase of a truck for his farming business. The agreement was a conditional sale agreement, with payments to take place over 36 months. The defendant heard rumours that the plaintiff was in serious financial trouble and might go bankrupt. When the truck arrived, the defendant demanded full cash payment before turning it over to Jankins. The plaintiff sued and the Court held that the plaintiff was entitled to delivery of the truck as the contract stated.

STOP IN TRANSIT

If the goods are shipped but not paid for, the seller may reroute the goods to another destination or stop the goods from being delivered. The seller must be careful in doing this, because if the goods are stopped wrongly, the seller may be guilty of breach of contract. Only an unpaid seller may effect this remedy against an insolvent buyer.

RESELL THE GOODS

The seller may notify the buyer that unless he or she takes possession of the goods, they will be sold elsewhere. This is of particular importance if the goods are perishable, because they must be sold before they perish. The law requires the unpaid seller to take action to minimize the loss. The buyer may be liable for the difference between the agreed price in the contract and what the seller was able to get in the available market. The seller cannot sacrifice the goods, meaning the seller must attempt to obtain the best price possible under current conditions.

SUE FOR BREACH OF CONTRACT

A sale of goods contract is enforceable just like any other contract. Neither party can avoid the contract at will. The seller may sue the buyer either for specific performance or for damages. Specific performance is one of the remedies open to both parties under a sale of goods contract.

More than price may be sought by the seller in some jurisdictions. In Alberta, British Columbia, and Saskatchewan, the seller may also sue for interest on the price from the date of tender of the goods.

REMEDIES OF THE BUYER

If the buyer feels that the seller is guilty of breach of contract in some manner, there are various remedies available. The buyer is sometimes forced to choose between trying to enforce the original contract and abandoning the contract and suing for damages.

SUE FOR SPECIFIC PERFORMANCE

If the buyer wants the terms of the contract carried out, the buyer may sue for specific performance. The buyer asks the court that, as a remedy, the seller be required to deliver the goods at the agreed price. Specific performance will be granted where the goods were distinct or irreplaceable, such that the buyer cannot obtain them elsewhere.

SUE FOR DAMAGES

As an alternative to specific performance, the seller can be sued for damages. If the buyer suffers financial loss because the seller fails to deliver as agreed, damages can be sought. In the event that the buyer must buy the same goods elsewhere at a higher price, the buyer may recover these increased costs.

In *George Reed Inc. v. Nelson Machinery Co.* (British Columbia, 1973) the plaintiff purchased a used rock crusher from the defendant. The contract stated: "All equipment to be reconditioned as necessary." The crusher repeatedly broke down, causing the plaintiff to incur expensive work stoppages. The Court held that the defendant was in breach of a warranty to provide a properly reconditioned machine.

RESCIND THE CONTRACT

If the buyer does not receive the goods, and it appears that the seller is not going to be able to deliver on time or according to agreed conditions, the buyer may notify the seller that the entire contract is being cancelled and that the buyer is going to look elsewhere for the goods.

In *Marinovich v. Riverside Chrysler Ltd.* (Ontario, 1987) the plaintiff sought to cancel the purchase of an automobile from the defendant. He also sought the return of his deposit. The automobile was delivered with a defective paint application. The defendant offered to repaint the car locally, but the plaintiff refused to accept this.

The Court ruled in favour of the plaintiff, saying that a local paint job could not equal factory painting. The plaintiff's refusal to accept the car was reasonable.

SEEK A PRICE ADJUSTMENT

If the seller substantially performs the contract but does not fulfil it completely, the buyer may seek an adjustment to the purchase price to compensate for the seller's failure to deliver the total amount of goods as agreed. The amount of damages would be roughly equal to the amount necessary to put the seller in the same position as if the contract had been completed.

CONDITIONAL SALES

Under an absolute sale, title passes immediately to the buyer upon the conclusion of the agreement. A **conditional sale** is one in which the title does not pass to the buyer until certain conditions are met, the most important being payment of the total price, which includes an interest charge. Entering into a conditional sale contract is also known as paying on the instalment plan.

THE CONDITIONAL SALE CONTRACT

The conditional sale contract is a lengthy document and we will not attempt to examine all of the possible terms in detail. The most important information to be included in the contract falls into the following general categories:

1. Identification of the goods and acknowledgment by the buyer that they have been received.
2. The total price and all other items, including interest, instalment payments, etc. The interest rate must be expressed as a true annual percentage.
3. A statement that the seller remains the owner until the buyer makes the last payment.
4. Authority for the seller to repossess if the buyer does not make the payments.
5. The right of the seller to resell the goods if the buyer does not redeem them within a certain period. In most provinces the buyer must redeem the goods by making up missed payments within 20 days. Some contracts have "acceleration" or "balloon" clauses which require the buyer to pay the remaining balance if one payment is missed.
6. The obligation of the buyer to make good any deficiency still remaining after resale.
7. A promise by the buyer not to remove, resell, or dispose of the goods in any way without the written consent of the seller. In some contracts the buyer promises to insure the goods as well.

REGISTRATION OF A CONTRACT

The person who buys goods under a conditional sale contract obtains use of the goods but not title to them. The seller has a concern that the buyer will resell the goods to an unsuspecting person who does not know that the goods belong to the seller. To prevent this, provincial law permits the registration of a conditional sale contract at the registry office. The seller must register the contract within a set period, ranging from 10 to 30 days, to protect his or her interest. The purpose of registration is to give notice to any potential buyer of the goods that the goods belong to the original seller and not to the person who presently has them.

In most provinces, goods that are sold to a dealer for resale pass to the subsequent buyer with good title, even though a contract may have been registered. Thus, if Green buys a car from Brown Motors, Green gets good title even though Brown may not have paid the manufacturer. The most expansive application of the rule is in British Columbia where the rule of **market overt** is the provincial law. Where goods are sold in an open market, according to the usage of the market, the buyer acquires good title provided that he or she buys in good faith and without notice of any defect or problem of title on the part of the seller. A market overt is an open, public, and legally constituted market. Thus, a person who buys something in a shop or store, during business hours, need have no concern about acquiring title to the goods.

CANADIAN IMPERIAL BANK OF COMMERCE v. PEAKER

British Columbia, 1989

The defendant borrowed money from the plaintiff bank to buy a used car. The loan was secured by a promissory note and a chattel mortgage on the car. Unfortunately, the car turned out to be stolen and it was returned to its rightful owner. The chattel mortgage was rendered worthless, but the bank sued upon the promissory note.

The defendant argued that the bank was negligent in not checking the vehicle's registration before approving the loan. The bank argued that it relies upon the borrower's representations and does not make any inspection of the vehicle or check title.

The Court held that the defendant must repay the money. The bank's policy of not checking the vehicle registration may be unwise, but it is not negligence. The defendant was buying the car and the defendant had the duty to check the registration.

A serious problem is posed by out-of-province liens. People sometimes sell goods in one province that are subject to liens in other provinces. These may not show up in a search at the Registry Office. The unpaid creditor often has a considerable advantage by a provision in the law of most provinces that allows this creditor to register his or her lien within a certain time period after learning that goods have been moved to another province. If the creditor does this properly, the lien is deemed to have been registered all along, even though it was not.

In Ontario, a security interest in one province can be perfected (completed and made enforceable) in Ontario within 15 days after the secured party receives notice that the goods are now in Ontario. In British Columbia, the creditor has 21 days to register. Therefore, it is extremely dangerous to buy goods from a person who has recently moved from one province to another. A national registry system would help solve this problem, but no such system exists.

PERSONAL PROPERTY SECURITY REGISTRATION (PPSR) SYSTEM

Alberta, British Columbia, Saskatchewan, Ontario, and Manitoba have developed a computerized registration system that makes it quicker and easier to determine who owns goods that are being resold. When the original sale is made, the seller registers the contract by completing a financing statement, which is fed into a computer. The information is available to all Registry Offices in the province. The information is filed under two headings: under the name of the debtor, and under a description of the goods. For the payment of a small fee, a potential purchaser can learn if any properly registered claim against the goods exists anywhere in the province. For the payment of a slightly higher fee, the office will provide a certificate guaranteeing that, as of the date and time of inquiry, the goods were free from any claim.

If it later turns out that the Registry Office made a mistake, there is an insurance fund to reimburse the purchaser for any loss incurred as a result of trusting the accuracy of the information. In the case of a motor vehicle, the search can be made by the serial number of the vehicle. The system can check not only conditional sale contracts but also can determine if the goods being sold have been pledged as security for a loan.

When a PPSR system is adopted, other legislation with respect to personal property security is repealed. For example, legislation involving conditional sale contracts and chattel mortgages will be rescinded. The PPSR system replaces numerous security documents with a single registration document. The property to which the security interest attaches is generally called the **collateral**. The security agreement then perfects the creditor's interest.

ASSIGNMENT OF CONTRACT

It is a common practice for sellers to assign conditional sale contracts to finance companies. Most auto dealers make the arrangement with the manufacturer's own financing company. Thus, a person who buys a General Motors product will ultimately finance the car through General Motors Acceptance Corporation (GMAC). In reality, the dealer is the seller, who then assigns the contract to GMAC. The seller does not require the consent of the buyer to assign the contract. The buyer must be notified of the assignment and to whom to make payment. The debt of the buyer cannot be increased by the assignment.

REPOSSESSION

The seller has the right to repossess the goods if the buyer does not carry out the condition of making the payments. Keep in mind that the seller owns the goods and is only recovering his or her property, not taking something that belongs to the buyer. Seizure of the goods is legal, without any further due process of law. It is seldom done (with the possible exception of vehicles which can easily be removed from the street), because violent objection is quite possible. If the debtor refuses to give up the goods, the creditor can revert to the courts.

In most provinces, the seller must notify the buyer that repossession is going to take place. A few provinces do not allow repossession without a court order. In Ontario, New Brunswick, and Nova Scotia, the seller may not repossess if the buyer has paid two-thirds of the purchase price or more, except by permission of a judge. Manitoba places the same restriction if 75 percent of the price has been paid.

The question arises as to how much force can be used to repossess. The contract itself may contain terms that allow the seller to break locks or enter premises to repossess. However, the use of excessive force is frowned upon by the courts, as the following case illustrates.

R. v. DOUCETTE

Ontario, 1960

Doucette was one of three men who were repossessing a television set. The men were bailiffs, but were acting privately and not in their legal capacity as bailiffs at the time. It was a common practice for bailiffs to hire out their services to private companies for this kind of work.

When the buyer vigorously protested the repossession, Doucette punched him. Doucette claimed that he thought the buyer was going to assault him, so he struck first. The judge convicted Doucette of assault saying:

> *Even though a person enters property lawfully for the purpose of repossession, if he assaults someone he becomes a trespasser. Once it was made clear that the television set would not be removed without resistance, they grossly exceeded their authority and abused the buyer's rights and became trespassers.*

In Alberta, British Columbia, Manitoba, and Newfoundland, the seller must "seize or sue" but cannot do both. That is, if the seller decides to repossess his or her goods, the seller forfeits the right to sue for any deficiency or amount still owed under the contract.

BUYER'S RIGHT TO REDEEM

Once the seller has repossessed the goods, the seller must give the buyer an opportunity to redeem (get back) the goods. The seller must keep the goods for the period stated in the provincial law, ranging from 14 to 21 days in most provinces. In Saskatchewan, Newfoundland, and New Brunswick, the buyer may redeem the goods by paying the amount due on the contract price, rather than the entire unpaid balance. No "balloon clauses" are allowed. Upon request, the seller must give the buyer a statement showing all pertinent details, to include the amount still owing, interest charges, storage charges, etc. The seller may charge the buyer for the cost of repossession, storing, and insuring the goods.

SELLER'S RIGHT OF RESALE

If the buyer does not redeem the goods, the seller has the right to resell them. The resale may be made by private sale or auction. The seller cannot sacrifice the goods, which means to sell them for any low price possible just to get rid of them. Nor may the seller purchase the goods personally.

If the amount obtained on resale is less than that still owed by the buyer, this is called the "deficiency upon resale." In those provinces where there is no "seize or sue" law, the buyer remains liable for this deficiency. The seller cannot buy the goods himself or herself at a low price. For example, a seller may be the owner or principal shareholder of several companies. If the buyer does not redeem the goods, the seller may be tempted to sell the goods to another of his or her companies at a very low price, in effect sacrificing the goods. The rule is that the subsequent sale must be "at arm's length," meaning to a truly independent third party at a fair price.

In *Vlakhas v. Broadstreet* (Ontario, 1973) the buyer failed to pay for office furniture that had been sold on the instalment plan, then repossessed for non-payment. The seller owned both a new office furniture store and a used office furniture store. The furniture was resold at a very low price to the company that operated the used furniture store. In effect, the seller had resold the goods to himself. The Court refused to hold the buyer liable upon the deficiency, saying that the resale was a sham.

CHATTEL MORTGAGE CONTRACTS

A **chattel mortgage** is a contract under which the owner of goods assigns title to the goods to another person in consideration of a debt. A **chattel** is any form of tangible, personal property other than land or buildings. The chattel mortgage was the first form of debt which allowed the borrower to maintain possession of the goods. For example, if Brown wants to borrow money from the Steady Bank, the bank would like some security, or collateral. If Brown owns his automobile, the bank could ask Brown to sign a chattel mortgage on the vehicle. The document transfers legal title of the vehicle to the bank, but this is not a true sale, because the title must be returned upon payment. The car is still in Brown's possession and is still registered in his name with the provincial motor vehicle registration office. However, Brown cannot legally sell the car to someone else, because the bank now holds title to it. The bank, in order to protect its interest, must register the chattel mortgage at the local registry office so any perspective buyer can learn about the chattel mortgage.

For example, suppose that Brown now decides to trade in his old car and buy a new one. If the automobile dealership is careful, it will use the serial number of Brown's car to check for any such liens. The chattel mortgage will prevent Brown from concluding the sale. Brown could make arrangements with the Steady Bank to discharge the chattel mortgage on the old car and sign a new mortgage on the new car.

If payments are not made, the mortgagee may take possession of the goods and sell them. As is true with any resale, the mortgagee must sell the goods at arm's length and not sacrifice the goods at a very low price.

A chattel mortgage may be assigned if the mortgagee so desires, and this may be done without the consent of the mortgagor. The formalities of assignment must be complied with and the mortgagor must be notified of the assignment.

BILL OF SALE

A **bill of sale** is a document representing the sale of goods of any type. In some situations, the normal status is reversed: rather than the buyer taking possession of the goods with the promise to pay the seller later, it is also possible that the buyer pays for the goods but the seller temporarily keeps possession of them. In this case, the buyer would require some proof that the goods in the seller's possession actually belong to the buyer.

It is for the buyer's protection, then, that a bill of sale is signed. It may be registered to prevent the seller from selling the goods again to another person.

REVIEW: POINTS OF LAW

1. Title to goods passes to the buyer when the goods are in a deliverable condition, but the seller does not have to deliver them.
2. Once goods have become ascertained, risk passes to the buyer.
3. A condition is an essential part of a sale contract. Failure to fulfil a condition can mean failure of the entire contract.
4. A warranty is not an essential part of the contract. It is a separate agreement that runs alongside the contract.
5. Even if no specific warranties come with goods, there are implied conditions and warranties that apply to all goods.
6. A disclaimer clause can limit the liability of the seller, but it cannot excuse the seller from all responsibility.
7. Under a conditional sale contract, the seller remains the owner of the goods until the buyer makes the last payment.
8. A seller may repossess goods if the buyer does not make payments. However, in some provinces, the seller must "seize or sue" but cannot do both.
9. If the seller repossesses the goods, they may be resold and the buyer will be liable for any deficiency remaining.
10. Before purchasing used goods, a potential buyer should check the local Registry Office to determine if the seller holds valid title to the goods.

LEGAL BRIEFS

1. D buys a travel trailer from R Trailer Sales. D wants certain details changed before accepting the trailer. D pays $5000 down and agrees to pay the final $3000 when the changes are made. R telephones D two weeks later and says, "Your trailer is ready." No prior discussion had been held about pickup or delivery. D replies, "I don't have my trailer hitch installed yet. Can you deliver it?" R agrees to deliver the trailer, without additional fee. While towing the trailer to D's home, a sudden, powerful wind tips the trailer over. Neither party has insurance on the trailer. Who bears the loss?

2. R ships a quantity of hogs to B, a packer in the United States. A U.S. Customs officer stops delivery of the hogs because there is no veterinarian's inspection certificate with the hogs. R then faxes a message to the U.S. buyer that the hogs have been delivered and can be picked up at the customs point. B refuses to accept this as delivery. Who will succeed?
3. G purchases a used truck from M. The truck is sold with a minimal, 30-day warranty. During the first 30 days, the truck breaks down twice and M makes the repairs. After the 30-day period has expired, the truck breaks down so often that it is useless. G demands that M take back the truck and refund the money. M refuses, saying that the warranty was for 30 days and it was duly honoured. After 30 days, G bears the risk. G argued that the truck was so bad there was a total failure of consideration. Who is correct?
4. W sells goods to V and ships them by rail. W hears that V is close to bankruptcy and reroutes the shipment elsewhere. Without the goods, V loses a good customer and goes into bankruptcy. V sues W, arguing that it was close to bankruptcy but it was W's action of not delivering the goods which actually pushed the company over the edge. W counterargues that its information was correct—V was going bankrupt—and therefore rerouting was justified. Who will succeed?
5. O is thinking of buying a used car. P, the seller, has the provincial registration card for the vehicle and an insurance card. O believes that this is sufficient to obtain good title to the car. Advise O.
6. F purchases a carload of lumber from W. F's representative inspects the first 20 bundles offloaded from the car and finds them very satisfactory. F accepts the shipment and makes full payment to W. Two weeks later, as F's employees open the bundles, they find that the lumber in the centre is of a lesser grade and quality than the lumber on the outside. It appears that the bundles were deliberately made up to conceal the poor lumber in the middle of the bundles. What recourse has F?
7. S bought a new car and made three payments to a finance company. S is involved in a major auto accident and the bank learns that shortly after buying the car, the company insuring the car cancelled the insurance policy because S had concealed previous accidents when completing the application form. S drove the car without insurance, contrary to the terms of the loan agreement. The bank demands the balance of the loan, to which S replies, "You can have the car. Repossess it." Is S correct that the bank has no recourse other than taking the wrecked car?
8. H buys a car on credit and is making payments to the K finance company. H then tries to borrow money from the B Bank and offers to pledge the car as collateral. The bank refuses to grant the loan. H does not understand the problem. Explain to H why the bank denied the loan application.

APPLYING THE LAW

KAVCAR INVESTMENTS LTD. v. AETNA FINANCIAL SERVICES

Ontario, 1986

The plaintiffs took over a hardware business in 1980. The business was losing money, but the plaintiffs believed they could make it profitable. The Federal Business Development Bank gave them a loan of $270 000 conditional upon their being able to borrow $800 000 from a bank. Aetna approved an operating loan of $900 000, with the Toronto Dominion Bank participating on the first $300 000. The remaining $600 000 was to be paid on sums advanced at prime plus 6 percent.

As security, Aetna took a demand debenture for $1 million plus an assignment of book debts, personal guarantees, an assignment of life insurance, and the pledge of savings bonds of one of the partners.

Problems arose when Kavcar repeatedly exceeded its credit limit with the bank. It was clear to Aetna that Kavçar did not have the necessary capital to operate under the line of credit the financing company was prepared to offer. Aetna believed that Kavcar would lose $30 000 in the first year of operation and then become profitable. It was shocked to receive financial statements showing that Kavcar lost $200 000 in its first year. The lender decided to call the loan.

Aetna wrote to Kavcar demanding $746 000, indicating its intention to put the borrower into receivership. The debenture contract contained a clause that said the lender could call the loan if it deemed itself to be "insecure." Aetna then put Kavcar into receivership the same day, without giving the company any chance to respond to the demand. The assets of the company were seized and sold by the receiver. The sale netted $91 000 more than was required to retire the loan. In its suit, the plaintiffs asked for $1.7 million in damages for trespass, breach of contract, and unlawful conversion of property.

The Court ruled in favour of the plaintiffs, noting that a debtor must be given reasonable time to respond to a demand by a creditor. It was reasonable that Kavcar could have found alternative financing.

Questions

1. The borrower had not failed to make any of the payments on its loan. What, then, was the basis for the lender demanding full payment?
2. It was once a common practice for lenders to demand payment of a loan

and seize assets the same day. Why did such a practice exist?

3. Why did the Court rule that the defendants had trespassed and unlawfully seized the property of the plaintiff when the debenture gave them that right?
4. Relying upon this case, what is the rule regarding a lender demanding full repayment from a creditor?

PARLBY CONSTRUCTION v. STEWART EQUIPMENT

British Columbia, 1971

The defendant, an equipment auctioneer, sold at auction a Caterpillar tractor that had been consigned to him for sale by someone unknown. The defendant had prepared a flyer in which the machine was described as "very good" and its undercarriage as "new."

Persuaded by these descriptions, the plaintiff bought the tractor at the auction. Its condition was found to be poor and not as described in the flyer. The defendant sought to rely upon a catalogue that accompanied the flyer and upon the registration card that the plaintiff had signed when he had come to the auction. The card included the words: "I agree to abide by the said conditions in accordance with the published conditions of sale. I further agree that there is no representation, warranty, collateral agreement or condition affecting my purchases other than as expressed herein in writing." Before the sale started, the auctioneer read these words aloud.

The Court held that the plaintiff was entitled to cancel the contract and to have its money refunded. There was no doubt that both the flyer and the catalogue contained misrepresentations as to the condition of the tractor and that the plaintiff had been enticed by those words to buy it. The conditions of sale on which the defendant relied had been brought to the plaintiff's attention, but the evidence showed that the defendant could not have had an honest belief in the truth of them. The defendant's conduct amounted to fraud, which disentitled him to the protection of the disclaimer clause upon which he relied.

Questions

1. What is a disclaimer clause?
2. Under what circumstances will a disclaimer clause protect the seller? When will it not protect the seller?

3. In this case, the defendant published a flyer containing claims that the machine was in good condition, then put a clause in the contract saying that it made no claims. This is a contradiction. How did the Court handle this?
4. This case occurred before the *Photo Production* case. If it had been argued after that case, would the decision have been the same? Give reasons for your answer.

PRINCIPLES AND CASES

Case 1: Legal Principle

A warranty is not an essential part of the sale agreement. A warranty is a collateral agreement that runs alongside the sale agreement. A warranty is not automatically imposed by the seller. In some situations the buyer must request it or register the purchase.

Case Facts

The plaintiff purchased a mobile home, receiving a warranty card that was not effective unless returned to the manufacturer. The defendant dealer did not point this out to the plaintiff, but only said: "Here is your warranty card."

The plaintiff believed he had a full warranty, but did not mail in the card. The mobile home developed moisture problems. The manufacturer suggested a solution which was rejected by the plaintiff, who wanted the contract rescinded and a full refund. The plaintiff sued the manufacturer and the dealer.

Possible Decisions

A The plaintiff is entitled to a refund because the dealer did not point out to him that he had to register the warranty.

B The plaintiff is entitled to a refund because the implied conditions and warranties in the *Sale of Goods Act* would apply.

C The plaintiff is not entitled to a refund because the warranty was conditional upon registering the warranty.

D The plaintiff is not entitled to a refund because the warranty is not part of the basic sale contract. It is a separate agreement.

Case 2: Legal Principle

There is an implied condition under the *Sale of Goods Act* that goods will correspond to the description given of them. However, a seller must inspect the goods within a reasonable period of time.

Case Facts

The plaintiff corporation agreed to purchase from the defendant a number of cowhides described as being of No. 1 and 2 grades. Delivery was to be made to the premises of Canada Packers, where the hides were stored. The buyer did not go and inspect the hides at Canada Packers as it did not know if it would be permitted to inspect them there. The hides were moved to the premises of the buyer and were inspected immediately upon delivery. They were defective and of a low grade.

The buyer telephoned the seller and told him the hides were not being accepted. The buyer then sent a letter to the seller to come and pick up the hides. The seller did not reply to the letter, so the buyer took the hides to the seller's place of business. The seller refused to take them back.

The seller sued for the purchase price and alleged that delivery had taken place at Canada Packers and the agreement was binding. Testimony was given by a representative of Canada Packers that the buyer could have inspected the hides there if it wanted to do so. The buyer argued that it did not have reasonable opportunity to inspect the hides until they were moved to its premises.

Possible Decisions

A The seller is entitled to payment because the buyer failed to inspect the goods within a reasonable time and notify the seller of any defects. The buyer made no real effort to inspect the goods at Canada Packers.

B The seller is entitled to payment because the act of the buyer in moving the goods to its own premises was acceptance.

C The buyer is entitled to cancel the contract because the goods did not match the description in the contract.

D The buyer is entitled to cancel the contract because the buyer notified the seller by letter that the hides were defective and did so in a reasonable period of time.

YOU BE THE JUDGE

1. The plaintiff suffered food poisoning after eating in the restaurant owned by the defendant. The normal course in such a case is to bring an action based upon negligence. However, the plaintiff brought the action based upon breach of contract under the *Sale of Goods Act*. The Act provides that there is an implied condition that goods supplied under a contract of sale are reasonably fit for the purpose for which they are required. There is also an implied condition that the goods will be of a merchantable quality. The defendant argued that the *Sale of Goods Act* did not apply to restaurant meals. Who would succeed?

2. The plaintiffs, after reading an advertisement placed by the defendant pool manufacturer, had a swimming pool installed at their home. The advertisement stressed the durability of the pool and emphasized a 15-year warranty. The plaintiffs were not given a warranty, but were given an advertisement in which the warranty was reproduced. It appeared as an impressive-looking, legal document but the words were not legible in the advertisement without a magnifying glass. The pool was installed by a local contractor who was the authorized dealer of the defendant. The pool deteriorated due to improper installation. In court, the defendant relied upon the wording in the warranty that restricted the defendant's warranty to the quality of the individual components, but did not cover improper installation. Who would succeed?

3. The plaintiff bought a new truck from the defendant with the intent of expanding his business. The new truck caused problems from the beginning and the plaintiff took it back many times. Some problems were corrected, but some were not, including a vibration and rear end bounce. The plaintiff took the truck to numerous specialists but none could solve the problems. The plaintiff's drivers refused to have anything to do with the truck, which they considered unsafe. The plaintiff returned the truck to the defendant and demanded a new truck or his money back. The defendant would not comply and relied upon a clause in the contract that said that there were no conditions or warranties, express or implied, in the contract. Who would succeed?

4. The plaintiff repossessed three trucks which had been sold to the defendant under a conditional sale contract. The vehicles had a book value of $110 000 but the plaintiff resold them for $32 000 to another

trucking company, claiming: "The market for used trucks is very poor right now. I was lucky to get anyone to buy them." The plaintiff also sued the defendant for the deficiency. The defendant learned that the trucking company, to whom the trucks had been resold, was owned by the plaintiff's brother and that the plaintiff owned a 15-percent share of the trucking business. Who would succeed?

5. The plaintiff placed an order with the defendant to purchase a large supply of compact disc players. The contract did not specifically state that the devices would comply with Canadian Standards Association (CSA) requirements. However, the plaintiff assumed that the players would meet these standards because they had been imported into Canada from the Far East. When the players arrived, they contained stickers which read "CSA Approved." The plaintiff sold the players to its customers and, when one of the players caught fire, it was learned that the players had never been checked by the CSA and that the stickers were bogus. The plaintiff sued for cancellation of the contract and refund of its money. The defendant argued that the contract did not specifically call for CSA approval and therefore its absence was not breach of contract. Who would succeed?

6. The plaintiff bought a used car from the defendant car dealer. The odometer had a low reading on it and the defendant told the plaintiff that it was "a good car." The plaintiff bought the car without test-driving it and without having a mechanic check it over. The contract said that the car was sold "as is" and that there was no warranty on the car of any kind. The car developed serious problems within a week and the plaintiff sought to have the contract rescinded and his money refunded. The plaintiff argued that there was a fundamental breach. The defendant argued that the car was repairable and that he was not aware of the problem when the car was sold. Who would succeed?

7. The defendant ordered printed envelopes from the plaintiff printer. The envelopes were to have the return address of the defendant printed in the top left corner. When the envelopes were delivered, it was discovered that the plaintiff had misspelled the defendant's name. The defendant rejected the entire shipment of 100 000 envelopes. The plaintiff sued, arguing that the envelopes were usable as envelopes and the spelling problem was a minor matter that might entitle the defendant to a price reduction, but was not justification for refusing to accept the envelopes. The defendant argued that the spelling error was embarrassing and a fundamental breach of the contract. Who would succeed?

C H A P T E R   N I N E

CONSUMER PROTECTION

> *"Advertising is still the cheapest way to sell worthless goods."*
>
> Sinclair Lewis, author

FEDERAL CONSUMER PROTECTION LAWS

Throughout most of recorded history, consumer protection was almost unknown. The accepted belief was that consumers had to look out for themselves and if "a fool and his gold are soon parted," then so be it. Parents told fables, such as "Jack and the Beanstalk," to children to warn them against dishonest strangers who might persuade them to trade a cow for a handful of beans.

During the period from 1960 to 1980, however, governments enacted a virtual blizzard of consumer protection legislation. The breathtaking scope of these laws demonstrate that the basic sale of goods legislation was inadequate to regulate dishonest consumer practices.

The rules of the marketplace, having worked so well for centuries, suddenly appeared outmoded. What had happened to make them obsolete? There are many possible answers to this question, but five factors have contributed toward the demand that government intrude directly into the marketplace:

1. **Increasing array of packaged goods**: Traditionally, buyers examined the goods they bought before they accepted them. This is seldom possible today, since many goods are packaged in cardboard or plastic, or sealed in metal containers, which cannot be opened. Therefore, the consumer has to accept the quality of the goods as they are described rather than being able to examine the goods themselves. Only when the package has been opened does the consumer learn what he or she has purchased.
2. **Growth of the international economy**: In early times, goods were generally sold close to their place of manufacture. If buyers did not like the quality of the things they bought, they could go to the manufacturer and complain of the poor quality. Today, international trade has expanded to the extent that many products available to the consumer are of foreign manufacture. Some products, such as automobiles, contain components from a half-dozen countries. Consumers find that the agent of a foreign manufacturer can play a cagey game of passing blame for a defective product onto the distant manufacturer, knowing that the consumer cannot communicate directly with the manufacturer.
3. **Obscure manufacturers**: Today, consumers commonly purchase products marked "Manufactured for the ABC Corporation." The label "ABC Corporation" on a product does not indicate who actually made the product. General Electric no longer produces household appliances, but many are sold with the GE label. IBM does not manufacture the computer printers that bear its name. The reverse is also true: many no-name products are actually made by major manufacturers, including such items as paint, automobile

tires, and television sets. The consumer cannot rely upon a brand name for quality in the true sense.

4. **Complexity of products**: Advances in modern technology have resulted in consumer products that are so complicated that consumers cannot evaluate them. They must rely upon the claims made by the manufacturer or by reports and opinions published by consumer advisory services.
5. **Media power and influence**: Two hundred years ago, advertising consisted of a seller standing in a marketplace and shouting at passers-by. Today, television, radio, and newspaper advertising reaches millions of potential consumers. Deceptive advertising can net the seller millions of dollars, while injuring honest competitors and disrupting the marketplace. Although advertising is a form of expression, governments must act to prevent wide-scale fraud that can span continents.

DEFINITION OF A CONSUMER

Although there are numerous statutes that use the word **consumer**, very few statutes offer a definition of the term. For example, the federal *Bills of Exchange Act* does not define "consumer," but defines a "consumer purchase" as follows:

> 188. In this Part, "consumer purchase" means a purchase, other than a cash purchase, of goods or services or an agreement to purchase goods or services
> (a) by an individual other than for resale or for use in the course of his business, profession or calling, and
> (b) from a person who is engaged in the business of selling or providing those goods or services

Various provincial laws tend to follow the same course, defining the transaction rather than the consumer. This is not an omission on the part of the various legislatures, but rather a recognition that the transaction is more readily defined and recognized.

A notable exception to the rule is the Ontario *Business Practices Act*, which defines a consumer as: "a natural person, but does not include a natural person, business partnership, or association of individuals acting in the course of carrying on a business."

It is uniformly accepted that a consumer is a natural person rather than a company or a corporation. It is generally viewed that an individual who engages in some form of transaction for a business is not acting as a consumer. A person who buys a vehicle for personal use is a consumer. If the same person buys a vehicle for the use of his or her business, the person is not acting as a consumer and the protective statutes may not apply. Also, business partnerships, companies, and corporations are not considered to be "natural persons" and are not covered by the legislation.

Not only is there no clear-cut definition of a consumer, there is also no clear distinction, under the *Constitution Act, 1867*, as to which level of government should protect the consumer. Each government must try to legislate within a field specifically assigned to it by the Constitution. For example, the federal government may legislate in the fields of weights and measures, postal services, bills of exchange, interprovincial trade and others. In this section, we will not attempt to deal with every such statute, but only with those that most directly affect consumer protection.

BILLS OF EXCHANGE ACT

The *Bills of Exchange Act*, modelled after a similar law passed in England, defines what are considered to be bills of exchange or negotiable instruments. The negotiable instrument used most often in consumer transactions is the promissory note, which is discussed more fully in Chapter 12.

Promissory notes are commonly signed when a person buys something on the instalment plan. The note is a promise to pay, which is enforceable solely on its face. No other conditions need to be proven to enforce collection. Notes can be transferred to another party, such as a bank or finance company, and can be collected by that party as a **holder in due course**. A holder in due course is a person who has taken a bill in good faith and for value, complete and regular on its face, without notice that it has been previously dishonoured.

The promissory note lends itself well to a dishonest selling scheme. The seller persuades the buyer to sign a conditional sale contract and a note. The note is then assigned to a finance company. The buyer, realizing the sales scheme is not honest, tries to stop making his or her instalment payments. However, the finance company can collect upon the note. Any dispute between the buyer and seller is a personal dispute that does not involve the finance company, which is legally classed as an innocent holder in due course. The buyer is outflanked by the team of the seller and the finance company.

Faced with numerous complaints about the abuse of promissory notes, the federal government amended the *Bills of Exchange Act* in an important way that greatly restricts their use as part of dishonest sales schemes. The amendment provided that notes given in connection with consumer purchases must be legibly marked on their faces with the words "Consumer Purchase." Where a promissory note is so marked, the purchaser has the same defences against the claims of a holder in due course as he or she would have had against a claim made by the seller. Finance companies may no longer rely on the status of holder in due course and insulate themselves from disputes between buyers and sellers over delivery, performance, service, quality, warranties, and other aspects of sale contracts. This does not imply that the buyer is always right. The court must still hear the case on its merits. If the buyer does not have a legitimate grievance, the buyer must pay the note.

Dishonest vendors can no longer operate as they did in the past because they will have trouble persuading finance companies to take notes off their hands. Not all transactions are consumer purchaser transactions. If a person borrows money from a bank and signs a promissory note, the note need not be marked. Nor does the law extend to business transactions.

CANADIAN IMPERIAL BANK OF COMMERCE v. LIVELY et al.

Nova Scotia, 1974

One of the defendants, Roberts, had sold some chinchillas and related equipment to the defendant Lively. The purchase was financed by a bank loan secured by a promissory note. Roberts arranged the bank loan through a contact at the bank. The money was paid by the bank directly to Roberts and the bank took the promissory note from Lively.

The defendant Lively did not make any money raising chinchillas and stopped payment on the note. Lively argued that Roberts had deceived him about the potential profit of the business just to unload the equipment and animals on him. The bank then brought an action against both Lively and Roberts.

It was argued for Lively that the note had been given on a consumer purchase and, since it had not been marked "Consumer Purchase," it was void. The Court held that the plaintiff bank could collect upon the note. The purchase of the chinchillas and equipment was not a consumer purchase, but rather was for use in a business.

FOOD AND DRUGS ACT

It is a basic right of Canadians to consume food and drugs that are safe, free from contaminants, and properly labelled.

The origins of the *Food and Drugs Act* can be traced back to England where it was once commonplace for merchants to try to hide deterioration in food by the use of spices and other ingredients. Food was often found to contain arrowroot, chicory, plaster of Paris, and peppermint. In 1861, the British Parliament passed the first law prohibiting the adulteration of food and drink. In 1874, the Canadian Parliament passed the *Adulteration Act*. It required that food be clean and safe to eat and no poisonous additives be used. This law was replaced by the present statute in 1920.

The passage of laws against adulteration has not prevented its occurrence, often with disastrous results. In 1985, the government of Austria learned that some of its wine producers had put antifreeze into wine to speed up its fermentation. In 1990, the Italian government discovered the same thing had been done by some of its producers. Consumers of these wines could suffer nerve damage or blindness. In 1985, a Spanish company sold refined motor oil as cooking oil. Hundreds of consumers suffered permanent nerve damage or death.

The *Food and Drugs Act* is largely concerned with the use of drugs that are considered sufficiently dangerous to require restricted use. These drugs are controlled and can be obtained only by prescription. Drugs can be sold without prescription only if they are registered under the *Proprietary and Patent Medicine Act*. These products are subject to testing and general inspection, but not to the same extent as are prescription drugs.

Canadian law also requires that doctors and pharmacists advise consumers if a prescription drug can be purchased under its generic (basic chemical) name. These drugs are usually sold for a lower price, but contain the same elements. However, consumers should also be aware that generic-brand drugs are not as rigorously checked as the brand-name drugs. In 1989, the United States Food and Drug Administration learned that many generic-name companies had falsified the samples they submitted for testing. The *Food and Drugs Act* also covers food, household chemicals, cosmetics, medicines, and vitamins. It prohibits the advertisement of false cures for certain diseases including alcoholism, cancer, venereal disease, diabetes, leukemia, and many others. The Act provides that no drugs shall be sold that were prepared in unsanitary conditions. All drugs must be labelled under regulations prescribed by the Governor in Council.

As the next case illustrates, the power of the government to regulate the food industry is not absolute.

LABATT BREWERIES v. A.G. OF CANADA

Supreme Court of Canada, 1979

The plaintiff marketed a product called Labatt's Special Lite beer. The beer did not qualify as a "light beer" under federal regulations. Among other things, the regulation required that light beer have a maximum alcoholic content of 2.5 percent. Labatt's Special Lite beer contained 4 percent alcohol.

Although s. 91(2) of the *Constitution Act, 1867* makes the federal government responsible for trade and commerce and s. 91(27) makes the federal government responsible for criminal law, the Supreme Court of Canada held that the compositional standard for beer could not be justified as an exercise of either the trade and commerce power or the criminal law power. The Court thus invalidated an important feature of the *Food and Drugs Act*—the power of the federal government to set specific standards for what may be contained in food or drink.

The decision in the *Labatt* case did not mean the federal government could no longer regulate food and drink. The Court ruled that the government cannot tell manufacturers how to make their products. For example, the government could not publish "approved recipes" for ketchup, peanut butter, etc. However, the law does require that the ingredients be listed on the label to alert people with allergies which foods to avoid. The government can continue to inspect food and drink for cleanliness and safety, and also insist upon proper labelling so that consumers are aware of what they eat. For example, the common product "hamburger" may contain a certain quantity of fat and other wastes, and perhaps a small amount of pork. However, if pork was substituted for beef, then the meat would be dangerous because it might not be cooked in the proper manner.

Special problems arise with products that have secret recipes. Coca-Cola has never disclosed its recipe. Kentucky Fried Chicken claims that its coating is a secret blend of herbs and spices. Present regulations do not compel disclosure of recipes. Restaurants often spray their salad bars with a chemical known as potassium metabisulphite. This chemical slows the deterioration of raw vegetables. The same chemical is used to sterilize many glass bottles and jars. This spraying is lawful under present regulation. However, approximately 10 percent of Canadians are allergic to this chemical.

COMPETITION ACT

The *Competition Act* is a law of general application that establishes basic principles for the conduct of business in Canada. The purpose of the Act is to maintain and encourage competition in Canada in order to promote the efficiency and adaptability of the Canadian economy, expand opportunities for Canadian participation in world markets, ensure that small enterprises have a fair opportunity to participate in the economy, and provide consumers with competitive prices and product choices.

The legislation applies to all sectors of the Canadian economy and consequently affects service, resource, and manufacturing industries. All business activities are subject to the law, with the exception of a few activities such as collective bargaining and amateur sport. The Act is binding on Crown corporations.

The Act gives the Director of Investigation and Research responsibilities in relation to criminal offences, and reviewable matters including mergers, notifiable transactions, and representations to regulatory boards

Part VI of the Act prohibits a number of criminal offences, including bid-rigging, conspiracy to lessen competition unduly, price maintenance, and misleading advertising.

Part VIII identifies a number of matters reviewable by the Competition Tribunal, including mergers, abuse of dominant position, refusal to deal, tied selling, delivered pricing, and specialization agreements. The Tribunal is a specialized group composed of judges from the Federal Court of Canada and lay people appointed by the Governor General. Only the Director may bring an application to the Tribunal.

ENFORCEMENT PROCESS

Each year, numerous complaints are received from members of the public concerning conduct that may be subject to the *Competition Act*. The Director is required to commence an inquiry whenever he or she has reason to believe an offence has been or is about to be committed, that grounds exist for the Tribunal to make an order relating to a reviewable matter, or that a person has contravened or failed to comply with an order. The Director must also conduct an inquiry if the Minister of Consumer and Corporate Affairs directs the Director to do so, or when six Canadian residents make an application for an investigation. Any person may request an investigation, which the Director may carry out if the complaint appears to have merit.

Once an inquiry has begun, the Director may use a number of investigative tools provided in the legislation. He or she may apply to a court for authorization to enter and search premises and seize records identified in a warrant. The Director may also obtain a court order requiring any person having information relevant to an inquiry to produce records, to provide written information under oath or affirmation, or to appear before a presiding officer appointed under the Act and be examined on oath or affirmation. In *Thomson Newspapers v. Director of Investigation and Research* (1990), the Supreme Court of Canada held that this requirement to produce documents and give sworn evidence is not contrary to the *Charter of Rights and Freedoms*. The Court held that the power to compel testimony is an essential part of the investigative machinery established by the Act. The inquiry is inquisitorial rather than adversarial in nature and does not violate the protection against self-incrimination. The case was actually argued under the *Combines Investigation Act*, which was later replaced by the *Competition Act*, but the issues were the same.

The inquiry may be discontinued at any time. In criminal cases, the Director may refer the matter to the Attorney General of Canada, who decides if criminal charges should be laid. Each offence provision of the Act stipulates the amount of fine and term of imprisonment that may be imposed upon conviction. For example, the possible penalty for misleading advertising is a fine of $25 000 or imprisonment for one year or both. The maximum penalty for offences other than misleading advertising is a fine of $10 million or imprisonment for five years or both. In 1988, two companies were each fined $200 000 for rigging bids to supply business forms to the Nova Scotia government.

In addition to any penalty imposed upon conviction, the court may issue an order prohibiting that person from continuing or repeating the offence. Prohibition orders may also be issued without securing a conviction. The person subject to the order may challenge the order in court.

A person who has suffered loss or damage as a result of conduct contrary to the criminal provision of the Act may bring a civil action for damages. In *Westfair Foods v. Lippens* (Manitoba, 1989) the Manitoba Court of Appeal held that a breach of the *Competition Act* can be used to support an independent civil cause of action for unlawful interference with economic interests and conspiracy. That is, violation of the Act may give rise to an action in tort.

CRIMINAL OFFENCES UNDER THE ACT

The *Competition Act* makes it an offence for people to conspire, combine, agree, or arrange to unduly lessen competition. In establishing that a conspiracy exists, it is not necessary for the Crown to prove that competition would be completely eliminated from the market. The Crown must still prove the existence of an agreement.

The Act prohibits bid-rigging, which is the act of people agreeing not to submit a bid in response to a call for bids in order to allow a competitor to respond to that bid with a very high price. The parties involved in the conspiracy divide potential contracts among themselves and agree not to compete against each other. Another method is for every company except one to enter excessively high bids, then have the company that wins the contract share the profits with the other companies in the conspiracy. There have been such conspiracies in everything from harbour dredging to contracts to supply light bulbs. In a recent Ontario case, the conspirators were caught when a government department called a company to ask why it had not bid on a contract. The surprising reply was, "It's not our turn to win the contract."

R. v. BEVERAGE SERVICES LTD. et al.

Manitoba, 1988

Two companies pleaded guilty to bid-rigging in relation to an agreement to sell soft drinks in the Brandon trade area. The accused were the bottlers for the major soft-drink brands. The accused divided the area into two zones and declined to bid in each other's zone. The effect was to push up the price of soft drinks. Each company was fined $50 000.

However, in 1989, a number of Nova Scotia pharmacists, accused of fixing prices of drugs paid for by insurance companies, argued successfully that the conspiracy section of the *Competition Act* offends the *Charter of Rights and Freedoms.*

One of the most important areas in the Act is the one that deals with price maintenance or price discrimination. **Price discrimination** exists when a supplier charges different prices to competitors who purchase similar volumes of an article. Firms are competitors if they sell in the same market. Price discrimination does not include temporary concessions to help a new business get started or to conduct warehouse clearances. **Predatory pricing** is selling products at unreasonably low prices to eliminate a competitor. **Price maintenance** is an attempt by suppliers of goods, by agreement, threat, or promise, to force their buyers to raise the prices at which goods are sold or to maintain them at high levels. It is illegal to refuse to supply a product to any person because of his or her low pricing policy. It is also illegal to attempt to induce a supplier to engage in price maintenance. Price maintenance penalties include a fine or imprisonment for a term not exceeding five years, or both.

REVIEWABLE TRADE PRACTICES UNDER THE ACT

The Tribunal has jurisdiction to deal with and make orders concerning certain trade practices. One of these, **refusal to deal,** represents a major concern for a small business that finds its source of supply eliminated. The most common reason this occurs is that a large retailer makes an exclusive agreement with a producer to cut off supplies to its competitors. The Act permits the Tribunal to order a supplier of a product to accept a specified person as a customer on the usual trade terms. The supplier may raise certain defences, such as the inability to produce sufficient numbers of items to meet all demands.

The practices of exclusive dealing, market restriction, and tied selling are very common and it is likely that most businesses will encounter these problems at some time. **Exclusive dealing** is defined as the practice whereby a supplier requires his or her customers to deal only in products provided by that supplier. **Market restriction** is a practice whereby a supplier requires a customer to sell its products only in a defined market. Examples have occurred in heavy equipment industries where it has sometimes been the practice of dealers to sell only in a certain geographical region. **Tied selling** is defined as the practice whereby the supplier of a product requires a customer to buy a second product as a condition of obtaining supplies of the first product.

Competition has a somewhat contradictory nature. On the one hand, each company should strive to outproduce and outsell its competitors. If one company succeeds too well, however, it will destroy the competition.

In many industries, there are large and small companies. Most notable are the automobile, drug, and computer industries. The Act prohibits the **abuse of dominant position**, which can be defined to include squeezing a supplier to prevent another company from entry into or expansion into a market, selling articles at a loss to eliminate a competitor, and many other practices. In 1991, the Competition Tribunal ordered the NutraSweet Company to end its monopoly on the sugar substitute, Aspartame. Aspartame is a key ingredient in diet soft drinks and low-calorie foods. The Tribunal said NutraSweet could no longer enforce contracts that required customers to buy all their Aspartame from NutraSweet.

Working hand in hand with the dominant position concern are the provisions of the Act that deal with approval of mergers. Mergers are now a civil matter, reviewable by the Tribunal. The Act provides a broad definition of merger to include, "any direct or indirect acquisition or establishment of control over a significant interest in the whole or part of the business of a competitor." The primary test is whether a merger prevents or lessens competition substantially. In making this determination, the Tribunal may not rely solely on the basis of evidence of market share; there are many factors that may be considered. In 1989, the Director announced the approval of a merger between Molson Companies and Elders IXL Limited. The merger would create the largest brewer in Canada and number six in North America, but would not lessen competition within Canada.

MISLEADING ADVERTISING/DECEPTIVE PRACTICES

The misleading advertising and deceptive marketing practices provisions are contained in sections 52-60 of the Act. These provisions apply generally to anyone who promotes the supply or use of a product or promotes any business interest.

However, certain provisions apply solely to representations in the form of advertisements. It is an offence to make representations that are false or misleading in a material respect. However, this section of the Act has been subject to many challenges on the ground that it places the burden on the accused to show that the advertisement was not a deliberate falsehood.

R. v. WHOLESALE TRAVEL GROUP AND CHEDORE

Ontario, 1989

The accused corporation and one individual were jointly charged with five counts of false or misleading advertising in contravention of the *Competition Act*. Under s. 60(2) of the Act, no person shall be convicted of an offence under s. 52 if he (or she) establishes that:

(a) the act or omission giving rise to the offence with which he is charged was the result of error;
(b) he took reasonable precautions and exercised due diligence to prevent the occurrence of such error;
(c) if he, or another person, took reasonable measures to bring the error to the attention of the class of persons likely to have been reached by the representation or testimonial; and
(d) the measures referred to in paragraph (c), except where the representation or testimonial related to a security, were taken forthwith after the representation was made or the testimonial was published.

The Ontario Court of Appeal held that the words "he establishes that" were contrary to s. 7 of the *Charter of Rights and Freedoms* because they create an absolute liability offence. The provisions impose an obligation on the accused to make a retraction as a precondition of raising the defence of due diligence to the charge. That is, the accused must retract everything before he or she is allowed to argue that the advertisement was not false at all. Without the retraction, the accused is not permitted to raise the defence of due diligence that should be available to every advertiser.

It is unlawful for a person to give a false testimonial about the quality of a product. A testimonial is a statement by a person that he or she has used the product and has found it to be of high quality.

The practice of **bait and switch** is also prohibited. This practice involves a seller advertising a product for sale at a bargain price that the seller does not supply in reasonable quantities. The seller draws the consumer into the store with the false advertisement, then tries to switch the consumer to a different, higher-priced product. In some instances, the seller has the advertised product available, but it is so inferior that the seller knows the consumer will not buy it.

It is unlawful to sell a product at a price higher than the price that is currently advertised. Despite this prohibition, the courts have given recognition to the honest-mistake defence where advertisements contained misprints. Retailers often print retractions or corrections to avoid prosecution. However, the consumer who has made a trip specifically to buy that item at that price remains very inconvenienced.

The statute specifically deals with promotional contests and provides that no person shall, for the purpose of promoting the sale of a product, conduct a contest, lottery, or game of chance or skill, unless:

1. There is adequate and fair disclosure of the number and approximate value of the prizes, of the area to which they relate, and of any fact within the knowledge of the advertiser that materially affects the chances of winning;
2. Distribution of the prizes is not unduly delayed;
3. The selection of participants or distribution of prizes is made on the basis of skill or a random basis in any area to which prizes have been allocated.

In 1985, Simpsons Limited conducted a one-day "mini casino" promotion, during which game cards were distributed to customers. Both the cards and newspaper advertisements stated that the customer could save from 10 to 25 percent on practically everything in the store. The advertisements did not disclose that 90 percent of the cards were printed with 10 percent under all four tabs, which would not allow the holder to save more than 10 percent. The company was fined $100 000.

During periods of high inflation, the problem of **double ticketing** is widely reported. This is the practice of retailers putting new price tags over old tags. The practice causes consumer complaints, particularly when tags are hastily applied in a manner that allows both prices to show. The Act provides that no person shall supply a product at a higher price than the lowest of two or more prices at which it is marked or represented on a wrapper or advertisement.

One of the concerns of a small business is that a supplier or manufacturer of products will attempt to influence the price at which products are sold by the retail business. Manufacturers do not like to see their products sold too cheaply, or used as loss leaders by retailers. A **loss leader** is the name given to a product that is sold at a loss, for the purpose of drawing customers into the store in the hopes that they will buy other products. Manufacturers feel that selling a product too cheaply lowers public esteem for the product. As well, other retailers will complain about being undercut and may engage in a price war.

Despite these concerns, the principle of competition allows retailers to set their own prices without outside interference. The Act states that no person who is engaged in the business of producing or supplying a product or service shall attempt to influence upward or to discourage the reduction of the price. The section also prohibits credit card companies from trying to discourage retailers from giving discounts to customers who pay cash. The suggestion by a producer of the resale price, without a statement that the retailer can ignore the suggestion, is considered proof of an attempt to coerce the retailer. In *R. v. Toshiba of Canada Ltd.* (British Columbia, 1989) the company pleaded guilty to two charges of trying to influence upward the price at which retailers were selling Toshiba microwave ovens, and had refused to supply the product to certain retailers unless they raised their prices.

The Act prohibits pyramid selling and referral selling. **Pyramid selling** is like a chain letter, operating upon geometric progression. For example, one person draws in 10 people to resell goods, and these people must each recruit 10 others. The profits flow to the top of the pyramid. Not all sales organizations that link people are pyramids. A pyramid requires new members to make regular payments to the people at the top, without any regard to actual sales figures. The pyramid is based upon a process of constant recruiting of new participants and drawing funds from them, not upon increased sales. Companies such as Amway do not operate pyramids, as there is no compulsion upon any sales representative to purchase a set amount of company products.

Referral selling is a practice by which a seller asks a customer for the names of other potential customers. If any of these people buy a product from the seller, the first customer receives a bonus or rebate.

WEIGHTS AND MEASURES ACT

Section 91 of the *Constitution Act, 1867* specifically grants the Parliament of Canada the power to legislate in the field of weights and measures. This ensures a uniformity of standards all across Canada. The *Weights and Measures Act* permits inspectors to examine any device used for measurement, including scales, gasoline pumps, parking meters, and automatic washers and dryers in laundromats. The Act prohibits tampering with odometers on cars for the purpose of concealing the true number of kilometres they have been driven.

Inspectors may investigate whether the mass of a product has been altered by such tactics as adding waste or removing some part of the product. That is, even though the scales are accurate, the seller may be engaging in tricks such as placing waste inside poultry or removing choice steaks from a side of beef.

Under the General Agreement on Tariffs and Trade (GATT), a food manufacturer need ensure only that the consumers receive, on average, the declared quantity on the label. Thus, individual packages in a lot may be slightly over or under, as long as the average is the stated quantity. The information must be in metric, but may be in imperial measurement as well.

HAZARDOUS PRODUCTS ACT

The *Hazardous Products Act* provides standards for the manufacture and labelling of hazardous products in Canada, and prohibits the sale of imported goods that do not meet the required safety standards. Toys have specific standards regarding the use of flammable materials and toxic paints. Clothing and bedding must meet rigid flammability tests, particularly baby clothing.

The Act requires that products be marked with a symbol or warning sign indicating that the product is explosive, flammable, corrosive, or poisonous. If special instructions are needed for the sale or use of a product, these instructions must be clearly printed on the product. There are also restrictions on the sale of hazardous products to children.

CONSUMER PACKAGING AND LABELLING ACT

The *Consumer Packaging and Labelling Act* protects consumers from misleading packaging, either in size or shape. The package must state the quantity of the product by count, mass, or capacity. If the product makes a claim that it will provide a certain number of servings, it must indicate the mass of each serving.

TEXTILE LABELLING ACT

It has been estimated that more than 600 names have been invented to describe the approximately 30 basic contents of fabrics. These names can cause confusion about their care and characteristics. To eliminate confusion, the *Textile Labelling Act* requires the labelling of clothing, rolls of cloth, and household textiles to be made in the generic name of the fibres used. Therefore, nylon is marked as nylon, not "Krinklenot" or some other trade name. Labels must indicate by the use of symbols how the fabric is to be cleaned and treated.

POST OFFICE ACT

The *Post Office Act* prohibits the sending of unsolicited goods COD (cash on delivery) to any person resident in Canada. This section was enacted to stop the unscrupulous practice of sending goods to recently deceased people. The relatives of the deceased often paid for the overpriced goods, believing that the deceased had ordered them.

PROVINCIAL CONSUMER PROTECTION LAWS

Provincial governments have constitutional authority over a number of fields that are related to the issue of consumer protection. An obvious example is the sale of goods within a province. Although the federal government has exclusive responsibility over banking and bills of exchange, the provinces can legislate in the fields of conditional sales, credit, and credit reporting. Clearly, consumer protection requires the joint effort of both federal and provincial governments.

Provincial governments began enacting extensive consumer protection legislation in the 1960s. The primary area of concern was the matter of disclosure. With growing frequency, consumers were signing complex contracts with many hidden or confused terms. Contracts did not disclose the total price of purchases or the interest rate charged. Often the consumer did not know the true identity of the seller. The parol evidence rule was a weapon in the hands of dishonest sellers who made oral promises not contained in the written contract.

DISCLOSURE OF TERMS AND CONDITIONS

The first concern of legislators was to regulate interest on loans. Contracts involving payment by instalment sometimes contained such high interest rates that they were unjustified by any business standard. Almost all the provinces passed statutes entitled the *Unconscionable Transactions Relief Act*, which permitted a court to set aside a contract that charged a debtor a rate of interest that was harsh and **unconscionable**, a word that means "unreasonable" or "beyond conscience."

This legislation was not sufficient to deal with transactions that were somewhat unfair, but fell short of the harsh standard of being totally unconscionable. The basic problem, as legislators saw it, was the failure on the part of the seller or creditor to tell the buyer or debtor all the facts. There was a need for more "Truth in Lending" and "Truth in Selling." New York and several other states had taken the lead in passing such legislation with very positive results.

Most provinces now require a minimal amount of information to be clearly explained in writing. Typical is Ontario's *Consumer Protection Act,* which requires every executory contract to be in writing and to state:

1. The name and address of the seller and the buyer;
2. A description of the goods or services sufficient to identify them with certainty;
3. The itemized price of the goods or services and a detailed statement of the terms of payment;
4. Where credit is extended, a statement disclosing the true cost of borrowing;
5. Any warranty or guarantee applying to the goods, and where there is no warranty or guarantee, a statement to this effect.

The Ontario Act requires a full disclosure of how costs and interest are calculated. The Act specifies that every lender must furnish to the borrower, before giving the credit, a clear statement in writing showing:

1. Where the transaction is a loan, the sum expressed in dollars and cents actually received by the borrower, plus insurance or official fees, if any;
2. Where the lender is a seller, the amount of the cash price for the goods or services, including any insurance or fees;
3. Where the lender is a seller, the sum actually paid as a down payment or credited in respect of a trade-in or paid or credited for any reason;
4. The cost of borrowing expressed as one sum in dollars and cents;
5. The percentage that the cost of borrowing bears to the sum borrowed;
6. The amount, if any, charged for insurance or official fees;
7. The basis upon which additional charges are to be made in the event of default.

An **executory contract** (a contract for which some terms remain to be carried out) is not binding upon the buyer unless the contract is signed by the parties and unless each of the parties has a duplicate copy of the original contract.

The British Columbia *Consumer Protection Act* requires that the lender pay the cost of this disclosure. In addition, the British Columbia *Trade Practices Act* gives a consumer the right to sue for damages if there has been deception. Thus, the seller is under very strict controls to disclose important information.

SCHOFIELD MANUEL LTD. v. ROSE et al.

Ontario, 1975

Rose, the defendant, contracted with the plaintiff for the supply of interior decorating services. The contract did not comply with the *Consumer Protection Act* in that it was not signed by the plaintiff and did not contain a warranty or a statement that no warranty was given. The goods were delivered and the services performed.

The defendant made several payments on account, and then defaulted. The plaintiff sued for the balance owing, but the defendant argued that the contract was not enforceable because it did not comply with the Act.

The plaintiff was successful. Although the original contract had not been in compliance with the Act, the performance of the contract by the plaintiff acted to execute it and removed it from the requirements of the statute, because it was no longer an executory contract. The contract was then binding on both parties.

In Ontario, the disclosure rule has been extended by special legislation to such contracts as motor vehicle repair estimates and dancing lessons. In cases involving complaints about dancing lessons, consumers had signed contracts, and prepaid, for more than 20 years of lessons, when the incidence of dance studios going bankrupt was in excess of 90 percent.

EXEMPT TRANSACTIONS

Consumer protection laws do not apply to all contracts. Real estate transactions are exempt, as are business-to-business transactions. Landlord and tenant contracts are governed by separate legislation. Manitoba, New Brunswick, and Saskatchewan exempt any transaction relating to farm implements and services related to agriculture. Banks are not subject to provincial laws, but have adopted disclosure policies regarding the true cost of a loan.

As the *Schofield* case illustrated, it is important to keep in mind that most consumer protection laws do not apply to executed contracts. For example, if the consumer pays the total cash price for goods, the requirements for disclosure, etc., are of no importance. The contract must be executory to be protected.

Every province has a monetary limit as well, reflecting the belief that the law need not protect the consumer from very small financial loss. Such amounts would cost more to enforce than they are worth. Ontario sets a minimum of $50; Alberta, $25. In British Columbia, the amount is $20.

RIGHT TO RESCIND

The popularity of door-to-door selling has caused the provinces to effect cooling-off periods. Many consumer complaints arose after consumers signed agreements, usually in haste, following high-pressure sales presentations during evenings or on weekends. These presentations nearly always contained the proviso that the offer was good only once and that the consumer must sign the contract immediately. Should the consumer want to seek outside financial advice, it was not immediately available. The cooling-off period was devised to eliminate this sales tactic.

The **right to rescind** means that a buyer may cancel a contract that is not signed in the seller's permanent place of business by delivering a notice of rescission (notice of cancellation) in writing to the seller. Most provinces require that this right to rescind be printed in bold letters on the contract form.

The period varies from province to province. Ontario and Manitoba have the shortest period—only two days. Alberta and Saskatchewan permit four days. In British Columbia and Prince Edward Island it is seven days. New Brunswick allows five days, while Nova Scotia, Quebec, and Newfoundland have the longest period—ten days.

Some provinces also allow the consumer to rescind the contract if it is not completed within a certain period. Alberta law, for example, permits cancellation "not later than one year after the date on which the copy of the sales contract was received if all the goods and services are not provided within one hundred and twenty days after the date the sales contract was signed by the buyer and no date for delivery or performance was set."

ONTARIO BUSINESS PRACTICES ACT

One of the most extensive pieces of consumer protection legislation is the Ontario *Business Practices Act*. This statute has two basic functions: (1) it identifies business practices that are deemed unfair and thereby prohibited, and (2) it establishes special defences for consumers who enter contracts unwisely because of their own physical or mental inabilities or lack of understanding of the contract.

More than 20 unfair practices are identified in the Act. Some typical examples are as follows:

1. To misrepresent that goods have characteristics, ingredients, or capabilities they do not have;
2. To misrepresent that used goods are new when they are not;
3. To misrepresent that service and parts are available when they are not;
4. To misrepresent an important fact in some way or to fail to mention it in order to deceive.

The statute has been called a "catalogue" of nearly every dishonest practice ever devised in the past 50 years. Some critics argue that the law makes the consumer mentally lazy in not looking out for his or her own interests. The statute also affords protection to consumers who:

1. Were unable to understand the contract for such reasons as ignorance, infirmity, or illiteracy;
2. Were grossly overcharged;
3. Did not receive a substantial benefit from the subject matter of the contract, or where the contract was so heavily weighted against the consumer that it was unfair.

The effect of the statute is to eliminate many of the procedural arguments that might have been raised under the historic rules of the sale of goods. For example, the rule of *caveat emptor* (buyer beware) has been virtually eliminated. The court can ignore disclaimer clauses and the parol evidence rule, and give legal effect to salespersons' puffing. The consumer can cancel a contract that is based upon his or her own personal characteristics, such as ignorance.

SANDILANDS v. GUELPH DATSUN

Ontario, 1981

The plaintiff purchased a used vehicle from the defendant for $1400, stipulating that the vehicle be certified as safe and be equipped with new tires. No warranty was given with the vehicle. Four months later, the vehicle's licence plates were removed by the Ministry of Transportation, which declared the vehicle unsafe. An inspection had revealed holes in the chassis, brake lines ruptured from rust, and a leaking exhaust. The plaintiff claimed rescission and damages on the ground that the defendant had made false and misleading representations and had engaged in unfair practices.

The Court awarded the plaintiff $1600, to represent the purchase price and costs. The defendant had violated the *Business Practices Act* and the *Sale of Goods Act.* There was an implied condition that the car be roadworthy and fit for the purpose for which it was sold. As well, the defendant had made misleading representations about the condition of the vehicle.

Consumers who want to assert their rights under the Act must do so within six months. The statute further provides for a maximum fine of $2000 or imprisonment for not more than one year, or both, in the case of an individual engaging in an unfair practice. The maximum fine for a corporation is $25 000. The Ministry of Consumer and Commercial Relations can order any company or individual to cease any unfair practice.

The Newfoundland *Trade Practices Act* is nearly identical to the Ontario law.

BRITISH COLUMBIA TRADE PRACTICES ACT

The British Columbia *Trade Practices Act* applies to any transaction that can be called a "consumer transaction." The term includes the borrowing of money or the purchase of goods and services, as long as the intent of the transaction is to acquire something that is personal or for a family or household. It does not include business-to-business transactions.

The Act does not cover any real estate transactions or loans to purchase real estate. Insurance contracts and personal transactions between two consumers are also exempt from the statute.The Act makes it an offence to engage in deceptive or misleading practices. These practices include any oral, written, visual, descriptive, or other representation; failure to disclose; and any conduct having the capability, tendency, or effect of deceiving another person. The Act contains a list of specific practices that are recognized as deceptive. The Director of Trade Practices may request a court injunction to have deceptive practices stopped.

The British Columbia law is unique because it allows consumers to obtain compensation for damages that they suffer as a result of deceptive or unconscionable practices. One section allows punitive damages. The Director of Trade Practices may bring an action to ask the court to declare that a particular merchant has engaged in a deceptive practice. Once this declaration is obtained, a consumer can sue for damages and the declaration is absolute proof that the merchant has engaged in a deceptive act. In practical terms, the two actions may be combined into one.

ALBERTA UNFAIR TRADE PRACTICES ACT

The Alberta *Unfair Trade Practices Act* is intended to prevent unfair business practices and to aid consumers in recovering losses caused by such practices. Like other provinces, Alberta's law does not cover business-to-business or real estate transactions.

The Act recognizes four distinct types of consumer services: services provided to maintain or repair goods; services provided to an individual involving the use of social, recreational, or physical fitness facilities; moving, hauling, and storage services; and certain kinds of education services.

Three major transactions are identified by the Act as being so objectionable that a court may declare the entire transaction unfair, cancel the contract, and award damages for loss:

1. The subjection of the consumer to undue pressure by the supplier to enter into the contract;
2. The inability of the consumer to understand the nature of the transaction and the fact that the supplier takes advantage of that lack of ability;
3. The existence of a major defect in the goods that prevents the consumer from obtaining value for his or her money.

CREDIT BUREAUS

The popularity of buying on credit has brought about the need for some means of keeping track of users and abusers of credit. As a result, credit bureaus have been established in Canada and the United States to provide employers and merchants with information about prospective employees and customers. These private companies keep files on individual consumers. Stores and lending institutions may become members of a credit bureau by paying an annual fee. They also pay a fee for each request for information that they make to the bureau. The credit bureau gives an interested member a report of a consumer's credit history. That information is then matched against the credit granter's own standards for extending credit. Credit bureaus do not make the decision to grant credit. They only provide the information they have in their files.

The provinces have enacted legislation to prevent the abuse of credit reporting. These statutes were passed to protect consumers from secret and hidden files, which often contained damaging information that prevented people from obtaining credit or employment. The laws vary from province to province, but most are very similar to the Ontario *Consumer Reporting Act* which contains the following important provisions:

1. All reporting agencies must make a reasonable effort to find proof to back up unfavourable personal information in their reports;
2. Reporting agencies are restricted as to whom they may give access to information;
3. No information about a bankruptcy that is more than seven years old may be included in the report. This restriction does not apply to a person who has declared bankruptcy more than once;
4. No information as to race, creed, colour, sex, ancestry, ethnic origin, or political affiliation may be included;
5. Any person knowingly supplying false information in the preparation of consumer reports is liable to prosecution;
6. Consumer reporting agencies may not use any information that is not filed or electronically stored in Canada;
7. Every consumer has the right to see his or her own file and can insist that the file be corrected if there are any inaccuracies.

In the past, married women have found it difficult to obtain credit. Many lenders insisted that the woman's husband guarantee the loan, even though provincial laws state that a married woman may contract in her own name. Several provinces have developed guidelines for lenders that prohibit discrimination against married women.

Ontario and Nova Scotia law prohibits anyone from reporting information on criminal convictions that are more than seven years old. In Saskatchewan, a job applicant is not protected from the disclosure to an employer of details about a personal bankruptcy if it happened less than 14 years earlier.

There is no credit reporting legislation in Alberta and, therefore, a person has no right to see, obtain, or change a credit record in that province. However, the policy of credit reporting agencies in Alberta is to apply the same rules as in other provinces.

The British Columbia *Credit Reporting Act* states that any person who has been denied credit may demand the name of the agency from which the information was received. The person may then demand from the agency the nature of all information on file, the source of that information, and the names of people who have been given that information within the past 12 months.

COLLECTION AGENCIES

Collection agencies are essentially debt collectors. They do not lend money and therefore do not obtain promissory notes. A person who is owed money and is unable to collect it may engage the services of such an agency. Where court action is taken by a collection agency on the creditor's behalf, it cannot be taken without the consent of the creditor.

Creditors often "sell" their unpaid accounts to a collection agency for a portion of the amount owing. For example, the Classic Record Club might have 200 delinquent accounts. It sells these accounts to the Effective Collection Agency for 10 cents on the dollar. If the collection agency can collect all of the money owed, then it will reap a large profit. However, the likelihood of collecting from more than 15 percent of the accounts is improbable.

Collection agencies have various methods of collecting the money that is owed, usually involving a combination of letters, telephone calls, and personal visits. Complaints about extreme collection methods caused provincial governments to legislate controls over these methods. The methods used by a collection agency cannot be threatening and above all cannot hint at criminal action should the debtor refuse to pay. Collection agencies cannot send letters containing excerpts from the *Criminal Code* as a way of intimidating debtors. Nor can the agencies use letterheads or forms that look like court documents.

Newfoundland, Nova Scotia, Saskatchewan, Quebec, and British Columbia have the strongest legislation regarding collection agencies. The British Columbia *Debt Collection Act* prohibits harassment of a debtor by such tactics as communicating with the debtor or the debtor's family or employer in a manner that causes alarm, distress, or humiliation. British Columbia is one of the few provinces that allows the government to act directly on the behalf of debtors by making arrangements with creditors for the repayment of debts. The other provinces have much weaker legislation that relies upon government licensing to stop unacceptable collection tactics.

SPECIAL LEGISLATION

Each province has enacted special legislation to deal with consumer complaints. The variations are too numerous to list all of them. They include prepaid funeral plans, dance lessons, and automobile repairs.

SUBSTITUTE ACTIONS

One of the problems that a consumer faces in a quarrel with a company is that the cost of a lawsuit is a deterrent.

Alberta and British Columbia have enacted legislation that permits the provincial government or one of its agencies to enter into the lawsuit directly and substitute itself for the consumer. This is called a **substitute action**. Thus, the power of the government can be brought into the legal battle against a powerful corporation or financial institution engaged in a legal dispute with a consumer.

The government normally intervenes only when the matter affects many consumers and when the government believes that the company has not attempted to resolve the matter fairly.

VOLUNTARY COMPLIANCE

Most provinces permit a supplier to enter into an agreement of voluntary compliance. This agreement is a contract between the enforcement authority and the supplier, by which the latter voluntarily promises to refrain from deceptive or unfair conduct and to reimburse some consumers. The federal government has the same policy.

Voluntary compliance removes the matter from the courts without having made a specific determination as to whether the act was indeed unfair. That is, there is no admission of wrongdoing, but only an agreement to discontinue the action because it has caused complaints. For example, in 1988, the Ontario government entered into a voluntary agreement with a company to stop advertising that one of its products would increase furnace efficiency by 25 percent. The company's tests showed that the device worked, but government tests found no change in furnace efficiency.

CLASS ACTIONS

The *Rules of Practice* in all provinces appear to permit class action suits, but in many provinces it is nearly impossible to bring a successful class action. A **class action** brings together the claims arising from a common complaint among a number of people against the same defendant. The action can be brought by a group or by one plaintiff who asks to be allowed to bring the action on behalf of all of the other people who have the same complaint. If the latter occurs, the other class members are not strictly parties and cannot be ordered to pay the costs. Class actions are very common in the United States.

The class action has two advantages: (1) a class action eliminates the possibility that different courts will reach opposite decisions on the same question of fact, and (2) by joining together, the cost of suing the defendant is greatly reduced for each person involved.

There is a disadvantage to a class action. If it is badly handled, the action prevents other people from suing on their own behalf. There is a danger that a class action may prejudice many class members who wanted to sue individually. In theory, the defendant could pay one plaintiff to start a class action and to deliberately lose the case. This would wipe out all possible future claims from other plaintiffs. For this reason, the courts are very strict about whether they will recognize that certain individuals constitute a class. The British Columbia *Trade Practices Act* is the most specific in its wording regarding class actions. Thus, the obstacles that are common to most class actions have mostly been overcome in that province. In *Chastain v. British Columbia Hydro & Power Authority* (British Columbia, 1973) a class action was brought on behalf of more than 23 000 utility users who had been charged security deposits by the authority. These deposits were required from people who were regarded as poor credit risks and who might not pay their hydro bills. The action was successful and the deposits were returned.

UNSOLICITED GOODS

If a consumer receives goods in the mail or by delivery that he or she has not ordered, the law often permits the consumer to keep or dispose of the goods as desired, without paying for them. In Ontario, the consumer is under no legal obligation for their use, loss, or theft unless the consumer knows that the goods were intended for some other party. The consumer must not withhold them from the correct party.

The British Columbia *Consumer Protection Act* states that if unsolicited goods are mailed or delivered, the sender "has no cause of action for any loss, use, misuse, possession, damage, or misappropriation in respect of the credit card, the goods, or the value obtained by the use of either." In short, unless the consumer acknowledges acceptance of the goods, they can be kept or disposed of as the consumer wishes.

CREDIT CARDS

The use of a credit card comes under the general law of contracts. When a person applies for a credit card, that person fills out an application form agreeing to be liable according to the terms of the agreement accompanying the card. The *Bills of Exchange Act* has no bearing upon payment by credit card.

The card remains the property of the bank or company that issued it. The consumer agrees not to charge more than a certain amount with the card. The credit card company does not accept responsibility for the goods bought under the card system. The sale contract between the card holder and the merchant remains their exclusive agreement. The burden is on the consumer to make purchases wisely, because payment cannot be withheld from the card company as a means of putting pressure on the merchant. There is no method of stopping payment on a credit card charge as there is with a cheque.

If a card is lost, the holder should report the loss immediately. In most provinces, the law states that the liability of the card holder is limited to $50 if the loss has been reported and the card is used by whomever found it. If the loss is not reported promptly, the liability may extend beyond the statutory limit, perhaps up to the credit limit of the card. The liability is stated in the contract with the card company.

The combination of credit cards with bank withdrawal cards gives the card a dual characteristic. If the card is lost, and the finder is able to use it to get money from a bank, the normal liability limit is not in effect.

PLATER v. BANK OF MONTREAL

British Columbia, 1988

The plaintiff had a MasterCard that allowed withdrawals from an automatic banking machine. The plaintiff ignored the warning not to write his personal identification number (PIN) on the card or a piece of paper carried with the card. The plaintiff lost his wallet and the finder took $400 from his account. The plaintiff argued that he should have to pay only the $50 liability set by provincial law. The Court held that the plaintiff must bear the full loss. A card used to get cash is not a true credit card and the provincial limit did not apply.

COMPUTER BILLING

The charging of interest on computer statements has caused considerable confusion and complaint. Some billing problems have occurred because companies have not allowed sufficient time for statements to be received by the consumer, so that payments can be forwarded and applied to the account before the end of the billing cycle. British Columbia has dealt with this problem in its *Consumer Protection Act* which provides that statements must be received by the consumer at least 10 days prior to the date payment is due. No creditor is to charge interest if the 10 days were not allowed.

Interest can be calculated many different ways. Therefore, the consumer should read the contract with the supplier or card company to determine how the interest is calculated. Many suppliers of credit now calculate interest daily. Payments must be received within a certain number of days after a purchase in order to be included in the current statement. Each lender must provide the consumer with a clear statement of how interest is calculated.

REVIEW: POINTS OF LAW

1. It is generally recognized that a consumer is an individual person rather than a company, and that the person is acting in a personal capacity rather than engaging in some form of business activity.
2. The *Competition Act* prohibits such acts as misleading advertising, price fixing, tied selling, or bid-rigging.
3. The *Bills of Exchange Act* requires that promissory notes given as part of a consumer transaction be marked with the words "Consumer Purchase." The buyer has the same rights and remedies against a holder in due course as against the original seller.
4. The federal government is responsible for checking all weighing and measuring devices to make certain they are accurate.
5. Federal law requires that hazardous products be marked with a symbol to warn consumers of specific dangers.
6. Pyramid and referral selling schemes are unlawful in Canada.
7. All provinces require "truth in lending," which means that the supplier of credit must disclose the true facts about the cost of borrowing.
8. Provincial legislation identifies unfair trade practices and permits cancellation of contracts if such practices are used.
9. Credit reporting agencies must make a reasonable effort to verify the truthfulness of records and allow consumers to challenge inaccuracies.
10. A collection agency cannot use or threaten the use of criminal action to collect a debt.

LEGAL BRIEFS

1. A retailer marks an item on the shelf with the price $1.39. When the product passes over a scanner at the check-out counter, the scanner reads the Universal Product Code on the item and prints $1.69 on the sales slip. The customer pays $1.69, then later complains of the discrepancy. The store manager replies: "The price on the package doesn't matter. It could be

months old. It's what is in the computer that matters." The manager points to a sign stating this policy. When the customer complains about "double-ticketing" the manager replies: "That rule doesn't apply. There is only one price on the product, not two. We reserve the right to change our prices at the check-out." Is the manager correct?

2. S is a very large grocery chain. In certain communities, it lowers all prices severely—selling many products at a loss—every time a competing store is opened in that community, and keeps its prices low until the other store goes out of business. S then raises its prices again. Fair competition?
3. L, a luggage manufacturing company, approves a magazine advertisement in which a car supposedly backs over one of its suitcases without crushing it. The ad shows the suitcase directly beneath the rear tire of the car. An independent testing agency tries to re-enact the same "accident" and finds that a car cannot back over the suitcase because the suitcase is pushed aside by the tire. The advertising agency admits that the car did not actually drive up on the suitcase. The agency jacked the car up, slid the suitcase under the wheel, then lowered the car onto the suitcase. The agency denies the ad is false, arguing that the point of the ad is to show that the suitcase is strong enough to hold a car, which is true. False advertising?
4. G, a supermarket, ran a full-page ad with many supposed specials. Each food item had a large notation in the corner saying, "50% Off!" Only by using a magnification device was the reader able to see the words "Up To" next to the numerals. Most of the items in the store were discounted 10 to 12 percent. False advertising?
5. Two newspaper chains compete in two large Canadian cities. Neither is operating profitably. Each chain agrees to close one of its operations, keeping one city for itself and surrendering the other. The result is that advertising and subscriber rates rise, returning both papers to profitability. Consumers, however, no longer have a choice of newspapers. "It just makes good business sense," the owner of one newspaper argues. "We were both beating our brains out and neither was making a dime." Have any laws been broken?
6. O signs a contract to purchase home furnishings. The contract and advertisement read: "No payments or interest for six months." However, after six months, O learns that he must immediately pay six months of principal and interest payments. Was the ad deceptive?
7. A company claims that its service personnel are "factory trained." The factory is in Japan, but the service personnel are trained in Toronto by Japanese technicians using factory assembly manuals. Are the personnel "factory trained"?
8. The M Dance Studios sell 20 years of dancing lessons to a woman who is 88 years of age. Have any laws been broken?

APPLYING THE LAW

HOME-GUARD v. DAVIES

Nova Scotia, 1976

A salesperson, representing the Home-Guard Company, gave a security system demonstration to the Davies family. The defendants were very elderly and concerned about a fire in their home. Since they both wore hearing aids, they feared that they might not be awakened by most systems. The salesperson showed them a complex system that combined smoke and heat detectors, alarms that involved both sound and flashing lights, and a sprinkler system that could be installed in the basement only. There was also an intercom system, through which a person in one room could alert a person anywhere in the house of a fire.

The salesperson quoted prices for separate parts of the system, but did not give a total price. He filled out a form and presented it to Mr. Davies, who had poor vision and could not read it. He gave it to Mrs. Davies who read it for a while, but did not say anything. Finally, she asked, "Well, what do you think?" Mr. Davies shrugged. Both signed the contract without having read it.

The system was installed the next week. It took three days to drill holes through the walls and to wire each room. The defendants had not realized that so many wires were required and were distressed at the holes being drilled. Not all of the wires could be hidden, so they were stapled to walls and baseboards. The defendants would testify that if they had known how ugly the system would be, they would not have bought it. The company presented a bill for $2800, which the Davieses said was higher than they were told it would be. The system worked well. When the defendants did not pay the bill, the company sued. Because the system was unique, it was not possible to compare it to other alarm systems.

The Court held that the defendants must pay the bill. There had been no misrepresentation as to what the system would include. If the couple had been confused about the total price, they could have asked for clarification. They were not grossly overcharged. As to the problem of exposed wires, the company had used due diligence in its method of installation.

Questions

1. When dealing with elderly people, how should a salesperson conduct negotiations to ensure that there will be no later disagreement?

2. The Davies did not read the contract and the salesperson knew that. Why did the Court not allow the contract to be rescinded?
3. Although the system could not be compared to others in terms of price, it was clear that simpler systems were available for less. The Davies perhaps bought more than they needed. Should this have been a factor in the case?
4. Do you think the case was rightly decided? Give a reason for your answer.

R. v. HOFFMAN-LaROCHE OF CANADA

Ontario, 1980

The accused company was charged with predatory pricing. The accused was the Canadian subsidiary of a large multinational drug company and, over a one-year period, had engaged in a policy of giving its best-known product, Valium, to hospitals, free of charge. The generic name for Valium is diazepam, and the accused company had first developed diazepam and wanted to protect its market from competitors who would be inclined to copy it.

The company gave away the equivalent of $2 .6 million of the drug at an annual cost of $900 000. The policy turned out to be a financial disaster, costing far more than it could conceivably be worth. Nonetheless, competing companies complained to the federal government.

The accused argued that it had a right to protect its invention by engaging in a promotion that would develop "customer loyalty." The Crown argued that, while price cutting is a proper form of competing against other companies, cutting prices to zero is not fair competition, it is predatory pricing. The company was convicted and fined $50 000, even though the company had voluntarily discontinued the practice before the charges were laid.

Questions

1. What is predatory pricing?
2. Ordinarily, there is nothing illegal about giving something to someone. The company bore the expense and hospitals obtained the benefit of free drugs. Why were the company's actions considered illegal?
3. What was the company trying to achieve by giving away its product?
4. The hospitals that accepted free drugs must have known, or would have strong reasons to know, that the accused drug company was engaging in an unfair practice. By accepting the drugs, were the hospitals not breaking the law as well? Why or why not?

PRINCIPLES AND CASES

Case 1: Legal Principle

One of the definitions of misleading representation is that the consumer would reasonably believe that he or she received a benefit that, in fact, the consumer did not receive.

Case Facts

The defendant was charged with unlawfully making a materially misleading representation by advertising a bottle of shampoo as "Special, $1.49." The bottle in question held 365 mL. The label contained no mention of any regular price. Prices for this bottle ranged from $0.99 to $1.49 in various stores but nowhere was it sold for more than $1.49. The Crown's position was that the word "Special" meant nothing and was misleading because there was nothing special about the offer.

The company defended the action on the ground that this was an introductory offer of a new bottle. The 365-mL size was the largest bottle the company had ever used and it had originally intended to sell it for $1.85. Based upon the unit value of smaller bottles, a price of $1.85 would have been reasonable. However, in order to have the new size well received by the public, the company decided to introduce the new size at a special price of $1.49. Therefore, the word "Special" was an accurate description.

Possible Decisions

A The company is guilty of false advertising because a shopper would believe that he or she was being offered the bottle at a price below the price at which the same size of bottle is ordinarily sold.

B The company is guilty of false advertising because nothing on the label explains what is "special" about the price.

C The company is not guilty of false advertising because the word "special" has many possible meanings which need not be explained.

D The company is not guilty of false advertising because the offer was a genuine "special" offer.

Case 2: Legal Principle

It is unlawful for any company to act in a manner that will lessen competition unduly. However, the manner and extent to which a company will compete remains a company policy decision.

Case Facts

Two companies were charged with conspiring to enhance unreasonably the price of sugar in Canada and to prevent or lessen unduly competition in the product, transportation, and sale of sugar.

Evidence was led that there are only two large sugar companies in Canada. During World War II, their markets were allocated by the government and controlled by a Prices Board. After the war, the companies competed against each other for market share. They cut prices and offered special enhancements to try to take business from each other. One firm nearly went bankrupt, but was rescued after being taken over by another company. The effects of vigorous competition had resulted in no change in market share, but the very low prices at which sugar was made available to consumers had seriously weakened corporate finances.

The two companies abandoned the practice of trying to take business from one another and turned their attentions to trying to increase their business within their territories. That is, they tried to get consumers to eat more sugar. The result was that consumers could find only one brand of sugar in their stores. Once the pricing war ended, the price of sugar rose substantially, leading to a charge that the companies were engaged in price fixing.

Possible Decisions

A The companies are not guilty of price fixing because they never formally met and conspired to divide up the Canadian sugar market.

B The companies are not guilty of price fixing because there is nothing in the law that states companies must compete against each other in a manner that includes trying to capture market share.

C The companies are guilty of price fixing because the actual result of what they are doing is to totally eliminate competition in the sugar market.

D The companies are guilty of price fixing because, although competition was lessened, it was not lessened unduly.

YOU BE THE JUDGE

1. A funeral home sold expensive coffins for $1000. Before burial or cremation, the deceased were transferred to inexpensive coffins. The expensive coffins were refinished, relined, and then sold again. The funeral home took the position that the expensive coffins were for "display" only and not for final disposition. The contract of sale disclosed what the funeral home was doing. However, the wording was in small print on the back of the second page. Crown witnesses testified they had never read the wording and did not know the exchange would be made. The owner of the funeral home explained that "affordable funerals" were possible only by presenting the deceased in the most impressive setting, then quietly making the substitution. To do otherwise would add $5000 to the cost of a funeral at a time when families might not have the money. The family of a deceased person complained to the provincial government. Is the funeral home breaking the law?

2. The plaintiff signed a contract for a food plan that claimed the plaintiff would cut food costs by 20 percent. The food received was of good quality, but priced the same or slightly higher than in local stores. If a consumer carefully shopped store specials, the food plan was more expensive than store prices. The food was delivered once a week. The plaintiff sought to cancel the contract on the basis that the plan was a false representation. The defendant argued that the saving was in the "time saved by not having to go to the store and buy the food and in the cost of transportation." Who would succeed?

3. An appliance store sold many appliances at very low prices, with a five-year guarantee. It then went out of business. One month later, another store opened in a different location, under a different name. However, consumers noted that the owner and most of the employees were the same people who operated the first store. It was later learned that much of the inventory had simply been moved from one store to the other. Consumers with complaints about their appliances were denied repair service under their supposed five-year guarantees. "That has nothing to do with this store," the store owner insisted. The provincial government ordered the store owner to honour the guarantees, but he refused. He was then charged with an unfair trade practice. Who would succeed?

4. The defendant owned and operated a furniture store. He developed a sales technique of "selling" furniture to his employees, who took the furniture home. The employees then placed advertisements in newspapers, stating that they were relocating and would sell furniture at bargain prices. These employees had the original price tags and persuaded buyers that they were getting bargains because they were forced to sell this almost-new furniture at a loss of 30 to 40 percent. In fact, the price that people eventually paid was close to the price they would have paid in the store. The defendant was charged under a provincial law that prohibits misrepresenting material facts. Who would succeed?

5. The defendant published a directory of businesses in the city. These businesses were not aware of the directory and had not entered into any agreement with the defendant. The defendant then invoiced each business the sum of $190 for having its name in the directory. Approximately 30 percent of the companies billed paid the invoices without question. In most instances, the accounting office that paid the invoice did not consult with the advertising department but just assumed that the transaction had been approved. Evidence was led that the defendant relied upon this rather careless business practice to make money. The defendant argued that he had done nothing improper. He had provided a service and was entitled to be paid. Small print on the back of the invoices stated: "This is a request for payment, not an assertion of right to payment." The Crown argued that the entire plan was a fraudulent scheme. Who would succeed?

6. The defendant oil company was charged with price maintenance violation. The defendant required its dealers to sell gasoline at a fixed price, higher than competing gasoline stations charged. The defendant promised to make up the difference to the dealers for lost business. The dealers complained they were not receiving enough money to make up the difference, but when they lowered their prices to increase sales, the defendant threatened to cut off the supply of gasoline and the subsidy. The defendant argued that it was permitted to establish a voluntary pricing policy. The Crown argued that the *Competition Act* had been violated. Who would succeed?

C H A P T E R   T E N

INTELLECTUAL PROPERTY LAW

"Sometimes I have a nightmare that there's nothing left to invent."

Thomas Edison, inventor

INTELLECTUAL PROPERTY

A nation prides itself upon its achievements. Advances in science and medicine enhance the prestige of a nation in the global community and elevate its position in the eyes of the world. Of no less importance is the totality of a nation's literary and artistic output. As well, the export of creative materials represents an important source of earnings for the producing country.

Canada has much of which it can be proud. Its literary outpouring is impressive, and the talents of Canadian artists are second to none. Canadians explore, discover, and invent. Among many other items, Canadians have invented Teflon, the snowmobile, and homing devices for airplanes.

For lack of a better name, the value of such creativity is generally referred to as **intellectual property**. As the name suggests, a person has a right of ownership of his or her ideas once those ideas cease to be theory and become reality. The general purpose of intellectual property law is to provide incentive and protection for creative people. If a person is not confident of such protection, then that person will be reluctant to commit the time and energy required to produce a new work.

People commit themselves to creative activity for a variety of motives. Some do it for the prospect of earnings, while others feel a compulsive urging that cannot be ignored. Many pursue recognition and the desire to be identified as leaders in certain fields. The law does not, and cannot, take cognizance of the motivation of the inventor, artist, or writer.

The basic method of protection is to allow a person to have a monopoly with respect to the sale, display, and control of the work. Intellectual property law tries to protect creators from theft of their ideas. However, it can be argued that affording a monopoly to a creator deprives millions of people of reasonable access to that discovery. If a new drug is discovered that cures a serious illness, the drug may be priced so high that many sufferers cannot afford it. And, because of the monopoly awarded, no one else may produce that drug at a lower price. At a Copyright Symposium at Queen's University, Professor Vivian Nelles advanced the following argument:

> *The technology/information explosion is the new capital of our society. The copyright and patent protection push is an attempt to turn ideas into profit. Creators are the new landlords trying to build fences around ideas and claim them for themselves. Copying gives greater exposure to ideas and often inspires new works, thus increasing our total wealth of knowledge.*

The law tries to balance competing interests. On the one hand, it protects creative people so they will continue creating. At the same time, it tries to make discoveries as widely available as possible, because the purpose of intellectual property law is not to benefit a few, but to encourage public access to bring the most good to as many people as possible.

There are four basic areas of intellectual property law: patent, industrial design, trade mark, and copyright. A **patent** is a right to a new invention. An **industrial design** is the right to manufacture something of unique design. A **trade mark** is a mark used to identify a product. A **copyright** is the right to copy a literary or artistic work. The authority to legislate concerning intellectual property falls under the jurisdiction of the federal government. Statutes have been passed that apply to each of these rights. Canada has signed numerous international conventions that extend the protection to other countries.

It is extremely important that any person employed in an innovative field have an employment contract that clearly states whether the person's discoveries or inventions belong to the person or the employer. Numerous lawsuits have arisen in the drug, computer, and aerospace industries, where employees have claimed the rights to their inventions against counterarguments from employers that such discoveries are company property. The following case is an example.

CANAVEST HOUSE LTD. v. LETT

Ontario, 1984

The plaintiff sought to refrain its former employee, Lett, from infringing copyright in computer programs developed while the defendant was in the plaintiff's employ, and from competing in relation to contracts or emerging business opportunities. The Court found that ownership of the programs was vested in the plaintiff and, on this basis, the defendant could be restrained from providing other people with copies of the programs or of the notes and material leading to their creation. The Court also indicated that, by virtue of the plaintiff's ownership of copyright in the programs, the defendant could be restrained from copying, reproducing, or using the software.

INVENTIONS AND PATENTS

A patent is a grant from the Canadian government that gives an inventor the sole right to make, use, and sell an invention for a period of 20 years after the application is filed. A patent holder then becomes the owner of the invention. The right conferred by a Canadian patent extends throughout Canada, but not to foreign countries. Patent rights for other countries must be applied for separately. Under the *Patent Co-operation Treaty*, inventors may ask for patent protection in 43 countries, using a single international application that can be filed in Canada. A patent is granted for a product, composition, apparatus, or process that is new, useful, and inventive. Taken separately, these terms have the following basic meanings:

- **New**: First in the world
- **Useful**: Functional and operative
- **Inventive**: Not obviously related to what was previously known

Early patents in England were essentially monopoly rights granted by the Crown under **Letters Patent**. In some instances, they related to useful inventions. In other situations, they were simply privileges granted to a friend of the King or Queen for personal enrichment.

The first patent registered in Canada appeared in 1791. It was granted under the British patent law for a process to make potash and soap from wood ash. It was issued to Angus MacDonnel, a Scottish soldier garrisoned at Quebec City. The largest number of patents held by one Canadian is 180, granted to George Dorey of Montreal. Most of his inventions involved railway equipment. In 1923, Dr. Frederick Banting and Dr. Charles Best of Toronto received a joint patent, Number 234336, for insulin, used to treat diabetes.

Despite its British roots, Canadian patent law developed very much along U.S. lines. The practice in England was for the inventor to keep his or her invention a secret. There were many secret processes for dying cloth, making leather, and hardening steel. The U.S. concept was quite different. The inventor was required to reveal the secret of his or her invention to the government. In return, the government awarded monopoly rights for a fixed number of years. When the time period lapsed, the invention became public property—available to everyone.

In Canada, a person can obtain full details of any invention from the federal Patent Office. The information contained in patents can inspire further discovery, and can be useful to all those wishing to be informed of the latest technological advances. Although the patented invention cannot be copied, it may give ideas for new inventions that will work with previous ones. This is one of the most important aspects of our present patent system. For example, Alexander Graham Bell acquired just three patents for his "voice transmission devices." Thousands of other inventions have been patented that do not copy Bell's work, but continue its advancement.

WHAT CAN BE PATENTED

Protection under the present *Patent Act* is available to inventors of any new and useful art, process, machine, manufacture, composition of matter, or any useful improvement of the same. To "invent" means to produce something that is totally new. A slight improvement of an existing invention is not patentable.

An invention must also be new in terms of time. An invention that has been developed or used in public for more than two years cannot be patented. The purpose of this rule is to prevent one person from acquiring a patent on something which many people are already using. For example, in 1966, U.S. soldiers in Vietnam complained that the M60 machine gun jammed because the belt of bullets often snagged on a protruding piece of metal on the side of the weapon. Enterprising soldiers bolted an empty C-ration (food) can to the side of the gun. The belt of bullets rode over the side of the can and the gun no longer jammed. In 1968, the M60 was redesigned with a new part that performed the same function as the empty can. A patent was denied to the engineer who designed the part because the idea was already commonly in use and the engineer had not really invented it.

It is not possible to patent a theory or vague idea. Detailed drawings of the invention must be filed with the application. Models are seldom necessary, but may be requested if the drawings do not demonstrate the invention. The inventor must demonstrate that the invention, or the principle of the invention, works.

In 1980, the U.S. Patent Office expanded the concept of intellectual property into the field of mathematics. Mathematical algorithms—step-by-step procedures to solve complex problems—are now patentable, as long as they are described in the context of a computer system. The change in policy has made it possible to obtain patents in the United States on computer software. However, in Canada, software is protected by copyright, not patent.

WHAT CANNOT BE PATENTED

There are numerous grounds for not granting a patent. Some things that are not normally patentable are:

1. An improvement to a known device, which improvement would be obvious to any person skilled in the art;
2. A device or material whose only difference from older devices is a mere change in size, shape, or degree;

3. A device intended for an illicit or illegal purpose;
4. An inoperative device or a device which has no use;
5. The discovery of a naturally occurring substance;
6. Printed matter, which is protected by copyright;
7. A mere suggestion or idea;
8. A scientific principle;
9. A method of doing business;
10. A new variety of a horticultural plant;
11. New works of art;
12. New methods of treating a patient;
13. Recipes for food or beverages;
14. Designs.

Currently, several new areas of discovery and invention are creating new problems for the patent system. For example, it has normally been accepted that no one could patent a living organism. However, the advance of science in the field of biotechnology has given rise to the claim that people are inventing new forms of life. These new organisms have great commercial potential and the inventors claim ownership. For example, a new strain of virus was invented to be spread on strawberries. The virus protects strawberries from damage by frost.

In 1979, the U.S. Supreme Court upheld a lower court decision that micro-organisms which have been genetically engineered were patentable. The Court concluded that the fact that micro-organisms are alive is without legal significance. In 1982, the Canadian Patent Office accepted a patent application for a yeast culture that was engineered to digest waste products found in the effluent from pulp and paper mills. However, in *Pioneer Hi-Breds Ltd. v. Commissioner of Patents* (1988), the Federal Court of Appeal refused an application to register a new strain of soybean as an invention. The Court concluded that making a better soybean is not equivalent to inventing the soybean. Many seed companies produce new varieties of basic seeds through cross-breeding. These are not patentable unless they actually represent new plants.

Although recipes cannot be patented, cooking processes can be protected. Proctor & Gamble once won a patent-infringement case involving an unusual method of baking cookies that left them very soft. The company successfully sued a competitor for using the same method.

REGISTRATION OF A PATENT

An application for a patent may be made by the inventor or the inventor's agent. The rule is "First filed, first registered," which means that the first inventor to apply is entitled to the patent. This system replaced the former first-to-invent system, which often led to legal battles over who first invented something. Therefore, prompt application is important. Foreign inventors may apply for patent protection in Canada. It is always possible that two people may invent the same thing at approximately the same time.

As the preparation of a patent application is quite complex, most people are advised to use a patent agent trained in this specialized practice and registered to practise by the Canadian Patent Office. A list of registered agents may be obtained from the Commissioner of Patents. Some law firms specialize in intellectual property law. More inventors are turning to law firms because they not only assist in registering patents, but they are available to defend the patent against intruders. They serve in an advisory capacity to clients who want to know if a certain action will infringe someone else's patent.

After the patent agent files the application, it is considered by a technically trained examiner at the Patent Office, who may issue reports raising objections to the application. These reports by the examiner may also include references to prior patents that the examiner considers too close to the invention presently being claimed. The patent agent will study the reports and decide whether to amend the application in an effort to overcome the objections of the examiner, or to submit a written argument against the objections of the examiner. Such a written argument may include an explanation of the invention and exactly how it is different from all previous inventions. The inventor may appeal the decision to the Patent Appeal Board. If the patent is still denied, the inventor can take the matter to the Federal Court of Canada, but this is a very expensive undertaking. In addition to these tasks, a patent agent may also be asked to register a patent in a foreign country.

If two or more inventors work together and make an invention, they are joint inventors and should file a joint application.

Despite the fact that a foreign patent is not automatically valid in Canada, a Canadian cannot patent something he or she did not invent. For example, if a Canadian learns about an invention available in a foreign country that has never been registered in Canada, that person cannot patent it. A patent may be obtained by the true inventor only. In the application, the inventor must swear that he or she is the true inventor. However, a foreign invention never registered in Canada may be copied in Canada without any liability. An application will be made public 18 months after filing, even though the patent has not yet been granted. This policy allows technology to be shared at a much earlier date. If the patent is eventually granted, the patent holder may sue anyone who infringed the patent while the application was pending.

After the patent is granted, the patent holder may want to mark the product with the patent number, but marking is not specifically required. Once a patent is granted, a maintenance fee must be paid annually to maintain the patent. These fees allow for a shorter patent term if the invention proves uneconomical.

A patent is normally granted within three years of application. An inventor may mark goods with the words "Patent Pending" or "Patent Applied For." However, this has no legal purpose other than to notify others that the application has been made and therefore the inventor believes that he or she is first in line to receive the patent.

COMPULSORY LICENCES

As was previously mentioned, the concept of patent is that an inventor discloses his or her secret, rather than hides it, in return for a monopoly. Seldom does a person obtain a patent for something useful and then withhold it from the market. Should this happen, the public will be denied access to the invention for nearly 20 years.

One of the duties of the patent holder is to produce the invention to satisfy public demand for the new product. This is a public duty and presents important responsibilities for the patent holder. If the patent holder cannot obtain financing to manufacture his or her invention, the discovery will benefit no one. The *Patent Act* provides that, for certain inventions, a compulsory licence may be in order. For example, an invention patented in 1990 may be of benefit only if an invention patented in 1985 is also used. If the 1985 invention is not commercially available, later inventions that depend upon it cannot be brought to the market.

If the patent holder fails to "work" his or her patent to meet public demand for the invention, or if the price is unreasonably high, any interested party may apply to manufacture the invention under licence at any time after the patent has been in effect for three years. If the patent holder cannot refute the claim that the device is not readily available, the Patent Office may issue a licence to a subsequent applicant on whatever terms it deems reasonable. This usually involves the payment of a royalty to the inventor.

For many years, Canadian law permitted Canadian drug companies to copy brand-name drugs and market them under their generic names. The Canadian companies had to pay a mere 4 percent sales royalty to the inventor. Drug companies complained that they had invested millions of dollars inventing and testing new drugs, which were then copied by Canadian companies that invested nothing in research. In 1987, the law was altered to give the company that invents a drug between seven and ten years of exclusive rights to a drug. Afterward, other companies may copy it if they pay the 4 percent royalty.

In rare cases, where a patented item is not being made available to the public, the patent may be revoked.

PATENT RIGHTS AND INFRINGEMENT

The holder of a patent has the exclusive right to manufacture and sell his or her invention. The holder may elect to permanently assign or license the patent to someone else. A person who alleges that his or her patent was infringed may bring a civil action against the violator. The Patent Office has no responsibility for enforcing patent rights. The burden of proof is upon the patent holder to prove infringement. If the Court agrees that there was a violation, the Court may order the payment of damages and profits on sales.

LUBRIZOL CORP. v. IMPERIAL OIL

Federal Court of Canada, 1990

The Federal Court found that Imperial Oil had infringed the patent of Lubrizol Corporation regarding a chemical additive that made motor oil more efficient. The chemical was found in such brands as Esso Extra and Canadian Tire's Motomaster Oil. Lubrizol's carboxylic derivative compound keeps engine dirt in suspension, so it drains out when the oil is changed, thereby extending motor life. The Court rejected Imperial's argument that it had used a similar chemical of its own invention. Lubrizol also sued Exxon Corporation in the United States and settled out of court for $85 million.

A patent holder may also obtain a court order stopping patent infringement where a competing product is so similar that it represents only a variation of the patent. For example, in 1991, Imperial Tobacco Ltd., Canada's largest tobacco company, was ordered to stop selling roll-your-own cigarettes because another company held the patent on them. Rothmans Benson & Hedges Inc. convinced the Federal Court of Canada that it held a valid patent on the roll-your-own process. In 1982, two British engineers patented the windsurfing board. A resident of Holland successfully challenged the patent by showing that he had windsurfed for many years, using a homemade device almost identical to the one patented.

INDUSTRIAL DESIGN

Creative designing of industrial and commercial products requires time, effort, and skill to ensure that the end product not only fulfils the function it is intended to perform but also appears distinctive and attractive to the consumer. As a means of stimulating this creative output, creators are protected by the *Industrial Design Act*.

The Act provides legal protection for the appearance of a product for five years, renewable for an additional five years. The appearance can be changed by making it in a new shape, by substantially altering a well-known shape, or by applying some ornamental pattern to it. It is one or a combination of these features, applied to a manufactured article for the first time, that is protected.

It is sometimes difficult to determine if a design should fall under the protection of this Act or the *Copyright Act*. Most designs are drawn or reduced to some print form, so it is a difficult task to determine the true, unique nature of it. Copyright protection exists for 50 years, so many creators would prefer to have their designs copyrighted. If a single drawing or product is made, it may be protected by copyright as a work of art. But once the product goes into production (at least 50 items or sets must be produced), the work becomes an industrial design.

DORAL BOATS LTD. v. BAYLINER MARINE CORP.

Federal Court of Appeal, 1986

Bayliner sued Doral, a Quebec-based firm, for copyright infringement of its boat designs. Bayliner argued that the copyright in the plans for two of its boats was infringed when Doral made the same boats under different names. According to evidence presented at trial, Bayliner engineers constructed their boats by initially preparing design drawings which were then used to produce "plugs," which are three-dimensional renderings of the boats. Moulds were then made, and they were used in the actual boat manufacturing. Doral bought some of Bayliner's boats, took them apart, and made plugs for its own boats, thus avoiding the expense of designing the boats. The action was allowed at trial and Doral Boats appealed.

The Federal Court of Appeal allowed the appeal and held that boat design comes under the *Industrial Design Act*, not the *Copyright Act*. The issue was the appearance and shape of the boat, not some literal translation that is given to written drawings or plans. The boats had gone into production and hundreds had been built. The *Copyright Act* protects drawings only if they are not used as models or patterns to be multiplied by any industrial process.

REGISTRATION

Design protection is obtained through an administrative registration program operated by the Industrial Design Office. The designer must complete an application that contains a description of the original features of the design and drawings of the design as it appears in the manufactured product. If the design has already been made known to the public, it must be submitted within 12 months of the date when it was first made known.

An examiner studies the application to determine that the design is original and unique. If approval of the application is granted, the owner of the design has exclusive rights to the design for five years, renewable for a further term of five years. The owner must notify the public of registration by putting the letters "Rd" on a label marking the goods. The date and designer's name should also appear on the product. If registration is denied, the appeal process is the same as that for patents.

WHAT CANNOT BE REGISTERED

The Act protects the appearance of designs, not the function. The following are examples of designs that cannot be registered:

1. A process of manufacture;
2. Functional features of an article;
3. Materials used in construction;
4. Useful purpose of the design;
5. Colours;
6. Ideas;
7. Designs for articles that serve no useful purpose.

For example, a person cannot register a fork as a unique eating tool. The fork is a commonly used device. However, a person could design a unique, artistic handle for a fork and register the design.

REGISTERED TRADE MARK

For centuries, manufacturers have sought to develop consumer loyalty to their products. Early craftsmen and guilds developed unique marks as a promise of quality. They marked their products with these distinctive emblems to identify them. There was an obvious danger that competitors would try to copy the marks and sell inferior goods disguised as the real thing. Thus, the dishonest practice of **passing-off** (selling reproductions as originals) has a long and ugly history.

Today, passing-off has reached enormous dimensions. Technology makes possible the effective copying of labels, colours, shapes, and designs. Bogus watches, jeans, cameras, books, coins, and many other items flood the marketplace. Even if the trade mark is genuine, the registered owner of a trade mark can prevent other unlicensed people from using it. In *Mattel Canada Inc. v. GTS Acquisitions Ltd.* (1990), the Federal Court of Canada ruled that a company selling genuine Nintendo products without a licence from Mattel, which had the registered trade mark, was liable to Mattel. This ruling was based on the fact that Mattel had the right to protect the goodwill and reputation of the products developed through its own advertising and marketing programs, and that the sale of the products by unauthorized dealers damaged the goodwill developed by Mattel. Under the Act, the rights of a trade mark owner are infringed by a person not entitled to exclusive use of the mark who sells, distributes, or advertises wares or services in association with a confusing trade mark or trade name. The unauthorized marketing of genuine articles may be subject to legal action under the trade mark laws.

A **trade mark** is a word, symbol, picture, or a combination of these, used to distinguish the goods or services of a person or organization from the goods or services of others in the marketplace. A **trade name** is the name under which a business is carried on. A trade name can be registered under the *Trade Marks Act* only if it is also used as the trade mark. The Act defines a trade mark as "any mark used by a person for the purpose of distinguishing or so as to distinguish wares or services manufactured, sold, leased, hired or performed by him from those manufactured, sold, leased, hired, or performed by others."

A trade mark is registered for a period of 15 years from the date of registration. A renewal fee is payable to continue the registration for another 15 years. It can be extended indefinitely by paying the renewal fee. It is not absolutely necessary to register a trade mark. Those who have not registered their marks may still try to assert ownership under the common law. However, registration is the more effective way to prevent copying. A registered trade mark gives the owner the exclusive rights to its use in Canada. Registration in foreign countries must be done separately.

WHAT CAN BE REGISTERED

Any symbol, logo, drawing, or words that comprise a trade mark must be readily identifiable. If the mark is other than a word mark, drawings of the design must be submitted with the application. In some cases, unique combinations of everyday characteristics might create a trade mark. For example, sounds such as the NBC television chimes have been registered, as has Owens-Corning pink fibreglass.

WHAT CANNOT BE REGISTERED

There are numerous exclusions to registration. Such things as coats of arms of the Royal Family, the Red Cross symbol, the Canadian flag, and national symbols cannot be registered. The Canadian "Mountie" cannot be part of a trade mark. The Maple Leaf cannot be part of a trade mark, but can appear on products with the words "Made in Canada" just to show the country of origin.

Obscene symbols or pictures cannot be registered. More importantly, registration will be denied if the trade mark is too similar to an existing one and will cause confusion.

For example, a request to register a trade mark for a cleaner called "Klearex" was denied because a cleaner called "Clearex" already existed. Likewise, words that describe the place of origin are not registerable. For example, "London Perfume" is not registerable. A word describing the product itself cannot be registered, in any language. The word "Frutto" was not registerable because it means "fruit" in Italian. In 1990, the U.S. Patent Office issued a trademark to a California company for a peculiar scent that the company used in its yarn and thread. The company, OSEWEZ (pronounced "Oh Sew Easy") successfully argued that the smell enabled customers to identify its products.

Unique to trade marks is the "opposition proceeding." This is a process whereby any person having valid grounds for so doing may oppose a trade mark application that has been advertised in the *Trade Marks Journal*.

INSTITUT NATIONAL DES APPELLATIONS D'ORIGINE DES VINS v. ANDRES WINES

Ontario, 1989

The plaintiffs brought an action against the defendant winery, arguing that the word "champagne" was a French product associated with wine from the Champagne district of France and was a protected trade mark. The plaintiffs did not argue that Canadians were passing off their product as French champagne, but were making a very poor quality product and hurting the name "champagne" itself and the shared goodwill that French champagne producers had developed. The Court acknowledged that passing-off contains three elements: (1) reputation or goodwill exists in the product, (2) a misrepresentation is made, leading to deception, and (3) the misrepresentation leads to actual damage to that reputation or goodwill. The Court ruled that it was not passing-off as long as Canadian producers labelled their product as "Canadian Champagne." Since 1956, Canadian wineries have done so under orders from the federal government. All other champagnes are identified as "Imported Champagne."

The Court agreed that champagne had its origins in France, but the term has been effectively diluted for many years. The word "champagne" now describes a general product much as the word "wine" does, and is no longer distinct to one part of the world.

One of the problems that can occur if a product is very successful is that the trade mark name becomes the generic name, or the only name by which the product is called, no matter who manufactures it. If this occurs, the right to exclusive use of the name may be lost. For example, "Aspirin" was once the trade mark of a single company that made the pills. However, exhaustive use of the name caused the company to lose that exclusive right. "Linoleum" and "Scotch Tape" suffered the same fate.

In 1991, a Toronto jeweller named his new store "Diamonds R Us." He was promptly sued by Toys R Us and changed his store's name rather than engage in a costly court action. Even though no one could possibly mistake toys for diamonds, the catchy use of the letter R was distinctive.

OTHER MARKINGS

Several other marks also may be registered under the Act. **Service marks** are used by service industries that do not manufacture any products and therefore have nothing to which a trade mark could be affixed. A service company may register its logo and use it exclusively on such things as uniforms, delivery vehicles, etc.

Certification marks are used to distinguish goods of a certain quality. Such marks may describe grading, sorting, strength, or special treatment. For example, "Wolmanite" is a special process for treating lumber. Other companies can use similar treatments, but cannot use the same name.

Distinctive guise refers to unique packages and appearances of products that readily identify them. For example, when L'eggs pantyhose was first marketed, it was packaged in plastic eggs. The package design was registered.

COPYRIGHT LAW

The purpose of copyright legislation is to provide protection to creators of literary, photographic, and artistic works. The basic method of protection is to extend a monopoly with respect to the sale, display, performance, and control of the particular work. By using that monopoly the artist can recover the initial costs of creating the work, achieve personal profit, and advance his or her professional reputation. In the absence of protection, the prices of all literary works would be driven down to the level of basic printing, affording the creator nothing for the artistic effort that went into the work.

There is a long-standing difference of opinion, however, as to whether copyright protects the artist's soul or wallet. One view, which is expressed in the writings of French jurists, is that copyright protects the creative spirit of the artist. Infringement attacks the artist as a creative person. Taking an entirely different track, the British point of view has traditionally been that infringement represents an attack upon the artist's wallet and is primarily a financial matter. This difference of opinion is important when considering the issue of damages. If infringement did not bring the offender much profit, a British-minded court would award the artist very little. If the French view prevailed, the financial loss suffered would not necessarily be the basis of awarding damages. Present Canadian law recognizes the moral-rights point of view, as the following case illustrates.

SNOW v. EATON CENTRE

Ontario, 1982

Artist Michael Snow was commissioned to produce a sculptural work, consisting of 60 separate elements, each representing Canada geese. His sculpture, entitled *Flight Stop*, was positioned in the Eaton Centre in Toronto and was generally acclaimed as outstanding art.

Mr. Snow protested when employees of the Centre tied red ribbons around the necks of the geese as Christmas decorations. He demanded that the ribbons be removed, but the Centre refused. The Court ordered the ribbons removed, holding that an artist retains a measure of control over how his or her work is displayed. The purchaser of art must not alter or modify the work because this will injure the reputation of the artist. The artist can bring an action to preserve the integrity of his or her work to prevent modification, mutilation, distortion, or destruction.

Although the *Snow* decision strongly reinforced the moral rights of an artist, the Court managed to bring the topic of money into the decision by adding that distortion of artwork will negatively affect the artist's ability to earn a living if his or her reputation is injured. Moral rights were specifically recognized in the 1987 amendments to the *Copyright Act*.

The technology of copying has advanced much faster than the technology of protection. Nothing is safe from copying. Books can be photocopied. For every audiotape sold, 10 illicit copies are made. For every software program sold, 15 copies are made.

Commercial pirating takes on a grander scale. Two weeks after a best-selling novel is released, exact copies go on sale in many of the capitals of the world. These fakes, including identical covers, rob the author and publisher of millions of dollars. In 1990, Canadian police assisted two legitimate companies in a crackdown on other companies that produced unauthorized souvenirs and sold them at rock concerts. They seized 250 000 posters, 100 000 embroidered patches, 25 000 articles of clothing, and thousands of audiotapes. The total value of the bogus goods was in excess of $1 million.

One of the most troubling aspects of copyright law is the almost total absence of any case law. Between 1923 and 1987, copyright cases seldom came to court for two reasons: (1) the infringement was blatant and the parties settled out of court, or (2) the penalties were so minor that the copyright holder declined to pursue the matter in court.

In recent years, there have been some copyright cases involving computer language, but these cases did not deal with the most confusing aspects of the law. The result of this situation is an absence of clear definitions of terms used in the Act.

COPYRIGHT ACT

In Canada, the protection of literary and musical works exists under the *Copyright Act*. A major revision of the Act took place in 1923 and the law remained unchanged for more than 60 years. Finally, responding to a growing chorus of complaints from publishers, software companies, and recording companies, important amendments were enacted in 1987. Penalties for infringement were sharply increased and new areas of technology, such as computer software, were given specific protection. Bill C-60, *An Act to Amend the Copyright Act*, was hotly debated and represented a battle between creators, who wanted more protection, and users, who opposed greater restrictions on copying.

WHAT CAN BE COPYRIGHT PROTECTED

The Act contains numerous definitions as to what types of work can be protected by copyright. (It should be pointed out that every creator has immediate copyright of his or her work as soon as it is created. Although registration of copyright provides greater protection, it is not absolutely necessary. The author of a manuscript holds the copyright even before it is published.) There have been numerous cases in which one author was sued by another for copying parts of his or her manuscript. The author of the best-selling novel, *Roots*, settled out of court with another author who claimed that some of his work had been incorporated into the book. The same argument has been advanced against movie producers, alleging that movie plots were stolen from authors who were never paid. Section 2 of the Act lists the following interpretations of terms:

"architectural work of art" means any building or any model of a building;

"artistic work" includes paintings, drawings, maps, charts, plans, photographs, engravings, sculptures, works of artistic craftsmanship, and architectural works of art;

"book" includes every volume, part or division of a volume, pamphlet, sheet of letterpress, sheet of music, map, chart, or plan separately published;

"choreographic work" includes any work of choreography, whether or not it has any story line;

"cinematograph" includes any work produced by any process analogous to cinematography;

"collective work" means:
(a) an encyclopedia, dictionary, yearbook, or similar work,
(b) a newspaper, review, magazine, or similar periodical, and
(c) any work written in distinct parts by different authors, or in which works or parts of works of different authors are incorporated;

"computer program" means a set of instructions that is expressed, fixed, embodied, or stored in any manner and that can be used directly or indirectly in a computer in order to bring about a specific result;

"dramatic work" includes any piece for recitation, choreographic work or entertainment in dumb show, the scenic arrangement or acting form of which is fixed in writing or otherwise, and any cinematograph production where the arrangement or acting form or the combination of incidents represented give the work an original character;

"engraving" includes etchings, lithographs, woodcuts, prints, and other similar works, not being photographs;

"lecture" includes address, speech, and sermon;

"literary work" includes tables, compilations, and computer programs;

"musical work" means any combination of melody and harmony, or either of them, printed, reduced to writing, or otherwise graphically produced or reproduced;

"performance" means any acoustic representation of a work or any visual representation of any dramatic action in a work, including a representation made by means of any mechanical instrument or by radio communication;

"photograph" includes photo-lithograph and any work produced by any process analogous to photography;

"work of sculpture" includes casts and models.

As the reader can see, copyright exists in many forms other than print. It is found in a unique presentation of a play, a new dance, special musical arrangements, or a speech. When Washington, D.C., newspapers printed the entire text of Dr. Martin Luther King's "I had a dream" speech, he successfully sued them for copyright infringement.

In the case of *Randall Homes v. Harwood Homes* (Manitoba, 1987) the Court held that house plans are subject to the same copyright protection as works of art. The Court awarded damages to an architect whose prize-winning house was copied by a contractor. The Court found that the house had so many artistic innovations that it was sufficiently unique to be protected by copyright.

WHAT CANNOT BE COPYRIGHT PROTECTED

Facts, themes, ideas, mere titles, names, catch phrases, or short word combinations of no real substance cannot be protected by copyright. No one has the copyright to "2 + 2 = 4." No one can copyright the word "cool." However, there is nothing to prevent "copycats." For example, when the game Trivial Pursuit became a success, dozens of similar games were marketed. They did not copy the original game, but were based on the same theme of trivia recall.

BRITISH COLUMBIA et al. v. MIHALJEVIC

British Columbia, 1989

Following on the success of Montreal's Expo '67, Branko Mihaljevic guessed that Vancouver would have a fair to coincide with its 1986 centennial. In anticipation, he registered a copyright of the words, "Expo '86." In 1985, when he began selling hats and T-shirts of his own design, he was sued by the British Columbia Expo Corporation for breach of the fair's trade mark. He launched his own suit to have his trade mark registered and the government's trade mark cancelled. The Court held that "Expo '86" was not protected by copyright, but only by trade mark. Under the Act, the government had exclusive rights to the phrase "Expo '86." The Court held:

> *The defendant's copyright does not confer on him the right to exclusive use of the designs, nor does it give him a unique right to use each element of such designs. Copyrights cannot prevail once marks are registered and exclusive use is secured to the plaintiff.*

The Court expressed doubts whether the defendant had a copyright at all, as there is no copyright in mere words. Nor could the defendant claim to be the author of the words. However, as the case was decided on other grounds, this particular issue was not settled.

COPYRIGHT PROTECTION

The word **copyright** is defined in section 3 of the Act as follows:

> 3.(1) For the purposes of this Act, "copyright" means the sole right to produce or reproduce the work or any substantial part thereof in any material form whatever, to perform, or in the case of a lecture to deliver, the work or any substantial part thereof in public; if the work is unpublished, to publish the work or any substantial part thereof; and includes the sole right:

(a) to produce, reproduce, perform, or publish any translation of the work;
(b) in the case of a dramatic work, to convert it into a novel or other non-dramatic work;
(c) in the case of a novel or other non-dramatic work, or of an artistic work, to convert it into a dramatic work, by way of performance in public or otherwise;
(d) in the case of a literary, dramatic, or musical work, to make any record, perforated roll, cinematograph film, or other contrivance by means of which the work may be mechanically performed or delivered;
(e) in the case of any literary, dramatic, musical, or artistic work, to reproduce, adapt, and publicly present such work by cinematograph, if the author has given such work an original character; but if such original character is absent the cinematographic production shall be protected as a photograph;
(f) in case of any literary, dramatic, musical, or artistic work, to communicate such work by radio communication;

and to authorize any such acts as aforesaid.

It is surprising that the Act does not specifically deal with television or video recordings. It is unclear whether the word "cinematograph" includes television. Other commentators have suggested that the phrase "mechanically performed" includes video recorders because they have mechanical parts as well as electronic parts. The essence of the definition is found in the very first part of this section of the Act, which gives the creator the right to produce or reproduce. Nearly every case of alleged copyright infringement involves one person reproducing something that belongs to another person. "Copyright" must be given its literal meaning: the right to copy.

Copyright in Canada exists for the life of the author and for 50 years following his or her death. There are important variations of this rule:

- **Author unknown**: Copyright exists for 50 years from the date of first publication of the work.
- **Crown copyright**: Copyright in a work published by the Crown exists for 50 years from the date of first publication.
- **Recordings**: Copyright is for 50 years from the date of making the original plate.
- **Photographs**: Copyright exists for 50 years from the making of the original negative.
- **Work of joint authorship**: Copyright exists during the lifetime of the author who dies last and 50 years following his or her death.

Copies of each work do not have to accompany registration. However, the *National Library Act* requires that two copies of each book with a retail value of less than $50 that is published in Canada, and one copy of a sound recording manufactured in Canada, be sent to the National Library within one week of publication. Only one copy of a book with a retail value of more than $50 must be submitted. The Act also defines books to include documents, records, and tapes.

It is not necessary to mark a book with a copyright notation. However, other countries require that works be marked with a small *c* in a circle, the name of the copyright owner, and the year of first publication. Therefore, if the work will be published or sold in other countries, the work should be properly marked. The Crown can hold a copyright in the same manner as any private citizen, as the next case illustrates.

THE QUEEN v. LORIMER PUBLISHING

Federal Court of Appeal, 1984

The Crown published a study entitled *The State of Competition in the Canadian Petroleum Industry*. It comprised seven volumes and was priced at $70. The defendant printed a summary of this work, comprising one volume and priced at $14.95. The defendant acknowledged that it had taken the material for its book from the Crown study but argued that there was no financial harm because the smaller book would not diminish sales for the larger work. The defendant also argued that the information was public domain and that the Crown could not enforce copyright when it had used public funds to produce a book.

The trial judge refused an injunction but made an unusual ruling that the defendant would have to pay the Crown a percentage of sales. The Crown appealed. The Court of Appeal held that the injunction should be granted:

> *Once infringement has been established, the copyright owner is entitled to an injunction. That the owner suffered no damages is not basis for denying an injunction. There is no legal basis in the legislation for the trial judge to order the defendant to pay a percentage of sales to the plaintiff. The legislation does not envision some form of compulsory licensing of this nature.*

The Court also permitted the Crown to recover costs, saying that there is no longer any such rule as the "rule of dignity" that prevents the Crown from recovering costs.

DEFINITION OF "PRIVATE"

The *Copyright Act* states that certain actions are not infringement of copyright because they represent **fair dealing** with the subject matter. Section 27 begins by stating that **infringement** is doing anything that "only the owner of the copyright has the right to do." However, section 27(2)(a) declares fair dealing to be an exception to the normal prohibition against copying:

> 27.(2) The following acts do not constitute an infringement of copyright:
> (a) any fair dealing with any work for the purposes of private study, research, criticism, review, or newspaper summary;

The meaning of fair dealing has been subject to much discussion and speculation. Perhaps the most troubling word in this section is the use of the word "private." It is not infringement to copy something for "private study." The word "private" also appears in another important section that pertains to performances:

> 43.(1) Any person who, without the written consent of the owner of the copyright or of his legal representative, knowingly performs or causes to be performed in public and for private profit the whole or any part, constituting an infringement, of any dramatic or operative work or musical composition in which copyright subsists in Canada, is guilty of an offence, and is liable on summary conviction to a fine not exceeding two hundred and fifty dollars, or in the case of a second or subsequent offence, either to such fine or to imprisonment for a term not exceeding two months, or to both.

In section 27, the word "private" refers only to the word "study." It does not modify the other words because, if it did, it would produce absurdities. What would be a "private newspaper summary"?

So, what does the word "private" actually mean? Some writers argue that "private study" implies that only one person is involved. The phrase would then mean that a person may make a copy of something that he or she alone will study. There is no solid basis for this argument, however; it can be argued that the word "private" can have multiple meanings that do not refer to one person. For example, an artist may have a "private showing" of his or her work. A person may invite friends to a "private party." A building may have a "private entrance." What meaning does the word "private" have in these uses? Private can mean out of sight, removed from public view, not available for public use, or done confidentially. In none of these definitions would it be correct to say that the word means "confined to one person."

The opposite of "private" is "public" and section 43 refers to both terms. There are no useful case reports in Canada on this issue, but there are numerous U.S. and British cases that are instructive. The established law in the United States is that a work is performed publicly if it is performed at a place open to the public or at any event where a substantial number of people outside a normal circle of a family or its social acquaintances is gathered. Thus, a performance limited to members of a family and invited guests is not a public performance. The case law is that a performance is not public if the audience is limited to a small, particular group. Public means "open to a substantial number of persons."

However, it is important to consider how the audience was selected. If it is a club that anyone can join, it would be a public performance even though only club members were present. A restaurant that has an orchestra entertain customers is giving a public performance because anyone may enter the restaurant. If a hotel pipes music into the lobby, this is a public performance of that music. It therefore follows that a classroom is not a public gathering and thus whatever is shown or presented in the classroom is not a public performance. The class is not open to everyone and presence in the class is limited by enrolment. The British *Copyright Act* specifically declares that a school is not a public place.

If something is copied for the use of a small number of people, it may be argued that the material is still for private study because it is not being made available to the public and each person receiving a copy studies it by himself or herself.

Further confusion is found in the words "research" and "criticism." If a teacher gives students an assignment that requires them to research a topic or criticize a theory or work, then all of the supposed limitations become irrelevant. Material could be copied and made available to the student for the purposes of research. This conclusion would be of great importance to libraries as well as teachers. There is no Canadian case on this important issue, but a U.S. case dealt head-on with the problem.

THE WILLIAMS AND WILKINS CO. v. THE UNITED STATES

U.S. Court of Claims, 1973

The plaintiff company sued the U.S. Department of Health because its library staff made photocopies of articles in medical journals for research. The library subscribed to 3000 journals, receiving two copies of each. One copy was kept on reserve and the other was circulated. However, hundreds of researchers requested articles from the journals each week. To meet the demand, the library made photocopies of the articles. The library limited each request to one photocopy of the article, not to exceed 50 pages. Each copy was stamped with the words:

> **This is a single photocopy, made by the National Library of Medicine, for purposes of study and research in lieu of lending the original.**

In 1970, the photocopy budget was $86 000. The total number of pages copied was 930 000. The library also answered 127 000 requests for inter-library lending. The Court held that the number of copies made was not relevant to the main issue, and that medical science would suffer if the practice was stopped. Researchers could not buy subscriptions to all of the journals themselves, and would waste time reading articles to make notes.

The publisher had argued that copying injured it because the people requesting the photocopies were the publisher's market. However, no evidence was submitted as to how much injury this represented. It was only presumed that there was injury. The publisher did introduce the evidence of two people to the effect that, once they found that they could borrow articles from the library without fee, they cancelled their subscriptions.

The Court held that there had been no violation of copyright. The Court specifically declined to presume loss, saying:

> *To us, it is very important that the plaintiff has failed to prove its assumption of economic detriment. The record does not show any serious, adverse effect.*

The plaintiff was not entitled to recovery. The majority found that what the library was doing was fair dealing and protected by the right of people to copy for research. There was a dissenting opinion in which the minority held that this was a violation of copyright because the defendant was not copying, it was reprinting by modern methods and distributing the copies to a wide number of users.

Although the *Williams* case is significant, a Canadian court would not necessarily come to the same conclusion, because the Canadian Act protects the moral rights of the creator as well as the economic rights. In *Williams*, the plaintiff could not demonstrate to the satisfaction of the Court that there was serious economic loss. A Canadian court would not require such proof.

There is no easy answer to the problem of interpreting words such as "private" or "research." However, a government report on copyright, which was prepared as a forerunner to Bill C-60, suggested that fair dealing means: "A use that does not conflict with the normal exploitation of the work in subject matter and does not unreasonably prejudice the legitimate interests of the copyright owner." This has been taken to include three rules, or guidelines, for copying:

1. Copying must not be so substantial that it will materially reduce demand for the original.
2. The nature of the work may determine whether there was harm. The owner's expectation as to how the material was to be used is relevant.
3. The amount or extent of the copying is relevant. It would not be fair dealing to copy a work in its entirety. This is reprinting, not copying.

ART AND PHOTOGRAPHY

An "artistic work" includes works of painting, drawing, sculpting, and artistic craftsmanship, and architectural works of art, engraving, and photography.

It is very difficult for an artist to put his or her name or the word "copyright" on everything the artist creates. However, a photographer can stamp his or her name on the back of photographs. There are two rights—economic and moral—in artistic copyright. These have been clearly defined in the Act.

The economic rights include the right to sell or lease the work for illustration or other purposes. A photographer may sell a photograph to a magazine, but may do so with the contractual term that the magazine will use the photograph only once. Thus, the author or publisher of a textbook who wants to use a photograph taken from a magazine is often advised that the magazine does not have the copyright. The publisher must obtain permission for use from the photographer.

An artist also has moral rights. These rights include placing restrictions upon the manner in which the work is displayed. The *Snow* case made this abundantly clear even before the legislation recognized the principle. The artist has the right not to have his or her work altered, defaced, or destroyed. The Act states:

> 28.2(1) The author's right to the integrity of a work is infringed only if the work is, to the prejudice of the honour or reputation of the author,
> (a) distorted, mutilated, or otherwise modified; or
> (b) used in association with a product, service, cause, or institution.

A change in the location of a work or restoration is not infringement of the author's moral rights. It is important to keep in mind that moral rights continue even after economic rights have passed to another person, unless the contract specifically states that the creator gives up his or her moral rights. For example, a songwriter could prevent the use of his or her song to sell a commercial product.

No newspaper or magazine ever acquires reproduction rights to syndicated cartoons. The common practice of many organizations of highlighting newsletters, bulletins, and other publications with "Herman" cartoons and similar works, without permission of the cartoonist, violates the Act.

There are many ambiguities in the law. If a work of art is displayed in a very public manner, who controls the image? For example, Mr. Snow's geese have been photographed by many people who enter the Eaton Centre. Is copyright violated, or does something so open to public view become public domain? It is one of many unanswered questions.

What constitutes "art" is also subject to debate. In 1991, Henry Smith, a wood carver from New Brunswick, prodded the federal government into prosecuting a company that was copying his designs of lawn ornaments. Smith first created the "small boy with fishing pole" lawn ornament and later the "leaping salmon." Walton's Lawn Ornaments was fined $1200 for copying Smith's artwork.

COMPUTERS AND COPYRIGHT

Computer piracy consists of the unauthorized copying of machine language or computer programs. It is a violation of the *Copyright Act*, the *Criminal Code*, and the contractual licence between the user and the creator. Yet it is estimated by numerous authorities that, for every program sold legitimately, between 10 and 30 illegal copies exist. This huge inventory of illegal program copies has reduced the effective sales life of a newly released software package to no more than six weeks. For the hard-core pirate, it takes only three weeks to obtain an illegal copy.

Computerized information storage and retrieval systems are common in business, government, and education. There are two languages in each system—the machine language and the program language. There has never been a serious question that program language is protected by copyright and the courts have enforced the rights of the copyright holder in both criminal and civil actions. There have been important court decisions about machine language. The primary argument was whether machine language is a language at all, or whether it is just a series of mathematical computations. When computer scientists speak of computer languages, they do not mean a spoken language, but a series of commands. Do these constitute a true language?

GEMOLOGISTS INTL. LTD. v. GEM SCAN INTL. et al.

Ontario, 1986

Gem Scan, a newly established jewellery appraisal company, used the source codes, data disks, and other documents that its employees copied before they left the employ of Gemologists International to start their own company—Gem Scan. The Court heard how four of the five employees resigned without notice and immediately went into competition with their former employer, using a new name, but marketing the software misappropriated from Gemologists.

Gemologists had spent four years developing its software programs and had taken steps to protect its interests in the programs through security procedures and copyright. Despite warnings from their lawyer not to use the pirated programs, the defendants hired two computer programmers to write a new program which was little more than a slightly altered copy of the pirated software. The menus, sequence of operation, and structure of the new program were identical to the old program. The Court issued a permanent injunction against further use of the software.

In *Apple Computer v. Mackintosh Computers* (1990) the Supreme Court of Canada also ruled that machine language—the system by which the operating system of the computer operates—is protected by copyright. Machine language is a language, albeit a mathematical language rather than a spoken language, and can be registered as a literary work. The decision was rendered even though the *Copyright Act* had been amended to specifically protect machine language. The ruling clarified that the protection extends to all copies made before 1987.

Not all software copying is illegal. The best-known practice is what is generally called "making a backup." Software is sold on diskettes that are either permanently transferred to a hard disk drive or loaded for each use in the disk drive of the computer. Careless storage, rough handling, or the unhappy transfer of a computer virus to a system can erase or damage programs. Thus, users are advised to make a second copy of the program and data diskettes in order to prevent permanent loss.

Licensing agreements permit this and, if the user does nothing more, there is no legal problem. The 1987 amendment to the Act specifically authorizes the making of backup copies. Section 27 permits a person who is in lawful possession of a computer program to make a reasonable number of reproductions, provided that not more than one of the reproductions is used at any given time and the reproductions are destroyed when the person ceases to be entitled to use the program.

Other ambiguities exist in the law. One problem lies with the practice of borrowing for evaluation. Although the licensing agreement does not authorize lending or renting software, there is a dispute over allowing a person to borrow software to evaluate it. The Act is silent on this issue, but a British case considered a similar problem. In *CBS v. Ames Records and Tapes, Ltd.* (1981), the Court of Exchequer held that a retailer who rents tapes and records and also sells blank tapes bore no personal responsibility if its customers illegally copied the tapes and records. Ames displayed signs in its stores warning against illegal copying and did not encourage its customers to break the law.

Another question that arises is whether software is sold for one particular computer. If a corporation purchases software, may its employees take the software home and run it on a personal computer? Or must the software be used only on the company computer? The Act is silent on this issue but many licensing agreements specifically authorize or prohibit the physical transfer of the software. For example, Microsoft Canada permits its programs to be used on only one computer at a time. The agreement prohibits software from being put into a "network" which can be accessed from other workstations. If this is what the purchaser wants to do, it must obtain special licensing permission from the software company.

It is important to read the license agreement that accompanies software. In nearly every instance, software is not sold to the user, it is licensed. Ownership remains with the software company. If the user violates the terms of the agreement, the software company can demand that the software and manuals be destroyed. Failure to comply could lead to a civil action by the software company.

LIBRARY PRESERVATION

One of the most often-cited reasons for the photocopying of print material is library preservation. A library has two major limitations: (1) space, and (2) funding. A library cannot purchase five, ten, or more copies of every bound volume or magazine because it does not have ample shelf space to store so many copies of different works. Also, a library is limited in the funds available and cannot reasonably buy multiple copies of every useful book on every subject.

The space problem is reduced by purchasing just two copies of a book, preserving one, and lending the other. Many books, journals, and magazines are transferred to microfilm. This copying, done primarily to preserve literary work, would appear to violate the law.

More importantly, a library is truly a collection of books. Some of these may be irreplaceable at any cost. The library's instinct is to hoard the books and not let anyone touch them, which hardly serves the purposes of a library. However, books are inevitably damaged or lost. There are cases of people signing out very rare books, claiming they lost them, and offering to pay for them at the original price. Having learned that these books cannot be purchased anywhere, collectors turn to libraries as a source. Although the library appears to have been compensated for the loss, in reality rare books disappear into private collections this way. It is also a common problem in schools that many students are often researching the same topic at the same time—straining the resources of the library. The students are tempted to steal the books or tear pages from books so that assignments can be completed. Regrettably, these students have no concerns about depriving future generations of the use of a particular work.

It is a unique feature of libraries that they reduce the sales of books by lending them to readers who might otherwise buy them. In 1986, the federal government recognized this problem by creating the Public Lending Right Commission, which administers a program of payments to Canadian authors for their eligible books catalogued in libraries across Canada. Payments are determined by a sample of holdings of a representative number of libraries.

TELEVISION, VIDEOTAPE, AND AUDIOTAPE

The use of videotape and audiotape in the home, school, and business is growing at the rate of 15 percent per year. Programs can be purchased, rented, or taped off the air. Surprisingly, the 1987 amendments to the *Copyright Act* did not contain a single reference to taping. However, the Act does refer to copying by "other contrivance," which might include a video or audio recorder. It should be stressed that performing rights are distinctly different from copying rights.

The most pertinent, and debatable, section of the Act is the section pertaining to public performances, section 43, which was cited earlier in this chapter.

There are three terms that are highly debatable in this section. The first is "performance," which is defined in the Act as "any acoustic representation of a work or any visual representation of any dramatic action in a work, including a representation made by means of any mechanical instrument or by radio communication." The 1923 legislation limited players and musicians from playing music in public. This does not readily adapt itself to videotapes. As was already mentioned, the word "public" is debatable. In *R. v. Burko* (Ontario, 1969), a provincial Court held that a school classroom is not a public place. It is the property of the Board of Education. Therefore, showing a videotape in a classroom to a select number of students registered in a class is not a public performance.

Lastly, the public performance section requires that the performance be given for private profit. "Profit" has been defined as a "direct or indirect commercial advantage." Therefore, it must be proven that the person showing or playing the tape is profiting by it. A business that plays taped music for its customers does profit, because the music may increase business. However, there is no private profit in a private home or a classroom. Despite arguments to the contrary, no person in Canada has ever been sued for, or convicted of, an unlawful public performance because that person showed a videotape or played an audiotape in a home or classroom.

In the unusual case of *Bishop v. Stevens* (1990) the Supreme Court of Canada ruled that a television company did not have the right to make an "ephemeral recording" of a song in the studio and then have a performer "lip sync" to the music on television. The television company had properly purchased the right to have an entertainer perform the song, but there was no authorization to record the song first. The fact that the tape would later be erased was not a defence. If the television company wished to have the music pre-recorded, it would have to purchase recording rights as well as performing rights.

COPY COLLECTIVES

The *Copyright Act* and the *Competition Act* specifically permit authors and publishers to join together to administer their rights for the benefit of all—both in granting licences to copy and in taking action against copyright infringers. Collective administration also benefits users, who often face difficulty in finding copyright owners to obtain permission to copy works.

The Canadian Reprography Collective (CANCOPY) is a federally incorporated, non-profit organization that has been formed to administer photocopying and other reprographic rights for authors and publishers. It issues licences to users of photocopied material and collects the money for authors and publishers. These licences contain guidelines specifying limits on permitted copying. In 1991, the Government of Ontario paid $2 million to CANCOPY to permit teachers to photocopy certain materials for their classes. A teacher may copy one chapter of a printed text, or 10 percent of the text, whichever is the smaller. Workbooks may not be copied. A publisher that does not want a work copied must specifically state this in the book, or ask that a book be placed on a register of books not to be copied. The Government of Quebec has a similar plan that includes both print materials and videotapes.

Collectives have existed in European countries for many years. Music syndicates operate along the same lines. Creators and publishers can refuse to join a collective.

CIVIL AND CRIMINAL PENALTIES

Unlike other intellectual property laws, the *Copyright Act* contains specific penalties for infringement. Also, the copyright holder may ask the Crown to prosecute offenders. Many sections still retain the small penalties enacted in 1923. For example, a violation of the public performance section can bring a fine of $250. However, the 1987 amendment established much tougher penalties for "commercial pirating":

> 42.(1) Every person who knowingly:
> (a) makes for sale or hire any infringing copy of a work in which copyright subsists;
> (b) sells or lets for hire, or by way of trade exposes or offers for sale or hire any infringing copy of any such work;
> (c) distributes infringing copies of any such work either for the purpose of trade or to such an extent as to affect prejudicially the owner of the copyright;
> (d) by way of trade exhibits in public any infringing copy of any such work; or
> (e) imports for sale or hire into Canada any infringing copy of any such work is guilty of an offence and is liable:
> (f) on summary conviction, to a fine not exceeding twenty-five thousand dollars or to imprisonment for a term not exceeding six months, or to both; or
> (g) on conviction on indictment, to a fine not exceeding one million dollars or to imprisonment for a term not exceeding five years, or to both.

In addition, the courts have applied the fraud section of the *Criminal Code* to commercial pirating. In *R. v. Kirkwood* (Ontario, 1983) the accused was convicted of fraud and sentenced to two years in prison for renting out pirated videotapes through his video store. Kirkwood had acquired these tapes by copying ones he had rented from other stores, thereby saving himself the expense of buying them. However, the Supreme Court of Canada held in *R. v. Stewart* (1989) that confidential information is not "property" and cannot be stolen. The Court compared confidentiality to fresh air. It can be enjoyed, but it cannot be owned. The Court was also troubled by the problem as to who would decide what was confidential. A person could be convicted for just having read something he or she was not supposed to have read. A person who was allowed to read confidential information by his or her employer could be called a thief if the person left that employment and still had the information in his or her head. It is unlikely a case of copyright infringement could be prosecuted as theft.

REVIEW: POINTS OF LAW

1. A patent is the exclusive right to make, use, and sell an invention for a period of 20 years.
2. To be patentable, an invention must be new and useful, not an improvement of an existing invention.
3. Ideas, facts, principles, and designs are some of the things that cannot be patented.
4. If two people invent the same thing, the first patent registered will take priority. The rule is "First filed, first registered."
5. An industrial design protects the unique appearance of a product, not its function.
6. A trade mark is a word, symbol, or picture, or a combination of these, used to distinguish the goods or services of a person or organization.
7. A trade mark cannot be registered if it will be confused with an existing trade mark.
8. Copyright is the sole right to produce or reproduce original literary, musical, or artistic work.
9. Copyright protection exists during the life of the author and 50 years after the author's death.
10. Copyright exists from the moment the work is created even if it has not been registered.
11. Some limited copying is permitted under a section of the Copyright Act referred to as "fair dealing."
12. Computer machine language and software are specifically protected by Canada's copyright legislation.

LEGAL BRIEFS

1. T produced a directory of Greek residents in the Toronto and Hamilton areas. Two years later, M published a "Greek Telephone Guide" for the Toronto area. The guide contained advertising and was almost identical to T's directory. T sued M for passing-off. M argued that he was simply competing with T. Is this passing-off?

2. H started a club called the "Music Swap." Members of the club would buy tapes and compact discs of music, and then lend them to each other. Many members made duplicate copies of the tapes. Some members taped only certain songs from the tapes. H acted as the "clearing broker" to make certain that all tapes were returned to their owners. H was charged with a violation of the copyright laws. Has H committed an offence?
3. L, an artist, sold a painting to the F Gallery. When L visited the gallery, he found his painting in a dark corner, in a cracked frame, and covered with dust from recent renovations to the building. L demanded that the gallery treat his work with proper respect. Must the gallery comply?
4. P drew some charcoal sketches of the "Tall Ships" when they visited Canada. P took them to a print shop to have 50 copies made, which she sold. The print shop made 50 additional copies and gave them to good customers. P demanded payment for the extra prints. Is P correct?
5. The International Button Makers Union has a new logo designed that incorporates the letters "IBM" inside a circle. Advise the union regarding its new logo.
6. R approached a newspaper with an idea for a promotional contest. The idea was to print a different number on each copy of the weekly TV guide sent out with the Sunday paper. Each Wednesday, winning numbers would be published and subscribers who held winning numbers could mail in the cover of their TV guide for a cash prize. The newspaper did not accept the idea. However, the paper then ran its own contest. Each TV guide had several letters printed on the cover. Subscribers clipped the letters and, when they could make a word with these letters, pasted them on a form and mailed it in. The contest was a take-off on the board game Scrabble. The newspaper was sued by both R and the company that markets Scrabble. Liability of the newspaper?
7. D, a high school student, was given permission to paint a large mural on a wall outside the art classroom. D painted an unusual depiction of rock singer Sting. It was partly original, partly taken from a concert poster. Two years later, it was announced that the school would be repainted and the mural painted over. D insists that the painters work around his mural and not cover it. Is D's demand justified?
8. Q developed a computer game for law students that operated on an Apple computer. When Q marketed the game, she put a distinctive Apple logo on the game. A representative of Apple Computer Canada warned Q to take the logo off the game because it gave the appearance that Apple produced and guaranteed the quality of the program. Q explained that she only meant the game operated on an Apple system, something potential buyers would want to know. Must the logo go?

APPLYING THE LAW

KEARNS v. FORD MOTOR COMPANY

U.S. District Court, 1990

The plaintiff brought an action against the defendant company on the grounds that the defendant had violated his patent rights. The plaintiff held patents on a device known as the "intermittent windshield wiper."

The Court heard evidence that the plaintiff designed the wiper, which was powered by a vacuum pump, and installed a set on his 1962 Ford Galaxy. In 1963, he showed it to Ford engineers, who questioned him at length about the design. The plaintiff was optimistic that Ford would buy the invention, but it never did. The plaintiff continued working on his invention and replaced the vacuum pump with electric switches.The plaintiff tried to interest other companies in his invention, but none showed any interest.

In 1969, the first intermittent wipers appeared on European cars, soon to be followed by North American and Japanese manufacturers. The plaintiff sued Ford, General Motors, and Chrysler, seeking damages of $50 per car for a total of $300 million. The plaintiff had not registered his patent in Europe or Japan. The defence argued that the plaintiff's patents should be set aside because he never demonstrated that he could actually manufacture or market the system. Further, the plaintiff's design was extremely bulky and inefficient. The plaintiff was trying to patent an idea, not a design or invention.

The judge held in favour of the plaintiff, ordering Ford to pay him $5 million in damages. The plaintiff had done more than patent an idea or concept: his invention was quite specific and workable. The fact that he did not have the financial resources to set up his own company, build a factory, and market his product did not necessarily defeat his patent. Although the systems eventually used by Ford were different in many aspects, they were basically modifications of the plaintiff's invention.

Questions

1. The defendant argued that the plaintiff had patented an idea, not an invention. Why did the Court disagree?
2. Was it relevant that the first intermittent wipers appeared on European cars? Why or why not?

3. The plaintiff did not invent the windshield wiper. Was his invention truly new?
4. The plaintiff did not attempt to mass-produce his invention. Why not? Was this a bar to his recovery of damages? Why or why not?

ROLEX WATCH CO. OF CANADA v. PALMER

Federal Court of Canada, 1989

The plaintiff brought an action against the defendant, Palmer, seeking an injunction against the importation and sale of fake Rolex watches.

The plaintiff represented Montres Rolex SA, the Swiss watchmaker whose expensive watches represent a luxury product. The defendant imported and sold similar watches that included the well-known crown design of Rolex. The name "Rollex" appeared in very small letters on each watch.

The defendant raised the unusual argument that he was not passing-off his watches as genuine. Rolex watches sell for $2500 to $10 000. Rollex watches sold for $40. The defendant provided each buyer with a card that included a disclaimer, stating that the Rollex was not a Swiss Rolex. The card identified it as an imitation.

"No one really believed he was buying a genuine Rolex for $40. This is simply another form of imitation art," the defendant testified. "People may fool their friends into believing they own a Rolex, but they were not fooled by me." The defence produced considerable evidence about the thriving industry generally known as "imitation art." Everything from famous oil paintings to rare books are artistically reproduced and sold as imitations. Art galleries sell oil paintings that are clearly marked as reproductions, not originals.

The Court issued the injunction, ruling that the defendant had infringed the Rolex trade mark and the watch's well-known design. The judge said Rolex had spent substantial funds and energy in promoting its trade marks, and the company's products were recognized as luxury products of quality and distinctiveness. The sale of imitation products was hurting the value of the goodwill associated with these products and misleading the public.

Questions

1. Imitation art is a very large industry, employing thousands of artisans around the world. As long as the products are labelled as copies, what harm is done? What laws are broken?

2. The defendant did not represent his watches as being genuine: he clearly advised buyers they were not buying a Rolex. Why did this defence fail?
3. The judge said the defendant deceived the public. Did the judge mean that it is unacceptable for the buyer to fool his or her friends? What did the judge mean by "public"?
4. It would be hard to argue that Rolex lost sales of genuine watches because the people who bought Rollex watches at $40 probably could not afford a genuine Rolex. What, then, is the basis of the injury to Rolex?

PRINCIPLES AND CASES

Case 1: Legal Principle

Where the Crown prosecutes one person under the *Copyright Act* for infringement, but does not prosecute others who are committing the same acts, it is not abuse of process unless it can be shown that the accused was singled out for unusually harsh treatment.

Case Facts

The accused, a disc jockey, had been in the practice of using compilation tapes made up of selections from previously recorded cassette tapes and record albums. He became concerned that this practice violated the law and had approached the recording industry association about the possibility of obtaining a licence. He was erroneously advised that no licensing procedure existed.

Subsequently, a former employee, who had a grudge against the accused, approached the association and made an agreement to assist in the investigation of the accused if she was granted immunity. The association advised the RCMP of the situation, but never told the RCMP about the informant or the secret agreement. The police executed search warrants and seized all of the accused's equipment, putting him out of business.

The accused argued that the purpose of the police raid was not to seize evidence, but to put him out of business. The accused also noted that many people do the same type of re-recording but no other person had been raided. The police, according to the accused, had been deceived by the association. Defence counsel stressed that the police had been "used" by a disgruntled former employee to take revenge on the accused.

Possible Decisions

A The accused should be convicted. How the police came to learn about his unlawful activity is irrelevant.

B The accused should be convicted. The fact that other people had not been prosecuted for similar acts is not relevant to his case.

C The accused should be acquitted. Because the search and seizure were motivated by the malice of the association and its informant, the entire matter is abuse of process.

D The accused should be acquitted. He had been falsely told that no licensing procedure existed, so he believed that his activities were lawful.

Case 2: Legal Principle

A patent can be issued only to the person who is the true inventor of a new and useful product. Invention is synonymous with "new discovery from research and experimentation."

Case Facts

The plaintiff entered a hospital suffering from cancer of the spleen. The spleen removes old blood cells but, in the diseased state, it fills with malignant white blood cells that kill healthy cells. The plaintiff's spleen was removed by the defendant doctor. The plaintiff recovered his good health.

The defendant doctor used cells from the plaintiff's spleen for medical research. He discovered disease-fighting cells in the plaintiff's spleen and then found a way to make these cells multiply. The plaintiff returned to the hospital several times to give the defendant blood, skin, and bone marrow. The doctor patented his discovery, called "Mo cells."

The financial benefit of the discovery was shared by a private company, the university where the doctor did research, and the defendant doctor.

The plaintiff sued, arguing that the spleen was genetically his and that the cells used for research belonged to him.

The defence argued that the plaintiff lost all rights to his diseased organ when it left his body. The defence also argued that human cells are not patentable. Only what is discovered using those cells is patentable and the plaintiff played no role in that whatsoever.

Possible Decisions

A The plaintiff is entitled to a share of the patent proceeds because his cells were the building blocks of the invention.

B The plaintiff is entitled to a share of the patent proceeds because he did not relinquish ownership of his spleen. He consented only to its removal.

C The plaintiff is not entitled to a share of the patent proceeds because he did not invent anything.

D The plaintiff is not entitled to a share of the patent proceeds because nearly all medical research is based upon raw materials that are otherwise not useful.

YOU BE THE JUDGE

1. The defendant university installed a photocopy machine in a library, allowing unlimited use of the machine by students. The school paid for the supplies used by the students. There were no warnings or other notices on or near the machine warning against copyright infringement. The school did not supervise the use of the machine. The students copied many books and articles that were protected by copyright, and an action was brought by a publisher against the school. The school contended that it was not responsible for the actions of its students. Who would succeed?

2. A television network initiated a new fishing program for ardent anglers. The host used his knack for fishing to teach viewers improved methods and to market some specific products such as fishing line, mosquito repellent, and fishing tackle. The host wore jeans, a checkered shirt, baseball cap, and moccasins. He used fishing jargon and told jokes. The program was called "Teaching You to Fish." Another network started a similar program. It, too, had an experienced host who discussed fishing techniques and good fishing spots. However, the network went so far as to have its host dress exactly the same as the first network's host. The judge referred to the situation as a look-alike contest. The program was called "We Teach You to Fish." The first network sued. Who would succeed?

3. The plaintiff company sought an injunction against the defendant company for infringement of its computer software copyright. The plaintiff had developed a software system for a credit union. The program was unique in many ways and was very costly to develop. The plaintiff was trying to sell it to other financial institutions. The defendant company was a small software company that approached the credit union for a loan. The manager of the credit union described the software system that it was using in glowing terms. The defendant's software engineers wanted to know more about it, so the credit union manager allowed them to spend two weeks studying the software and manuals. The defendant then developed its own software, which was basically an improvement of the plaintiff's program, and began marketing it to other prospective buyers at a very low price. Who would succeed?

4. The plaintiff company produced a publication about horse racing. It contained detailed information about the races to be run the next day. The plaintiff kept very detailed statistics about horses and jockeys, including comments about the performance of horses on muddy tracks, length of each race, weight of the jockeys, entries by post position, and purses. The defendant published his own newsletter. He took the data that the plaintiff printed, rearranged it, then added interviews with jockeys and trainers, betting odds, and many comments useful to the handicapper. The defendant contended that his was an unusual and unique publication. The plaintiff argued that the defendant was merely rearranging its information in a new format. Who would succeed?

5. A small city sponsored a summer festival in which street entertainers were employed to perform tricks, play music, and tell jokes to tourists throughout the city. The practice originated in England centuries ago and entertainers of this type are called "buskers." The idea had been used in other cities with great success. Posters were printed showing a clown in a top hat juggling three balls. An organization called "Buskers International Festivals Incorporated" filed suit, claiming exclusive rights to buskers and to the logo showing the clown. The city argued that buskers have existed for centuries and no one can claim exclusive rights to the concept. Who would succeed?

TORONTO LOCAL
CUPW
ON STRIKE

C H A P T E R   E L E V E N

LABOUR LAW

> *"By working eight hours a day you can become the boss and work twelve hours a day."*
>
> Robert Frost,
> author

LAW OF MASTER AND SERVANT

The *Constitution Act, 1867* assigns the power to legislate in the field of labour to the provinces. This creates a wide difference of laws across Canada from province to province, particularly with reference to the formation and operation of unions.

However, the federal government can legislate in the field of labour law with regard to people who are either directly employed by the federal government, Crown corporations, or federally chartered businesses. Nearly two million Canadians fall into the federal sphere.

UNDER THE COMMON LAW

The traditional common law term used to describe a person who works for another person is **servant**. The terms more commonly used today are worker or employee. The employer is referred to under the common law as the **master**. Despite its harsh sound, the phrase "master and servant" describes the nature of the employment contract, not the relationship between the two people.

The common law developed very few rules that protected the rights of employees. Courts consistently refused to interfere in such matters as wages and working conditions, holding that it was for Parliament to regulate such things. As well, there was a strong belief that government had no right to intrude into contracts of employment. Commerce, it was said, should be free from all government interference. The laws that did exist penalized workers for numerous actions. For example, workers could not quit their jobs without the permission of the employer. To do so was an offence—the offence of desertion of employment. If a worker damaged a machine while operating it, the worker had to pay for it. If an unsafe machine injured a worker, there was no liability upon the employer. The absence of any comprehensive legal protection helped speed the development of the labour union movement.

An **independent contractor** is a person who is not under the direct control of the person who does the hiring. Generally, someone who employs a contractor to do a particular job does not supervise or control the details of the work or the manner in which it is done. Ordinarily, the contractor provides the equipment, materials, and workers to carry out the contract. An independent contractor can be a company or a single individual.

At times, it is difficult to determine whether the relationship between parties is that of master and servant or employer and independent contractor. Typical of such grey areas are franchises, which the owner/manager seems to operate independently but is actually under the strict control of the franchise owner. In

Re Becker Milk Company Ltd. (1973) an Ontario Court concluded that the central issue is control. If the franchise owner controls the work schedule, activities, fixtures, merchandise ordering, and many other aspects of operating the business, then the store manager is an employee, not an independent contractor. If the person is an employee, then he or she is entitled to the protection of any provincial laws governing employees.

CONTRACT OF HIRE

The **contract of hire**, or employment contract, is a contract between the master and servant for services or labour. It is not a contract involving materials or goods, even if the worker must provide his or her own tools, transportation, or any other items. It is a contract like any other and is subject to all of the rules pertaining to contracts. All pertinent details, such as hours of work, duties to be performed, and rate of pay, should be included in the contract. A contract of hire may be oral or in writing. Most Canadians are employed on the basis of an oral contract.

A contract of hire is binding as soon as it has been accepted by the worker. If the employer does not honour the contract, the employer could be liable for civil damages, particularly when the worker has given up other employment to take the new position.

QUEEN v. COGNOS, INC.

Ontario, 1990

Douglas Queen was recruited by Sean Johnston, an employee of Cognos, for a position at its computer software development plant in Ottawa. Queen was told the project would run for a number of years and that the project would be well funded. Based on these representations and a signed contract, Queen quit a secure job in Calgary and moved to Ottawa.

When he arrived, he learned that Cognos had not completed feasibility studies or approved financing for the project for which he was hired. For 18 months, Queen was given odd jobs to do while the company studied the market potential of the software. The decision was made to cancel the project and Queen was let go. Johnston was fired at the same time.

Queen sued Cognos for "wrongful hiring." This was a unique lawsuit—the first of its kind in Canada. The suit alleged that the defendant had committed a tort by hiring Queen when it did not have a project for him to do. He could not get his previous job back, had incurred expenses moving to Ottawa, and had suffered career injury by wasting 18 months doing almost nothing. The plaintiff was awarded damages and the company appealed.

The Court of Appeal recognized that there is such a tort as "wrongful hiring" and that Queen's action could have succeeded, except for one crucial point—the written contract of employment. The contract which Queen had signed included a clause that said the company could terminate the employment without cause on one month's notice. The Court concluded that Johnston honestly believed the project would proceed when he hired Queen. There was no misrepresentation.

Queen had won a victory of sorts, but in the final analysis lost the case, because the written contract was deemed to be enforceable against him.

TERMINATION

A contract of employment may have a fixed term. If a person is hired for two years, the contract ends at that time and there is no obligation on either party to renew it. If the contract of hire is indefinite and has no fixed ending date, it is assumed that the two parties may continue in the contract as long as they are both satisfied with the relationship. Should either party want to end the contract, the common law would require that the party wanting to end the contract give the other **reasonable notice**. What constitutes reasonable notice depends upon a variety of things, including the availability of a replacement, the frequency of pay periods, and other factors. Many provincial laws also contain sections setting forth the requirement for giving notice.

In *Zimmer v. Cascade Construction Ltd.* (Alberta, 1985) the defendant company told the plaintiff that he "might be laid off" if business did not improve. When a major project was completed, the company abruptly fired the plaintiff. The Court held that this was not proper notice. Telling a person that he or she *might* lose a position is not notice, it is just a possibility. This requirement of reasonable notice applies equally to the master and the servant.

SYSTEMS ENGINEERING v. POWER

Newfoundland, 1989

Two computer technicians, Ken Power and Gerald Guy, resigned from their jobs with Systems Engineering without notice. They formed their own company and persuaded a third employee to join them. Systems was under contract to its clients to provide technical services and was liable for failure to meet its obligations. Systems had to hire an independent consultant at the rate of $550 per day. For a while, it hired Gerald Guy on the same basis.

Systems sued Power and Guy, claiming that it lost $75 000 in lost profits and $30 000 in actual costs when the two technicians left without notice. The Court awarded the company just $16 000, which it calculated as the amount that would have been lost if the employees had given reasonable notice, which the judge estimated would have been two weeks.

There are exceptions to the reasonable notice rule. For example, the master may fire the servant without notice for absenteeism, dishonesty, incompetence, or insubordination. The servant may quit without notice for reasons such as not being paid, unsafe working conditions, being assigned duties that are degrading, being assigned illegal tasks, or sexual harassment. The employer also may be held liable for not acting promptly to protect one employee from the wrongful actions of another. In *Brennan v. Canada and Robichaud* (Supreme Court of Canada, 1988) the Court held an employer, the Department of National Defence, liable because it did not take any action to stop a supervisor from sexually harassing a female employee. The Court concluded that only an employer can take action against its supervisory personnel and provide its workers with a safe and healthy work environment.

WRONGFUL DISMISSAL

Every employment contract, whether written or oral, contains a tacit understanding that the employee will not be fired without notice or reason. An employee who is fired without cause, reasonable notice, or pay in lieu of notice may sue the employer for **wrongful dismissal**. The lawsuit may ask for damages for loss of income, loss of professional status, cost of locating another job, punitive damages, retraining for another job, and relocation expenses.

The area of wrongful dismissal has been called "explosive." The number of people suing former employers has grown enormously and the awards have been very large. Employers can no longer dismiss people at will. Employers are taught at special seminars to "dehire" employees carefully rather than fire them. As well, employers are taught to maintain very detailed files on employees to support the decision to terminate employment. The wrongful dismissal avalanche began with the following case.

PILON v. PEUGEOT CANADA

Ontario, 1980

The plaintiff, a mechanic by trade, had worked for the defendant as a service manager for 17 years. The defendant had given its employees an assurance of lifelong security, and the plaintiff had rendered faithful and loyal service. The plaintiff was suddenly fired. In an action for damages, the plaintiff sought further damages for mental distress, anxiety, vexation, and frustration caused by the defendant's breach of contract. The Court held:

> *Discharge from one's position is frequently the cause of mental distress to an employee. I am not suggesting that such distress is actionable in all cases of termination. Had Peugeot discharged the plaintiff legally by giving him either 12 months' notice or payment in lieu thereof, I doubt that he would have any right to recovery, because there would have been no breach of contract. I think the right to recover damages for mental distress is conditional upon there being an actionable breach of contract. If Peugeot had wished to avoid legal responsibility for damages for mental distress, which they must have contemplated as a result of the sudden termination of Pilon's employment, they ought to have discharged him lawfully by proper notice.*

Pilon also received one year's wages but no compensation for what he called loss of job opportunity because of his age. He had argued that Peugeot fired him so late in life that his chances for developing a career with another company were nil. The Court did not accept this argument because there were no statistics to support this claim.

The case law which emerged after the *Pilon* case is massive and cannot be dealt with totally here. However, some important determinations were made that must be mentioned.

In *Ponzo v. Sawicki* (Ontario, 1985) the plaintiff sued for wrongful dismissal and defamation in the same action. The plaintiff had been a very successful bartender who brought so much business into his employer's place of business that he was allowed to give free drinks to regular customers and his friends. The defendant employer suddenly fired him, claiming that he was charging for two drinks when only one drink was served and pocketing the difference and taking bottles from the bar after closing. After he was fired, regular customers were told the plaintiff was fired for stealing. The issue for the Court was whether an action for wrongful dismissal and defamation could be brought as one action. The Court ruled that it was permissible and awarded damages to the plaintiff under both heads (types) of damage.

An employer may force an employee to resign by making the working conditions intolerable. This is referred to as **constructive dismissal.** Radically changing a person's job description and responsibilities, or reducing pay, may constitute constructive dismissal.

In *McNamara v. Price Wilson* (British Columbia, 1985) the plaintiff was transferred by his employer from Ontario to British Columbia, then fired. The Court took into consideration that the plaintiff had sold a house in Ontario, bought a house in British Columbia, and would now have to repeat the expensive process in reverse. As well, the plaintiff's wife had given up a secure job in Ontario that she could not get back. The employer was required to pay substantial damages.

The extent of damages reached absurd levels when an Ontario Supreme Court judge ordered the Canadian Development and Investment Corporation (CDIC) to pay its former chief executive officer $3.3 million in damages for wrongful dismissal. In the case of *Bell v. CDIC* (Ontario, 1990) the Court concluded that the plaintiff had been fired for political reasons which violated a promise of job security and tenure that he had been promised when hired.

The issue of emotional injury, begun in *Pilon*, was eventually heard by the Supreme Court of Canada in a different case. The Court was concerned about the direction that wrongful dismissal cases were taking. Rather than being matters of contract, the cases were becoming tort actions. The Court effectively put the brakes on this process in the following case.

VORVIS v. INSURANCE CORPORATION OF B.C.

Supreme Court of Canada, 1989

The plaintiff sued the defendant corporation after being dismissed from his job as legal counsel. Problems had arisen between Vorvis and his supervisor and he was ultimately fired. He was offered salary and benefits for eight months, which he refused. The action alleged wrongful dismissal, lost pension benefits, mental distress, and punitive damages. The Court accepted the plaintiff's claim for lost wages and pension benefits, but refused to make an award for the other two claims. The judgment read:

> *In my view, while it may be very unusual to do so, punitive damages may be awarded in cases of breach of contract. It would seem to me, however, that it will*

be rare to find a contractual breach which would be appropriate for such an award. ... As the name would indicate, punitive damages are designed to punish. In this, they constitute an exception to the general common law rule that damages are designed to compensate the injured, not to punish the wrongdoer.

The Court stressed that the issue between the two parties was a contract. It was a very impersonal, business matter that should be about money, not about personalities. The Court concluded that the case should be confined to the issue of lost earnings. The Court should not consider injured feelings or the manner of termination. If the employer slandered the employee, this could form an independent cause of action.

The decision in Vorvis brought the focus of a wrongful dismissal action back to the basic nature of the matter—breach of contract.

It would be wrong to leave the impression that the employee always wins a wrongful dismissal case. The evidence suggests the opposite. If the employer has cause to terminate the employment, then an action by the employee has little chance of success. In *Ball v. MacMillan Bloedel* (British Columbia, 1989) the plaintiff was fired for making 90 long distance telephone calls and charging them to his employer. The Court upheld his dismissal for dishonesty. Employees have been properly terminated for padding expense accounts, driving company vehicles for personal use, making sexual advances toward clients, and numerous other reasons.

If general economic conditions are poor, employers can lay off workers if they give notice. Outside of an employment contract with specific promises, no job is guaranteed and workers can be dismissed, with notice, for genuine business reasons.

LIABILITY OF MASTER TO SERVANT

At one time, the common law generally did very little in the way of allowing servants to sue their masters for injuries received at work. Every job was assumed to have some risks, and if those risks resulted in a predictable injury, there was no liability on the part of the master. There were almost no laws regarding health, safety, or working conditions. Workers were killed and maimed in factories and mines and had little recourse. They also suffered from industrial diseases. During the twentieth century, the courts finally determined that a master could be liable for the injuries suffered by a servant under two conditions:

1. If the master was personally negligent in not providing the servant with a safe place to work or a safe system of work;
2. If the master was personally negligent in not hiring competent co-workers.

The immediate problem that the servant faced was in trying to prove that the master was personally negligent in these matters, since most servants worked for a manager, supervisor, or other representative of the company.

PARIS v. STEPNEY BOROUGHS COUNCIL

England, 1951

The plaintiff was a mechanic in a garage owned by the defendant. The plaintiff was blind in one eye, a fact well known by his employer. While working on a truck, he used a hammer to loosen a rusted bolt. The hammer knocked away a piece of metal which blinded the plaintiff's other eye, rendering him 100 percent sightless. He sued his employer on the ground that his employer failed to provide him with goggles to protect his eye.

The defendant argued that the accident was freakish, that none of the other mechanics wore goggles, and that the employer owed no greater duty of care toward an employee with one eye than toward employees with two eyes. The trial judge held in favour of the defendant, saying that a "one-eyed man is no more likely to get a splinter in his eye than a two-eyed man."

However, this decision was overturned by the Court of Appeal, which held that the gravity of harm was so severe that a reasonable employer would have shown greater concern for a one-eyed employee and required him to wear goggles even if the other employees did not. The plaintiff had a special need of protection that was known to the employer.

The servant's right to sue his or her master has been greatly reduced by the establishment of workers' compensation plans across Canada. More will be said about these plans later in this chapter.

LIABILITY OF THE MASTER TO THIRD PARTIES

In common law, if a servant commits a tort while acting within the scope of employment for a master, the master is liable in tort to the third party who is injured. The master can, in turn, sue the servant and recover any money paid out because of the servant's negligent actions. In *Mayers v. Palmer and Smith* (British Columbia, 1990) a packaging company, whose senior salesman had copied the account cards from his former employer and used the confidential information to steal customer accounts, was held liable for his behaviour even though it did not know what he was doing. The Court held that the employer has a duty to check that employees are not improperly using confidential information from an earlier contract.

EDWARDS v. DONATELLI BROTHERS, LTD.

Ontario, 1989

The defendant company hired a man to operate a bulldozer. The construction supervisor did not ask if the man was qualified to operate a bulldozer. On the job application form, the man had stated that he was experienced in the use of heavy earth-moving equipment. The truth was that he had only taken a correspondence course from a school in the United States. The course, entitled "Construction Methods," was not recognized by any construction association in Canada or the United States. The school was no longer in existence. The new employee had never operated anything larger than a small front-end loader, and he had only operated it for four hours.

The employee was loading earth into a dump truck when he negligently dropped the shovel-blade onto the cab of the truck, injuring the driver. The defendant was held liable for the negligence of its employee. The false statement on the application form was no defence against an injured third party.

The injury must arise within the scope of employment. If the incident is unrelated to employment, the employer is not liable. In *Jennings v. CNR* (Ontario, 1925) a ticket collector got into an argument with a passenger and hit him. The trial judge did not hold the employer liable, but the appeal court did. It was held that the assault arose while the collector was arguing about a ticket with the passenger. Therefore, the assault arose from an "act of employment" and required the CNR to be responsible for the tort of its employee.

HUMAN RIGHTS AND LABOUR LAW

Examination of the history of human rights in Canada reveals a spotted record. At times, various legislatures made very definite attempts to discriminate. Discrimination has long existed against Asians, blacks, Jews, Indians, and other groups. Just before the end of the nineteenth century, British Columbia passed laws prohibiting Asians from working in the mines or forests. Asians could not obtain business licences in British Columbia or Saskatchewan. Saskatchewan also made it illegal for an Asian to hire a non-Asian, female employee. In 1939, a black man was denied service in a Montreal bar. He sued the owner under a provincial law that required restaurant owners to serve "travellers," but the Supreme Court of Canada held that a merchant is free to deal as he or she chooses with any member of the public.

Discrimination in employment was once widespread across Canada. A person could be denied a job for any reason the employer chose. Employers hung out signs listing the groups of persons who need not apply for work.

The first province to deal with the issue was Saskatchewan, which passed its *Bill of Rights* in 1947. The bill dealt with housing, employment, and accommodation. By the mid-1950s, similar legislation was in place in all of the provinces. The federal government had policies against job discrimination for many years, but formalized them in 1978 when it passed the *Canadian Human Rights Act*. In 1982, the *Charter of Rights and Freedoms* became part of the Canadian Constitution, but its interpretation and application with regard to labour law has been complex and sometimes confusing. The Charter is difficult to apply to labour law because numerous sections can be brought to bear upon the issues.

FEDERAL LABOUR LEGISLATION AND HUMAN RIGHTS

The federal government has jurisdiction over labour matters involving people directly employed by the federal government, Crown corporations, and industries directly regulated by the federal government, such as banking.

The *Canadian Human Rights Act* prohibits discrimination in employment. Like most provincial legislation, the Act lists prohibited grounds of discrimination, including race, national or ethnic origin, colour, religion, age, sex, marital status, family status, disability, and conviction for which a pardon has been granted. The Act specifically declares that sex discrimination includes discrimination related to pregnancy or childbirth.

RE KATHY MacRAE

Canadian Human Rights Commission, 1988

The Canadian Armed Forces was required to pay a woman $10 000 in damages on the ground that she was refused a position as a helicopter mechanic because of her gender. Kathy MacRae, a machinist, filed a complaint after she was told by a recruiting officer that she would have to accept a clerical position because women could not be hired as mechanics.

The Act also requires that males and females be paid the same wages if they are performing **work of equal value**. This is a difficult principle to apply. The principle which had been used for many years was **equal pay for equal work,** which required that a male person and a female person must be paid the same if they do exactly the same job. However, it did not address the problem that females were confined to lower-paying job categories.

In trying to assess whether two people are performing work of equal value, the arbitrator may go outside the workplace and look at very different industries. The arbitrator need only assess three basic criteria for determining what the pay should be: skill, effort, and responsibility. To apply the law properly, employers must have detailed job descriptions and evaluations. The burden is on the employer to justify unequal pay scales.

PROVINCIAL LABOUR LEGISLATION AND HUMAN RIGHTS

All provinces and territories have enacted legislation that establishes certain prohibited grounds of discrimination in the workplace. Most commonly, the grounds are race, colour, ancestry, place of origin, citizenship, ethnic origin, creed, family status, sex, religion, marital status, age, handicap, and record of legal offences. The grounds vary considerably across Canada. Ontario and British Columbia have adopted the work of equal value method of pay equity.

CASES UNDER THE CHARTER

When the *Charter of Rights and Freedoms* was enacted in 1982, it was very difficult to predict the types of cases that would come before the courts, because the Charter could potentially touch upon many aspects of labour. Must employees work on days of religious observation? Did unions acquire a fundamental right to strike? Is compulsory retirement discrimination against the elderly?

The Charter does not apply to private matters—disputes between individuals. It applies only to the action of governments and its agencies. However, the Supreme Court of Canada has held that it will interpret provincial human rights laws in the same manner as the Charter, and provincial laws do cover three categories: discrimination, freedom of association, and mobility rights.

DISCRIMINATION

Section 15 of the Charter prohibits **discrimination**. It reads as follows:

> 15. (1) Every individual is equal before and under the law and has the right to the equal protection and equal benefit of the law without discrimination and, in particular, without discrimination based on race, national or ethnic origin, colour, religion, sex, age or mental or physical disability.
>
> (2) Subsection (1) does not preclude any law, program or activity that has as its object the amelioration of conditions of disadvantaged individuals or groups including those that are disadvantaged because of race, national or ethnic origin, colour, religion, sex, age or mental or physical disability.

Discrimination means many different things to different people. Section 15 of the Charter prohibits discrimination, but trying to reach a consensus upon its meaning is very illusive. In the following case, the Supreme Court of Canada tried to provide both a general definition of discrimination and guidelines for recognizing it in the workplace.

ANDREWS v. LAW SOCIETY OF BRITISH COLUMBIA

Supreme Court of Canada, 1989

Andrews brought an action against the law society because it would not permit him to become a member of the bar as a practising lawyer. The reason was that Andrews was not a Canadian citizen and the provincial law stated that no person could become a lawyer unless that person was a citizen. The Supreme Court declared the law unconstitutional because it violates section 15 of the Charter. The Court defined discrimination as follows:

Discrimination is a distinction which, whether intentional or not but based on grounds relating to personal characteristics of the individual or group, has an effect which imposes disadvantages not imposed upon others or which withholds or limits access to advantages available to other members of society.

The Court stressed that distinctions based on personal characteristics attributed to an individual solely on the basis of association with a group will rarely escape the charge of discrimination, while those based on an individual's merits and capacities will rarely be so classified.

The law society had argued that because "citizenship" is not specifically listed in section 15, it is not a prohibited ground of discrimination. The Court disagreed, ruling that the list in section 15 is only a partial list of those grounds that occur most often. This is the effect of the words "and, in particular." The section prohibits all discrimination on any recognizable grounds.

The Court concluded by saying that, procedurally, the burden is on the complainant to show that he or she has been discriminated against. If the court finds that there has been discrimination, the employer must show that the discrimination can be justified under section 1 of the Charter, which states that the rights of a person can sometimes be violated if the action is demonstrably justified.

In the *Andrews* decision, the Supreme Court of Canada specifically rejected what had been called the "similarly situated test." This test would have held that people who are similar in some manner could be treated differently from everyone else. The Court ruled that "a bad law will not be saved merely because it operates equally upon those to whom it has application." The Court also said that section 15 is aimed at protecting those people who are most often disadvantaged. It is not aimed at protecting the privileged or economically strong.

The guidance provided by the Court in *Andrews* was considerable, but it does not answer every possible Charter issue. One of the most difficult issues has been the **bona fide occupational requirement test** of discrimination. This means that an employer may establish legitimate, meaningful qualification tests for employees or job applicants. If the employee does not have the job qualifications, then it is not discriminatory to refuse to employ the person.

In the case of *Re Bhinder and CNR* (1985) the Supreme Court of Canada heard the case of a Sikh who was terminated from his job because he would not wear a safety helmet in the train yard. As a Sikh, Bhinder had to wear a turban. Even though he agreed to absolve his employer of any liability should he be injured, the employer fired him. The Court ruled that the hard hat was a bona fide safety requirement, established to protect workers, and not aimed against the complainant because of his religion. However, in 1990, the Court reached a very different decision in the following case.

CENTRAL ALBERTA DAIRY POOL v. ALBERTA HUMAN RIGHTS COMMISSION

Supreme Court of Canada, 1990

The Dairy Pool fired Jim Christie for refusing to report to work on one of his religion's holy days. Mr. Christie was a member of the World Wide Church of God. The church recognized several holy days throughout the year and expected its members to avoid working on those days. Christie refused to work Easter Monday.

Christie filed a complaint with the Alberta Human Rights Commission under the province's *Individual's Rights Protection Act*, which prohibits discrimination on the grounds of religious belief. However, the Act states that requiring an employee to do something that is a bona fide occupational qualification is not discrimination.

The Board of Inquiry found that the Dairy Pool could easily have accommodated Christie without any hardship, and awarded him compensation for lost income. The Dairy Pool appealed and the case eventually reached the Supreme Court, which upheld the award. The Court held that an employer must accommodate an employee's special requirements, such as religious observation, to the point of undue hardship. The factors to be considered include financial cost, disruption of a collective agreement, interchangeability of the work force, the size of the employer's operation, and the nature of any safety risks. Madam Justice Wilson wrote:

> *If the employer could cope with an employee being sick or away on vacation on Mondays, it could surely accommodate a similarly isolated absence of an employee due to religious obligation.*

Madam Justice Wilson went on to say that the Court's decision in *Bhinder* was "probably wrong." The Court has clearly put the burden upon the employer to show why a person should not be hired or promoted. It is not enough to allege that the person cannot perform a job—it must be proven. In *Ede v. Canadian Armed Forces* (Canadian Human Rights Tribunal, 1990) a three-person tribunal upheld the decision of the Canadian Army not to accept a man who was too short. The minimum height requirement is 152 cm. Ede stood just 143 cm. The Army was able to show that Ede could not use army equipment and vehicles properly.

In the following case, a very important issue was considered by the Supreme Court. The Charter prohibits discrimination on the basis of sex, but does not define "sex." Various courts had held that "sex" does not include pregnancy, it only refers to gender. The Court concluded this interpretation was too narrow.

BROOKS v. CANADA SAFEWAY

Supreme Court of Canada, 1989

Brooks brought an action against her employer because the company benefits plan denied any sickness benefits to pregnant supermarket cashiers. The company plan did not recognize the medically proven fact that pregnancy can be difficult and accompanied by sickness. The Supreme Court of Canada held that discrimination on the basis of pregnancy is a form of sexual discrimination:

> *Pregnancy discrimination is a form of sex discrimination because of the basic biological fact that only women have the capacity to become pregnant ... Imposing a disproportionate amount of the costs of pregnancy on women is one of the most significant ways in which women have been disadvantaged in our society ... If the medical condition associated with pregnancy does not provide a legitimate reason for absence from the workplace, it is hard to imagine what would provide such a reason.*

Numerous cases have been brought by people contesting mandatory retirement programs. Doctors, firefighters, and professors have all sought to continue working beyond the mandatory retirement age in a contract of employment or union agreement. In *University of British Columbia v. Harrison* (1991) the Supreme Court of Canada upheld mandatory retirement programs as a legitimate infringement of the *Charter of Rights and Freedoms*, justified because the practice benefits society as well as the majority of employees. The Court's ruling permits employers and collective agreements to require workers to retire at a certain age, where the practice is permitted by provincial laws. However, if a provincial law prohibits mandatory retirement, workers may continue working until other factors force retirement. Manitoba has such a law and Quebec allows workers to work to age 70 to receive higher benefits. In a peculiar about-face, the Supreme Court of Canada held in 1991 that the federal government cannot deny unemployment insurance benefits to jobless people over age 65. The Act has since been amended.

In *Tomen v. FWTAO* (1989) the Ontario Court of Appeal held that a female teacher does not have a right to join a male teachers' union. Margaret Tomen lost her bid to join the Ontario Public School Teachers' Federation, a male teachers' association. The by-laws of the Ontario Teachers' Federation require her to belong to the Federation of Women Teachers' Associations of Ontario. Ms. Tomen had argued that this was sex discrimination. The Court held that there is no obligation on a government body to prevent private organizations from discriminating against its members.

FREEDOM OF ASSOCIATION

Section 2 of the Charter guarantees **freedom of association**. Since a labour union is an association, it was predictable that cases would arise regarding the establishment and operation of unions. In particular, the courts were asked whether the right to strike is a constitutionally protected right.

In *Dolphin Delivery v. Local 580* (British Columbia, 1985) the British Columbia Court of Appeal ordered a union to stop "secondary picketing" the plaintiff. The Court held that although there is a constitutional freedom to form a union, this does not mean that every union activity is protected by the Charter. The Supreme Court of Canada was more direct in the following decision.

RE PUBLIC SERVICE EMPLOYEE RELATIONS ACT

Supreme Court of Canada, 1987

The Lieutenant Governor of Alberta referred a constitutional question to the Supreme Court of Canada. Two provincial laws prohibited public servants from taking strike action and imposed arbitration in any labour dispute. The Court held that the laws do not violate section 2 of the Charter. Freedom of association does not include a guarantee of the right to bargain collectively or the right to strike.

The union had argued that a union must have the right to strike or the union has no meaningful existence. However, the Court concluded that the right to form a union is found in specific provincial legislation. It was not a common law right or freedom prior to the enactment of special laws. In the absence of any specific statute recognizing the right to strike, it does not exist.

In 1990 the Court took its earlier decision one step further. The Court held in *Professional Institute of the Public Service of Canada v. Northwest Territories* that section 2 of the Charter does not protect the right to bargain collectively. The action was brought by the Institute because it wanted to continue to represent 32 nurses employed by the federal government. However, the nurses were told they could not have the union of their choice. They would have to join the Public Service Association.

The Court, in denying the action, held that while individuals may form the associations they wish, the government does not have to recognize them or bargain with them. The Court said: "A government does not have to bargain with anyone and there can be no constitutional impediment to its choosing to bargain with someone."

MOBILITY RIGHTS

The third group of cases falls under the heading of **mobility or economic rights**. Section 6 of the Charter guarantees the right of a person to move to and take up residence in any province and to pursue a livelihood in any province or territory. However, despite the strong wording of this part of the section, it also states that it is subject to "laws or practices of general application in force in a province." This means, for example, that a province may require a licence, work permit, test, or other procedure before allowing someone to work in that province, as long as the requirement is applied equally to all.

In *Re Demaere and the Queen* (1985) the Federal Court of Appeal ruled that a person does not have the right to apply for a promotion if it involves a job transfer. The appellant was an air traffic controller who had applied for a promotion in another zone but was told the job was open only to people already working in that zone. The Court ruled that section 6 does not create a "right to work." It prohibits governments only from trying to restrict people from relocating.

In *Wilson v. Medical Services Commission* (1988) the British Columbia Court of Appeal struck down a provincial law which required doctors who recently graduated from medical school to practise in remote communities. If doctors refused to comply with the requirement, the province would not issue them a billing number for the medical insurance plan. Without such a number, a doctor could not earn a living. The Court held that the government plan violated the right of a doctor to practise his or her chosen profession. As well, many new graduates were female and the plan was discriminatory toward young, female doctors as compared to older, male doctors who had established practices.

Some legal experts believe that the decision in *Wilson* gave legal recognition to **economic rights**—to the idea that a government cannot act in a manner that injures a person's profession or livelihood. Considering other decisions in which the courts have held that there is no right to work in Canada, this interpretation is tenuous. However, the Court did appear to consider the economic impact that the law had upon doctors.

The freedom of a professional person to advertise his or her business was given a strong boost by the Ontario Court of Appeal in *Rocket v. Royal College of Dental Surgeons* (1988). The Court struck down a regulation which prohibited dentists from advertising other than in the telephone directory. The Court ruled that advertising is a guaranteed form of expression that is Charter-protected. Although the Royal College of Dental Surgeons could regulate the content of ads to keep them dignified and fair, it could not ban advertising totally.

SPECIAL LABOUR LEGISLATION

In numerous areas of law, the sheer number of problems or potential cases has led the legislative branch to effect a system of compensation that removes the matter from the courts and transfers it to an administrative agency. An example would be no-fault insurance. Such plans try to reduce some of the harsh aspects of the traditional workplace.

WORKERS' COMPENSATION

It is obvious that a single injured worker does not have the financial strength to engage in a lawsuit against a large employer. It is a very uneven contest. This basic fact of life provides the primary argument for an alternative plan that seeks to compensate rather than to fix blame. The largest of these plans is workers' compensation.

The plan is similar in all the provinces, although there are many variations and differing rules across Canada. The plan provides compensation where there is personal injury by accident arising out of and in the course of employment. In some cases, compensation is paid for illness caused by an industrial disease, such as black-lung disease. Compensation includes payment of wages, medical expenses, surviving spouse's benefits, and funeral expenses. The cost of the program is financed by payments by employers. No employee deduction may be made to pay the costs of the plan.

To qualify for compensation, the injury must have occurred on the job or in some act related to the job. The two major exceptions that prevent a person from receiving benefits are:

1. Where the injury does not disable the worker beyond the date of accident from earning full wages at the work at which the worker was employed;
2. Where the accident is attributable solely to the serious and wilful misconduct of the worker and does not result in serious injury or death.

Workers' compensation generally does not attempt to put the blame on any particular person for the injury, although a negligent employer can be fined for a poor safety record.

If the Workers' Compensation Board must pay compensation, the Board has the right to recover the cost from any third person who caused the injury to the employee. A worker injured on the job must report the injury to the employer immediately. Failure to do so may jeopardize the worker's claim to have been injured on the job. There have been false claims submitted by people injured at home who later claimed that the injury occurred at work.

PAST v. WORKERS' COMPENSATION BOARD

British Columbia, 1990

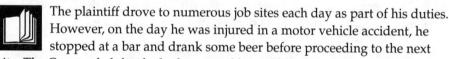

The plaintiff drove to numerous job sites each day as part of his duties. However, on the day he was injured in a motor vehicle accident, he stopped at a bar and drank some beer before proceeding to the next site. The Court ruled that he had removed himself from the course of his employment by making the unauthorized stop.

In each province some occupations are not covered, including the employees of banks and trust companies, agricultural workers, and domestic workers. Casual and occasional employees are not covered. Most provincial plans award compensation on the basis of physical impairment and lost wages. The Ontario plan differs somewhat in that it also compensates workers who suffer permanent injury for loss of future earnings and loss of non-work-related aspects of life.

Because an injured worker is compensated by the plan, the worker cannot also bring a private lawsuit against the employer or the person who caused the injury. This would amount to double compensation. In some instances, the removal of the right to sue has resulted in a hardship for the worker and the worker's family, because compensation under the plan is not always considered adequate. In the following case, the constitutionality of a plan that removes the right to sue was challenged.

RE SS. 32 AND 34 OF THE *WORKERS' COMPENSATION ACT*

Supreme Court of Canada, 1987

Samuel Piercey, a bakery employee, was electrocuted while carrying out his job duties. His widow sued the employer, claiming Mr. Piercey's death had been due to the company's negligence. The bakery cited s. 32 of the Newfoundland *Workers' Compensation Act*, which states that the compensation paid by the plan exempts the employer from any further liability. S. 34 states that any arguments about whether a person may sue or claim benefits from the plan are to be decided by the Board, not by the courts. Mrs. Piercey felt that the compensation she received from the plan was only a small fraction of what she should have received because of the death of her husband. If her husband had been killed in a motor vehicle accident, she would have been able to sue the other driver for much more money.

Counsel for Mrs. Piercey argued that the law was of no force and effect because it denied her access to the courts and thereby infringed her s. 15 Charter right to the equal protection and benefit of the law without discrimination.

The Court held that the legislation is not unconstitutional. It is a viable scheme falling within the scope of provincial legislative authority. It provides workers with many advantages that are not available to plaintiffs in common law damage actions, including rehabilitation and medical programs. Plaintiffs do not have their awards reduced for contributory negligence. In fact, the issue of liability is not considered at all. The removal of a common law right to sue is justified if a statutory compensation plan is created in its place.

Although a worker is barred from suing for compensation, the legislation seldom excludes other types of damages. In *McIntyre v. Atlantic Hardchrome Ltd.* (1991) the Nova Scotia Supreme Court awarded punitive damages to employees who were injured on the job. The workers had complained that the process of electroplating was dangerous and that safety equipment supplied by the company was inadequate. The workers suffered injury from chromium fumes and sued for punitive damages. The Court held that while an employee could not sue for accidental injury, an employee could sue for injuries caused by the employer's misconduct.

In an important decision, a tribunal of the Workers' Compensation Board of Ontario held in 1990 that workplace stress could be considered an "injury" and could be compensable. In *WCAT Decision 918* the tribunal also found that "chronic pain" is a compensable injury. The award was made to a man who suffered a permanent back injury when he fell from a wall. The physical injury healed, but the pain never went away.

UNEMPLOYMENT INSURANCE

Unemployment insurance is the responsibility of the federal government. It took a constitutional amendment to establish the plan after the Supreme Court of Canada held that the federal government had no constitutional authority to enter so extensively into the field of labour.

The basic concept of the plan is that the worker and employer contribute to a fund that provides insurance against loss of employment. The plan provides benefits for unemployment, pregnancy leave, sickness, and some retirement benefits. Exact details of how the plan operates can be obtained from the nearest office of Employment and Immigration Canada.

There have been few legal challenges to the plan, but those that have arisen have been based primarily upon discrimination. At one time, the plan contained certain provisions that awarded benefits to some, but withheld them from others.

In *McKinley v. Minister of National Revenue* (1989) the Tax Court of Canada struck down a section of the *Unemployment Insurance Act* which said that a person who is employed by his or her spouse is not eligible for unemployment insurance. The plaintiff was employed by her husband to run a restaurant that he owned. Their marriage broke up and she was "fired" by her ex-husband and denied unemployment benefits. The Court held that this was discrimination based on marital status and that there are many situations in which a spouse could make a legitimate claim that he or she lost a job.

In *Schacter v. R.* (Federal Court of Canada, 1988) the Court held that a section of the *Unemployment Insurance Act* discriminates on the basis of sex. If parents adopt a child, the Act provides benefits for either parent to stay home for 15 weeks to become acquainted with the child. If parents have their own child, however, only the mother is eligible for maternity benefits. Schacter, a new father, wanted to take some time away from his job to get to know his newborn child. Under the Act, there was no such benefit. The Court held that this was sexual discrimination.

CANADA PENSION PLAN

Established in 1966, the Canada Pension Plan is a contributory social insurance plan designed to make retirement more secure and to afford financial assistance in case of disability or death. The plan operates in all parts of Canada except

Quebec, which operates its own similar plan. The two plans are transportable if a worker moves to or from Quebec.

To be eligible, a worker must be between the ages of 18 and 70 and must earn wages above a minimum level called the "Basic Exemption." Workers contribute on employment income only, which includes salaries, wages, and tips. Self-employed people must contribute to their own, individual plan.

Benefits under the plan include retirement pension, disability benefits, and survivors' benefits. If spouses divorce, the credits accumulated under the Canada Pension Plan can be divided as part of the family assets.

EMPLOYMENT STANDARDS

Every province regulates the conditions or standards of employment. In most provinces, this is accomplished by the terms of the *Employment Standards Act* or *Labour Act*. The federal government has similar provisions in the *Public Service Employment Act* and other legislation.

This legislation mandates hours of work, minimum wage, public holidays, overtime and vacation pay, severance pay, and many other requirements. Employers who violate the law are subject to fines. The law does not apply to the various professions, farmers, teachers, Crown employees, and other groups. There are many variations across Canada.

In recent years, employers have initiated a series of special tests which may intrude upon the privacy of employees. The most controversial are lie detector tests and drug tests. Ontario law specifically prohibits employers from administering lie detector tests to employees or job applicants. Polygraph tests do not provide reliable measurements of truthfulness and honesty and the use of such tests is a poor substitute for basic background checks. Drug tests are also controversial. The first widespread drug testing program was established for amateur athletes, most notably Olympic athletes. The generally supported rationale for testing was to prevent cheating by using chemical substances to enhance performance. Testing then moved to professional athletes. The accepted concept was that athletes are role models for young people and should be drug-free. The third phase has been to test all workers whose job performance is related to safety. For example, a worker operating earth-moving equipment would be a danger to other workers and the public if the worker used drugs.

The Federal Court of Canada stopped mandatory urine testing of prison inmates. In *Jackson v. Joyceville Penitentiary* (1990) the Court said that mandatory testing was an unconstitutional search of inmates that violated the *Charter of Rights and Freedoms*. Private employers are also interested in drug testing. The extent of such testing is small in Canada compared to the United States where such tests are almost routine. Keeping in mind that the Charter does not apply to purely private matters, the decision by an employer to implement a mandatory drug test program would be subject to only two possible constraints: (1) any union agreement, and (2) specific legislation prohibiting the practice. To date, no province has enacted any legislation regarding drug testing. In 1991, the Toronto Dominion Bank announced plans to start drug testing in 1992 because "banking is a public trust involving large sums of money."

LABOUR LAW AND UNIONS

The development of labour law has two distinct aspects—laws involving the individual worker and laws regulating collective bargaining.

The earliest English statutes gave the authority to local judges to set wages. This power was accompanied by legislation that prohibited collective bargaining. Such statutes provided a criminal penalty for breach of a contract of employment and were vigorously enforced.

Parliament and the courts also viewed organizations of workers as criminal conspiracies in restraint of trade. People who tried to organize labour unions were convicted of offences and deported, usually to Australia. Anyone who attempted to picket a workplace was arrested for "watching and besetting a place." In 1871, however, the British Parliament declared that labour unions did not constitute a conspiracy in restraint of trade. In 1872, the Canadian Parliament passed the *Trade Unions Act* and amended the *Criminal Code* to remove penalties for union activity. These actions did not authorize or encourage unionization, they only removed the government from the arena. The battles would now be between the workers and employers.

It was not until the middle of the twentieth century that governments began to actively recognize collective bargaining. Strikes were often violent, resembling small wars, with factories and mines as the battleground. The United States was first to conclude that a mechanism was needed to bring order to the process of forming unions and negotiating as a group. The U.S. Congress passed the *Wagner Act* of 1935, which was sweeping legislation that eliminated effective employer resistance to unionization. Workers were given the right to organize and employers were prohibited from using unfair practices to impede the organization of unions.

These innovations were incorporated into the *Canadian Wartime Labour Relations Regulations* of 1944, which required employers to bargain with unions and prohibited strikes or lockouts until arbitration had been attempted. These principles would form the basis of provincial laws across Canada.

RIGHT TO ORGANIZE

The provincial legislatures generally have the responsibility for recognizing unions and granting them legal status. Most provinces have a specific statute that provides rules for the recognition of a particular union as the collective bargaining agent for a group of workers. At the same time, some restrictions are placed upon this right. For example, workers in a particular profession may be required to belong to a particular union or association and workers in essential services may be denied the right to strike.

Typical of provincial legislation is the Ontario *Labour Relations Act*. The main points covered by the legislation are:

1. Every employee is free to join a union and participate in its lawful activities.
2. No employer may discriminate against an employee because of union membership. Such discrimination would include: refusing to employ or continue to employ a person because of union membership, imposing any condition to restrain an employee from joining a union, and using the threat of dismissal or any other means to compel an employee to leave a union or to refrain from becoming a union member.
3. An employer cannot participate in or interfere with the formation or administration of a union or contribute financial support to it.
4. Where a union has been certified as the bargaining agent by the employees, the employer must deal only with that union when negotiating a collective agreement.
5. Collective agreements must contain a provision stating that there will be no strikes or lockouts while the agreement remains in force.
6. Collective agreements must contain a provision for settlement by arbitration, without stoppage of work, of all differences between employer and employees arising from the interpretation, application, or alleged violation of the agreement.
7. Members of a union cannot be expelled or penalized because they refuse to take part in an illegal strike.
8. Where an employee is wrongfully dismissed, the employer may be compelled to reinstate the employee and pay compensation for loss of earnings.
9. Both employers and unions are liable to penalties for refusing or failing to comply with the provisions of the Act.

There are many other provisions, and many variations across Canada, of this basic concept. A union becomes certified by a vote of the workers. The employer cannot try to prevent or intimidate workers against taking a vote. This prohibition includes threatening to go out of business if the workers form a union. By the same method, the workers can vote to dissolve their union or to have another union represent them.

The *Industrial Relations Act* of British Columbia differs in some important ways from the basic model. The Act prohibits union-employer contracts from containing any provision that requires the employer to purchase products from, or contract out to, unionized firms only. If a union goes on strike, it is limited to picketing the main plant or head office of the employer. It cannot picket subsidiary plants or customers of the employer, a practice called "secondary picketing." The Act permits the government to intervene in a dispute if basic services or the economy are threatened.

In *International Association of Machinists and Aerospace Workers v. Dominion Chain* (Ontario, 1988) the union successfully sued the employer for closing its plant in Stratford, Ontario, and re-opening it in Lindsay, Ontario, without any discussion with the union. The Court ruled that the company made the move just to break its contract with the union and to avoid negotiating a new one. The company was ordered to pay $1 million in damages to the affected workers.

However, in *Paccar of Canada v. Canadian Association of Industrial, Mechanical and Allied Workers* (1989) the Supreme Court of Canada upheld the decision of the employer to unilaterally change terms and conditions after a collective agreement expired. The two parties had a collective agreement that said the terms of the previous contract would remain in effect during negotiations, but also gave either side the right to terminate the contract with written notice. The employer did so and the Court held that the contract was binding.

STRIKES AND OTHER UNION ACTIVITIES

When a current labour agreement expires, the parties are required by law to bargain in good faith in an effort to reach a new agreement. If this cannot be accomplished, the union may serve notice on the employer of its intention to strike. This normally requires a vote of the members to take strike action, but this is not universally true across Canada. In some provinces, the employer has a right to make its final offer directly to the workers.

Workers often speak of their "right to strike" and some labour leaders once believed that the freedom of association guaranteed in section 2 of the *Charter of Rights and Freedoms* extends to the right to strike. They argue that, without the right to strike, unions have no economic power and membership in a union would bring no meaningful benefit to the members. However, the Supreme Court of Canada has held that union activity is not constitutionally protected, as illustrated by some of the cases previously discussed in this chapter. The Court has handed down these important decisions regarding union activities:

1. Governments may impose wage and price controls to restrain inflation.
2. Governments may impose compulsory arbitration to settle disputes with government employees.
3. Governments may prohibit strikes by private sector employees if the strike will hurt the economy or endanger public safety.
4. There is no right to strike within the guarantee of freedom of association.
5. There is no right to bargain collectively within the guarantee of freedom of association.
6. The right to form a union is not a common law right. It is specifically sanctioned by legislation. The right to form a union does not mean that every activity the union undertakes is lawful or protected.
7. A union may not picket a courthouse, as this impedes the access of the public to justice.

Specific performance is a remedy against a union engaged in an unlawful strike. That is, a court may order a union to go back to work. Specific performance is not a remedy against one individual—the court may not order one person to go back to work. To do so, in the view of most jurists, would amount to the imposition of involuntary servitude.

The contract that a union signs is binding on its members. In some provinces, employees cannot be compelled to join a union, but they may have union dues deducted from their pay under the Rand Formula. This agreement stipulates that employees do not have to join a union, but that the employer must deduct the dues because all workers receive the same benefits under the union contract.

Although the Supreme Court has given little weight to freedom of association as a legal argument for union activity, it has recognized picketing as freedom of expression. In *SDGMR v. Dolphin Delivery Ltd.* (1986) the Court held that picketing, for any reason, is protected by the guarantee of freedom of expression. This could include secondary picketing. However, the Court then went on to say that picketing could be restricted by the legislature or the courts. A court may issue an injunction against a union to curb violence or to prohibit such practices as mass or blockade picketing.

If a union conducts an illegal strike, it can be held liable for the losses suffered by the employer and also losses suffered by other companies against whom the strike is brought. Union leaders can be held personally liable for failure to comply with a court order ending an unlawful strike. A union is a legal corporation and may sue or be sued in its own name and its funds can be seized by the court to pay penalties assessed.

PRINCIPAL AND AGENT

A different type of relationship from that of employer and employee is that of principal and agent. An **agent** is a person employed to act on the behalf of another person, called the **principal**. The relationship is such that the agent's actions, done within the scope of the authority given by the principal, bind the principal the same as if the principal had acted himself or herself. The rule of law is: "What one person may do may be done through another."

The primary difference between an agent and a servant is that a servant cannot enter into contracts in the master's name, but an agent can sign contracts in the principal's name. While an agent can be given definite guidelines under which to operate, the principal does not direct the work of the agent closely. There are generally three classes of agents:

- **Universal**: Appointed to act for the principal in all matters;
- **General**: Appointed to act in a transaction of a class (e.g., an employment agent);
- **Special**: Appointed for one purpose only.

Any person capable of contracting may be a principal. Since the agent acts for the principal, the agent need not be someone capable of contracting. Therefore, a minor can be an agent.

Spouses are not automatically agents entitled to represent each other in personal or business matters. If one spouse is dependent upon the other, that spouse may pledge the other spouse's credit to obtain necessaries of life.

CREATION OF AGENCY

The relationship of agency may be created in numerous ways. The first is by **express appointment**, by which the principal directs the agent to act on his or her behalf and gives authority and instructions. This is often done in writing, either by an employment contract or by a document known as a **power of attorney**. The agreement should spell out precisely what the agent may do and give the agent signing authority to contract for the principal. The signature of the agent is final and the principal cannot escape the contract because he or she does not like the terms.

A second method is by **estoppel**. Anyone who allows another person to act as his or her agent, even though never appointing that person for this purpose, is estopped (prevented) from later denying the agency. When a person learns that someone is acting on his or her behalf without authority, the person should immediately deny the existence of any agency and advise anyone that might be affected that such contracts will not be honoured.

An agency may also be formed by **necessity**. Any person who must act out of necessity to benefit another person is said to be doing so as an agent by necessity. For example if someone witnesses an automobile accident and calls an ambulance for an injured motorist, the injured person must pay for the ambulance. The witness acted as an agent by necessity for the injured person.

An agency may also be created by the act of **ratification**. If a person enters into a contract on behalf of someone else, without any authority, the principal cannot remain silent or accept any part of the agreement. If the principal gives approval to the contract after the fact, the principal ratifies the agreement and must live up to its terms and pay the agent.

A person may bind the principal, even if that person has no power to do so, if the person acts within his or her **apparent authority**. If a principal puts a person into a position that carries certain powers, it is reasonable for third parties to believe that the person is an agent. The principal will be bound by any contract that falls within that apparent authority, even if the agent exceeded his or her true authority. For example, to most parties a company sales manager has the authority to make sale agreements. The company cannot escape a contract by arguing that the sales manager was required to have all sales approved by the president. A principal is liable for torts committed by the agent, if they are committed in the course of employment. This might include such torts as fraud or misrepresentation.

An agent should sign all documents to clearly indicate that it is the principal who is being committed. The agent should sign the principal's name first, then sign his or her own name and the capacity in which the agent signs. An example might be: *R.J. Rogers Ltd., per Garry Wilson, General Manager.* However, in some situations, the principal might want to remain secret. The agent may then enter into the agreement in his or her own name, or indicate in some way that the agreement is being undertaken for an unnamed principal. In recent years, works of art have been purchased by agents for secret principals so art thieves will not be able to locate the artwork.

There is a danger in representing a hidden principal. If the agent does not disclose the existence of a principal, the agent could be personally liable to the third party for breach of warranty of authority.

AGENTS' RESPONSIBILITIES

Agents are bound to carry out the instructions of their principals diligently and with reasonable skill. If an agent obtained a position by saying that he or she had special talents, the agent must demonstrate those talents. Agents must also be loyal to their principals. To a certain extent, this is a fiduciary duty. They cannot accept secret commissions from others or work against the interest of their principals. For example, an agent cannot hide from the principal that he or she is actually engaged in the same business and is secretly doing business with the principal under the guise of a company name. If agents are given money by their principals, they must account for the money.

KRAMER v. COOPER

British Columbia, 1975

The defendant, Cooper, listed vacant lots for sale with a real estate agent. The plaintiff, Kramer, was an employee of the real estate agent. He told his employer he was interested in buying the lots himself, but for a lower price than the defendant was asking. Kramer signed a purchasing agreement which stated that he held a licence in real estate, but did not disclose the name of his employer.

When the sale was completed, Kramer received part of the commission that Cooper paid to the agency. At no time did Cooper know that Kramer was employed by the agency handling his sale. Cooper instructed his lawyer not to close the deal. Kramer sued for specific enforcement of the sale.

The Court refused to order the sale completed. The conflict of interest was obvious. The plaintiff wanted to buy the property at a low price; the defendant wanted to sell at a high price. If the plaintiff made no serious effort to sell the property, the defendant would lower his price. The failure to disclose the fact that he was employed by the agency put Kramer into a conflict of interest, because he suppressed material facts and deceived the principal.

In some situations it is a breach of the agent's duty not to tell the principal that the agent is acting for other principals at the same time. If an agent is disloyal, the principal may take action even if the principal did not suffer any loss because of the agent's actions. In *Bank of Montreal v. Ng* (1989) the Supreme Court of Canada heard the unusual case of a currency trader who had authority to make transactions with a limit of $40 000 000 per day. Kuet Ng had authority to make trades for clients and for his employer, the Bank of Montreal. However, he secretly took money from his clients' accounts and invested it in his own name. He also made secret transactions for two of the bank's clients with the arrangement that he would receive half the profits. Ng did not lose any money; he made large profits. However, his actions were unethical and possibly illegal. The bank fired him and sued for all the profits. The Supreme Court upheld the bank's action on the grounds that Ng had acted fraudulently and had no right to the profits he made.

In *Sennecke v. Sutherland* (Ontario, 1991) Sennecke had been looking for a house and employed the defendant, a real estate agent, to find one. Sennecke decided to make an offer on a house in Toronto. He alleged that Sutherland lied, telling him that there was already a firm offer for the house at $150 000 and that he must make a higher offer. Sennecke offered $151 000, which was promptly accepted. Sennecke never closed the deal because he felt something was wrong. He forfeited his $2500 deposit. The house soon sold for $138 000. Sennecke felt his suspicions had been confirmed that the real estate agent persuaded him to make a high offer so she could earn a larger commission. He sued Sutherland for breach of her duties as his agent, but the Court dismissed the case saying that as long as Sutherland honestly believed the firm offer existed, there was no breach of her duties.

RIGHTS OF AGENTS

Agents have the right to be paid for their services, provided they carry out their duties properly. They are also entitled to collect for reasonable expenses. A principal cannot fire an agent just to avoid paying a fee or commission.

TERMINATION OF AGENCY

Like any contract, a contract to create an agency may have a predetermined date after which it is void. The agency contract can also be ended by either party giving reasonable notice to the other. A principal should notify interested third parties that a particular agent is no longer employed.

If the principal dies, is disabled, goes bankrupt, or is declared mentally unfit, the agency ends. Since the principal can no longer contract, the agency cannot contract on the principal's behalf. One exception to the rule of mental competency involves a power of attorney. If the power of attorney specifically states that the agency continues despite the incompetence of the principal, then the agency is not ended. Indeed, some people sign powers of attorney specifically so their affairs can be managed if they become incompetent.

REVIEW: POINTS OF LAW

1. A worker who is fired without notice or without cause may sue the employer for wrongful dismissal.
2. A worker who quits a job without notice may be liable to his or her employer for financial injury the employer suffers.
3. A worker may be dismissed without notice for dishonesty, absenteeism, incompetence, or insubordination.
4. An employer has a common law duty to provide employees with a safe place to work, a safe system of work, and competent co-workers.
5. Job discrimination on the basis of race, religion, sex, age, and other characteristics is unlawful.
6. The Supreme Court of Canada has held that an employer must make a reasonable effort to accommodate the various religious holidays of workers.
7. Under provincial workers' compensation plans, the worker is compensated for injury but loses the right to sue the employer or any third party. The Supreme Court of Canada has upheld the constitutional validity of the plans.
8. The Supreme Court of Canada has held that there is no constitutional right to strike or bargain collectively. There is a right to picket, but it is a right that may be restricted.
9. An agent is a person who represents another person, the principal.
10. An agent must carry out the principal's instructions diligently, must account for all funds, and must be loyal to the principal.

LEGAL BRIEFS

1. R, a real estate agent, was employed to sell a house for T. R showed the house to B, who made an offer. Two days later, R telephoned B and told him that T had accepted the offer. B then signed an agreement to sell his existing home. In fact, T had not accepted the offer, and B ended up with no place to

live. R admitted the mistake, but argued that he was T's agent and owed a duty to T, not B. Is R liable to B?

2. E was employed as a secretary by a small law firm with three lawyers. One of the lawyers was E's husband. When the senior lawyer retired, the other two lawyers decided to seek employment with larger firms. The law firm went out of business and E was unemployed. She filed for unemployment insurance. Benefits were denied when the Unemployment Insurance Commission learned that E had been employed by her spouse. Should E receive unemployment benefits?
3. A hair salon advertised a position for a hairdresser. The ad did not make any declaration about the gender of the person sought, but when P went for a job interview, the owner of the salon said he wanted to hire a female because he presently had four male employees and one female employee and needed a better "balance" because some customers preferred a female hairdresser. Has the salon owner broken the law?
4. W was employed by a computer consulting firm. She was in line for promotion to head up a large project. W, however, was five months' pregnant and would soon be leaving on pregnancy leave. She did not receive the promotion. It went to a male who was her subordinate at the time. Her employer said the decision was made for "obvious business reasons." Has W a valid complaint against her employer?
5. H was employed by a large company as the manager of a division with 25 employees. H considered himself a very friendly, extroverted person, particularly toward female employees. He spoke in a booming voice. He hugged, patted, and kidded them about sexual matters. He complimented their appearance in semi-vulgar terms. Most of the female employees considered H harmless, but two filed complaints about his conduct, particularly his habit of patting them and suggesting that if they tired of their boyfriends H would show them a good time. Should H be fired?
6. L was the manager of a service station in a small town. Each fall, it was traditional that the station be closed every Saturday afternoon for three hours because nearly everyone went to the local high school football game. The area supervisor found the station locked up and L at the football game, sitting at the top of the bleachers. The supervisor shouted to L that he was fired as of that moment. Wrongful dismissal?
7. C was dismissed from his job as a labourer because he could not speak English very well. The foreman who fired him said C disobeyed orders. The evidence was that C did not deliberately disobey orders, but sometimes did not understand them. The company then argued that C was fired because he did not understand English and that the provincial law does not prohibit discrimination on the basis of language. Should C be reinstated?

APPLYING THE LAW

PATZNER v. PILLER DELICATESSENS LTD.

Ontario, 1990

The plaintiff had been employed by the defendant as a meat-packing foreman for 24 years. He was a loyal, hard-working employee with an excellent work record. When he joined the company, there were four employees. There were now 180 employees. The plaintiff worked shoulder to shoulder with the original owners (since retired) to build the company from scratch.

One day his section was given a large order for hams and beef. His crew was short-handed because of staff illness, but the plaintiff worked them very hard to fill the order. After the shift ended, the plaintiff went into a cold storage room and brought back four beers that had been left there after a social function. He gave a beer to each of his workers, told them they did a good job, and drank one himself. They were not on duty at the time, as their shift had ended.

The next day the plant manager confronted him about the empty bottles. When told why they had been consumed, the manager said: "I could fire you for this." Indeed, the plaintiff was fired the next day. The company offered to reinstate him in a night job, cleaning machines, at half the salary. He resigned and sued for wrongful dismissal.

The trial judge held that the plaintiff had been wrongfully dismissed. The plaintiff committed an error in judgment, but not one that justified the way he was treated after 24 years of loyal service. He had not brought the beer into the building and did not drink any while working on his shift. No employee was endangered because no machine work was underway. A reprimand would have been more than proper in the circumstances. The plaintiff had been fired in a "draconian [harsh or cruel] manner" and was entitled to 18 months' severance pay.

Questions

1. What grounds would the employer have for firing the plaintiff?
2. Is there a rule, written or unwritten, that says a worker must be given a warning or reprimand rather than being fired?
3. The plaintiff was not fired, he resigned. Why did the Court conclude he had been wrongfully dismissed?

POULIN v. HAREL et al.

Quebec, 1988

The plaintiff entered into a contract with a resources company to cut timber from the company's land. The plaintiff and eight workers set up a camp and began the cutting. The campsite was invaded by two dozen members of a lumber workers' union who accused the plaintiff of "scabbing" their jobs. The union members made several return visits, damaged equipment, and threatened the plaintiff to the point that he sought court protection. He eventually obtained an injunction against the union, but no one would work for him because the threats continued. The plaintiff abandoned the project and sued the union for damages.

The Court ordered the union to pay the plaintiff $75 000 in damages for economic interference, including $25 000 in punitive damages. The union was responsible for the conduct of its members when they appeared to be acting in a concerted manner that was directly related to employment.

Questions

1. The union did not order its members to take the action they did. Why should the union be liable?
2. Why did the Court include punitive damages in its award?
3. Do you think the union leadership could have stopped its members? Did it have a legal duty to do so?
4. What is economic interference?

PRINCIPLES AND CASES

Case 1: Legal Principle

A union must demonstrate that it retains the confidence and support of its members in order to continue to represent its members.

Case Facts

The plaintiff union brought an action before the Court asking that the employer be compelled to accept binding arbitration of a dispute. As well, the union asked that the Court find the employer in violation of the provincial law because the employer had hired replacement workers during the strike.

When the strike began, there were 77 employees on strike. However, as the dispute dragged on, 43 of the 77 workers broke ranks and returned to work over the direct orders of their union not to do so. The other 34 workers remained on the picket line. The company ordered them to return to work or they would be fired and replaced. Two weeks later, the company carried out its threat. The union insisted that the strike was still on and that it represented all of the workers.

Possible Decisions

A The union is correct because it had not been decertified as the bargaining agent for the workers.

B The union is correct because the company engaged in strike-breaking tactics by hiring some of the workers back.

C The company is correct because when the majority of union members return to work, they are indicating that the strike is over.

D The company is correct because individual rights take precedent over collective rights.

Case 2: Legal Principle

A demotion or drastic change in job description can constitute wrongful dismissal.

Case Facts

The plaintiff was the accountant for a large automobile dealership. When the dealership was sold to a new owner, the contract contained a clause requiring the purchaser to "offer employment at the time of closing on terms and conditions then in effect to all employees." The purchaser could, however, "alter job functions and method of remuneration in order to encourage productivity."

Soon after the sale was completed, the new owners asked the plaintiff for complete financial statements. He worked two weekends and completed them. He was advised that the new owners already had an accountant and did not need him as an accountant. He was handed a letter offering him a job as a car salesperson, on commission. He left the building and never returned. He sued for wrongful dismissal.

Possible Decisions

A The plaintiff was wrongfully dismissed because the demotion was so severe that it was constructive dismissal.

B The plaintiff was wrongfully dismissed because to offer an accountant a job as a car salesperson is degrading.

C The plaintiff was not wrongfully dismissed because the sale contract said the new owners could alter job functions.

D The plaintiff was not wrongfully dismissed because there is no evidence that he could not obtain the same income selling cars.

YOU BE THE JUDGE

1. The plaintiffs were key senior management employees of the defendant company. While in the defendant's employ, they entered into negotiations to purchase a company that would compete directly with the defendant. When the president of the defendant company found out what the plaintiffs were doing, he called them in and accused them of "disloyalty." They denied these allegations and said that they were only considering going into business for themselves and had taken no action that was harmful to the defendant's business. The meeting ended with the president demanding the plaintiffs' resignations, which they submitted. They later sued for wrongful dismissal. Who would succeed?
2. A law firm employed five legal secretaries. Three took maternity leave at the same time, leaving the firm's legal work in a chaotic state. The firm hired three temporary secretaries, one of whom was highly proficient. When the plaintiff secretary advised the firm that she, too, was pregnant, she was terminated and given six months' severance pay. She was given a letter stating that she was discharged because she had voluntarily made a decision to become pregnant, knowing that the firm was experiencing enormous staffing problems and that she had disqualified herself from further employment. The firm wanted to offer the temporary secretary full-time employment and could do so only if it terminated one employee. The plaintiff sued the firm. Who would succeed?

3. The defendant hotel employed two categories of beverage and cocktail employees with different pay scales. The male employees were generally placed in Category 1 and were paid $4 more per hour than Category 2 employees. The female employees and two males were in Category 2. When the Employment Standards Branch investigated a complaint about this discrepancy, the hotel manager explained that Category 1 employees had to perform two difficult tasks not assigned to Category 2 employees. One task was to tap beer kegs. The second was to "bounce" unruly patrons. The investigation showed that tapping beer kegs took four minutes. Unruly patrons were not a common problem. In fact, on the one occasion the investigator happened to see a problem with a patron, it was a female employee who evicted the patron from the premises. Who would succeed?
4. When the defendant was absent from his home for a lengthy period of time, he asked his neighbour to look after his house. A windstorm severely damaged the roof of the house. The neighbour called a roofing company and told them to effect the necessary repairs. The roofing company inspected the roof and told the neighbour that it would be a waste of money to repair the roof because it needed to be completely renovated and new shingles applied. The neighbour called in a second company for an opinion and received the same advice. The neighbour obtained three bids for the job and authorized the company with the lowest bid to do the work. When he returned, the defendant thought the work was unnecessary, the bill was excessive, and that he could have done the work himself. He refused to pay the bill and denied that the neighbour had the authority to order the work. Who would succeed?
5. The plaintiff suffered a broken hip from an automobile accident when he was very young. When he applied for a job with the defendant company, he disclosed this fact. He was turned down for the job. The reason given to him was that the defendant's insurance company would not accept him because he would very likely have a medical problem resulting from the earlier accident. The provincial law prohibited discrimination on the basis of physical or mental disability. The company argued that the plaintiff was a high risk, but not disabled, and therefore there had been no discrimination. Who would succeed?
6. The plaintiff was hired as a cook for a railroad work crew. He performed his work very well and there were no problems until he inadvertently told another worker that he had tested positive for the AIDS virus. Although scientific evidence is conclusive that AIDS cannot be transmitted to anyone through the preparation of food, the work crew refused to eat anything the plaintiff prepared. He was subsequently fired and he sued for wrongful dismissal. Who would succeed?

7. The plaintiff owned an apartment building. She employed her nephew as the building supervisor. He made repairs and generally looked after the building. He had no authority to collect rent from the tenants nor to spend money for repairs. These activities were done only by the plaintiff. The plaintiff suffered a lengthy illness and was in a hospital for five months. She sent a letter to her tenants stating that her nephew would temporarily look after her business affairs. Tenants were advised to pay their rent to the nephew. When the plaintiff regained her health, she did not specifically notify the tenants that she was again managing her affairs. The nephew continued to collect rent money from some tenants for three months. The plaintiff prepared notices to these tenants that rent was overdue, but the nephew did not deliver the notices. The nephew left town, taking the money with him. The plaintiff sued 16 tenants for unpaid rent, which they had actually paid to the plaintiff's nephew. The plaintiff argued that her nephew had no authority to continue to act for her. Who would succeed?
8. The defendant company sought to avoid a contract which had been entered into by its sales manager with the plaintiff company. The plaintiff's purchasing agent had met with the defendant's sales manager to discuss the terms for the purchase of a large quantity of newsprint. The price was higher than competing bids, so the sales manager said that he would authorize a 15 percent reduction in price if the plaintiff bought a six-month supply. The plaintiff accepted these terms and a contract was signed. However, when the sales manager told the president of his company the terms he had agreed to, the president said they were too generous and that the company could not afford to sell at such a low price. He fired the sales manager and sent the plaintiff a letter, stating that the contract would not be honoured because the sales manager had "exceeded his authorization in entering into such a contract." The plaintiff sued to enforce the contract. Who would succeed?
9. The plaintiff, a professional football player, sued his club, demanding a bonus be paid to him for playing two more games than his contract required. The plaintiff had been represented by an agent who signed a contract under which the plaintiff agreed to play "all regular season games, playoff games, and championship game." At the time, the regular season was 14 games. However, as two new teams were added to the league, the regular season was extended to 16 games. The defendant club knew that this change would take place, as did the agent. The plaintiff argued that he was entitled to more money because his agent had not properly represented his interests and the defendant knew this at the time. Who would succeed?

ONE
ONE
THE GOVERNMENT OF THE PROVINCE OF ALBERTA
PROSPERITY CERTIFICATE
DATE OF ISSUE
AUGUST 5, 1936
A 216880
THE PROVINCIAL TREASURER WILL PAY TO THE BEARER THE SUM OF ONE DOLLAR ON THE EXPIRATION OF TWO YEARS FROM DATE OF ISSUE HEREOF UPON PRESENTATION HEREOF PROVIDED THERE ARE THEN ATTACHED TO THE BACK HEREOF ONE HUNDRED AND FOUR ONE CENT CERTIFICATE STAMPS
GOVERNMENT OF THE PROVINCE OF ALBERTA OF CANADA
OFFICE OF THE PROVINCIAL TREASURER
DEPUTY PROVINCIAL TREASURER
ONE DOLLAR
William Aberhart
PREMIER
C. Cockroft
PROVINCIAL TREASURER
ONE
ONE
WESTERN PRINTING & LITHOGRAPHING CO LTD CALGARY

CHAPTER TWELVE

BILLS OF EXCHANGE

> *"Virtue has never been as respectable as money."*
>
> Mark Twain,
> author

BILLS OF EXCHANGE ACT

Modern society has devised numerous methods of dealing with the basic business problem of safely transferring large or small sums of money. Money, in any form, can be lost, destroyed, or stolen. Centuries ago, merchants realized the need for "substitutes for money" to reduce this problem. They developed a system of using paper documents upon which instructions were recorded that represented an exchange of value. These documents are of many types, but are generally known as **bills of exchange**.

The first detailed law regarding the use of bills was drawn up in England under what was called the *Law Merchant*. The British Parliament later incorporated bills of exchange into a separate law. Canada's *Bills of Exchange Act* deals with the same subject and was first enacted in 1890.

The oldest known cheque to have been drawn on a British bank was made payable to a Mr. Delboe by Nicholas Vanacker. It was issued in 1659 and was prepared in almost exactly the style of a modern cheque, the amount being written out first in words and then in figures.

The concept of a bill of exchange is simple. Rather than transfer money from person to person, the parties would pass pieces of paper back and forth which contained the names of the parties and the amount of money involved. Each merchant, and later each merchant banker, made an entry into a book, adding or deducting the sum from the account of the person. The actual money remained locked in vaults or money boxes where it was less vulnerable to theft. Legislation was necessary to regulate matters such as form, transfer, forgery, and collection. The *Bills of Exchange Act* defines a bill of exchange as follows:

> 17. (1) A bill of exchange is an unconditional order in writing addressed by one person to another, signed by the person giving it, requiring the person to whom it is addressed to pay on demand or at a fixed or determinable time, a sum certain in money to or to the order of a specific person or to bearer.

This definition sets down certain necessary requirements that a bill of exchange must meet in order to be valid. The bill must be:

- **Unconditional**: The drawer or preparer of the bill is not making the payment on the condition that something be done in return. The bill requires the payment of the money without question.
- **In writing**: The bill must be written or printed. It cannot be oral. No particular form is required as long as all of the necessary information is provided. Standard forms have been developed for convenience and everyday use, but they are not mandatory. For example, a cheque could be

written on anything. A lumber company once carved its final mortgage cheque on a log and floated it down the river to the bank.
- **Signed by the person giving it**: The signature of the person who drew the bill is necessary to show that it represents that person's true wishes. The signature can be handwritten or printed.
- **Paid on demand**: The person who holds the bill may demand payment by presenting it to the bank upon which it was drawn any time after the date on the bill.
- **Payable at a fixed or determinable time**: The bill is either dated, after which it is valid, or a future time is set that is determinable. For example, "July 1, 1992" is a fixed time. An example of a determinable time would be "30 days after date." An indeterminable time would be "30 days after I inherit my uncle's estate." This is indeterminable because no one knows upon what date the uncle will die or whether the drawer will in fact inherit the estate.
- **For a sum certain**: The amount must be expressed in exact dollars and cents. It cannot read, for example, "Half the value of my house."
- **Payable to a person or bearer**: The bill must indicate who is to receive payment. A specific person may be named or just "bearer," meaning anyone having physical possession. A corporation is a "person" within the meaning of the Act. A bill payable to a deceased person is not negotiable as that individual is no longer a legal person.

Bills of exchange generally fall into three classes: cheques, promissory notes, and drafts. The consumer and commercial credit markets have made drafts obsolete, so this discussion will centre on cheques and promissory notes.

It is important to distinguish bills of exchange from legal tender. **Legal tender** consists of bank notes (paper money) and coins in limited amounts. Payment by coin may not exceed $0.25 in copper coins and $10 in silver coins. There is no specific limit upon the number of $1 coins that may be used, but it is presumed that practical considerations will limit their use.

Any creditor may insist upon payment in legal tender if that form of payment is preferred. There is no obligation upon any person to accept payment by cheque.

Parties to an agreement may specify how payment is to be made as a term of the contract. For example, a party may require payment by cheque and may refuse to accept cash. This is a contractual matter and is outside the effect of the *Bills of Exchange Act*. For example, a university may require students to pay tuition by cheque and not accept cash because it does not want the danger of handling so much cash.

CHEQUES AS BILLS OF EXCHANGE

The *Bills of Exchange Act* defines a **cheque** as "a bill of exchange drawn on a bank, payable on demand." The word "bank" historically meant only a chartered bank of Canada. However, the Act was amended to specifically allow other financial institutions, such as credit unions and trust companies, to offer chequing accounts to customers. A cheque has three phases in its life cycle: (1) issue, (2) negotiation, and (3) payment.

ISSUE OF A CHEQUE

A cheque is issued when it is written out and delivered to the intended recipient. It may be handwritten or printed. One person may sign a cheque for another person if he or she has the authority to do so. For example, a company treasurer has authority to sign company cheques.

The essential information that a cheque must contain was discussed under the definition of a bill of exchange. Generally, a cheque is prepared by the person who owns the bank account (**drawer**) ordering the bank (**drawee**) to pay a sum of money to another person (**payee**) on or after the date shown.

The person who signs a company cheque or promissory note may be held personally liable by the payee if the cheque does not clearly indicate that the person signing it is doing so in a representative, not a personal, capacity. It is for this reason that a company cheque should be prepared in a different format than a personal cheque. A company cheque should have the company's name above the line where the drawer signs and the word "per" just before his or her name. This indicates that no personal liability is intended.

ALLPRINT v. IRWIN

Ontario, 1982

The plaintiff sued Grant Erwin personally as the drawer of three cheques in favour of the plaintiff. Except for the dates and the amounts, the cheques were identical in form. In the top left corner the name of Erwin's company, "Edumedia Holdings Limited," was printed. The company name was also printed just above the signature line. However, the word "per" did not appear and Mr. Erwin's title as company president and signing officer was not stated. A dispute arose between the parties and payment on the cheques was stopped. Allprint sued Erwin personally. The trial judge held Erwin personally liable under s. 52 of the *Bills of Exchange Act* which reads:

52. (1) Where a person signs a bill as drawer, endorser or acceptor, and adds words to his signature indicating that he signs for or on behalf of a principal, or in a representative character, he is not personally liable thereon; but the mere addition to his signature of words describing him as an agent, or as filling a representative character does not exempt him from personal liability.
(2) In determining whether a signature on a bill is that of the principal or that of the agent by whose hand it is written, the construction most favourable to the validity of the instrument shall be adopted.

The Court of Appeal reversed the trial judge's decision, holding that the cheque was clearly a corporate cheque only. The cheque was drawn on the corporation's bank account, the computer code attached directed the cheque to the corporate account only, and the name of the corporation was in boldface above the signature. The line on the cheque was clearly for the signing officer.

NEGOTIATION OF A CHEQUE

Since many bills of exchange are transferred to other parties, they are also called **negotiable instruments**. The process of negotiating a bill to someone else varies, depending upon how the bill is drawn. If the cheque says, "Pay to bearer," then whoever has the cheque can negotiate it merely by handing it to someone else. For this reason, bearer cheques are risky. If they are lost, they can be cashed by anyone who happens to find them.

If the cheque is drawn "Pay to R. Green" or "Pay to the Order of R. Green," negotiation requires more than handing over. There must be a written transfer to explain why a person other than R. Green now has the cheque. The process required is called **endorsement**. An endorsement is a signature, usually with words of explanation and direction, transferring the cheque to someone else. Endorsements are usually written on the back of a cheque so as not to obscure the writing on the face. The most common forms of endorsement are blank, special, restrictive, and qualified.

BLANK ENDORSEMENT

A **blank endorsement** requires only that the payee sign on the back. The legal effect of a blank endorsement is to change the cheque into a bearer cheque. A blank endorsement is normally used when the payee presents the cheque for payment at either his or her own bank or at the bank on which the cheque is drawn. For this reason, the endorsement should not be written prior to going to the bank, in case the cheque is lost. A person may write a cheque on his or her own bank account, normally payable to "Cash," and then endorse the back with his or her own signature. Such a cheque works the same as a withdrawal slip.

SPECIAL ENDORSEMENT

A **special endorsement** negotiates the cheque to a specific person, not just to anyone. That person becomes a holder and must further endorse the cheque in some manner. A special endorsement might read: "Pay to Fred Green (signed) William Brown." There is no limit upon the number of special endorsements that may appear on a cheque. Brown could further negotiate the cheque to Black.

RESTRICTIVE ENDORSEMENT

A **restrictive endorsement** limits future endorsements in some manner. Where the drawer, or the payee, for some reason does not want the cheque negotiated to other people, a restrictive endorsement prevents further negotiation, usually by the use of the word "only." If the holder deposits cheques by mail, to prevent theft the holder can use a restrictive endorsement such as "For deposit only." If the cheque is stolen, it can only be deposited, not cashed.

QUALIFIED ENDORSEMENT

An endorser may sign a cheque in a manner that excuses the endorser from any later liability. This is a **qualified endorsement**. For example, a person negotiating a cheque may declare that he or she accepts no responsibility if the cheque is not honoured. An example would be: "Pay to Fred Green, without recourse to me (signed) William Brown."

PAYMENT OF A CHEQUE

Assuming that there is nothing wrong with the physical appearance of the cheque, it must eventually be presented to the drawee (bank) for payment. If the bank finds nothing amiss, it stamps the cheque "Paid" and pays the money to the person presenting it. The bank is under a contractual obligation with the drawer to make payment. If the bank fails to honour a valid cheque, the drawer may be liable for breach of contract with the payee. The bank may refuse to honour a cheque under the following conditions:

- The cheque is not in proper form or has been altered.
- The person presenting it cannot produce identification.
- The drawer does not have sufficient funds in his or her account to cover the cheque. If the account does not have enough funds, the cheque is stamped "NSF" (Not Sufficient Funds).
- The cheque is stale-dated. A cheque becomes stale-dated if it is not presented for payment within six months of the date on it. A common problem time is the beginning of each January. Many people, as a matter of habit, write the year as the preceding year. This makes the cheque a year old.
- The account has been frozen by court order.
- Payment has been stopped by the drawer.

A cheque is **certified** when the drawee bank immediately debits the drawer's account by the amount of the cheque. The cheque is then stamped "certified." This cheque carries the bank's guarantee that there are sufficient funds in the bank to pay the cheque. In this case, the holder has a claim against the bank for payment. A cheque is usually certified at the request of the drawer, who wants to assure the payee that the cheque will be honoured by the bank and that the drawer has the funds he or she claims to have. For example, real estate transactions almost always require certified cheques because of the large sums of money involved.

The *Bills of Exchange Act* is silent on the subject of certified cheques. Therefore, the actual legal consequences have been left to the courts to try to sort out. Certification can be done at the request of the drawer or the payee. There is a distinct difference as far as the bank is concerned.

Usually it is the drawer who takes his or her own cheque to the bank and has it certified before it is issued to the payee. Such a cheque is not yet a negotiable instrument, because it has not been delivered. In fact, the cheque might never be delivered. The drawer may change his or her mind and have the bank cancel the cheque. In this situation, the bank has certified the cheque and has set aside funds to cover the cheque. The bank, however, has no relationship with the payee because it does not know if the payee has the cheque. In the second possible situation, the payee may bring the cheque to the bank and ask that it be certified. This is normally done with postdated cheques. In this case, the bank knows the payee has the cheque and by certifying the cheque is making a promise to the payee that the money will be available. The bank has become liable on the bill.

If the drawer wants to stop payment on a certified cheque, it is possible only if the drawer can demonstrate to the bank that the payee is no longer entitled to the funds. If the payee has committed a serious act of misconduct, such as fraud, the bank would be correct to refuse payment. However, banks are very reluctant to accept stop-payment orders on certified cheques and insist upon a strong body of evidence as to why the cheque should not be paid.

MORE ABOUT CHEQUES

A bank will not pay a cheque that is drawn against a depositor's account if the bank has been notified that the depositor is deceased. In this case, the normal practice is for the payee to present the cheque to the estate of the deceased and ask that a new cheque be issued by the executor of the estate. If the payee dies before cashing the cheque, the executor asks the drawer to issue a new cheque payable "in trust" to the estate of the deceased.

If two people, such as spouses, have a joint banking account, it is prudent for them to sign a **Survivorship Agreement** with the bank. Under the terms of such an agreement, one spouse can continue to write cheques on the account after the other has died. Without such an agreement, the entire account could be frozen upon the death of one spouse, leaving the surviving spouse without access to current funds.

Minor errors in the preparation of a cheque can be accommodated. For example, if a person dated a cheque "June 31, 1992," the cheque is valid even though there are only 30 days in the month of June. It would be assumed that the cheque could be cashed on July 1, 1992. If the payee's name is misspelled, the payee may endorse the cheque by writing the name correctly on the back, or may sign it twice—first with the name as it appears on the cheque and then a second time, spelling the name correctly. Either method is acceptable.

A minor can legally have a chequing account. However, most banks insist that the account be a joint account with an adult to prevent any problems arising over the minor's legal capacity to contract.

If the sum in figures is not the same as the sum in words, the rule is that the words must take precedent. However, most banks will not honour the cheque until the controversy has been clarified.

DISHONOURED CHEQUES AND THE HOLDER IN DUE COURSE

A cheque that the drawee bank refuses to pay is said to be **dishonoured**. The question then arises as to who will suffer the loss. The person holding the cheque is known in law as a **holder in due course**. At one time the person was called the "innocent holder" but the word "innocent" is seldom used today.

Generally, the holder in due course should be able to collect the money if he or she acts promptly. To be regarded as a true holder in due course, the person holding the cheque must meet the qualifications contained in the *Bills of Exchange Act*, which are as follows:

> **56. (1) A holder in due course is a holder who has taken a bill, complete and regular on the face of it, under the following conditions, namely:**
> **(a) that he became the holder of it before it was overdue and without notice that it had been previously dishonoured, if such was the fact;**
> **(b) that he took the bill in good faith and for value, and that at the time the bill was negotiated to him he had no notice of any defect in the title of the person who negotiated it.**

This definition indicates that the holder in due course is a person who accepted the bill of exchange on its "face." This means that the person obtained the bill as a piece of paper in the normal course of business. The person obtained the bill for value, which means that the person had given something to the previous holder. Every holder in due course has the same rights as the previous holder.

The holder must act quickly when he or she learns that a cheque has been dishonoured. The immediate action should be to give Notice of Dishonour within one business day to the drawer and all previous holders whom he or she intends to hold responsible for the amount. Any previous holder who is not notified cannot be held liable on the cheque.

Notice can be given orally or in writing, as long as it clearly indicates the bill that was dishonoured. It is a better practice to given written notice. A bill must be formally protested at the place where it was dishonoured. If the bill is returned by mail, it may be formally protested at the place it was received. In most provinces, a lawyer or notary can prepare a formal, written protest. If the protest is mailed to the drawer or other holders, it is advisable to use registered mail as proof of the date and time the notice was mailed.

The importance of protesting a dishonoured bill is that the holder may sue upon the bill itself, and not have to discuss the reasons (usually a contract) for which the bill was given. If the protest is not made, then the parties can argue only about the terms of the contract. If the holder in due course has given proper notice of dishonour, the value of the cheque can be recovered from any of the previous holders, or from the drawer.

Writing a bad cheque knowing that there is not enough money in the account to cover the cheque is a criminal offence. However, the holder should not assume that every bad cheque represents a criminal act. It is abuse of process to threaten criminal charges in order to force payment of a civil obligation. A lawyer should be consulted before making a criminal complaint.

DEFENCES

The fact that the holder protests the dishonour of the bill does not guarantee that he or she will recover the money. Defences can be raised against a holder in due course. However, some defences are good against all holders while others have limited application. There are two basic types of defences. Some relate to the appearance of the bill itself. These are called **real defences**. A good example of a real defence is a cheque on which an additional number has been inserted with a different colour of ink. Other defences relate to the reason for which the bill was given. These are called **personal defences**. Generally, real defences are successful against any holder in due course. Personal defences are usually valid only against immediate parties.

REAL DEFENCES

After the drawer has written a cheque, something may have happened to the cheque that causes the drawer to stop payment on the cheque. Another possibility is that the bank identifies a problem with the face of the cheque and refuses to honour it. Real defences include forgery, alteration, lack of delivery, and incapacity of an infant.

- **Forgery**: When a cheque is forged, the person whose name was forged is not liable. However, an endorser of a forged cheque can be held liable by a subsequent holder. Each party gives a guarantee to the next person of its genuineness. The holder in due course must notify all previous endorsers about the forgery. The holder can then claim from any endorser, usually the nearest endorser. In most cases, unless the forger can be found, the first person to take the cheque from the forger will be the ultimate loser.

KELLY FUNERAL HOMES v. CIBC

Ontario, 1990

Lorne Kelly first started banking with the Canadian Imperial Bank of Commerce when he began his business, Kelly Funeral Homes, in 1954. As the business grew, he opened four more funeral homes in the Ottawa area. The volume of work required him to hire additional managerial help and in 1964 he hired Patrick Larkin. Larkin had been recommended by the parish priest, even though it was known Larkin had been in some trouble. For 20 years, Larkin lived with the Kelly family and was treated like a member of the family. He worked hard and the business flourished. Kelly turned most of the operation of the business over to Larkin.

Larkin was a close friend—and a thief. He stole $240 000 from the business. As the chief financial officer, Larkin paid himself and his wife high salaries and self-declared bonuses. The cheque cashing authorization that the business had with the defendant bank stated that every cheque over $1000 was to be signed by both Larkin and Kelly. However, the rule was not closely enforced and Larkin wrote cheques to fictitious people, which he cashed. He paid personal expenses with company cheques and forged endorsements on cheques.

The contract between the plaintiff and the defendant said that the customer is responsible to check bank statements and to notify the bank within 30 days of any discrepancies. Kelly did not do this until Larkin had stolen money over a period of eight years. When Kelly discovered the thefts, he sued the bank for negligence.

The action was dismissed. The funeral home was bound by the terms of the agreement which said it would check its statements and let the bank know of any problems within 30 days. During the eight years in which most of the money was stolen, the bank processed more than 30 000 cheques. It was unreasonable to expect every bank employee to be on the lookout for irregularities which the customer's own trusted employee was causing. The judge held that the fault lay with Kelly's faulty bookkeeping procedures and his failure to check his bank statements closely.

- **Material alteration**: Once a cheque is drawn, any attempt to change the information written upon its face or to change any of the endorsements on the back will result in dishonour, and the drawer will remain liable only for the original amount as ordered paid to the original payee.

- **Lack of delivery of an incomplete instrument**: A partially completed cheque that is taken without the drawer's consent and then filled in at a later date would be subject to a real defence. It is, of course, careless to leave cheques lying around partially completed. However, if an incomplete cheque is delivered on the understanding that the holder will complete it according to certain terms, then the cheque is valid. Thus, if Brown writes a cheque for Green and asks Green to fill in the amount later, the cheque is valid.

- **Incapacity of an infant**: An infant can write cheques but cannot be held liable as an endorser. An infant cannot rely upon his or her incapacity to avoid basic banking problems that could happen to any customer, regardless of age.

BANK OF NOVA SCOTIA v. PASSERO

Ontario, 1990

The infant defendant, Maria Passero, had a bank account with the plaintiff. She asked that her account be transferred to a different branch. The bank mistakenly transferred the account of the defendant's grandmother, who was also named Maria Passero. The defendant was surprised to find so much money in her account, so she withdrew most of it and gave it to her mother.

When the bank learned of its error, it repaid the grandmother and demanded $6300 from the defendant and her mother. Counsel for the defendant submitted that since Maria was an infant at the time the incident took place, no contract was enforceable against her. Her mother argued that she was not liable for her daughter's actions and that she had no privity of contract with the bank. The Court ordered Maria to repay the money.

The principle of unjust enrichment was applied to the facts of the case. The bank made an honest error and notified the defendant as soon as it learned of the error. The granddaughter had no legal or moral right to take the money. The action against the mother was dismissed. Even though the mother ended up with the money, restitution is available against the payee, not a third party who may have received the eventual benefit.

PROMISSORY NOTES

While a cheque is an order to pay, a **promissory note** is a promise to pay. Apart from this essential difference, promissory notes are subject to the same requirements of a bill of exchange as are cheques. The person who signs a note is generally called the **maker**. A promissory note is normally given as a promise to pay a debt such as a bank loan. It is also common to have such a note as part of a conditional sale agreement. It does not have to follow any particular form, but must include the names of the parties, the current date, the due date, the amount owed, the payment schedule, and the rate of interest charged.

Unlike cheques, promissory notes may contain a requirement to pay interest as well as the principal amount stated. If a note says "pay on demand" it must be paid whenever the holder demands the money.

If a note is payable at a future time, the debtor is permitted three business days after the given time to make payment. These are called "days of grace." Although the holder may have the right to demand payment of the note, the holder does not have an unqualified right to seize and dispose of assets if the borrower cannot pay.

A promissory note can be endorsed to someone else, who may enforce payment as a holder in due course. If the note is not paid, the holder may sue upon it in much the same way as the holder of a cheque, except that in this case there is no abrupt time limit such as one business day.

The defences mentioned earlier, personal and real, generally apply to notes in the same manner as to cheques.

The signature of an infant on a promissory note as either the maker or as an endorser is not binding, even if the note is given for necessaries.

THE INNOCENT HOLDER IN DUE COURSE

A genuine holder in due course is believed to be unaware of any defects and has no knowledge of the circumstances regarding the issue of the note. Such a person is innocent and protected by the court because he or she accepted the note in good faith. This privileged status must be maintained in order for business to function, otherwise no one would dare trust any promissory note. The question of prior knowledge can cause the holder in due course to lose his or her protected status.

FEDERAL DISCOUNT CORPORATION v. ST. PIERRE

Ontario, 1962

St. Pierre agreed to purchase a home knitting machine from Fair Isle Knitting Ltd. for $365. She paid $35 in cash and signed a contract and promissory note to make 12 monthly payments of $27.50 each. One clause of the confusing contract said that Fair Isle would buy her finished work, thus guaranteeing that she would earn enough money to pay for the machine and then earn additional money in the following years. St. Pierre paid two instalments and shipped what she believed to be $150 worth of knitted goods to

Fair Isle, for which she was not paid. Fair Isle notified her that they were going out of business. She then received a letter from Federal Discount saying that they held her note and requested payment. The letter they sent her was stamped with the words: "Promissory note payments must be made regardless of amount earned from knitting."

The trial judge ruled that Federal Discount was not a true holder in due course. The Court of Appeal upheld the ruling saying:

> *The plaintiff was fully aware of the general course of operation employed by Fair Isle, as indicated by the notation stamped on the letter. The course of dealings between Federal Discount and Fair Isle indicates a relationship much more intimate than in a normal commercial transaction. To pretend that they were so separate that the transfer of the note constituted an independent commercial transaction ignores the true substance of their pre-existing arrangements.*

The preceding case illustrates the rule that a true holder in due course does not know the nature of the contractual agreement that existed between the original two parties. A holder in due course merely buys "commercial paper" as part of its business.

The potential abuse of promissory notes by dishonest sellers is obvious. The buyer could be "outflanked" by the teamwork of the seller and the holder in due course. The seller could cheat the buyer, quickly sell the note to the holder in due course, then go out of business. The buyer must pay the holder in due course because his or her argument is with the seller. The note is an unconditional promise to pay that is not dependent upon a good relationship with the seller.

In the 1960s, Canadians were victimized by a dazzling array of dishonest schemes, including overpriced appliances, pyramid sales schemes, and work-at-home schemes. Mrs. St. Pierre bought a loom and hoped to augment her family income by weaving.

Canadians bought floor sanders, water softeners, and vacuum cleaners at inflated prices. In every instance, the victims made small down payments and signed promissory notes which they never expected to pay because they expected to earn sufficient income through these schemes to render the payments unimportant. In reality, they were stuck with full payment plus interest. Although most finance companies are reputable, a number of finance companies co-operated with the con artists running these dishonest schemes. They readily bought the notes signed by victims and took legal action to get the money. Equally annoying to the victims was the fact that the law was solidly on the side of the crooks.

The abuse of promissory notes led to a change in the *Bills of Exchange Act* to eliminate the ease with which buyers were cheated. Present law requires that all promissory notes attached to conditional sale contracts or given as security for an instalment purchase be marked with the words "Consumer Purchase." Various provincial laws were also changed to adopt this new requirement. Although a note can still be negotiated to a third party, the law now permits the maker to refuse to pay a third party, or holder in due course, if there is a valid complaint against the original seller. Thus, with regard to consumer purchases, the holder in due course has lost his or her traditionally safe position. A note signed as part of a business purchase need not be so marked. For example, if Brown borrows money from the Steady Bank, the note will not be marked with the words "Consumer Purchase" because it is not a consumer transaction. To a certain extent, the law makes it very difficult for any person to buy a note marked with these protective words. On the one hand, the person cannot contact the maker of the note and ask questions as to whether there is any complaint or problem with the product or contract because a holder in due course is not supposed to know these details. On the other hand, if a person accepts such a note without additional information, he or she runs a great risk of not being paid.

ROYAL BANK v. SIEMENS

British Columbia, 1978

The defendant and her boyfriend borrowed $3000 from the plaintiff bank. The purpose of the loan was to enable the boyfriend to buy a new Dodge Charger. The defendant and her boyfriend signed a promissory note and a chattel mortgage on the new car. The defendant also signed a chattel mortgage on her own car as security for the loan. The money was placed in the defendant's bank account. She then paid for the new car for her boyfriend, who promptly took the car and left the province. The boyfriend made no car payments and the bank demanded full payment from the defendant.

The defendant did not want the bank to seize her own car, so she worked out a new payment plan with the bank. She took out a new loan, with smaller payments over a longer period of time, and pledged additional security. The initial loan was cancelled. The defendant found the payments too difficult to make by herself and sought to avoid the entire agreement on the basis that she had received no consideration for the second loan agreement and that the promissory note was invalid because it was not marked with the words "Consumer Purchase."

The Court held that the note did not have to be marked with the protective words. The bank lent money to the defendant, who paid cash for the car. The promissory notes were a bank loan only; they were not tied in any way to the purchase of the car. The cancellation of the first note and the signing of the second note were valid, because the bank gave forebearance in not immediately seizing the defendant's car.

However, the judge then discovered that when the first note was cancelled, the bank relinquished its claim upon the Charger and forgot to reassign it to the defendant when the second note was signed. By this error, the bank relieved the defendant of liability for the new car and had no further claim against her.

JOINT NOTES

When two people sign a note that reads, "We promise to pay," then the two people are signing a **joint note**. This means that, in default of payment, the holder must sue them both as one defendant and can hope to obtain only one judgment. However, if the note reads, "I promise to pay" and is signed by two people, the note is a **joint and several note**. In a joint and several note, the makers sign both together and individually. They promise to pay the note together, but each maker also promises separately to make good the entire note personally if the other maker does not fulfil his or her obligation. In the *Siemens* case the couple signed a joint and several note and when the boyfriend disappeared, Ms. Siemens was personally liable for the entire sum, not half of it.

When suing upon a joint and several note, the holder is not limited to one judgment, but could if necessary sue the two makers in separate actions to recover the full amount. If one maker of the note is required to pay the full amount, that maker may, in turn, sue the other maker for half that amount. This assumes that the other maker can be found and has the money.

GUARANTEEING A NOTE

If a borrower has a weak credit rating or is very young and has no assets, the lender may require that another person guarantee the note. The legal effect of such a guarantee is that the guarantor accepts liability for the note if the maker defaults. Some people regard such guarantees as mere formalities or just a way of saying that the maker is a good risk. This is untrue. Should the maker fail to pay, the guarantor will have to pay the note.

The courts have traditionally held that a wife could not guarantee a husband's loan unless she had received "independent legal advice." This concept presumed that the wife had no experience in business, would be unduly influenced by her husband, and could not exercise an independent will free of her husband. In some situations, this is quite true. In the British Columbia case of *E. &. R. Distributors v. Atlas Drywall Ltd.* (1981) the Court held that the holder must show that the wife received a proper explanation of the legal significance of the note before she signed it. However, in *Royal Bank v. Poisson* (1977) the Ontario Supreme Court saw no reason why a wife should not be held liable for guaranteeing a note when the wife was familiar with banking agreements and had considerable business experience. The judge concluded: "There is no magic to independent legal advice and each case must be considered on the facts."

REVIEW: POINTS OF LAW

1. A bill of exchange must be in writing, signed by the person giving it, and for a sum certain.
2. A cheque is not legal tender. A creditor does not have to accept a cheque as payment of a debt.
3. A cheque may be negotiated to another person by endorsing it on the back.
4. A cheque may be written on anything. It does not have to be written on a blank cheque form.
5. A person who signs a company cheque should do so in a manner that makes it clear that the person accepts no personal liability for the cheque.
6. A cheque is stale-dated after six months and cannot be paid.
7. Forgery is a real defence that is valid against any holder in due course.
8. A promissory note that is part of an instalment purchase must be marked with the words "Consumer Purchase," which gives the maker the same defences against a holder in due course as against the original seller.

LEGAL BRIEFS

1. R borrowed $10 000 from his sister, E. No formal paper was signed, but E kept a small notebook in which she wrote down each instalment payment made by R. When R had repaid only half of the money, he died. E sought the remainder of the money from R's estate, using her notebook as evidence. Will E receive the money?
2. H pressured T into signing a contract that T did not really want to sign. T signed the contract and the promissory note that accompanied it, but deliberately misspelled his name. There was a witness to the signing. Later, T tried to avoid the contract by pointing out that the name on the papers was not his true name. Has T cleverly avoided liability?
3. B left his pay cheque on the seat of his car. His cousin, M, found it and decided to steal the money. M forged an endorsement to himself and cashed the cheque. M then left town. B did not advise his bank or his employer about the lost cheque because he thought he had just misplaced it and would eventually find it. When B received his monthly bank statement, he learned what had happened and demanded the money from the bank. Must the bank comply?
4. P borrowed $5000 from his father and repaid it over a period of two years. P signed a note when he borrowed the money and, when he made the last payment, wanted the note back. His father said he had lost the note. P considered the matter settled. When the father died, the executor of the estate found the note and notified P that the estate wanted the money. Advise P.
5. L had a bad habit of not signing her cheques when she paid bills, etc. One day she decided to cure the problem by signing all the blank cheques in her book. She lost the book. What action should L take?

APPLYING THE LAW

TD BANK v. CAISSE POPULAIRE STE.-CAMILLE

Quebec, 1975

The case arose from the fraudulent manipulation of cheques by a third party, M, acting jointly with several accomplices. M asked J, who had an account with the plaintiff bank and owed him some money, to deposit $44 000 in cash in his account. J then had two cheques certified. One was for $40 000 and the other for $4000. M then altered the second cheque to also read $40 000 and J cashed the forged cheque and gave the money to M. In order to cash the first cheque for $40 000, M used another man, S, who was a regular customer of the defendant credit union, to present the cheque for payment. S was a customer in good standing with the credit union.

The manager of the credit union wanted to verify the cheque with the plaintiff bank. He told the assistant manager to contact the plaintiff, but the assistant manager had trouble getting in touch with someone who could provide the information.

The manager, hearing nothing further about the matter, and in the belief that everything was in order, accepted the cheque. He paid S $5000 in cash and credited his account with $15 000 and the account of a company belonging to M's wife with $20 000. The manager was later able to contact someone at the plaintiff bank who said that the bank had indeed issued a certified cheque for $40 000 and that it was valid.

The plaintiff paid the money to the defendant credit union, but later realized that a forgery had taken place when the second cheque showed up. The plaintiff sued to have the money repaid. The trial judge dismissed the plaintiff's action, finding that the defendant had acted in good faith and that the cheque actually presented to the defendant was not the forged cheque.

The plaintiff appealed, arguing that it was not important to decide which of the cheques was the forged one—the important point was that the entire scheme was a fraud. Forgery and fraud represent real defences that are valid against a holder in due course.

The Court of Appeal upheld the decision of the trial judge. The cheque which the credit union had honoured was a true cheque. The credit union had acted carefully and in good faith. Whatever claim the plaintiff had was against J, M, and S.

Questions

1. The cheque cashed by the credit union was genuine, so why did the plaintiff believe it could recover the money?
2. Did the credit union fail to act properly in any way in this case? Why or why not?
3. Why were two cheques involved in this plan?
4. Although the plan seemed complex, do you think the forgers ever had a chance of getting away with it? Give reasons for your answer.

PRINCIPLES AND CASES

Case 1: Legal Principle

A minor cannot be held liable upon a promissory note, even if given for necessaries. An adult who guarantees such a note has no similar protection.

Case Facts

The defendant's daughter, a minor, wanted to borrow money from the plaintiff bank. The daughter signed a promissory note, which was then co-signed by her mother, who guaranteed the loan. The daughter repaid most of the loan. While still a minor, the daughter returned to the bank and borrowed a much larger sum. The second note was not guaranteed by the defendant. When her daughter told her that the bank had loaned her more money, the defendant was surprised. Her daughter did not have a secure job and was not using the money for a good purpose. What the defendant did not know was that the first note was worded in such a way that it bound the defendant to all future loans.

The defendant's daughter moved to another province and did not repay the money. The plaintiff bank brought an action against the defendant, who accepted liability only for the first loan, but denied liability for the second. She stated that she had never been told she was making a commitment for further loans or advances.

Possible Decisions

A The defendant is liable because the wording of the loan agreement was clear and unambiguous.

B The defendant is liable because, once an adult guarantees the debt of a minor, the creditor may continue to look to that adult for payment.

C The defendant is not liable because she did not receive independent legal advice.

D The defendant is not liable because a crucial term of the agreement was not explained to her.

YOU BE THE JUDGE

1. The defendant was a farmer who ordered a prefabricated steel building from the C Steel Company. He paid $100 down and signed a note for $5412. He thought the contract included assembly, but was told that he would have to pay another $1000 for assembly. He signed a second note for $6523 and tore up the first note. The building was assembled by the steel company. While the work was underway, a representative of the I Credit Corporation called the defendant and asked if the defendant was pleased with the way the work was progressing. The defendant said yes. The building was assembled incorrectly and another company said it would have to be torn down. The defendant refused to make payment on his note to the steel company, but was surprised to learn that the credit corporation held the note. The defendant refused to pay them, too. The credit corporation sued on the note as a holder in due course. Who would succeed?

2. The defendant was sued by the executor of his father's estate for the amount unpaid on a promissory note. The defendant had borrowed $25 000 from his father to invest in his business. He had repaid $5000 on schedule. The father became very ill and from his hospital bed told his son, "You can just forget about what you owe me." The father's estate was to be divided among the defendant and his two sisters. The executor demanded that the remaining $20 000 be repaid to the estate. Who would succeed?

3. The defendant, a minor, purchased a used car from the plaintiff car dealership. The plaintiff did not know that the defendant was a minor and the question of her age never came up. The defendant paid for the car with two cheques. One was dated with the current date; the second was post-dated for one week. The defendant explained that she was expecting a tax refund that would cover the second cheque. The defendant smashed up the car within two days and had no collision insurance. The defendant negated the value of both cheques by closing her bank account. The plaintiff received the cheques back from its bank marked "NSF" and protested the dishonour. The defendant raised the defence of her minority. Who would succeed?

4. The president of a small company borrowed $150 000 from the plaintiff bank. He signed a promissory note with his name only. He did not indicate by his signature that he was signing for the company or that he was a signing officer. The president died and it was discovered that he had mismanaged the company and had spent a large sum of money for his own personal living expenses. The bank brought an action against the company and the estate of the deceased man. The company defended the action by arguing that the company by-laws prohibited the president from taking the loan without the approval of the board of directors. Counsel for the company argued that the bank should have insisted upon proof of authority from the president before extending the loan. Counsel for the deceased's estate raised the opposite argument. The deceased had undertaken the loan for the business and no personal liability was attached. Will the bank succeed against either defendant?

5. The defendant, an 18-year-old high school student, had a bank account with the plaintiff bank. The balance never exceeded $500. The bank made an error in assigning a corporate customer the same account number. Deposits made by the second customer were credited to the defendant's account. The defendant was surprised to find a balance of nearly $30 000 in his account. He withdrew $10 000 and bought a stereo and a motorcycle. He fully expected to be caught and did not know what would happen to him. When nothing happened, he withdrew more money. The situation extended for nearly 10 months without detection. By then, the defendant had spent almost $40 000 for frills and lavish living with his friends. Only $10 000 of this amount was recoverable. Counsel for the defendant argued that although the defendant knew he was not entitled to this money, the bank should not be allowed to recover it because both the bank and the corporate customer were negligent in not detecting the problem sooner. The defendant was unable to resist the temptation which was placed in front of him. Counsel for the defendant alternatively argued that the money was a perpetual loan with no specific repayment period. The bank relied upon the terms of the bank agreement which required customers to report discrepancies in their accounts within 30 days. The action was also brought against the defendant's parents, who did not take action when they saw their son spending thousands of dollars. Who would succeed?

6. The plaintiff was sued by the defendant bank and a third party for the amount of a cheque that the plaintiff had given to a third party. The plaintiff decided he had been cheated on the purchase of a boat and went back to the third party and demanded that his cheque be returned. The third party

refused, saying the deal was final. The plaintiff clearly told the third party that he would stop payment on the cheque. The following morning, the plaintiff called his bank and told the assistant manager not to pay the cheque. He was told he would have to come into the bank and sign a form. He was promised that the cheque would not be paid and gave the assistant manager the details. The assistant manager was delayed ten minutes by another phone call. Unknown to either the plaintiff or the assistant manager, the third party was already at the teller's window with the cheque. By the time the assistant manager went to the teller, the money had been paid and the third party had left the bank. The bank denied liability, saying that the plaintiff had acted too late. The third party continued to insist that the sale was valid and that he was not obligated to return the cheque. Who would succeed?

C H A P T E R   T H I R T E E N

BUSINESS ORGANIZATION

"The secret of successful investing is to keep your head while others are losing theirs."

John Paul Getty,
oil company president

FORMS OF BUSINESS

The decision to start a business enterprise is one that appeals to many Canadians. There are many matters to be considered, however, including the nature of the business, the financing of it, and the form it will take. It is important that the owner or owners of a business understand the legal responsibilities and rights that apply to the various forms of business organization. The three basic forms of business organization are the sole proprietorship, partnership, and corporation. There are variations of each of these, depending upon the size and nature of the business.

THE SOLE PROPRIETORSHIP

A **sole proprietorship** exists when an individual carries on business in his or her own name without involving any other form of business organization or the control of any other person. The individual is the sole owner and operator of the business. The proprietor cannot hire himself or herself as an employee of the business. All the benefits, such as profits, and all the obligations, such as debts, flow to this one person.

The sole proprietor is *personally* responsible for carrying out all contractual relationships relating to the business. A sole proprietorship does not afford the owner any protection against business losses. Accordingly, all business and personal assets of the sole proprietor may be seized to satisfy the debts of the business. A sole proprietorship is the simplest arrangement for carrying on a business and is used in a wide variety of circumstances.

In most provinces, a sole proprietorship does not have to be registered with the provincial government if the business is operated under the name of the owner. However, if the sole proprietor carries on business under a name other than his or her own, the law requires that people doing business with the proprietorship be provided with a mechanism to learn the name of the owner. If a person wishes to bring a lawsuit against a sole proprietorship, the action must name the business owner as a personal defendant. In Ontario, the *Partnership Act* requires a person operating a sole proprietorship under a name other than his or her own name to register with the Ministry of Consumer and Commercial Relations. If the business is not registered, the sole proprietor cannot file a civil action against any person.

The profit or loss from the business in a sole proprietorship in any year must be combined with the owner's income or losses from other sources during the year and taxed at the individual rate.

GENERAL AND LIMITED PARTNERSHIPS

When two or more people carry on business together, the relationship is called a **partnership** and the members of the business are called **partners**. A partnership is not a legal entity separate from its partners. Partnerships are commonly established by lawyers, accountants, and other professional people. The partnership does not necessarily give each partner an equal ownership of the business. There is no limit upon the size of a partnership. Corporations, as well as individuals, may be partners. A person may be a partner in more than one partnership.

There are two basic types of partnerships: a general partnership and a limited partnership.

GENERAL PARTNERSHIPS

In a **general partnership** the liability of each partner for the debts and other obligations of the partnership is unlimited. All provinces have a *Partnership Act* that defines a partnership as "the relation that subsists between persons carrying on a business in common with a view to profit." The law specifies that a corporation is not a partnership. The definition of a partnership contains three important elements that must be satisfied:

1. There must be a business, which is loosely defined as any trade, occupation, or profession.
2. The people in the partnership must have agreed to carry on business in common. A partnership must be distinguished from business relationships such as employer and employee, principal and agent.
3. The partnership must operate with a view to profit. This eliminates clubs, social organizations, or charities. The partners must agree to share the profit, not the gross revenue.

Most partnerships are formed by signing a formal partnership agreement. However, a partnership may exist by virtue of what the people intended and were doing. If two or more people carry on a business in common, contribute property or labour to the business, and share in the profits or losses, then it is safe to assume that a partnership exists, even in the absence of any formal agreement.

A partnership has a legal existence, but it is not a separate legal entity from the partners who compose it. Under the common law, this was not the case. A partnership was not a legal entity and lawsuits could not be brought against a partnership, only against the partners. The partnership could not sue in its own name. As partnerships grew in size, sometimes having dozens of partners, this rule became unwieldy. By special statute, partnerships have been given specific legal recognition but are still not formally divorced from the partners themselves. The rules of practice permit a partnership to sue or be sued in its own name, but stop short of declaring that a partnership is a corporation. Another effect of the rule that a partnership is not a separate legal entity is that a person cannot be a partner and an employee at the same time. The basic reason is that a person cannot enter into a contract with himself or herself.

Joint ownership of property does not, by itself, create a partnership, even if the owners share in the profits generated by the property. In *A.E. LePage Ltd. v. Kamex Developments Ltd.* (Ontario, 1977), the Court held that the issue was whether the two parties intended to carry on business together or merely to share the profits of a jointly owned property.

The decision to enter into a partnership with another person or persons involves substantial risk. The concept of a partnership is that each partner is the agent of the partnership and the other partners when acting within the normal scope of the partnership's business. Thus, the action of one partner legally binds all of the partners. Only when it is apparent that the partner acted outside the firm's normal business, or when a third party knew the partner had no authority to act for the firm, will the other partners escape liability. In this sense, each partner acts as an agent for the partnership—the principal. The potential liability of each person who enters a partnership is total. Each partner is *personally* liable to the extent of all of the assets that the partner contributed to the partnership and all of his or her personal assets. The stupidity or dishonesty of one partner may bankrupt all the partners. This liability includes contracts, torts, and fiduciary duty. Partners are jointly liable for debts of the partnership. This means that in order to sue the partnership, it is important to name all of the partners as defendants.

The rights and duties of the partners should be carefully stated in the partnership agreement. Generally, as with most agreements, the parties must conduct themselves in a manner that is of the utmost good faith to the firm and other partners. Each partner must render an accounting to the other partners of any money or information received. Partners must not engage in other businesses that compete directly against the firm.

A partner is not liable for anything done before he or she became a partner. A retired partner remains liable for the partnership's debts incurred before retirement unless the partner is discharged by an agreement between himself or herself and the firm's creditors.

When a partnership is formed, the partners often contribute money or other assets to the partnership. This property becomes the property of the firm, and it is no longer the property of the partner who contributed it. The partner's right is to a share of the profits of the firm according to the partnership agreement.

A partnership may be dissolved by the application or one or more partners to the court. Grounds for such application include mental incompetence of a partner, a partner's persistent breach of the partnership agreement, or when the partnership can be carried on only at a loss. In British Columbia, the death of a partner does not dissolve the partnership unless the agreement specifically provides for such dissolution.

In the absence of any specific terms in the partnership agreement, a partnership is dissolved:

1. On the expiration of the term set for its existence;
2. On the death or insolvency of a partner;
3. On a partner giving notice to the other partners of his or her intention to dissolve the partnership.

Some provinces require that a partnership be registered. In Alberta, Ontario, and British Columbia there is no requirement to register a partnership unless it is engaged in mining, trading, or manufacturing. However, an unregistered partnership may be barred from suing third parties, which is a strong incentive to register any partnership.

Partnerships are regulated by each province and, historically, no province was prepared to recognize or permit an interprovincial partnership. In the following case, the Supreme Court of Canada found this restriction unacceptable.

LAW SOCIETY OF ALBERTA v. BLACK

Supreme Court of Canada, 1989

The Alberta Law Society had two rules that prohibited Alberta lawyers from being partners in more than one firm and from entering into partnerships with non-residents. The Supreme Court held that these rules were an unjustifiable violation of the mobility rights under s. 6 of the *Charter of Rights and Freedoms*, which guarantees to Canadian citizens and permanent residents the right to pursue a livelihood in any province. The decision opened the door to the establishment of large, national, full-service law firms across Canada. The decision also means that a person can be a partner in more than one province and can be a partner in a business in a province without actually living there.

The case arose when a large Ontario law firm, McCarthy & McCarthy, opened an office in Calgary. It used the name "Black & Company," but its

Calgary lawyers were also partners in McCarthy & McCarthy. The province insisted that the lawyers in Black & Company sever all ties with McCarthy & McCarthy. The province argued that the quality of legal service would suffer if law firms were not exclusively Alberta-based. Black & Company successfully contested the ruling and then merged with McCarthy & McCarthy.

LIMITED PARTNERSHIPS

The most important feature of a **limited partnership** (as compared to a general partnership) is that the liability of each limited partner is restricted to the amount of money or other assets the partner contributes or agrees to contribute to the limited partnership. A limited partner may contribute money or property, but not services.

Limited partnerships are governed by the *Limited Partnership Act* of each province. To a certain extent, they are also governed by the *Partnership Act* and the common law. A limited partnership must consist of one or more people who are general partners and one or more people who are limited partners. However, a person may be a general partner and a limited partner at the same time. A "person" can include a corporation.

A limited partnership is formed by filing a declaration with the Registrar of Partnerships, signed by all of the partners and stating the firm's name, business address, nature of business, names and addresses of all partners, and the money or property contributed by each partner. A new declaration must be filed every five years.

A limited partner is more of a passive investor of the firm rather than a person who directs the operation of the business. Limited partners may provide active service to the firm, but once the person becomes a partner, he or she is no longer an employee of the firm. The limited partners share in the profits of the limited partnership according to the terms of the partnership agreement. If the agreement is silent on this matter, the limited partners share according to the proportion of money or assets contributed. It is very important to note that profits cannot be paid out to a partner if the payment would reduce the assets of the firm to an amount that is inadequate to discharge the liabilities of the firm.

A limited partner may do business with his or her firm and may lend money to the firm. The partner will rank as a creditor along with all other creditors. One restriction is that a limited partner cannot hold the assets of the partnership as security or collateral for a loan. If the partnership is dissolved, the limited partners are entitled to receive the amount of their contribution after all debts have been satisfied. Any remaining surplus should then be divided in proportion to the amount each contributed to the firm. A limited partner has the same rights as a general partner to inspect the financial records of the company. The limited partner may also investigate the state of the firm's business and contracts and give advice as to the conduct of business.

A limited partner may apply to the court to have the partnership dissolved. If a general partner dies, the partnership is dissolved unless the partnership agreement specifically authorizes the firm to continue business if all of the remaining partners agree. If the partnership is dissolved, the payments are made, in the following order, to:

1. Limited partners in respect of their profits and other compensation;
2. Limited partners in respect of their contributions;
3. General partners other than for capital and profits;
4. General partners in respect of their profits;
5. General partners in respect of capital.

A partnership itself is not a taxable entity. The income or loss of the firm's business is calculated and then each partner is allocated a share of the profits for tax purposes.

THE BUSINESS CORPORATION

The concept of an incorporated company evolved in Europe several centuries ago. What was needed was a system under which a large number of people could be involved in a business without actually running it. The major stumbling block to such an idea was the matter of liability. Traditionally, every person who was considered an owner of a business was liable for its debts and other liabilities. The problem was solved by enacting special legislation that declared that an incorporated company has a separate legal personality from the people who own the shares of the company. In short, a company was declared a legal person that can sue or be sued in its name. General Motors Canada, Imperial Oil, and Alcan are not just corporations, they are legal "persons."

LEGAL ENTITY

A corporation is a separate legal entity, sometimes called "an artificial person." It may sue or be sued in its own name. It has perpetual existence and can be dissolved only by a court order, order of the government official who administers the Act under which it was incorporated, or by a vote of the majority of the shareholders. It is possible for an individual to be an owner of a corporation, a shareholder, and an employee. The management is separate from ownership. There is no legal requirement for directors and officers to own any shares of the corporation.

A corporation is liable for the wrongful acts of its employees "within the scope of employment."

HAWES v. RYCZKO et al.

British Columbia, 1988

Douglas Terpsma was shot to death by his employer, John Ryczko. An action was brought on behalf of Terpsma's children against Greenridge Holdings Ltd., of which Ryczko was the president. Greenridge owned and operated a farm. The victim cut and baled hay from this farm and paid the farm corporation so much per bale. When the two men had a fight over the price of the hay, Ryczko shot and killed the deceased.

The Court held that the corporation was vicariously liable for the tort committed by its president because the argument arose over a business transaction, not a personal dispute. Thus, the defendant was acting within the scope of his employment when he killed the victim.

A corporation has many of the rights and freedoms under the *Charter of Rights and Freedoms*. A specific exception is section 15—discrimination. The Supreme Court of Canada has held that section 15 applies only to the "individual" and a corporation is not an individual. In some cases, a corporation can be held criminally responsible. Although the corporation cannot be imprisoned, it can be convicted and fined.

WHERE TO INCORPORATE

A business may be incorporated under federal or provincial law. For example, a business incorporated under the laws of Ontario will be registered under the Ontario *Business Corporations Act*. A business incorporated under federal law will be incorporated under the *Business Corporations Act of Canada*.

INCORPORATION PROCEDURE

Every business, as a matter of right, is entitled to form a corporation whether under federal or provincial law. This is accomplished by delivering **Articles of Incorporation** in the form prescribed to the appropriate government department, together with the necessary supporting materials. If all of the information is in order, a **Certificate of Incorporation** is issued and the corporation comes into existence on the date shown in the certificate. There are companies that specialize in helping businesses incorporate. For a basic fee, they will prepare all the documentation and process the application. For a small business, the process is very straightforward. The articles must set out the following information:

1. Name of the corporation;
2. Location of the registered office;
3. Capital structure of the company;
4. Share transfer restrictions;
5. Names of the first directors;
6. Restrictions, if any, on the nature of the business.

Once the corporation is registered, the names of officers and directors are registered on a continuing basis, and the registered information is a matter of public record.

NAMING THE CORPORATION

Every company is given a number and if the company wishes, it can decline to have any name at all. It can simply remain a "numbered company." Ontario requires that every company use a descriptive word along with the chosen name such as "Limited" or "Incorporated." The standard abbreviations may also be used, e.g., "Ltd." However, the name chosen must be consistently applied. Thus, "Great Northern Ltd." cannot also call itself "Great Northern Limited."

Although the name of the province or "Canada" may be part of the company registration, the name cannot imply that the company has a government affiliation. For example, the name "Power Corporation of Canada" is acceptable. However, a subtle change such as "Canada Power Corporation" might be rejected because the name implies it is a Crown corporation.

The decision to have a corporate name will slow the process of incorporation because a search must be made to determine if the name has already been adopted by another company. Two companies cannot have the same name.

A name cannot be approved if it is already in use, refers to the Crown in any way, is obscene, incorrectly describes the nature of the business, uses another person's family name, or would be confused with another company with a similar-sounding name.

An application for incorporation must be accompanied by a computer search of names to demonstrate that the above requirements have been met. There are several companies that provide this service.

CORPORATE ADDRESS

Federal and provincial statutes provide that a corporation must, at all times, have a registered office in the locality specified in its Articles. If the company is federally incorporated, its head office must be in Canada.

CORPORATE DIRECTORS

Provincial and federal laws generally permit a company to have just one director. If the company intends to sell securities to the public, it must have at least three directors. One-third of the directors must not be employees of the company. There is no limit upon the maximum number of directors allowed.

The qualifications to be a director are rather basic. The person must be 18 years of age or more, mentally competent, and not an undischarged bankrupt. Ontario law also requires that the majority of directors be resident Canadians.

The initial directors are named in the Articles, but as soon as possible there must be an election by the shareholders. A director is elected for a term not exceeding three years. It is permissible to stagger the terms so that not all the directors are running for office at the same time.

For many years, people such as former provincial premiers accepted directorships as a way of lending their names to corporate public relations. These individuals seldom attended meetings and collected fees simply for allowing their names to be used on the company letterhead. Some individuals were directors of more than 40 corporations. However, in view of recent court decisions that imposed personal liability upon directors, this practice is not as common as it was in the past.

The directors of a company are required to manage or supervise the management of the business of the company. Ontario law holds directors personally liable for the unpaid wages of employees. Directors owe a fiduciary duty to their companies and can be liable of they do not act in good faith or are negligent. The leading case on this point is the following one.

CANADIAN AERO SERVICE LTD. (CANAERO) v. O'MALLEY

Supreme Court of Canada, 1974

O'Malley and Zarzycki were employees and directors of Canaero. They were involved in negotiating a contract involving the aerial mapping of Guyana. The two men suddenly resigned their jobs and directorships and set up their own company, Terra Surveys Limited. They were awarded the contract by the Government of Guyana.

Canaero sued, alleging a total breach of trust of two employees and directors who abused inside information for personal profit. The Court awarded damages to the plaintiff:

> *It follows that O'Malley and Zarzycki stood in a fiduciary relationship to Canaero, which in its generality betokens loyalty, good faith and avoidance of a conflict of duty and self-interest. Descending from the generality, the fiduciary relationship goes at least this far: a director or senior officer like O'Malley or Zarzycki is precluded from obtaining for himself, either secretly or without the approval of the company, any property or advantage either belonging to the company or for which it has been negotiating; and especially is this so where the director or officer is a participant in the negotiations on behalf of the company.*

The second type of general obligation placed upon a director is the common law duty to maintain a reasonable standard of care in carrying out his or her responsibilities. The federal and provincial statutes generally state that a director must "exercise the care, diligence, and skill that a reasonably prudent person would exercise in comparable circumstances." Failure to meet this standard exposes a director to personal liability for damages arising out of his or her negligence.

Directors may be personally liable for failure to obey securities laws. For example, it is illegal for directors to declare a dividend if the company cannot pay its liabilities. A director would not be liable for a breach of this requirement if he or she was given false accounting information.

SHARE CAPITAL

The Articles must define the capital structure of the company. Generally, if there is only one class of shares, it is assumed that the rights and privileges attaching to the shares are equal. However, there may be more than one class of shares. The classes and maximum number of shares authorized under the Articles need not actually be issued. Therefore, it is wise to specify a wide variety of shares that might be issued in the future in the original application. For example, a small company might want to establish common and preferred/special shares as follows:

- Common: Unlimited number, no par value;
- Special: Unlimited number, 6%, non-voting, non-cumulative, redeemable.

This means that common shares will be issued in any number that the directors vote to issue. Each certificate will have "no par value," meaning that it has no face value if the company is wound up. Ontario does not permit shares to be issued with a par value.

The second type of shares will be preferred shares, paying a 6 percent dividend. They will also be issued in whatever amounts the directors decide. If the directors vote not to pay a quarterly dividend, the obligation does not accumulate in the shareholder's account. The shares are redeemable (to be cashed in) at a given date at a fixed price. The company must issue common shares, but does not need to issue the special shares unless the need for special financing arises.

CAPITAL STRUCTURE OF A CORPORATION

The capital structure of a corporation has three basic components: bonds and debentures, common shares, and preferred shares.

BONDS AND DEBENTURES

When a company issues a **bond or debenture**, it borrows money from investors and promises to repay the money on the **maturity date** of the bond. As well, the company pays the investor interest on the loan. In terms of safety, bonds rank ahead of common and preferred shares. This position of safety is enforced by the requirement that the interest on the bonds be paid before any dividends are paid on shares and the fact that the bondholders rank ahead of the shareholders in a claim upon the assets of the company should the company wind up business.

If a company cannot pay the interest on its bonds, the company must declare bankruptcy or reach a new agreement with the bondholders. For example, the venerable Canadian corporation, Massey Ferguson Ltd. (now called Varity Corporation), faced bankruptcy in the mid-1970s. The company avoided bankruptcy by persuading bondholders to exchange their bonds for shares in the company. The rate of interest on a bond is fixed and not subject to change. During periods of inflation, low-yield bonds have proven to be poor investments because the investor is locked into a fixed rate of interest.

PREFERRED SHARES

A company may decide to issue **preferred shares** which represent ownership of the company but are often not voting shares. Investors who buy preferred shares rank behind bondholders but ahead of common shareholders in terms of receiving a return upon investment. The dividend of the preferred share is fixed at a specific percentage. It does not increase even if the company profits soar. However, preferred shares are given a prior claim on assets ahead of the common shares in the event of the winding up of the company.

The word "preferred" means a preferred claim upon assets and profits. The dividend must be paid to the preferred shareholders before any dividends can be paid to the common shareholders. However, if the company loses money and pays no dividends, the preferred shareholders will suffer the same fate as the common shareholders, which is the cessation of dividends.

COMMON SHARES

Ownership of **common shares** is usually evidenced by registered, transferable shares in a company. The word "Limited" in a company name indicates that common shareholders of that company have only limited responsibility for the debts of the company. Each share usually carries one vote, which allows the holder to vote for the directors of the company. Each year, a company must conduct a shareholders' meeting and if the shareholders are not satisfied with the progress of the company, they may vote to remove the directors. A shareholder has the right to attend the meeting, to ask questions, and to introduce motions.

A shareholder who cannot attend may give another person his or her vote by **proxy**, a document which allows one person to cast the vote of another shareholder. When one group of shareholders believes a company is not well managed, it may solicit the votes of other shareholders in what is often called a **proxy fight**. If the group obtains enough proxies, it will have the votes to dismiss the present board of directors.

A common shareholder is not guaranteed any return upon investment. This decision is purely at the discretion of the directors who may elect to declare a common share dividend if the company profits warrant such payment. Since debt holders and preferred shareholders have prior claims on earnings, it is obvious that the common shareholders receive only what is left. In good years, this may be an attractive return, but in poorer years it may be nothing. Dividends are not a contractual or legal obligation upon the company.

PURCHASE OF A BUSINESS

The decision by a person or company to purchase all or part of another company is a complex matter that should be carried out only with the assistance of competent legal and accounting counsel. There are many potential pitfalls and tax problems. The following discussion is not a complete blueprint, but only a brief overview of some matters that must be considered.

PURCHASE OF ASSETS

A buyer might want to purchase the assets of another business, but not the shares. The assets will be transferred and the former business will most likely cease operation. The actual process is complicated because various provincial laws pertaining to bulk sales apply, debtors may have liens or claims on those assets, and the shareholders will have to agree to the contract.

The parties will agree upon a list of assets. The contract should also contain basic representations and warranties that confirm the accuracy of the information. If land is involved, the title to that land must be searched. The inventory should be physically checked to make certain it is accurate. The accounts receivable should be examined to determine how old the debts are and what percentage is uncollectable.

A particular problem may arise with regard to employee agreements. If the employees will lose their jobs, the labour-management agreement must be studied to determine if they are entitled to severance pay. Some provincial laws require severance pay. This represents a lien (financial claim) upon the assets of the company.

Usually, the purchaser intends to operate the business formerly carried on by the seller. To be successful, the purchaser will want to retain the customers and contracts of the seller. It is prudent to include a non-competition clause that prohibits the seller from setting up a new business in the same area and competing directly with the buyer. This is particularly important when the buyer paid for the goodwill of the company as one of the assets.

Most provinces have a *Bulk Sales Act*. This legislation is designed to protect the creditors of the company. If the purchaser buys assets in bulk from the seller without complying with the Act, the purchaser is liable to the creditors for the value of the assets. The seller cannot sell the assets of the company, take the money, and then leave unpaid creditors behind.

PURCHASE OF SHARES

In the 1980s, the news media confronted Canadians with an array of puzzling terms, such as "leveraged buy-out," "takeover," "management buy-out," and "junk bonds." The sums of money were enormous, reaching more than $24 billion in the takeover of RJR Corporation in the United States.

The takeover process is not complex. One company decides to acquire all of another company. It borrows money from investment bankers to make the purchase. Once the purchase is completed, the company has a large amount of debt owed to the bankers. It proceeds to sell off some of the assets it recently acquired to pay down the debt. Another method is to finance the purchase by selling high-interest bonds, giving the company more time to pay down its debt load. These bonds specifically state that they are not backed by the assets of the company in case of default. Hence, the name **junk bonds.** During periods of economic expansion and high profitability, the process is often very successful. During periods of recession, very large debt payments can drive a company into bankruptcy.

As strange as it may sound, one of the reasons to buy a company is to put it out of business. Investors look for companies that have very under-valued assets on their balance sheets. Assets are normally carried at the original cost. The investors buy the shares of the company, then sell all the assets for a total return greater than the cost of the shares, thereby making a very large profit.

If a foreign company wants to acquire control of a Canadian company, the purchase might first require approval by a federal agency, Investment Canada. Direct investment of $5 million or more or indirect investment of $50 million or more requires approval. Under the *Investment Canada Act*, the federal government will evaluate the "net benefit to Canada" that the investment will provide.

FRANCHISES AND LICENCES

Both licences and franchise agreements are methods of transferring information or intellectual property rights from one person to another. The purpose is to permit the second person to engage in a commercial activity that would otherwise be the exclusive right of the first person. A **franchise** is an agreement whereby the franchisor grants to the franchisee the use of a trade mark or trade name in connection with the supply of goods and services. The franchisee must conduct its business in accordance with prescribed methods developed and generally controlled by the franchisor. The franchisee makes use of the experience, training, accounting systems, site selection, construction, and equipment methods of the franchisor. The franchisor maintains a continuing interest in the franchisee's business by monitoring compliance with standards and operating methods required by the contract. The franchisor has the right to receive compensation from the franchisee through fees, lease payments, or by its sale of products to the franchisee for resale.

A **licence** is a contractual agreement whereby the owner of a trade mark, patent, or copyright grants to another person the right to use this intellectual property for a royalty fee. The licensor has little control over how the licensee conducts business because there is seldom any ongoing involvement between the two parties. Both licensees and franchisees are independent contractors, not direct employees of the other party.

Disadvantages to the franchisor arise from the difficulty of maintaining standards throughout the various franchises and the transfer of technology that may create potential competitors. Terminating a franchise is difficult, because the franchisor must retrieve confidential information, repurchase stock, try to collect debts, and solve any public relations problems.

Disadvantages to the franchisee may include the degree of control exercised by the franchisor and the ongoing financial drain of payments to the franchisor. When the franchise suffers poor sales, there is often a dispute as to which party is more to blame. Franchises are sometimes sold to people by exaggerated claims of potential business.

No special legislation deals specifically with franchising. The courts simply treat the matter as a business contract and apply common law rules.

Restrictions in a franchise agreement may be challenged on the ground that they are a restraint of trade and violate federal or provincial law. For example, the franchisee may be compelled to purchase all supplies from the franchisor. Even though prices are inflated, the franchisee cannot purchase from another, less-expensive source. In *Stephens v. Gulf Oil Ltd.* (Ontario, 1976) the operator of a gas station tried to break his agreement with Gulf Oil because he was being charged a very high, non-competitive price for petroleum products. The contract also gave Gulf the right of "first refusal" if the plaintiff wanted to sell the station. The Ontario Court of Appeal held that the agreement was not a restraint of trade. A restriction upon the franchisee's ability to trade freely is not a restraint of trade, except in the most extreme cases.

REVIEW: POINTS OF LAW

1. A sole proprietorship is the simplest form of business organization, but the proprietor is personally liable for all debts of the business.
2. A partnership has a legal existence, but is not a separate legal entity from the partners that compose it.
3. Each partner is personally liable for all of the debts of the partnership and is therefore vicariously liable for the mistakes of other partners.
4. A partnership is not a taxable entity. Each partner is allocated a share of the profits for tax purposes.
5. A corporation is an artificial person and has a separate, perpetual, legal existence.
6. The directors of a corporation are required by law to act in good faith for the benefit of the corporation.
7. Although a corporation may issue several types of shares, only the common shareholders may vote to elect directors.
8. A person who wants to take over a corporation may either buy only the assets of the corporation or buy control of the corporation by the purchase of more than half the common shares.

LEGAL BRIEFS

1. Y operated a family restaurant as a sole proprietorship for many years. Y had three children, but only one of them, H, took an active part in the operation of the restaurant. It was always "understood" that H would eventually take over the business, but there was no written agreement to this effect. Y died and H believed he now owned the business. Advise H.
2. N worked for an insurance agency for many years. The business was operated by R and W as a partnership. As R was nearing retirement, N was asked if she wanted to become a partner and buy out R's interest. She was interested and took the necessary licensing courses. Papers were prepared to effect the transfer. Before the agreement was signed, R died. W suddenly declined to accept N as a partner and invited P to establish a partnership with him. What rights has N?

3. John Hilton purchased a small motel and wanted to rename it "Hilton Inn." John explained his decision by simply asserting, "Well, that's my name." What possible problem might arise?
4. P bought $10 000 in bonds of a company that has reported large financial losses. "Bonds are guaranteed by the government," P insists. "I got a great price. Can't lose with bonds, because I get paid off first." Is P correct?
5. G and K are partners in a restaurant business. G formed a partnership with two other people to open a restaurant in another city. Must G tell K about this?
6. M learned that his partners, J and Y, were engaged in illegal misuse of client funds. Rather than report this to the authorities, M retired. J and Y continued the partnership, bringing in a new partner, L. J and Y were arrested and convicted eight months later. L lost all of his investment as the partnership was hit with expensive lawsuits. L sued M for not warning him about the situation. What liability would M have to L?

APPLYING THE LAW

ATLAS SUPPLY CO. v. YARMOUTH EQUIPMENT

Nova Scotia, 1991

Atlas Supply Company, an auto parts manufacturer and subsidiary of Imperial Oil, decided to start a string of franchises for auto parts. Atlas's manager for Atlantic Canada prepared a brochure to interest people in acquiring franchises. He sent a copy to the head office. The national sales manager studied the brochure and financial figures, accepting some, but not all. He particularly felt that the economic forecasts for Yarmouth, Nova Scotia, were too high. The area manager suggested a franchise could profit $33 000 per year. The national manager said that a profit of only $11 000 was likely.

Yarmouth Equipment was interested in obtaining a franchise to add to its existing hardware business. The area manager showed the owner the forecast of $33 000, not the $11 000 figure that the head office had used. Yarmouth started a franchise and lost money. It sued Atlas, saying the company had tricked it into an unconscionable contract by using false figures. The printed contract, however, stated that the franchisee entered into the agreement without any warranty or promise of profit of any kind.

The inventory was sold by bulk sale to pay a bank loan and Atlas then sued

Yarmouth for the cost of the inventory, about $200 000. According to the franchise agreement, Atlas had the first right to recover unpaid inventory and to buy back inventory that had been paid for. The trial judge ruled in favour of Yarmouth and Atlas appealed. The Court of Appeal upheld the trial judge, saying:

> *The contract was entered into by a large company with international connections and a small businessman with little experience. It is clear that Atlas had information that would have dissuaded any but the foolhardy to enter into the agreement and it withheld the information from Yarmouth. To enforce the exclusionary clause in these circumstances would produce an unconscionable bargain. There are echoes here of the old doctrine of fundamental breach, breach of collateral warranty, reliance on the seller's skill and judgment, but unconscionability says it all.*

Questions

1. Atlas did not know that the area manager had shown Yarmouth the wrong figures. Why would Atlas not be able to collect what it was owed?
2. The printed contract stated that there was no warranty about how much profit the franchise would earn. Why did the Court not uphold this clause?
3. The franchise might have failed because of mismanagement more than any other reason. Why did the Court not weigh that possibility?
4. In your opinion, was the franchise agreement unconscionable?

PRINCIPLES AND CASES

Case 1: Legal Principle

A partnership exists when two or more persons carry on a business in common with a view towards a profit.

Case Facts

Robert established a new business as a plumbing supplies retailer. He was not experienced in business matters and had little cash. Thomas, the president of Arrow Plumbing Supplies, took an interest in Robert's problem. They made an oral agreement that Thomas would advise Robert if Robert would buy at least half of his supplies from Arrow. Thomas provided business assistance and advertising and helped arrange bank loans. Robert negotiated contracts with builders. Robert ran the store, but everyone knew that business deals had to be made with Thomas. Most people thought Thomas was a part-owner of Robert's store.

For two years the arrangement was successful and both businesses prospered. Arrow made money because Robert purchased nearly 90 percent of his supplies from Arrow. Robert made money because Thomas made solid contracts with large buyers. The two men became good friends and talked about starting a new company together. However, when an economic recession hit, Arrow barely survived and Robert went broke. Robert could not pay his bank loan. He also had supplies on hand for which he had not paid Arrow. The bank seized the inventory, claiming rights to it. Arrow insisted that the inventory must be returned. The bank then sued Robert and Thomas personally on Robert's loan, arguing that the two men were partners.

Possible Decisions

A Robert and Thomas are jointly liable because a partnership was created by their joint efforts to profit.

B Robert and Thomas are jointly liable because Robert allowed Thomas to manage his business affairs.

C Only Robert is liable because his business dealings were with Arrow, not with Thomas.

D Only Robert is liable because there was no formal relationship with either Arrow or Thomas.

YOU BE THE JUDGE

1. The plaintiffs invested in a dishonest land-flip deal and lost a large sum of money. They brought an action against a lawyer and his two partners. The lawyer had allowed his name, and the name of his firm, to be used in the documents that the plaintiffs examined before deciding to invest. The scheme was dreamed up by a trickster who persuaded 300 people to buy vacant land on the promise that others would immediately buy it at a higher price. The land was sold and resold in a plan of "wash trading" that pushed the prices very high. The scheme collapsed when no new victims could be found. The defendant lawyer handled all of the land transfers and

collected large fees for the work, all the while knowing it was a sham. The partners were aware that a large volume of business was involved, but were unaware there was anything dishonest in these transactions. The partnership was dissolved, and the defendant lawyer was unable to cover all of the losses. His partners denied liability. Who would succeed?

2. The plaintiff sued his former employer for wrongful dismissal. The plaintiff had been a vice-president and director of the defendant company for 14 years. The other directors learned that the plaintiff was making frequent contacts with the president of a competitor. These contacts included weekend trips to the head office of the competitor, golf matches, fishing trips, and luncheon meetings with the sales director of the competitor. The plaintiff denied there was anything improper about these activities as they were purely personal activities between friends. The defendant company argued that such contacts were detrimental to the best interests of the company and that important, confidential business matters could be discussed at these so-called personal meetings. Who would succeed?

3. The plaintiff, a commodity trading house, brought an action against the defendant for the debts and losses incurred by the defendant's partner. The partnership traded commodities, particularly foreign currencies. The exchange rules required that all transactions be supported by a minimal commitment of money, usually 10 percent. This is generally called "margin." If the value of the client's position drops, the client is given a "margin call" and required to put up more cash. If the cash is not immediately paid, the trading house must liquidate the client's position. The defendant's partner took on a very large position in Japanese yen. When the market went against him, he was called upon for more margin. The defendant immediately went to the offices of the plaintiff and gave the broker a postdated cheque. The cheque had to be signed by both partners, so the partner forged the defendant's signature. In accepting this cheque, the broker went against the trading rules, because postdated cheques might not be honoured. The broker accepted the cheque because he did not want to irritate a good customer. The partner bought more yen contracts. He continued to lose money and could not put up more margin. When the position was liquidated, the partnership owed the trading house nearly $600 000. The defendant's partner committed suicide. The defendant refused to pay, arguing that he did not know what his partner was doing and could not be held liable when the trading house broke the rules of the exchange and allowed a client to buy contracts with a postdated cheque. Who would succeed?

NO
TRESPASSING

CHAPTER FOURTEEN

REAL PROPERTY

"Buy land. They're not making it anymore."

Will Rogers,
comedian

LEGAL CONCEPTS OF PROPERTY

Primitive society was primarily nomadic. Humans then did not think much about the limits to land, because there did not appear to be any. When humans formed more complex social groupings, they began competing for food with other groups and staked claims to the physical land to ensure their own survival.

The idea of landholding did not originally extend to individuals. The land belonged to the group and, eventually, to the leaders of the groups. The leaders may have taken different names, but nearly all societies settled upon the concept of a king or queen.

In Europe, feudalism was a system under which landholding was extended by the king to individuals in return for services. Actual ownership did not pass to the individual: every bit of land was held by the Crown. The word **tenure** represented the relationship of the **tenant**, or holder of land, to the Crown. Since land represented the only source of wealth, the tenants formed an aristocracy called the "land lords." When the *Doomsday Book* (the first census) was compiled in 1086, it was learned that the whole of England was held by 1500 people.

In Canada, originally, all land was first vested in the Crown. The *Constitution Act, 1867* then transferred to each province the federal Crown's interest in all land within the respective provincial boundaries, with the exception of lands retained for certain federal purposes. The provinces, under the "property and civil rights" section of the Constitution, can regulate the way in which the land is held, recorded, used, and transferred.

Land is referred to as **real property** to distinguish it from all other types of property. In the early days of English law, real property meant any property so unique that monetary damages could not be used to compensate for it. Since ownership of land was nearly always the subject of such cases, "real property" became an accepted term for land, including any buildings on the land. A person involved in a dispute over real property could bring a **real action** to recover it. Where other forms of property were concerned, only a **personal action** could be brought.

Land has a permanent, immovable location. Each parcel of land is unique with respect to every other. The law recognizes this special feature of land by allowing a purchaser of land to compel the seller to complete the sale, because no other parcel of land could be substituted for it. In common law, land includes not only the surface but all that is under and above the surface. More recently, land includes only that part below the surface that can be effectively used by the owner.

In nearly all grants of tenure the Crown reserves for itself the mineral rights under the surface of the land. The passage of airplanes through the air space well above the land is in the public interest and the law permits this without permission of the owners.

PUGLIESE v. NATIONAL CAPITAL COMMISSION

Ontario, 1978

The plaintiffs claimed that the ground water table below their properties was substantially lowered by the construction of a collector sewer on nearby lands owned by the National Capital Commission and that their homes and lands were seriously damaged by the resulting subsidence. When the water table dropped, the land under their homes also dropped. They also claimed that their properties were damaged as a result of drilling and blasting operations. An application was made to a Supreme Court judge to determine whether the plaintiffs had a valid cause of action in law, assuming that the allegations were true. The questions were: (1) Does an owner of land have a right to the support of water beneath his or her land, not flowing in a defined channel? (2) Does such an owner have a right of action in negligence or nuisance under the Ontario *Water Resources Act* from the pumping of water in excess of the amounts set out in permits granted under the Act, for any damage resulting from the removal of such water?

The Court of Appeal came to the conclusion that an owner of land does not have an absolute right to the support of subterranean water that was not flowing in a defined channel so that the removal of the water gave rise to a cause of action. The owner has a right not to be subjected to interference with the support of the water under his land amounting to negligence or nuisance. Infringement of that right could give rise to an action.

LANDHOLDING

The old concept of feudal tenure has given way to what in Canada is generally called "ownership" of land. The closest to private ownership of land in Canada is freehold estate in **fee simple**. The owner of land in fee simple may grant any or all interests in it to others, but if the person dies without a will and without relatives, the land automatically escheats (reverts) back to the Crown.

Another common form of landholding is a **life estate**, which lasts only for the life of the person holding the land. During that lifetime, the property may be enjoyed but not disposed of or materially altered. For example, a person might will land to a child, but give a spouse a life estate. The spouse may live on the land for the rest of his or her life, after which the child may claim it. The spouse cannot sell, divide, mortgage, radically alter, or otherwise dispose of the land.

The person who will eventually inherit the property is called the **remainderman**. As a general rule, life tenants who make improvements or repairs with full knowledge of the limitations of their title cannot obtain contribution to the cost from the remainderman. For example, if the life tenant is forced under local improvement legislation to pay for the cost of improvements in the form of sewers, sidewalks, or street lighting, the life tenant must pay the assessment and not look to the remainderman to pay these costs.

The use of life estates has diminished in recent years because governments have reduced inheritance and estate taxes.

TITLE TO LAND

In Canada, property rights are a provincial responsibility and so real estate transactions differ from province to province. Historically, land division and registration was a duty of each county. Areas under development were divided into concessions and lots and most deeds still refer to them by these descriptions.

REGISTRY SYSTEM

There are two main systems of recording the ownership of land. The system which has been in use the longest is called the **registry system**, and this prevails throughout most of Canada. The other is the **land titles system**, and is discussed in the next section.

Under the registry system, a registry office is maintained at the county or district court. The purchaser must make a title search of the property he or she wants to acquire. If a clear title is established from the original owner to the present owner, and there are no adverse claims against the property, the purchaser can assume that a good and clear title would be acquired.

A title search requires considerable reading and should be done by a lawyer, who can interpret the various documents. In most provinces, the lawyer must trace the title back 40 years to establish a "good root of title."

The registry system produces an inventory of instruments (documents) affecting title, whereas the land titles system produces a statement of title. The sheer volume of instruments has compelled the provinces to take rigorous steps to reduce the amount of paperwork involved in registering and checking titles.

Ontario has a unique problem in that both systems are used within the province. The province is attempting to develop shorter documents, an automated title record system, a better property mapping system, and a parcel numbering system. The province is also trying to reduce the number of types of documents by compiling them under single headings. The word "transfer" includes "deed" and "conveyance." The word "charge" includes "mortgage" and any other lien upon the property. The following is a description of the Ontario system, but all provinces using the registry system follow the same basic process.

The registration process must be carried out on prescribed forms. The descriptions of the land must be clear. If the description is complex or vague, the registrar may accept a sketch of the land. The main books in the registry system are the abstract index, the copy book, the by-law index, and the general register index.

The **abstract index** is an index to a number of particular pieces of land. It lists all instruments registered or deposited against each piece of land, with concise descriptions of the instruments and their dates of registration.

The **copy book** is the depository of the instruments. All registered instruments formerly were copied by hand in the copy book. It is now done on microfilm. The land registrar keeps a **by-law index** which is important for checking any restrictions upon land use, such as zoning. The **general register index** is a register of special documents that are not recorded in the abstract index.

The *Registry Act* states that documents take priority as of the date and time they are registered. Instruments are numbered as they are registered and this establishes the priority. Failure to register an instrument may cause the person to lose a claim or charge upon the land. In Ontario, seals are no longer required on any of these documents.

In most provinces, an owner of land may voluntarily apply to the Director of Titles to have the title to any land under the registry system investigated and certified. Subdivision plans must be certified because of the large number of parcels involved.

LAND TITLES SYSTEM

Unlike the registry system, the land titles system produces a statement of the title rather than an inventory of instruments. Each separately owned piece of land is called a "parcel" and each parcel has a number. Dealings with a parcel are registered in a book commonly referred to as a "register."

The system was first developed in Australia by Robert Torrens and is sometimes called the "Torrens System" in his honour. Torrens thought land should be registered in the same way that ships are registered. A log, or book, is kept on each ship and a person wanting to buy a ship would use this log to determine if there were any legal claims against the ship by some unpaid creditor. The system is used in British Columbia and Alberta and in parts of Ontario, Saskatchewan, and Manitoba. Variations of the system are being developed elsewhere, and eventually the inefficient registry system will disappear.

Only four documents need to be registered: a transfer, a charge, a discharge, and a document general.

The concept of the land titles system is totally different from that of the registry system. Each new transaction must be approved before registration. The government, acting through a Master of Land Titles, guarantees the accuracy of the title as shown on the record, which is kept up to date with each transaction. The essential difference between the two systems is that with the registry system the researcher must use personal judgment and must interpret the documents. If the researcher makes an error, the purchaser may not obtain a valid title to the land. The land titles system provides the purchaser with a declaration as to the legal situation involving the land. The legal work is done by the government and presented to the purchaser as a completed package, which is much easier to read. The chance of error is greatly reduced under the land titles system.

There is an insurance fund that will compensate a purchaser who did not obtain good title because the Land Titles Office made a mistake.

FUTURE DEVELOPMENTS

Several provinces are designing new registration systems that are simplified and computerized. Ontario's *Land Registration Reform Act* is an experimental project with the goal of streamlining registration into very basic statements. Alberta and British Columbia are studying similar ideas.

One objective is to create a new system of parcelization that will be applied to lands under both systems. Registered documents will be organized accordingly, with some effort to streamline older documents. Among the documents that will be eliminated are the many affidavits that lawyers must complete, such as declarations of age, spousal status, foreign residency, etc. Ontario has accomplished most of these changes.

Property identifiers, consisting of four digits, will be applied to each property. These will be used in conjunction with block numbers, consisting of five digits, to identify each property. If the description changes, a new identifier will be assigned. The property will continue to have a proper legal description drawn in accordance with the existing requirements, but the property identifier will be used to access the computerized description of a particular property. When the system is complete, a lawyer in one city will be able to use a computer and modem to check the title and status of a parcel of land in another city. Eventually, the system may link all the provinces together, allowing a check upon property anywhere in Canada.

CO-OWNERSHIP OF PROPERTY

Property may be owned by two or more people, each being entitled to full enjoyment of all of the property. A grant of land to two or more people in either joint tenancy or tenancy in common creates a single ownership. The primary difference between the two is the right of survivorship.

JOINT TENANCY

Historically, a **joint tenancy** was preferred to a tenancy in common because it was a simple tenancy to understand. If one owner died, there was simply one less person, but the estate remained the same.

If property is registered as "joint," the deed or transfer must specifically state that the owners are "joint tenants." In the absence of any specific direction, a tenancy in common will be presumed to exist. In a joint tenancy, the property is not physically divided in any way; each owner holds an undivided interest in the property. There is no such thing as "my half" or "your half." Should one of the tenants die, the other tenant or tenants automatically assume that person's interest. Most married couples have their deeds registered as joint tenants. When one dies, the other automatically becomes the full and absolute owner.

A joint tenancy can be severed under the laws of most provinces. It can be severed either at the request of the tenants themselves, or possibly by a creditor who seeks to recover from one of them.

TENANCY IN COMMON

Co-owners who hold an undivided interest in land have a **tenancy in common**. The main difference from a joint tenancy is that, when one of the tenants dies, the other does not automatically take over the deceased owner's interests. Tenants in common may sell their interest in the land and may will their interest to any person. This does not mean that they can divide or parcel the land.

BRYAN et al. v. HEATH

British Columbia, 1979

Mr. and Mrs. Heath, husband and wife, owned a house registered in joint tenancy. They decided together to sever the tenancy and each executed a will leaving his or her half to the other and to children by previous marriages. A transfer of title to tenants in common was not executed. The wife fell ill and they decided to sell their home and buy another which, the respondent husband argued, was to have been registered in joint tenancy. The wife died before the new home was purchased.

The beneficiaries under her will brought a petition for a declaration that the joint tenancy had been severed and that they now owned half the house. Mr. Heath argued that he was now the exclusive owner of the house because the couple had not been able to buy a new house as they originally intended.

The Court held in favour of the petitioners. The common intention to sever and the execution of wills that carried out the intention was sufficient to sever the tenancy. There was insufficient evidence of a further intention to return to a joint tenancy.

SPECIAL RIGHTS TO PROPERTY

A person may acquire a special right to real property without actually owning it. This claim often arises from the historic use of the property. These rights are referred to as **easements** or **profits.** Examples of easements include such things as rights of way and water rights. Profits include rights to cut wood, dig gravel, or hunt and fish. The use of the term "profits" has generally been discontinued.

EASEMENTS

An easement is a right that a person has obtained to use land for personal benefit. A right cannot exist without conferring a benefit upon the person claiming it. The benefit must also be one that can be practically and frequently utilized. Thus, a person living in Alberta could not claim a right in Nova Scotia unless he or she frequently went there and exercised that right.

Easements arise either by **specific grant** or **prescription**. A specific grant means that a landowner (grantor) says to some person (grantee) that the grantee may use the grantor's property for his or her benefit. A grant may be withdrawn by the grantor within a reasonable time. If the easement continues for a long time, it may become permanent unless the original grant specifically said that it could be revoked.

The legal basis of an easement by prescription is that if long enjoyment of a right is shown, the court will uphold the right by presuming that it had a lawful origin in the first place and that the right was once specifically granted as a permanent right. The common law, and some provincial statutes, recognize a rule that the uninterrupted use of land creates an easement. In most provinces, the time period is specifically stated in the *Limitations Act* or some similar law. The time period is usually 10 or 20 years. A claim to Crown land is governed by statute and may take as long as 60 years.

The whole question of easements, or possessory title, relates only to land under the registry system. When land is brought under the land titles system, existing possessory rights are not disturbed. However, no title can be acquired by easement or possession during any period of time while the land is subject to the land titles system. Therefore, no new claims of easement will be accepted once land is registered under this system.

The term most often given to a claim by one person to the use or possession of another person's land is **adverse possession**. Broadly speaking, in Ontario, an action to recover possession of land or of an interest in land must be brought within 10 years after the cause of action first arose, failing which the action can no longer be brought and the right in question is extinguished.

It is useful to understand the reasoning behind a rule of law that permits one person to lay claim to someone else's land by long-term use. Throughout Canadian history, economic depressions have caused families to abandon their farms and search for other opportunities. These families often disappeared and could not be found. The land might eventually revert back to the Crown, but in the meantime it had no productive use. Seeing that the land was unused, neighbours would often work the land and make improvements upon it. It was reasonable that these residents should eventually claim the land they had maintained and put into production.

In the case of a right of way, the rule is somewhat different. In order to establish entitlement to a right of way by user (the right to travel across land) it is necessary to establish uninterrupted use extending over a period of 20 years. A right of way can be extinguished only by evidence that the use of the land has been abandoned.

In actual practice, the person claiming a right cannot initiate the action. That is, the user of the land cannot bring an action asking the court to recognize his or her adverse possession. Rather, adverse possession is a defence that can be raised when the person holding title to the land tries to evict the person using it.

In the case of easements alleged to have been created by use, it is necessary to produce evidence establishing a well-defined area of the easement, such as a specific path of travel as opposed to a history of wandering through an area. For example, 20 years or more of using a trail for moving a tractor from a roadway across someone else's property to a field would give rise to an easement across the other property. If the population in the area increased and people began walking along the same path, they could be restrained from doing so as this is an entirely different type of easement. The path does not become a public road.

It is often said that the possession must be "adverse, open, continuous, and notorious." The meaning of "adverse" is simply that the possession must be of a type that is inconsistent with the rights of the owner of the land. The easement must be open and notorious, meaning that it was not hidden or done by stealth. It was in plain view to the owner if he or she cared to inspect the property and object. It is not necessary that the owner know of the adverse possession but it is necessary that the failure of the owner to take action was not because the easement was hidden. The easement must be continuous, not an infrequent use.

If the owner of land wants to allow neighbours to use part of it, but does not want to create a permanent right of access, the owner should adopt a practice of closing the land for a short period of time each year and notifying the neighbours of this fact. For example, if the owner allows neighbours to use a dirt road, the road might be closed by a gate periodically and its use cut off. This defeats any argument that use was continuous and uncontested.

The misplacement of boundaries often supports an argument of adverse possession. However, the boundary itself, such as a fence, is not sufficient. The land in question must be used. For example, if a fence is misplaced and the land in question simply lies fallow, this will not support a claim of adverse possession. If the land is cultivated or put to constant use, it will support a claim of adverse possession.

MATHERS v. BRISTOW

Ontario, 1990

The plaintiff sought to require the defendant to remove a chain link fence and to vacate a strip of land that lay between their properties. The defendant had erected the fence in 1979 when he constructed a swimming pool. The new fence followed the same line as the former wooden fence that was in place when he bought the property in 1971. No objection was made by the plaintiff until 1989 when the plaintiff decided to sell his home. He had the land surveyed and discovered that the fence was one metre on his property. The Court dismissed the action because the defendant had held an open and notorious possession of the land for more than 10 years. The time period began in 1971, not 1979. The fact that an old fence was replaced with a new fence did not alter the issue of using the land. The defendant had used the land since 1971 and now had possessory title to it.

Another form of easement is an **encroachment** which occurs when a building is erected over a boundary line. After 20 years, the property owner cannot demand that the building be pulled down or compensation paid. If the encroachment is upon vacant land, the right to continue encroachment may be established after just 10 years.

Some easements may be established by law or by subdivision plan. This is usually called a **dedication,** which means that the developer has set aside parts of the land for public use. These usually involve the right of service companies to enter or cross land to maintain sewers, hydro lines, and other utilities. It can also include access roads so that police and firefighters may enter to provide services to residents. It is important for a prospective buyer to find out about such rights before buying the property.

MINERAL RIGHTS

Historically, the right to the minerals below the surface of the land was possessed by the owners of the land in fee simple in most of the older provinces of Canada. More recently the Crown reserves mineral rights for itself. A person who acquires the mineral rights in the lands of another acquires an interest in land known as a ***profit a pendre*** which must be in writing. Since the removal of minerals normally requires some disturbance of the surface, the owner of the mineral rights must compensate the owner of the surface rights for the interference with the property. In Ontario, Quebec, and Alberta, the mineral rights on land must be made by special grant. In those parts of Canada under federal control, mineral rights must be leased from the Crown.

Typical of a problem in which the two rights conflict is the search for minerals under farmland. In Alberta, for example, farmers do not own the mineral rights to their lands and must negotiate with companies who want to explore and develop minerals. A government agency tries to arbitrate when the parties cannot agree. Oil companies may enter farmland, build roads, and drill wells. One well puts an average of four acres out of production. If oil is discovered, the land owner does not receive any share of the profits, but is paid an annual leasing fee.

WATER RIGHTS

A landowner does not own the water that either percolates through the land or flows across it in a defined channel. However, the common law allows the landowner to make unrestricted use of water percolating through the land without regard for any claims made by a neighbour.

However, the **riparian owner** (the owner of the land through which water flows in a defined channel) cannot take all of the water. The owner can make use of it for personal needs, but cannot dam it or divert it from its course so that a downstream neighbour is denied its use. Most provinces prohibit the construction of dams without a government permit. Nor can the riparian owner pollute or foul the water so that a neighbour cannot use it.

Where a natural watercourse becomes part of an artificial drainage system it is no longer natural, so the entire system must have a safe and proper outlet.

The right to use underground water for irrigation is more secure than the right to use a surface source. The owner of land containing underground water, which percolates by undefined channels and flows to the land of a neighbour, has the right, within his or her own land, to use the water for any purpose, and to divert or sell it, even if the neighbour is thereby denied use of the water.

The problem of boundaries in reference to water is a more complicated matter. Additional complications arise from the common problem of erosion and accretion. A parcel of land which abuts and fronts on a body of water gives the owner of the land riparian ownership. If the water is navigable, the ownership is limited to the water's edge. Navigability is a question of fact and there is no statutory guidance on this issue. Generally, a navigable stream in Canada would appear to be one actually navigated by boats or vessels. However, in *Coleman v. A.G. Ontario* (Ontario, 1983) the Court extended the rule by accepting argument that the potential recreation use of a stream made it navigable.

If the question of navigability is settled, there still remains much argument about the actual boundary. Many courts have concluded that the limit of a parcel having a boundary on a navigable body of water is the edge of the bed of the body of water in its normal condition. Such terms as "the bank," "the edge of the bed," "the low-water mark," and "the water's edge" occur frequently in court decisions.

If a body of water is not navigable, then the boundary line would ordinarily be the halfway point to the opposite shore. Just because water is navigable, does not mean that everyone is entitled access to it. For example, if the landowner owns all the land around a lake, the lake is, for all practical purposes, a private lake because the landowner can deny public access to it. If, however, the lake connects to another lake, persons may enter the "private" lake by the water route and could not be denied such activities as fishing.

Any landowner whose lands abut upon a natural watercourse has the right to drain those lands into the natural stream where the lands are wet because they lie in a watershed. Water must not be brought in from another watershed. If a landowner fills in a stream, or raises the level of his or her land to prevent flooding, he has interfered with the natural channel of the stream and may be liable for damages caused downstream.

LINE FENCES

Property owners in rural areas are required to establish and maintain good fences. "Good fences make good neighbours" is an old adage that implies a good neighbour would not let his or her animals stray into neighbours' fields.

When the owner of land wants to construct or repair a boundary fence, he or she can request "fence-viewers" to examine the boundary and arbitrate as to what portion of the fence the owner and his or her neighbour should pay. The award, if not paid, will be added to the owner's property taxes.

GIFTS OF REAL PROPERTY

A person may make a gift of real property to another, including to a spouse. Historically, this was the way in which a wife who was not employed outside the home acquired a claim to property purchased with her husband's income. If a husband bought property with money he earned, but registered the deed in both names, it was presumed that he had made a gift to his wife of one-half of the value of the property. This was called **the presumption of advancement.**

If a wife bought real property, possibly using an inheritance, and registered the property in both names, it was not presumed that she had made a gift to her husband. Rather, it was presumed that he held half the value of the property "in trust" for her. This was called a **resulting trust**.

With the reform of statutes involving the division of property, the issue of trusts has diminished considerably. Some provinces have specifically abolished the presumption of advancement.

However, trusts can arise by various means. A **constructive trust** can arise if one person performs actions that increase the value of real property of another person and where there was a tacit understanding that both parties would share the benefit. To allow one party to keep all of the profit would be unjust. In *Crisp v. Banton* (Ontario, 1989) the Court awarded a 40 percent share in a house to a woman who lived for 13 years with the man who owned the house. The woman performed domestic chores and looked after the man's three children. They never married. The Court held that spousal services, such as child care and household management, can create a constructive trust in property owned by the other person. The judge ruled that it was proper to take into consideration the "reasonable expectations of the parties."

MATRIMONIAL PROPERTY

At one time under the common law, a married woman could not own real property. Her husband acquired all rights to his wife's real estate and the income resulting from it during their marriage. This was changed by the *Married Women's Property Act*, passed in England in 1880, which provided that a married woman could own real property and dispose of it as she wished.

Serious inequities continued to exist. A husband could mortgage or sell the family home and keep all of the money. He might do so and desert his family, leaving the wife and children destitute. To reduce the severity of this problem, the provinces passed laws recognizing the right of **dower**. A wife's right of dower was the right to a life estate in one-third of her deceased husband's real property, which he acquired during the marriage.

Even with this change, however, it was obvious that the husband still controlled the family assets, including the home. The potential harshness of the situation was dramatized in the case of *Murdoch v. Murdoch* (Supreme Court of Canada, 1973) in which a farm wife worked extremely hard on the family farm for 25 years but was denied any interest in it when she divorced her husband. The entire farm was in her husband's name and there was nothing in the law that recognized her claim to it. The Court held that farm work is very hard for everyone and does not give rise to a claim of ownership.

The *Murdoch* case brought home the fact that the law gave little protection to married women in the matter of property. People living together who were not married would be in the same situation. Changes began occurring within four years and now all the provinces and territories have legislation recognizing the equal rights of husband and wife to matrimonial property.

Nearly all of these statutes contain a checklist of factors the judge should consider when dividing the assets. An important change is the recognition that work and services as homemaker and parent have an equal importance to financial contribution. The judge does not have to divide the matrimonial home equally. If there are compelling reasons why one spouse should receive a greater share, the judge may give recognition to those reasons.

LeBLANC v. LeBLANC

Supreme Court of Canada, 1989

The LeBlancs divorced after a marriage of 26 years, during which the wife worked extremely hard to build up a restaurant business, raise seven children, and buy a family home. The husband was an alcoholic who contributed nearly nothing to the family during the marriage. The family lived on welfare until the wife saved $12 000 to buy a restaurant and then built it into a thriving business with the help of the children. The family assets also included a cottage and boat, all registered in Mrs. LeBlanc's name.

The trial judge awarded the husband $6000, and all the rest of the assets, including the house and cottage, to the wife. The Supreme Court of Canada upheld the decision because the provincial law specifically allowed the Court to make an unequal division.

When people live together but are not married, it is very advisable to have a contract regarding the ownership of real property. These contracts, called by names such as "cohabitation agreements," are recognized in most provinces.

The Supreme Court of Canada has taken a somewhat accommodating attitude toward long-term relationships, applying a mixture of rules such as resulting trust and unjust enrichment to cases where a great injustice might be done. In *Pettkus v. Becker* (Supreme Court of Canada, 1980) the couple lived together for 19 years while building a profitable honey business. When they split, Mr. Pettkus claimed ownership of everything, but the Court upheld a lower court decision to divide the assets equally. The Court said: "I see no basis for any distinction, in dividing property and assets, between marital relationships and those more informal relationships which subsist for a lengthy period." However, the case is unique because it was first argued under Quebec law and both parties contributed money and labour to the enterprise. The Court treated the matter more as the break-up of a business partnership than of a personal relationship.

EXPROPRIATION BY THE CROWN

All land inherently belongs to the Crown, so the Crown may at any time assert this inherent power and take the land from the present owner. This action is called **expropriation** and may be defined as legal action by the government to compulsorily deprive a person of a right of real property belonging to that person.

Some 1200 federal statutes and several hundred provincial laws have allowed expropriation, the majority of them being for the purpose of building railroad lines. There are also statutes that allow the expropriation of land for enlarging harbours or cemeteries, building power lines, establishing national parks, or creating experimental farm stations.

The *Charter of Rights and Freedoms* contains no specific protections to the ownership of land, or to any property for that matter. By comparison, the *Constitution of the United States* provides that no state shall "deprive any person of life, liberty, or property, without due process of law."

A person has little recourse when his or her land is expropriated, other than to argue that the compensation awarded was insufficient. Most laws allowing expropriation require fair compensation. The process is not reversible. In the 1970s, hundreds of farms near Pickering, Ontario, were expropriated for the construction of a new airport that was never built. The original landowners brought an action demanding that they be allowed to return to their homesteads, but the Court held that there was nothing in the law that gave the original owners first claim to the expropriated land.

RESTRICTIONS ON LAND OWNERSHIP AND USE

The owner of land does not have an unrestricted right to use the land in any manner he or she wishes. Many restrictions may apply. The use of the land may be affected by zoning by-laws; for example, a factory cannot be operated in a residential area. However, such restrictions cannot be applied to people.

CANADIAN MENTAL HEALTH ASSOC. v. WINNIPEG

Manitoba, 1990

The City of Winnipeg established a zoning by-law that regulated the location and number of special facilities, generally called "group homes." The people affected by the law included the elderly, the disabled, drug addicts, and former prison inmates.

The by-law was attacked as a violation of s. 15 of the Charter because it discriminated against certain people. The Manitoba Court of Appeal held that the by-law was unconstitutional because the equality rights of the group home occupants were violated by telling them where they could live. It was a law that regulated people, not activity, and violated the Charter.

Provincial and federal laws prohibit discrimination in rental housing. Further, any restriction upon the sale of real property that discriminates against any person by reason of race, national origin, or religion is unlawful. In 1951, in the case of *Noble and Wolfe v. Alley,* the Supreme Court of Canada struck down such a provision in a deed that prohibited the sale of a parcel of land "to any person of the Jewish, Hebrew, Semitic, Negro or coloured race." Provincial statutes later banned such covenants in real estate transactions.

These protections are not absolute, and do not apply to foreigners. Concern about foreign ownership and the concentration of land in the hands of certain groups has caused several provinces to pass laws restricting the right to own land. The constitutionality of such laws was tested before the Supreme Court of Canada, which upheld a Prince Edward Island law that limited the ownership of land by non-residents. The case was argued before the enactment of the *Charter of Rights and Freedoms,* so it is not clear whether the same decision would be reached now.

The division and sale of farmland is subject to tighter restrictions than was true 30 years ago. Typically, a farmer would sell one or two acres each year to augment low farm income. The purchaser would drill a well, build a house, and enjoy a bit of the rural life. The farmer would also sell or give parcels of land to his or her children. The long-term effect of this action was to see farms cut up into "checkerboard" configurations which did not follow any intelligent plan. Further, good farmland disappeared under the growth of buildings and roads. Today, farms cannot be divided or sold for non-farming use without government permission, usually under a provincial *Planning Act*.

REAL PROPERTY FIXTURES

It is a rule of law that anything attached to the land is part of it. This means that if something is not attached, it may normally be removed. This is an important point if the property is sold and the previous owner removes things that the purchaser considers to be part of the land or building. Curtains do not belong to a house; curtain rods do. All trees and shrubs belong with the property.

Some things are difficult to assess. An article may be temporarily attached. Other things are very large and, while not attached, sit so heavily upon the land that they become part of it. Such things as sheds would fall into this category. A heavy machine may necessarily be bolted to a floor. Although it could easily be removed, the act of fastening it might change its status from a chattel to a fixture. Changing a chattel into a fixture could result in increased property taxes.

Problems arising over fixtures can be avoided by careful wording of the sale agreement to ensure that every item that should stay with the property is included in the Offer to Purchase.

REAL PROPERTY MORTGAGES

When the purchaser of real property cannot pay the full purchase price, a **mortgage** is taken out on the property. The lender of the money is called the **mortgagee** and the borrower is called the **mortgagor**. The mortgage is a conveyance, or transfer, of an equitable interest in property with a provision for redemption, meaning that if the loan is repaid the conveyance will become void.

It is important to understand that, under the registry system, a mortgage actually transfers ownership of the property to the mortgagee. An equitable interest means that the mortgagee has the right to physically recover the property from the mortgagor if the payments are not made. In those provinces where the land titles system is used, a mortgage does not convey title to the mortgagee; it places a charge upon the land and the word "charge" generally replaces the word "mortgage." The words "chargor" and "chargee" may be used in place of "mortgagor" and "mortgagee."

A mortgage is also a personal loan under which the mortgagor gives a personal promise to pay the principal and interest on the loan.

LOAN AGREEMENTS

When a person borrows money, the repayment of which is secured by a charge upon real property, the initial document to be completed is the loan agreement. It sets out the relevant terms of the contract, including the following:

1. Principal amount of the loan;
2. Interest rate;
3. Monthly or weekly payments;
4. Period over which the loan is amortized;
5. Term or maturity date of the loan;
6. Legal description of the property.

The term of a loan is not the same as the amortization period. The term of any charge is normally five years or less. The *Mortgages Act* states that, if the term is longer than five years, the mortgagor has the right, at any time after five years, to pay off the loan, together with three months' interest in lieu of notice. However, in *Dickson v. Bluestein* (Ontario, 1991) the Ontario Court (General Division) held that this penalty violates the *Interest Act* which states that no penalty can be applied if it has the effect of increasing the charge on the arrears beyond the rate of interest payable on the principal money not in arrears. In many instances, a three-month penalty would be a much higher interest rate than the original mortgage.

The **term** is the period after which the loan must be renegotiated. Presently, it can be as short as six months. The mortgagor usually tries to renew the mortgage at the current rate and, based upon interest rate forecasts, may select a longer or shorter term.

A loan is **amortized** (made dead) over a period of 20, 25, 30, or more years. In other words, using a monthly blended payment system, which combines principal and interest, it would take the specified number of years for the loan to be completely repaid.

TYPES OF MORTGAGES

There are four main types of mortgages:

1. A **National Housing Act (NHA) mortgage** is a loan insured against loss by the Canada Mortgage and Housing Corporation (CMHC). Borrowers must pay an application fee to CMHC and an insurance fee.
2. A **conventional mortgage** is a loan that does not exceed 75 percent of the appraised value or the purchase price of the property, whichever is the lesser of the two.
3. A **high-ratio mortgage** exceeds 75 percent of the appraised value or purchase price of the property, whichever is the lesser of the two. These mortgages must, by law, be insured.
4. A **collateral mortgage** is a loan backed up by a promissory note and the security of a mortgage on real property. The money borrowed may be used for the purchase of the property itself or for other purposes.

REGISTRATION OF A MORTGAGE

The mortgagee protects his or her interest in the property by registering the mortgage at the Registry Office. Any subsequent purchaser of the property assumes the existing mortgage, and registration denies such a purchaser the right to claim ignorance of the mortgage. If two mortgages exist on the same property, the first mortgage registered has first claim to the property.

Registration constitutes notice to all people claiming an interest in the land. If an instrument is not registered, it is void against a subsequent purchaser for valuable consideration without actual notice. If a person who owns land gives another person a mortgage which that person does not register, then the mortgage has no effect upon a third person who buys the land.

Once the mortgage is fully paid, the mortgagor should obtain from the mortgagee a **mortgage discharge**. This should be registered as proof that the mortgage has been paid.

ENFORCEMENT OF MORTGAGE SECURITY

When a mortgagor defaults upon his or her obligations, the mortgagee has a number of remedies from which to choose. The mortgagee can:

1. Sue for payment on the basis of the mortgagor's personal covenant in the contract;
2. Take possession of the property privately, by court order, or by a receiver appointed pursuant to the provisions contained in the mortgage;
3. Sell the property under either the power of sale contained in the mortgage or pursuant to a court order;
4. Obtain title to the property by means of a foreclosure action or by accepting a quit claim deed from the mortgagor to the property.

The exercise of a power of sale has several advantages as compared to a foreclosure action. The sale can usually be effected in less time and at a reduced cost. If after selling the mortgaged property under power of sale the mortgage debt has not been fully satisfied, the mortgagee is entitled to sue the mortgagor to recover the deficit. The same right exists in favour of the mortgagee after a judicial sale. However, by foreclosing, the mortgagee has elected to accept the property to satisfy the debt.

The advantage to the mortgagee under foreclosure is that the property may be worth much more than the outstanding balance of the loan. Under a foreclosure, the mortgagor is not entitled to any of the proceeds of the sale. Under a forced sale, any money remaining after the mortgage has been paid must be returned to the mortgagor.

If the property is registered in the name of more than one owner, both must sign the mortgage. If the house is a matrimonial home, in the name of one person only, the other person must sign the mortgage, because that person has an equal interest in the property. A married person must state if the mortgaged property is a matrimonial home. As the next case illustrates, false declarations can cause problems.

STOIMENOV v. STOIMENOV et al.

Ontario, 1983

The applicant wife and the respondent husband separated in October 1980. Shortly after separation, the husband placed large mortgages on the matrimonial home with Greymac Mortgage Corporation and another mortgage upon another house with Sterling Trust. Mrs. Stoimenov had moved out of the house and was living with relatives.

The mortgages were registered and the money paid to the husband, who left Canada and returned to his native Yugoslavia. The mortgage companies believed that the husband was free to place the mortgages because he signed false affidavits as to his marital status. The wife discovered the mortgages during the divorce action and sought an order to set them aside. Witnesses for the trust companies admitted that Mr. Stoimenov seemed in a hurry to complete the transactions, but he said he needed the money for an urgent business investment. The loan officers of the trust companies inspected the properties before granting the loans and saw no evidence of a wife or family living in the houses. Mr. Stoimenov said that he and his wife had divorced many years ago and that she had never lived in the houses and had no claim to them. They believed him.

The trial judge held that the mortgages were valid. However, the Ontario Court of Appeal overturned that decision and held that the trust companies knew that there was a Mrs. Stoimenov, that Mr. Stoimenov was in a hurry, and the companies should have undertaken a minimal investigation.

If the mortgagee does not want to follow through on a lengthy foreclosure procedure, negotiations could be undertaken to have the mortgagor execute and deliver a **quit claim deed** whereby the mortgagor gives up all rights in the property. Consider an example where a severe recession has left the mortgagor unemployed. He or she has little equity in the house and the present housing market is depressed. If the mortgagee tries to retake the property and sell it, there will be a deficit. It is even possible that the property cannot be sold at all in the near future. The mortgagor, wishing to relocate, would like to walk away from the house. A quit claim deed allows him or her to do so.

If there are multiple mortgages upon the property, any mortgagee who wants to force a sale or to foreclose must satisfy, to the extent possible, the other mortgages, in order of their registration. If the taxes are not paid on a property, the municipality may eventually force the sale of the property. This presents obvious problems for the mortgagee. For this reason, many lenders require the mortgagor to make tax instalment payments to the mortgagee, who then pays the taxes.

PURCHASING REAL PROPERTY

Most people who want to buy or sell real property do so through a real estate agent. This is not strictly necessary, because private sales are quite lawful. Most people use a real estate agent to expedite the process and because they are unaware of the proper steps to take. The following general overview of real estate purchasing assumes that a real estate agent is involved.

LISTING THE PROPERTY

Mr. and Mrs. Green want to sell their house. They list the property with the Reliable Real Estate Company and sign a contract called a **listing agreement**. The contract states that Reliable will be paid a commission only when the deal closes. The Greens declare a minimum price below which they will not sell the property. This is important to protect both parties, because the agent is required to present any offer made to the Greens. The listing agreement should state a time period, after which it is void. It is unwise to agree to a long time period because, if Reliable does not provide good service, the Greens cannot cancel the agreement until it expires. The asking price, or listing price, is set at $190 000. This price is not necessarily the lowest price the seller will accept. It should be kept in mind that the real estate agent acts on behalf of the seller, not the buyer.

OFFER TO PURCHASE

Reliable advertises the property at its own expense and shows it to prospective buyers. Mr. and Mrs. Brown are interested in the property and make an offer of $183 000. Reliable draws up a formal document, called an **Offer to Purchase** or an **Agreement of Purchase and Sale**. (Numerous other names are often given to this document.) Reliable requires a deposit from Brown payable to the realtor "in trust." The deposit meets the requirement for consideration. If the offer is refused, the deposit is returned. If the offer is accepted, but Brown backs out of the deal, the deposit would be forfeited to Green. The offer should include:

1. Full description of the property;
2. Price offered and the terms of payment;
3. What is included with the property;
4. Closing date of the sale;
5. Mortgage or financing arrangements. The offer is usually conditional upon the buyer obtaining mortgage approval;
6. Time period for acceptance by the seller;
7. Time period for the purchaser to check the title to the property, at the purchaser's expense.

Brown should have a lawyer check the offer before signing it. The realtor carries the offer to Green, who may accept it by signing it or refuse it. Green might sign it but change some of the terms (such as the price) of the offer, thus making a counteroffer. Like Brown, Green should have a lawyer check the offer before signing it. It is a common mistake to sign the agreement, and then have a lawyer read it. If there are serious errors, it is often too late to correct them.

The seller (or **vendor**) does not have to point out every defect in the property, but the seller cannot deliberately deceive the buyer about the true nature of the property. In the 1970s, many houses were insulated with urea formaldehyde foam insulation (UFFI). It was later discovered that this material is a health hazard which should be removed. It is common in a sale agreement that the vendor declare that the house does not contain UFFI.

CHECKING THE TITLE

Once the offer to purchase has been signed, the purchaser is allowed a period of time to check the title to the property. A check should be made of the following:

1. Property title, which should be registered and clear;
2. Mortgages, liens, or charges registered against the property;
3. Survey of the property boundaries;
4. Taxes paid;
5. Property in agreement with local by-laws;
6. Easements;

7. Oil or gas leases;
8. Builders' liens or city work orders;
9. Tenant leases.

If there are any defects in the title, the purchaser notifies the seller and gives him or her a chance to clear them away. If the seller cannot do so, the purchaser can refuse to go through with the sale.

If a tenant is in valid possession of the property, the buyer cannot evict the tenant until the lease period expires. In most provinces, a lease for a term exceeding seven years must be registered to be valid. In Ontario, a buyer can evict the tenant only if the buyer requires the property for his or her personal use, not to rent it to someone else.

STATEMENT OF ADJUSTMENTS

The next step for the lawyers of the two parties is to reach agreement on final payment. To do this a **Statement of Adjustments** is prepared. For example, taxes may be unpaid when the deal closes. Therefore, the seller should pay the purchaser for the taxes that are owing up to that date, since the purchaser will assume responsibility for payment. On the other hand, the seller may be leaving a full tank of heating oil and the purchaser should pay the seller for this.

CLOSING

The lawyers meet at the Registry Office on the date of closing. The new mortgage is registered and the old mortgage discharged. The deed is transferred to Brown whose lawyer gives Green's lawyer a cheque for the balance shown in the Statement of Adjustments. The lawyer later issues a cheque to Green representing the final payment minus the lawyer's fees and the realtor's fees. Both parties will receive from their lawyers a closing letter reviewing all that has taken place and accounting for all funds. The keys are handed over to Brown's lawyer, who will give them to his or her client. In some provinces, the purchaser must pay a land transfer tax.

Under the land titles system, the two lawyers do not meet at the Registry Office. The transfer of title is completed by an exchange of correspondence and binding trust conditions.

AGENT'S RIGHTS AND RESPONSIBILITIES

The real estate agent is entitled to a commission if the property is sold. Most forms of listing agreements contain the following provision: "I agree to pay you a commission of ____% of the sale price of my property on any sale or exchange from any source whatsoever effected."

Many lawyers add words such as "on closing only" because the contract appears to say that the agent receives a commission even if the buyer backs out of the agreement. The agent is entitled to a commission if the agent showed the property to a prospective buyer who did not buy the property during the period of the listing agreement, but who purchased the property later. This prevents the buyer and seller from making an agreement to cut the agent out of the commission by arranging a private sale at a later date.

Real estate agents must be registered with the provincial government and it is unlawful to act as an agent without being registered. It should be clearly understood that the agent represents only one of the parties, usually the seller. The agent cannot represent both parties and collect two commissions. If the agent is hired by a buyer to locate a property, the agent must inform the seller of his or her true status and not try to represent both parties. In some situations, the real estate agent may be personally liable for errors, omissions, or misrepresentations. For example, if an agent deceived the seller about the nature or existence of an offer, the agent could be liable. If the agent personally bought the property from the seller without disclosing who was the true purchaser, the agent could be liable.

In *Olsen v. Poirier* (Ontario, 1978) a newly arrived immigrant hired a real estate agent to locate a profitable dairy farm. The agent claimed to have knowledge of dairy farming and recommended a property, which the plaintiff eventually bought. The defendant agent failed to tell the plaintiff that the Milk Marketing Board has a rule that when a farm is sold to a person who is not related to the seller, the milk quota of the buyer is reduced by 25 percent. The agent was personally liable for this oversight.

BUILDING A HOUSE

The legal procedure involved in building a house differs from that in purchasing a house already constructed. The contract with the builder should be read by a lawyer. It is also important to obtain reliable recommendations regarding the choice of a builder. In some provinces, including Ontario, builders must be registered with the provincial government.

BUILDING CONTRACTS

The building contract should include basic provisions such as a declaration that the builder will follow all appropriate by-laws, building regulations, and standards. It should also stipulate the following:

1. **Specific date for completion**: While a completion date should be included, most contracts allow for delays caused by unavailability of materials or by labour stoppages. Completion dates may be missed by a wide margin and it is unwise to depend upon such dates by selling an existing home.
2. **Plans to be followed**: Clearly defined house plans should show the overall design of the house and details of construction and contain a specific list of what is included in the price and what will be extra. Plans can be purchased from professional design companies or prepared by an architect. There is no such thing as plans that are too detailed. The visual image of what the buyer expects may be very different from what the builder envisions. Therefore, to build a house based on nothing more than some pencil sketches would probably lead to many disputes between the parties.
3. **Materials to be used**: Although a builder assumes overall responsibility for the construction of the house, the builder normally subcontracts specialized work such as plumbing, electrical wiring, etc. There is no contract between the buyer and the subcontractor: the contractor remains liable to the buyer if the subcontractor does a poor job. The subcontractor looks to the contractor for payment. However, if the contractor does not or cannot pay, the subcontractor may file a lien against the property.

A **lien** is the right to hold or lay claim to another person's property as security for the performance of an obligation. In the case of a building under construction, the right of lien extends to labourers, contractors, and suppliers of materials. Each province has passed a statute allowing unpaid contractors or workers to bring their claims against a property, but requires that this be done within a certain time. In most of the provinces, the time limit is between 30 and 60 days. In Ontario, it is 45 days; 35 days in Alberta; 40 days in British Columbia.

HOLDBACK

There is a statutory requirement to hold back part of the final price until the time for filing a lien has run out. The amount varies from 10 to 15 percent. If no liens are filed within the time required, the buyer is relieved of any responsibility, and the contractor is paid the final percentage that is due. It is therefore important that any person considering placing a lien on property should consult a lawyer quickly.

WARRANTIES

Ontario has a *New Home Warranty Plan* that protects the buyer for up to seven years against major structural defects. All contractors must be licensed and registered with the plan. Any buyer who deals with an unlicensed builder is unprotected. Small defects are covered for up to one year. The Ontario plan protects deposits up to $20 000. Unfinished work is covered up to $5000 or 2 percent of the home's price. Alberta has a similar plan, but participation by builders is voluntary.

The British Columbia plan is operated as a private insurance plan under which the individual may buy, at an additional cost, an insurance policy to provide coverage for losses resulting from certain risk or defects.

The Ontario plan does not cover work that an individual does on his or her own behalf. For a new home to be qualified for coverage, it has to be a previously unoccupied new home and be enrolled before construction begins. This can create a problem when a builder constructs a new home for himself or herself, occupies it for a short time, and then sells it. Such a home would have no warranty.

One difficult area of law is when a buyer engages the services of a builder to partially construct a house and then takes it over with the intent of completing the house himself or herself. The courts have drawn many distinctions between the sale of completed or partially completed houses.

RAWSON v. HAMMER

Alberta, 1982

The defendants listed their home for sale and the plaintiffs went to see it, accompanied by the defendant's real estate agent. The defendants had built the house themselves. The plaintiffs noted the usual necessary items such as furnace, plumbing, etc. It was obvious that the fireplace was not finished. Mrs. Hammer told the plaintiffs that her husband would finish the fireplace. The linen closet had no shelves and baseboards were not installed. Mrs. Hammer told the plaintiffs that it was her husband's intention to build a deck around the house. She said they had experienced no problems with the house and that it had been appraised at $92 000. The plaintiffs were not told that the defendants were living in the house without having any permits for the installation of natural gas, electricity, plumbing, or sewage disposal. The plaintiffs purchased the house for $79 000 and moved in.

The contract stated there were no warranties of any kind. The plaintiffs found there were no air ducts to the furnace from the rooms of the house, basement walls were wet, and one basement wall had "bellied in." The defect had been hidden by pieces of plywood stacked against the wall. In addition to these problems, there were serious and dangerous defects in the wiring and gas system. The building was declared by an inspector as unfit for human habitation.

The plaintiffs sued for damages and based their claim on three arguments:

1. The defendants had breached an implied warranty that the house was fit for habitation;
2. Even if this had been a completed house, the defendants could not rely upon the doctrine of "buyer beware" because they had concealed the defects;
3. The agreement of sale notwithstanding, the defendants owed a duty of care to the plaintiffs to obey all building codes.

An important precedent for this case was *Fraser-Reid v. Droumtsekas* (Supreme Court of Canada, 1979) in which the Court held that there is no implied warranty on the sale of a completed house and refused to impose such a warranty, saying that this was a matter for legislative action. However, in that case, the weeping tile had not been installed and the contract required the defendant to reveal all outstanding infractions. The plaintiff succeeded because there had been a breach of contract. In the present case, the house was not a completed house. The Court held in favour of the plaintiffs:

> *I am of the opinion that the doctrine of buyer beware applies to houses purchased in an incomplete condition to be finished by the purchaser ... Turning to the second submission, namely, that even if this had been a completed house, the defendants were not entitled to rely upon the doctrine of* caveat emptor *as they concealed latent defects from the plaintiffs, I am of the opinion that there is merit to this argument. The plaintiffs knew they were not buying a completed house and I am of the opinion that the law applicable to latent defects not disclosed to the plaintiffs applies to this unfinished house.*

The judge refused to give any weight to a disclaimer clause that purported to excuse the defendants of liability. The judge ruled that there is no disclaimer clause that excuses a person from complying with the building codes.

MUNICIPALITY'S LIABILITY

In most communities, it is unlawful for any person to commence building a structure without a building permit. It is also unlawful to occupy a new building, residential or commercial, before the building inspector has issued an occupancy permit. Failure to comply with this requirement may result in eviction from the building and the imposition of fines.

Municipalities place restrictions upon how a building may be constructed. For example, there are minimum distance requirements for buildings. A house, garage, or other building must be kept a certain distance from the property line. A house may not occupy more than a certain percentage of the lot.

The local municipality is also responsible for enforcing building codes, construction safety, and many other matters. If the municipality is lax in enforcing standards, it may be held liable.

In *Kamloops v. Nielsen* (Supreme Court of Canada, 1984) the Court held that the City of Kamloops was partly liable for permitting a house to be completed and occupied by the builder, Hughes, even though it failed to meet numerous building standards. Hughes had told the city building inspector that it was his retirement home and would not represent a problem to anyone else. However, Hughes then sold the house to Nielsen who soon learned of the defects. The Court ruled that a building inspector has a public duty to prevent faulty construction, and if the inspector is in breach of that duty, the City is liable to any subsequent purchaser. Damages were assessed as 75 percent against Hughes and 25 percent against the City.

CONDOMINIUM OWNERSHIP

The term **condominium** (generally shortened to "condo") refers to a system of ownership within a multi-unit housing development whereby each unit is owned separately by the individual who purchases it. The common elements such as hallways, lobby, and exterior grounds, are held in common by all of the unit owners. Each owner has an undivided interest in the common elements, which is in a fixed proportion based upon the size of each unit or the value of the unit compared to the total project.

The common law does not fit comfortably with the concept of condos, so all Canadian provinces have enacted special legislation to provide a framework for the development of such projects. Typical is the Ontario *Condominium Act*. The concept was readily accepted as a means by which families could afford their own homes by sharing common expenses. Under the Act, owners can:

1. Register and mortgage their individual units, together with their interests in the common elements of the project;
2. Enforce legal obligations against one another for non-compliance with the declaration, by-laws, and rules;
3. Enforce a lien for arrears in common expense payments;
4. Pay individual expenses such as taxes, mortgages, and a share of common expenses.

REGISTRATION

A condo complex may be constructed and operated only by a registered condominium corporation. The approval process is complex and lengthy and there is no fixed period of time within which a developer can guarantee that the project will be registered. It is unlawful in most provinces to sell the units of the condo until the registration has been approved. However, a sales campaign can usually be started once draft approval has been received from the provincial government.

ABDOOL v. SOMERSET DEVELOPMENT and PRENOR EQUITY

Alberta, 1991

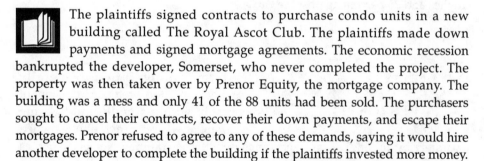

The plaintiffs signed contracts to purchase condo units in a new building called The Royal Ascot Club. The plaintiffs made down payments and signed mortgage agreements. The economic recession bankrupted the developer, Somerset, who never completed the project. The property was then taken over by Prenor Equity, the mortgage company. The building was a mess and only 41 of the 88 units had been sold. The purchasers sought to cancel their contracts, recover their down payments, and escape their mortgages. Prenor refused to agree to any of these demands, saying it would hire another developer to complete the building if the plaintiffs invested more money.

The Court ruled that the plaintiffs could cancel their contracts and mortgages, and were entitled to the refund of their deposits from Prenor, even though Prenor had paid the money over to Somerset. When Prenor took over the property to protect its investment, it became the "declarant" under the *Condominium Act* . Although it could be argued that Prenor was being penalized for the mistakes of Somerset, this is a risk that a mortgagee takes when financing a condo project.

DECLARATION AND DESCRIPTION

The condo declaration and description are registered once final approval has been obtained from the provincial government. The declaration contains many important legal matters:

1. A statement of intention that the land described in the description be governed by the Act;
2. A statement expressed in percentages of the proportions of the common interests;
3. An address for service and a mailing address for the corporation;
4. A specification of any parts of the common elements that are to be exclusive use areas for the owners of one or more designated units and not for all of the owners. For example, there may be limits upon using parking areas, balconies, or other exclusive use areas;
5. Provisions restricting gifts, leases, and sale of the units;
6. Specification of any allocation of the obligation to repair and maintain the units and common elements.

The extent of these provisions is subject to constant court challenge. For example, in *Re Peel Condominium Corp. No. 11 and Caroe* (1974) the Ontario Supreme Court held that a unit owner cannot be prohibited from leasing his unit to another person. In *York Condominium Corp. No. 216 v. Borsodi* (1983) it was held that a condominium corporation can force a unit owner to sell his unit if he violates a "no children" clause. The case was complicated by the fact that the complex contained three buildings. Two allowed children and one did not. The defendant was ordered to move from a "no children" building to a "children allowed" building.

In *Condominium Corporation 624 v. Ramdial et al.* (Ontario, 1988) the Court upheld a declaration that prohibited a unit owner from selling his unit to a buyer who had a 13-year-old child. The Court ruled that the provincial law prohibiting age discrimination did not apply to people under the age of 18 and the corporation did not discriminate against the seller or the buyer on the basis of family status.

There has been extensive litigation against unit owners who violate the "no pets" clause in the declarations, with mixed decisions that provide no clear guidance. In *Re York Condominium Corp. No. 288 and McDougall* (1978) the Ontario Supreme Court ruled that a "no pets" rule was not valid, but that the corporation could take action against individual unit owners who had noisy, dirty, or otherwise problem pets.

BY-LAWS AND RULES

The by-laws and rules, two other sets of documents in the condo constitution, are important. The board of directors of a condo corporation may pass by-laws, as long as they are not contrary to provincial statutes, governing the following matters:

1. Number, qualification, election, term of office, and remuneration of the directors;
2. Meeting, quorum, and functions of the board of directors;
3. Appointment, function, and removal of agents of the corporation;
4. Management of the property;
5. Maintenance of the units;
6. Collection of funds toward the common expenses.

The board of directors is elected by the unit owners. The board may then make further rules regarding the daily function of the condo. Any rules made by the board must be reasonable and consistent with provincial laws. Rules generally are aimed to promote the safety, security, and welfare of the unit holders and the property, and to prevent unreasonable interference with the use and enjoyment of the common elements.

The basic problem that any board of directors has is the simple fact that a unit owner cannot be evicted in the traditional sense of a tenant who rents a unit. If a unit owner conducts himself or herself in a manner that irritates the other unit owners, the board of directors is tasked with "disciplining" this person. However, it lacks any real teeth to do so, other than to bring a civil action.

LANDLORD AND TENANT

The historical origin of the term **landlord** is feudal law, which held that "all land which is held in any estate shall be of a lord." The word **tenant** means "one who holds tenure in land." The relationship did not originally involve the land so much as the people. The lord owed service and loyalty to the monarch. The tenant owed service and loyalty to the lord. In return, the lord permitted the tenant to occupy and use the land. The landlord could, at any time, evict the tenant from the land. Large tracts of land were held directly by the monarch to the exclusion of all others. For example, trespassing in the "King's Forest" was an offence punishable by death.

Two areas of law must be considered when discussing landlord and tenant matters. First, there is the common law going back many centuries. Second, each province has enacted specific legislation to regulate dealings between landlords and tenants. The nature of this legislation has changed over the years as the nature of tenancy has changed. Tenants no longer see themselves as holding land, but rather renting living units. Where there is a contradiction between the common law and the statute law, the statute takes priority.

Historically, the common law favoured the landlord, whose powers over the land were absolute. There are many examples of this, including the notorious "Highland Clearances," when Scottish landlords evicted tens of thousands of people to make room for more sheep. Many emigrated to Canada.

The statutes passed by the provinces have generally tried to establish a balance between the rights of landlords on the one hand and tenants on the other. Since the statutes in each province vary in many details, the following discussion will be general, with some specific references to a number of provincial statutes.

ESSENTIALS OF A LEASE

A lease creates a legal estate, good against the whole world. Leases first appeared in the thirteenth century. Although a lease theoretically can be for any number of years, British law eventually established a rule that a lease could not exceed 99 years.

A **lease** can be defined as a document creating an interest in land for a fixed period of certain duration in consideration of the payment of rent. Most provincial statutes refer to a lease as a **tenancy agreement.** For example, the Ontario *Landlord and Tenant Act* defines such an agreement as follows:

> Tenancy agreement means an agreement between a tenant and a landlord for possession of residential premises, whether written, oral, or implied, and includes a licence to occupy residential premises.

Not every document resembling a lease is necessarily a lease. Certain requirements must be met, either in specific words or implied actions. For example, there is a difference between a lease and an agreement to lease. The latter is a contract that says the parties will enter into a lease at a later date. It does not create an estate. A person who signs a lease, but who is denied possession of the property, may sue for possession. A person who signs an agreement to lease may sue for breach of contract but may not sue for possession of the property.

All leases, whatever form they take, must meet three basic requirements: exclusive possession, defined premises, and intent to create a lease agreement.

EXCLUSIVE POSSESSION

The purpose of the lease must be to grant exclusive possession. No lease is valid if the person granting the lease continues to occupy or have direct control over the property. In most provinces, a boarder or lodger does not have a lease. The Ontario law is an exception to this rule because it specifically includes a "boarding house, rooming house, or lodging house." A person who takes a room at a hotel or motel does not have a lease. Nor does a person who moves in with a relative or friend acquire a lease.

DEFINED PREMISES

The lease agreement must clearly identify just what the tenant is obtaining. An address, apartment number, or some other identification must be spelled out.

INTENTION

An agreement may be defective in some way, but if the court accepts that the intention of the parties was to create a lease, it will be interpreted as being a valid lease.

FORMAL LEASES

At common law, a lease could be granted orally and today many leases are still entered into on the basis of an oral contract. The original *Statute of Frauds*, passed in England in 1677, required that all leases be in writing. The situation today is generally that a lease of more than three years' duration must be in writing. Very long-term leases must also be registered. There are distinct differences between leases for commercial property and residential property. Commercial leases will be discussed in a separate section of this chapter.

A valid lease should contain certain essential information including:

1. Names of the landlord and tenant;
2. Date the lease begins;
3. Clear description of the property;
4. Duration of the term;
5. Amount of rent and how it is to be paid;

6. Specific terms of the contract, including who pays for utilities;
7. Limitations upon the use of the property;
8. Assurance of exclusive possession.

The landlord must give a copy of the lease to the tenant, or the tenant may refuse to pay rent. In Ontario, British Columbia, and Alberta, this copy must be provided within 21 days. Newfoundland adds a further requirement that the landlord must give the tenant a copy of the *Residential Tenancies Act*.

INFORMAL LEASES

In most provinces, leases for a term of three years or less may be informal, which means that they can be written, oral, or implied. However, the absence of a written lease may make it difficult for the tenant to prove there is a lease if the landlord later refuses to allow occupancy of the premises. For protection of rights, the tenant should make every effort to occupy the premises immediately or even move one personal belonging into the premises. The reason for this is that the tenant should demonstrate "part performance" of the contract, which makes it binding.

STANDARDIZED LEASES

Reform of landlord and tenant law has led to concern about the wording of leases that are complex and often one-sided. In response to these problems, several provinces have taken steps to make the forms of leases more uniform than they have been in the past.

The provinces of British Columbia, Newfoundland, Nova Scotia, and Saskatchewan have stipulated that certain conditions must appear in every tenancy agreement. The landlord and tenant may add additional terms to the form, but cannot delete the minimum terms. Ontario developed a standard form in 1980 as part of a revision to the *Landlord and Tenant Act*, but the Supreme Court of Ontario declared that much of the law was unconstitutional and the standard form was not adopted.

TYPE AND DURATION OF TENANCY

The period of time for which the tenancy runs is often a point of disagreement. The following are the most common leases based upon a certain time period.

LEASES FOR A FIXED PERIOD

Written leases for a fixed, or specific, period may run for any specified duration. The length of the lease is not important. What is essential is that both the date on which the lease begins and the date on which it ends must be stated or determinable. Leases for a fixed period are now of minimal importance. Virtually all of the important provisions about ending a lease are covered by provincial statutes and cannot be varied by the parties. Regardless of whether a termination date is specified, the tenancy is automatically continued until proper notice is given by either the landlord or the tenant, and the landlord may give notice only for specific reasons.

In most provinces, leases for a period greater than three years must be registered to be valid against third parties. For example, if the landlord sold the building, the tenant with a long-term lease could be evicted if the lease was not registered.

PERIODIC TENANCIES

A periodic tenancy is one that is renewed from week to week, month to month, etc. This type of tenancy can be created by express agreement or by implied behaviour of the parties, such as payment on a regular basis. Where no other agreement exists, the court may use the period of rental payment to determine the nature of the agreement. A yearly tenancy is one that begins with a period of at least one year and continues from year to year until ended by proper notice. The lease normally identifies such a period with the phrase, "for one year and so thereafter from year to year."

TENANCY AT SUFFERANCE

A tenancy at sufferance exists when a tenant occupies property without the owner's consent and the owner takes no action to remove the tenant. The owner may eject the tenant at any time and the fact that the tenant is allowed to remain does not indicate acceptance of the tenant's presence. Such tenants have often been called "squatters," a name that indicates people who occupy vacant land or buildings.

MULTIPLE TENANT AGREEMENTS

When more than one person is occupying rented premises, a problem may arise as to who is the tenant. If two or more people are tenants under one agreement, because they have all signed the lease, they are each liable for the whole rent, despite any arrangement among themselves as to how much is to be paid by each. If one of the tenants leaves, his or her share of the rent must be paid by the remaining tenants. If this person leaves without the consent of the other tenants, they could sue him or her for the share of the rent. This has no effect on the rent owed to the landlord.

MATERIAL COVENANTS

In a landlord and tenant agreement, it is important to distinguish between essential and non-essential promises. **Material covenants** (promises) are essential promises. They include such things as the landlord's duty to provide adequate heat, repairs, and quiet enjoyment. A material covenant is the tenant's promise to pay rent, to keep the premises clean and in good condition, and not to annoy other tenants. Violation of a material covenant is a serious breach of the tenancy agreement.

Non-material covenants might include repainting faded walls, keeping the lawn healthy and green, or removing graffiti from the elevator walls. These are nuisances, but they are not central to the tenancy agreement itself. Minor deficiencies and disputes are not grounds to withhold rent or evict tenants.

ASSIGNMENT OF A LEASE

A tenant who signs a lease for a fixed period is normally bound to pay the rent for the full term of the lease. If the tenant's employer transfers him or her to another city, there is no automatic right to cancel the lease. The tenant should first try to get the landlord to voluntarily release him or her from the lease. If this is not possible, the tenant might **assign** the lease to another person. This person becomes an **assignee tenant**. The original tenant is no longer liable to pay the rent should the assignee fail to do so. An assignment seldom occurs without the consent of the landlord, who may oppose the assignment for various reasons.

The tenant may find it more convenient to **sublet** the premises. Subletting differs from assignment in two important ways. First, the tenant does not give up all interest in the property. He or she may sublet for a period of time and then reoccupy the premises. Or the tenant may sublet only part of the premises and continue to occupy the remainder. Secondly, the tenant remains completely liable to the landlord for rent and damage. That is, the tenant cannot demand that the landlord accept rent from the subtenant. If the subtenant damages the premises, the landlord may look to the tenant for the cost of repair. Whereas an assignee has the same rights as the original tenant, the subtenant is in a weak legal position. The subtenant must pay rent to the tenant, who is required to pay it to the landlord. But, if the tenant fails to pay the landlord, the subtenant can be evicted. The tenant must request permission from the landlord before subletting. However, the landlord cannot "unreasonably" withhold permission. In most provinces, the statute specifically states that, unless the tenant is planning to sublet to a very undesirable person, the landlord must allow subletting.

There is no such thing as "lease-breaking," as the following case demonstrates.

APPLEWOOD LANE WEST LTD. v. SCOTT and HINDS

Manitoba, 1987

The defendants were tenants in a building owned by the plaintiff. The defendants wanted to move but they had a long-term lease. They decided to have themselves evicted by misconduct. They told their friends they were going to throw lease-breaking parties and warned a neighbour that he should not expect to get much sleep in the near future. The parties were indeed loud, lasting all night. The defendants were evicted. The landlord, however, preserved its rights under the lease, including the right to damages.

The landlord had to repair the apartment and lost a month's rent before it was able to find new tenants. The landlord sued for damages, lost rent, legal fees, and the cost of advertising for new tenants. The trial judge allowed all of the costs, except lost rent, holding that if a landlord puts the tenant out, the landlord cannot also sue for rent. The landlord cannot "seize and sue." The Court of Appeal ruled that the landlord was entitled to all of the damages, including lost rent. The Court said:

> *The action of the tenants in so provoking the landlord constituted constructive abandonment of the lease. Abandonment is a fundamental breach and entitles the landlord to assert a claim for lost rentals after the date of repossession.*

RENT AND RENT CONTROLS

The tenant must pay the rent on the dates stated in the lease. Rent is not payable in advance unless so stated, as it nearly always is. The tenant cannot withhold the rent because of a dispute with the landlord. The payment of rent is not conditional upon the tenant's total satisfaction with the landlord or the building.

Under the common law, the covenant to pay rent was very rigid and was applied even if the building was destroyed or damaged. For example, if the building burned down and the tenant had to find another place to live, the tenant still had to pay rent on the destroyed unit because there was nothing in the law that excused this obligation. Further, the tenant could not consider the contract to be ended and seek accommodation elsewhere because the tenant might be able to re-occupy the building after it was repaired. Today, the provinces have included tenancy agreements in provincial legislation dealing with the **doctrine of contract frustration**. Under present legislation, the tenant may stop paying rent if something happens that forces the tenant to vacate the building. As well, the tenant may permanently cancel the agreement and seek new accommodation elsewhere.

The amount of rent is negotiated between the landlord and tenant. However, nearly every province has passed legislation restricting rent increases. The controls normally limit the amount a landlord may increase rent and the frequency, usually once a year. Landlords may apply for exceptions because of special problems. The variety of rent control programs in Canada is very great and constantly changing. Therefore, current information must be obtained from the appropriate government office. In many provinces, landlords may increase rent above the rent control limits to pay for renovation and modernization. Tenants complain that these repairs are sometimes unnecessary and serve as a ruse to obtain rent increases.

Provincial statutes also provide that the landlord must give the tenant advance notice of any rent increases. In British Columbia and Newfoundland, a year-to-year tenancy requires three months' written notice. In Ontario the landlord must give 90 days' written notice.

Basic disputes can arise about what constitutes "rent." Landlords have tried to avoid rent control by establishing various "service fees" that they contend are separate from rent and therefore may be increased without any limitation. These include fees for parking, recreation, cable television, air conditioning, and security. Some provinces, including Ontario and British Columbia, have specific legislation that services and facilities cannot be billed separately and are included in rent. Therefore, a decrease in service is an increase in rent. However, unique charges such as "key deposits" crop up as fast as governments try to restrict them.

Another method by which landlords avoided rent controls was to convert a building from a rental unit to a condominium. Each tenant was told he or she would have to buy the occupied unit or vacate. Older buildings were demolished and new condominiums built where they had stood. The disappearance of rental units was a great concern and several provincial governments passed legislation requiring landlords to obtain permission before demolishing or converting rental units. The Ontario *Rental Housing Protection Act* requires that permission be obtained from the local municipality. The prohibition applies even if the building is vacant. The Act does not apply if there are four or fewer rental units in the building. In British Columbia, landlords must give evicted tenants reasonable moving expenses if the building is being demolished, plus up to a maximum of six month's rent toward the cost of new accommodation.

TERMINATING A TENANCY

A tenancy is terminated by either party giving **notice to quit**. Most provinces require that the notice be given in writing and personally served on the tenant. If the tenant is staying away from the premises or has sublet the unit, the notice may be served by mail or some other form of substitute service.

In Ontario the notice must be given 60 days in advance and the landlord must give reasons for terminating the tenancy. The tenant does not have to give reasons. The notice must include a statement advising the tenant that the tenant has the right to contest the eviction and does not have to move unless the landlord obtains a court order, called a writ of possession.

In Alberta the landlord must give the tenant three months' written notice. The tenant must give the landlord notice of one month if the tenancy is monthly or 60 days if the tenancy is yearly. Notice can be served personally or by registered mail.

In British Columbia written notice must be served on the tenant before the day the rent is due. For example, if the rent is due on June 1, the notice must be delivered before June 1 to require the tenant to vacate by July 1.

The landlord may terminate the lease before its expiry date, without notice, if the tenant engages in certain forms of misconduct. Ontario permits eviction if the tenant engages in criminal activity, damages the premises, or repeatedly disturbs the other tenants.

LANSDOWNE AVENUE HOLDINGS LTD. v. ELLINGTON

Ontario, 1991

Following a police raid on his apartment, Ellington was charged with possession of narcotics for the purposes of trafficking. He was immediately served with an eviction notice, which he contested, arguing that he had not been tried or convicted of any offence. The landlord introduced evidence that Ellington's drug business greatly disturbed other tenants. There had been one shooting incident in the apartment. The Court ruled that the burden of proof on a landlord who wants to evict is to demonstrate on a balance of probabilities that there had been a breach of the lease agreement or the *Landlord and Tenant Act*. Based on the evidence, the Court issued the eviction order.

RIGHTS AND DUTIES OF THE LANDLORD

Both the landlord and tenant have common law and statutory rights and duties. Historically, the landlord had nearly all the power and could evict the tenant at will. The effect of the statutory law over the years has been to restrict that power.

MAINTENANCE

The landlord is responsible for maintaining the premises in a good state of repair and keeping them "fit for habitation." Some provinces apply the fit-for-habitation rule only to furnished premises. The landlord must comply with all health and safety standards. Failure to maintain the premises is a breach of a material covenant. As well, failure to maintain services which the lease promised could be considered a major breach. In *Pajelle Investments Ltd. v. Herbold* (Supreme Court of Canada, 1976) the landlord had induced tenants into a rental agreement by including a swimming pool. The landlord allowed the condition of the pool to deteriorate until it became unusable. The tenants applied for a rent reduction and the Court ruled in their favour, saying that they had been denied something for which they had paid.

If a third person is injured on the property, the landlord is liable if the injury arises from a dangerous situation that it was the landlord's duty to repair. The landlord must inspect the property at reasonable intervals to determine its safe condition. The landlord is also liable if the tenant is injured by a dangerous condition about which the tenant had complained.

SAFETY OF TENANTS

The landlord does not owe any special duty to ensure the safety of tenants from the criminal acts of third parties. The duty may exist, however, if the landlord has guaranteed the personal security of the tenants, either by specific contract or implied words and actions.

ALLISON v. RANK CITY WALL LTD.

Ontario, 1984

The plaintiff was sexually assaulted by an intruder in the parking garage of her apartment building. Before leasing the apartment from the defendant landlord, the plaintiff had been assured by the defendant's agent that the parking garage was secure. In fact, it was not. It was quite easy for the person who attacked the plaintiff to gain access to the garage. The plaintiff had been told that the garage was patrolled by a security officer and under observation of a television camera. There were 38 television monitoring cameras on the premises, but there was no camera in the garage.

The lease contained a general exemption clause relieving the landlord from liability for personal injury suffered by the tenant "in any way." The trial judge, however, awarded the plaintiff damages against the defendant:

> *The negligence of the defendant consisted of failing to reasonably secure the garage premises once having represented their safe condition or alternatively of allowing the plaintiff to be lulled into a false sense of security —"You are safe." I repeat that the plaintiff's concerns had been clearly expressed. She was enticed to rent these premises and drawn into the contractual relationship by reason of the representations made by the reputation acquired by the complex and of the oral conversations at the time the plaintiff made her application to lease. The security measures were totally inadequate. Patrolling was insufficient, lighting was dim. There was no television device monitoring the parking area although there were 38 monitoring devices, mostly focused on the commercial entrances. Liability under the* Occupier's Liability Act *can be restricted according to its terms but the restriction must be specific and brought to the attention of the person whom the legislation is intended to protect.*

The judge held that the disclaimer clause could not protect the landlord from liability where there had been misrepresentation about the security of the premises.

SECURITY AND RENT DEPOSITS

Landlords are concerned about the non-payment of rent and damage to the premises. For many years, landlords tried to protect themselves by requiring the tenants to pay damage deposits and advance rent. These deposits were governed by the terms of the lease and usually stated that if the tenant vacated the premises without having damaged them, the deposit would be repaid. It seldom was. Although the deposit was not intended to pay for ordinary wear and tear, landlords nearly always kept the deposit and alleged that there had been damage. Most provinces have made security or damage deposits illegal. In Alberta, the landlord may collect one month's rent as a security deposit and must pay the tenant interest on the money. The landlord must give the tenant an accounting within 10 days after the tenant vacates and must state the nature of any deduction for damage. British Columbia forbids damage deposits that are automatically forfeited when the tenant vacates. The landlord must demonstrate that the tenant actually damaged the property.

Ontario permits the landlord to collect one month's advance rent, which is to serve as the payment of the final month before the tenant vacates. The landlord cannot withhold any of this money because of alleged damage.

RIGHT OF ENTRY

The landlord must respect the privacy of the tenant and the tenant's right to quiet enjoyment. The landlord does have the right of entry under certain conditions:

1. In a case of emergency;
2. When the tenant gives consent at the time of entry;
3. To inspect and repair the premises after giving the tenant notice;
4. To show the premises to prospective tenants after a notice to quit has been given.

Normally, the landlord can enter only during daylight hours after giving reasonable notice. In Ontario the tenant may insist upon 24 hours' written notice.

DISTRESS

If a tenant failed to pay rent, the early common law permitted the landlord to exercise a right of **distress**. This meant that the landlord could enter the premises and seize the tenant's personal property to **distrain** (hold for security) for unpaid rent. The tenant had to pay the rent to retrieve the property. If the rent was not paid, the landlord could sell the property.

Most provinces have abolished the right of distress as far as it applies to residential properties. The right of distress still exists in commercial leases.

RIGHTS AND DUTIES OF THE TENANT

The common law gave tenants very few rights. This situation has been corrected by legislation that declares that tenants have rights, including the right to privacy in their own homes. The tenant is entitled to quiet enjoyment.

ALTERATION OF LOCKS

Neither the landlord nor the tenant is permitted to alter the lock on any door that gives entrance to the premises without the consent of the other. The tenant cannot totally lock out the landlord and the landlord cannot lock out the tenant over disputes such as unpaid rent.

POSTDATED CHEQUES

The landlord may ask the tenant for a number of postdated cheques as a form of security that the rent will be paid on time. Alberta and Ontario prohibit this practice.

WITHHOLDING SERVICES

The landlord may not cut off essential services such as water and heat as a way of forcing the tenant to vacate. Most provinces impose a fine upon violators.

PETS

Many rental agreements prohibit the keeping of pets on the premises. It has never been easy for landlords to enforce this rule. Even if specified in the lease, the courts have often said that this is not a material covenant that justifies eviction. However, in 1989, an Ontario court ordered Marion and Richard Ryll to vacate their apartment because of the presence of their cat, "Fluffy." The Ontario Legislature then amended the statute to provide that tenants have a right to keep pets unless the pets cause a specific problem.

MAINTENANCE

Generally, a tenant is required to keep the premises reasonably clean and not to damage them. Ordinary wear and tear is not the tenant's responsibility. The tenant is responsible for damage caused by members of his or her family and by people the tenant allows on the premises.

IVERSEN v. PURSER and WALTER

British Columbia, 1990

The plaintiffs rented a house to Purser. Purser later told the plaintiffs that another man, Walter, would move in with him for a short time, and that both would be leaving at the end of the month. Walter started a fire with a cigarette that destroyed the house and killed Purser.

An action was brought against Walter and the deceased man's estate for negligence. The plaintiffs argued that Purser was liable for the damage caused by a guest whom he allowed on the premises. Counsel for Purser's estate argued that Walter was a co-tenant who was solely responsible for his own actions. The Court held that Walter was a guest and that Purser was vicariously liable for the damage his guest had caused.

REMOVAL OF FIXTURES

It is a common law rule that fixtures are the landlord's fixtures. When tenants vacate, they have the right to remove their chattel property only. They can remove personal property which is attached to the premises if they can do so without damage.

Tenants do not have a right to materially alter the premises. If a tenant embarks upon a decorating binge, the landlord may require the tenant to restore the premises to their original appearance. In one case, the tenant cut an archway through a wall, thinking it would be more convenient. The landlord insisted the wall be rebuilt.

A tenant who wrongfully takes fixtures from rented premises may also be prosecuted under section 441 of the *Criminal Code*, which makes it an offence to pull down, demolish, or remove all or any part of a building, including fixtures.

HUMAN RIGHTS

A landlord may not refuse to rent to a person on the basis of race, religion, creed, colour, sex, marital status, or ethnic origin. Various provinces have other specific prohibitions regarding discrimination. Ontario adds age, ancestry, receipt of public aid, handicap, sexual orientation, and family status.

A difficult area of law involves the exclusion of children. If a landlord states a policy that no children will be permitted in the building, most provincial laws do not prohibit this form of discrimination because such laws protect only people between certain ages, such as 18 to 65. In those provinces that prohibit discrimination on the basis of family status, the courts have generally struck down "no children" lease clauses. British Columbia law prohibits landlords from discriminating against tenants with children unless the unit is designated for senior citizens or disabled people. If a tenant increases his or her family by birth or adoption of a child, the landlord must give 24 months' notice to vacate.

COMMERCIAL LEASES

A commercial lease has unique and special features that distinguish it from a residential lease. Typical of such leases is the shopping centre lease and the following discussion will use that as a model.

RENT

Generally, tenants are required to pay a fixed annual minimum rent based upon a certain dollar figure per square foot of the premises. In addition to the minimum rent, the tenant may agree to pay a percentage rent consisting of the amount by which the tenant's revenue exceeds the minimum rent. In order to ensure that the percentage rent that the tenant has calculated is accurate, the landlord must have control over the method of reporting that the tenant uses and must have access to the tenant's books and records to conduct an audit.

Although shopping centre leases disclaim any liability upon the landlord for the success or failure of an enterprise within the centre, the reality is that many landlords compile detailed statistics about their tenants in order to attract other tenants. Eager to fill empty space, rental agents may take a wide latitude when it comes to representing the success of the shopping centre.

TWT ENTERPRISES LTD. v. WESTGREEN DEVELOPMENTS

Alberta, 1991

The plaintiffs, who owned TWT Enterprises, approached Westgreen Developments, landlord of the Kingsway Garden Mall, to discuss leasing space for a Ukrainian food kiosk in the mall's food fair. The landlord's leasing agent told the plaintiffs that the mall had the highest sales per square foot of any mall in western Canada. The agent claimed that the previous occupant of the kiosk had sales of $200 000 per year and that the customer rate in the food fair was 600 persons per hour. These estimates were grossly inflated and the Ukrainian food enterprise failed.

Evidence from other food operators was that the agent had made the same exaggerated claims to all of them. Some had gone out of business. The judge held that the agent had fraudulently and negligently misrepresented the viability of the business in the mall and held the landlord liable. The plaintiffs were awarded $186 000 plus costs.

COMMON AREAS

The common areas of the building are under the exclusive control and management of the landlord. The landlord is responsible for their maintenance and for controlling the people who enter. The landlord owns the parking area and may establish a controlled parking system to prevent non-customers from using the parking lot.

USE OF PREMISES

The tenant must declare how he or she will use the premises and must confine all activity to that declaration. Thus, a bulk food store could not begin selling cooked or prepared food.

Although the landlord has the right to rent vacant space to new tenants, the new tenants must not use the premises in such a way that it causes injury to existing tenants. For example, where a landlord rented the second floor of a building to a karate school, the restaurant operator on the first floor complained of the noise caused by bodies crashing to the floor (the restaurant ceiling). The tenant was justified in vacating when the problem was not reduced.

DISTRESS

Distress, a remedy for the landlord that arises when rent is not paid, is the seizure of the tenant's property by the landlord or his authorized agent. The landlord must sell the seized goods and apply the proceeds in satisfaction of rent arrears. Seizure of the goods does not terminate the lease. Seizure actually constitutes the landlord's recognition of the continuation of the lease.

Further, the remedy of distress is an alternative to an action for rent. As long as the landlord holds distrained goods, the landlord cannot sue for rent. The goods must be sold and if there are still arrears, the landlord may sue. The landlord is not permitted to change the locks on the door in conjunction with distress, since changing the locks constitutes a re-entry which terminates the landlord's right to distress. Distress following a re-entry is wrongful.

The landlord cannot seize an unreasonable amount of goods. In *Rawlins v. Monsur* (Ontario, 1978) the landlord was held liable when the value of the property seized greatly exceeded the arrears of rent.

FORFEITURE OR RE-ENTRY

A landlord can pursue the right of forfeiture or re-entry in one of three ways: (1) actual physical re-entry, (2) summary proceedings under the statute, or (3) an action for possession.

The landlord does not have to give a notice to vacate before taking over the premises. Re-entry is normally effected by changing the locks on the premises and giving the tenant written notice that the lease is at an end. The act of re-entry is a notice of the landlord's unequivocal intention to bring the tenancy to an end.

BAYWEST ENTERPRISES v. STRATHDEN PROPERTIES LTD.

British Columbia, 1991

The plaintiff company sued the defendant landlord, arguing that the landlord had seized its business and had made a large profit. The action was founded upon the principle of unjust enrichment. Baywest started a restaurant business in a new building owned by Strathden. While the building was being constructed, the landlord presented the plaintiff with a new lease, containing tougher terms. The plaintiff accepted the terms.

The plaintiff ran into financial trouble shortly after the restaurant was opened. The plaintiff abandoned the enterprise, saying, "To hell with it." The landlord was notified by a bailiff that the equipment and fixtures would be seized. The landlord could not locate the plaintiff and decided to effect a rescue of the business. It paid off the debts, brought in a management company to continue the restaurant, then sold the business at a profit. Baywest commenced an action for the value of the improvements it had made in the building and for unjust enrichment. It argued that the landlord had forced it into financial problems by the new, tougher lease. Counsel for the plaintiff said that this was economic duress.

The judge held that the plaintiff was not entitled to any relief. By the act of abandonment, the plaintiff had indicated to the landlord that the tenancy was at an end. The fact that a failed venture was subsequently made profitable in more capable hands was not grounds for the plaintiff to recover its investment.

REVIEW: POINTS OF LAW

1. All land belongs to the Crown. The closest thing to private ownership of land in Canada is an estate in fee simple.
2. Two land registration systems exist in Canada: the registry system and the land titles system.
3. Property may be owned by two or more people. In a joint tenancy, if one owner dies, the others automatically inherit that person's interest.
4. If a person uses another person's land in an adverse, open, and notorious manner, that person may eventually acquire a claim to the land.
5. A property owner is entitled to use water that flows across his or her property as long as that person does not substantially reduce its flow or pollute the water to the detriment of neighbours downstream.
6. All provinces have legislation which gives spouses an equal interest in the matrimonial home, regardless of how the property is registered.
7. Fixtures are those things which are permanently attached to real property and should not be removed when the property is sold.
8. A mortgage is both a charge upon the real property and a personal covenant by the borrower.
9. For a lease to be valid, it must give the tenant exclusive possession of clearly defined premises.
10. Although a written lease is advisable, oral leases are valid for short periods.
11. A tenant who must relocate may sublet the unit to another person. However, the tenant remains liable for such matters as payment of rent, damage to the premises, etc.
12. A tenancy is terminated by either party giving a Notice to Quit, which usually must be served personally on the other party.
13. The landlord is required to maintain the property so it is fit for habitation. The tenant is required to maintain the property to a standard of ordinary cleanliness.
14. A landlord may not refuse to rent to a person on the basis of race, religion, colour, and other personal features.

LEGAL BRIEFS

1. When G died in 1956, he left the family farm to his grandson, B, with a life estate to his son, K. The two men were to work the farm together and share the profits equally. B never worked the land. He moved away in 1958 and his father, K, worked the land alone until his death in 1988. K's widow, R, intended to remain on the farm and operate it with hired help. However, in 1989, B returned to claim "his" farm. He did not claim half the profits, agreeing that he was not entitled to them because he had not done any work. Who owns the farm?
2. A stream flowed through the lands of C and her neighbour Y. The water was clear and plentiful and there were small fish in the stream. C had a personal affection for water fowl, so she constructed a pond and diverted the stream into the pond. She then allowed the water to overflow, back into the original stream bed. Many birds were attracted to the pond and the result was that the water flowing to Y's property was fouled and dirty. There were no fish in the water because the birds ate them. What rights, if any, has Y?
3. Q owned a cottage on Gull Lake. There were 18 other cottages on the same lake. Approximately 50 m from the shore, in front of Q's lot, was a small island, with a good beach. All the cottagers went to the island by boat and could navigate through the channel between the island and the shore. They were surprised when Q began trucking in rock and dumping it in the water. He announced that he was going to fill in the lake between his lot and the island and make the island part of his lot. The other cottagers protested, but Q did not cease his action. Have the other cottagers any rights in the matter?
4. T offered to sell agricultural land to W. The contract described the land as 13.5 acres. The price was established, on the basis of $2000 per acre, at $27 000. When the land was surveyed, it turned out that it was actually 16 acres. T said to W, "The price will, of course, be $32 000 because you're getting more land than we both figured." W disputed this, saying the price was firmly agreed upon at $27 000. Who is correct?
5. When the R Construction Corp. was building a tall office building, it placed a large crane close to a building owned by M. The crane was used to lift steel beams and other materials to upper floors. Each time the crane did so, it swung its load through the air directly over the roof of M's building, an action which both worried and annoyed M. "If that crane drops something, it will crash right through my roof," he told his lawyer. The R Corp. said there was no other way to operate the crane in the limited space available. What rights has M in this matter?

6. When P rented an apartment from W, P noticed that the locks were of an inexpensive, poor quality type that could be easily opened. P wrote a letter to W requesting that the locks be changed. W never answered the letter. Seven months later, P's apartment was broken into and goods stolen. P demanded that W pay for the loss. Must W do so?
7. When N and H, a married couple, rented a house from S, only H signed the lease as tenant. Four months later, they quarreled and H moved out, leaving N in the unit. N continued to pay the rent and S accepted it. When the lease ran out at the end of the year, S refused to renew it, saying that the tenant was H and H had abandoned the premises. Must N vacate?
8. K rented a two-bedroom bungalow from G. K's mother came to live with her. Then K's brother lost his job and moved in with her, bringing his wife and one child. K's sister divorced her husband and also came to live with K, bringing her two children with her. At what point could G put a stop to K's generosity?

APPLYING THE LAW

LUNDIGANS LTD. v. PROSPER and BRAKE

Newfoundland, 1981

The respondents in this appeal had built and maintained a small hunting and fishing cabin on the land owned by the appellant corporation. The trial judge held that by virtue of use in excess of 20 years, the respondents had acquired a good possessory title to the land.

The law applied is the *Limitations of Actions Act* of Newfoundland which provides that, after 20 years has expired from the date adverse possession began, the possessor acquires good title. His possession must have been open, notorious, exclusive, and uninterrupted.

The respondents stated that they first built a log cabin on the land in 1956. This cabin was torn down in 1972 and a plank-board cabin built which measured 8 m by 10 m. This cabin was painted green with a black felt roof. The respondents cleared the land around the cabin to the extent of only 1 m. The cabin was used by the respondents and their families for hunting and fishing. The cabin is located 75 m from the Humber River, but is not visible from the river. It was discovered in 1980 by survey crews hired by the appellant. The crews were carrying out the survey for a proposed real estate development. The only access to the cabin was a footpath. The respondents believed that other hunters knew of the existence of the cabin but did not know if the appellant knew about it. The appellant argued that the cabin was hidden and therefore was not open and notorious.

The trial judge concluded that the respondents had not deliberately tried to keep the cabin a secret, thus the occupation had been notorious.

The Court of Appeal reversed the decision of the trial judge, holding that there was neither open nor notorious possession. The land in question is wooded and undeveloped. There was no knowledge of the existence of the cabin by the appellant.

> *I do not think that constructive knowledge can or should be imputed. The evidence is clear that the cabin was well hidden because it could not be seen from the air nor from the nearby river or ground area. That it was almost totally obscured may also be deduced from the fact that its location was unknown despite its proximity to Corner Brook, the Humber River and the Trans-Canada Highway. In all these circumstances, there is insufficient evidence of open or visible or notorious possession within the meaning given these words by the courts, so as to dispossess the legal title holder.*

Questions

1. The original cabin was torn down after 16 years. Would this affect the running time of the 20-year rule? Why or why not?
2. The respondents insisted they never tried to hide the cabin. The Court did not reject this evidence. Why, then, did the Court not accept the argument that occupation of the land was open and notorious?
3. What does the case reveal about adverse possession in a very remote, seldom-visited area?
4. Assuming it has some minimal value, what becomes of the cabin?

Q v. MINTO MANAGEMENT LTD.

Ontario, 1984

When a woman was sexually assaulted in her apartment in a building owned and operated by the defendant corporation, the police recommended that the defendant change all of the locks because it appeared that the attacker had used a key, possibly a master key. The defendant did not take this action. Two months later, a similar assault was made against the plaintiff in her apartment. The attacker was arrested and it was learned that he was an employee of the defendant and did use a master key.

The action was based upon negligence and occupier's liability. The defendant argued that it did not want to alarm its tenants. The investigation of the first assault was still underway and there was suspicion that the criminal was an "insider." To change all of the locks might have scared the criminal away, and, if he was an insider, he might very well have ended up with a master key that fit the new locks.

The Court held the defendant liable and awarded the plaintiff damages. The judge said:

> *It is one thing to act in such a way as not to alarm tenants but it is quite another thing to take no additional steps following the May incident and after being informed that the police consider that the culprit may have been an insider.*

The judge then noted that if the locks were not to be changed, the defendant owed a duty to the tenants to tell them to be doubly careful and to take additional security measures to patrol the building and account for all keys.

Questions

1. What duty does a landlord owe to the tenants regarding their personal safety?
2. Why was the landlord held liable?
3. Would the landlord be liable, by virtue of vicarious liability, because the criminal was its employee?
4. A landlord cannot change locks without the permission of the tenants. Would the landlord have to obtain the individual consent of each tenant before making such a change?

PRINCIPLES AND CASES

Case 1: Legal Principle

A claim by one person to an interest in the real property of another person can be based only upon establishment of a resulting or constructive trust, which requires

proof that the parties, at the time the agreement was made, intended that the property be shared.

Case Facts

The plaintiff and the defendant each contributed money to the purchase price of land and a house that was registered in the name of the defendant alone. The evidence was that the defendant and her mother wanted to buy a house and that the plaintiff, the defendant's boyfriend, wanted to help them. He found a good house for them, but it was more money than they could afford. The plaintiff said he would help financially and it was understood that he would also live in the house.

The transfer papers were drawn, showing the house in the names of the plaintiff and the defendant. The defendant became angry about this and refused to complete the purchase. She told the lawyer, "This is to be *our* house," referring to herself and her mother. The lawyer telephoned the plaintiff and told him the problem. The plaintiff then told the lawyer to put the house in the name of the defendant alone. He still contributed $5000 to the down payment.

The three people lived together in the house for a short time before the plaintiff moved out. He brought an action for a declaration that he was entitled to an interest in the house. The defendant argued that the money was a personal loan to her and had nothing to do with the house. The Court reviewed the law of resulting trusts and found that two things must be considered: (1) the nature of the conveyance, and (2) the common intention of the parties at the time of the transaction.

Possible Decisions

A The plaintiff is entitled to an interest in the house because, without his financial help, it could not have been purchased at all.

B The plaintiff is entitled to an interest in the house because he initially lived in it in a cohabitation arrangement.

C The plaintiff is not entitled to an interest in the house because he instructed the lawyer not to put his name on the transfer as an owner.

D The plaintiff is not entitled to an interest in the house because there was no common intention that he be a joint owner.

Case 2: Legal Principle

Breach of a material covenant in a tenancy agreement is a serious breach that permits the other party to terminate without notice. A material covenant is a matter that goes to the heart of the tenancy agreement.

Case Facts

The defendant operated a hardware store in a small plaza. There were only two stores in the plaza. The defendant leased one and the second unit was leased by a variety store.

The plaza had a very small parking lot. This did not represent a particular problem for the defendant because it was observed that when customers went into the variety store they stayed for less than 10 minutes on average. Although cars came and went frequently, ample parking space was available for the defendant's customers.

The variety store closed and the plaintiff landlord leased the premises to a restaurant. The restaurant did not offend the defendant by smells or other activity, but parking became a serious problem. Patrons of the restaurant remained on the premises for an average of 45 minutes. The result was that the parking lot was frequently full. Customers of the defendant's hardware store complained that they could not find a place to park and eventually took their business elsewhere. The defendant's lease had another 18 months to run, but he vacated without notice. The landlord sued for the rent.

Possible Decisions

A The plaintiff landlord will succeed because parking is not a material covenant of the lease, but rather just a collateral matter.

B The plaintiff landlord will succeed because the restaurant is not being operated in a manner that annoys the defendant's customers.

C The defendant tenant will succeed because it is obvious that parking space is essential to the operation of a hardware store or any commercial enterprise.

D The defendant tenant will succeed because the landlord failed to consult him before making a decision to lease to a restaurant.

YOU BE THE JUDGE

1. The plaintiffs purchased from the defendants a home that had a large fireplace in the living room. The defendants had never built a fire in the fireplace and stated that they did not know how well it worked. The defendants had purchased the house from the initial owner. There was nothing in the sale agreement about any warranty on the fireplace. In fact, the fireplace was a "show" fireplace only. It did not have a chimney. After the plaintiffs moved in, they built a fire in the fireplace that set the house on fire. They sued the defendants and the company that constructed the fireplace. The construction company defended the action saying that it had been specifically hired to build a show fireplace and assumed that each owner would tell each subsequent owner not to build a fire in it. A company representative testified: "Any fool should know if there is no chimney on the house, it is not a real fireplace." The defendants relied upon their ignorance of the facts and that they had given no warranty on the fireplace. Who would succeed?
2. The plaintiffs needed an appraisal of a house they intended to buy for their CMHC mortgage application.The bank engaged the services of the defendant to conduct the appraisal, at a cost to the plaintiffs of $165. The defendant drove to the house, walked around the outside, and quickly estimated that it had a value of $55 000. The report stated that minor cosmetic repairs were required. He gave a hand-written report to the bank and to the CMHC on which the following words were printed: "This appraisal is for mortgage purposes only and should not be regarded as a detailed building inspection with respect to the condition of the structure." After the plaintiffs moved in, they found that the building was in terrible condition and sued the defendant. The defendant appraiser relied upon the disclaimer in his report and also argued that he worked for the bank, not the plaintiffs, and therefore owed them no duty of care whatsoever. He did not even know their names when he did the appraisal. Who would succeed?
3. The plaintiff purchased an apartment building from the defendant for $1.9 million. The defendant showed the plaintiff an offer from another interested buyer for $1.8 million and suggested the plaintiff would have to "top it." It turned out that this offer was a fake document. The defendant provided the plaintiff with a list of all the tenants, all the lease terms, and the status of the rent payments. The list showed the units were 100 percent leased, and that most leases would run for at least one year or longer. It also showed that no tenants were behind in their rent. After the plaintiff bought

the building, the tenants began moving out because their leases had expired and the former owner had not kept promises to make repairs and improvements. The plaintiff eventually determined that 60 percent of the information on the list was not accurate. In fact, two units were empty and the defendant had paid the rent himself to make it appear they were rented. Three tenants were months behind in their payments. The plaintiff's problems were then compounded by the fact that revenue fell below what he needed to make his mortgage payments. The mortgage company forced a sale at $1.1 million. The plaintiff sued the defendant for his loss of nearly $800 000. The defendant admitted responsibility only for the units that were empty and not rented, saying, "I sold a building, not a bunch of people. Tenants move in and out all the time. That was not an important matter at all." Who would succeed?

4. The plaintiffs loved television, particularly the U.S. public broadcasting system. They rejected numerous houses in the city because these did not have cable television. They made it clear to the defendant real estate agency that they wanted cable television. They were shown a house by a different agent than the one they had been using. They asked the all-important question: "Does the house have cable television?" The agent looked at the listing agreement and showed them the notation: "TV:C." He said that meant the house did have cable television. They also saw the plastic wall outlets and wires for cable television. The plaintiffs bought the house and then learned that, although the house was wired for cable service, the service was not yet available on that street. They had to buy a satellite dish to receive the channels they wanted. They sued the real estate agency for misrepresentation or negligence. The agency argued that the plaintiffs could have easily telephoned the cable company before they bought the house to make certain it had service. Or, as an alternative, they could have connected a television to the cable to get the same answer. Who would succeed?
5. The plaintiff landlord sued four tenants for breach of the terms of their leases. The landlord had sought to avoid rent controls by inserting a clause in the lease that maintenance of the building would be calculated separately from rent. The clause stated, "The tenant agrees to pay a monthly maintenance fee to be calculated yearly, 1/12 of which shall be paid on the first day of each month." The landlord calculated the fee by totalling the repairs and maintenance costs for the year. He then assigned an equal amount to each tenant. Each tenant also paid monthly rent, limited by rent controls. The maintenance costs, accordingly, were not subject to controls. The tenants argued that they did not have to pay this fee as it was "hidden rent." The landlord argued that "rent" referred only to the basic fee for living in an apartment. Who would succeed?

6. The plaintiff, the widow of a man electrocuted by a pump motor, sued the defendant, her landlord, alleging that negligence caused her husband's death. The landlord had purchased and installed a sump pump in the basement of the rented house. The basement was very small, with an earth floor. One day the pump started making a great deal of noise and then stopped running. The deceased man called the landlord, but got no answer. Water began to accumulate in the basement so the husband went down to check the pump. He was not a qualified electrician nor an expert in pumps but had a basic knowledge of how pumps worked. When he touched the pump, an electrical short circuit gave him a fatal shock because he was standing in water at the time. The pump was later examined and it was found that the landlord had installed it incorrectly. The landlord defended the action by saying the deceased man should not have attempted to deal with something about which he had little knowledge. An expert would have cut the power to the pump before touching it. Who would succeed?
7. The plaintiff tenant sued the defendant landlord for an abatement (reduction) of rent because the landlord took no action to stop drug dealing in the apartment building. The plaintiff rented what he thought was a luxury apartment in a newly renovated building. He then discovered that the building was inundated with drug traffickers and users who had keys to the front door. He discovered that an all-hours drug bar was operating in the laundry room. He found used needles in the halls and was disturbed by people knocking on his door at all hours of the night looking for drugs. The problem centred around two other tenants who were known drug dealers. The landlord argued that he had taken all reasonable action to stop the problem, but could not catch the drug-dealing tenants in the act. Who would succeed?
8. The plaintiff landlord sought to evict the defendant tenant from her apartment. The defendant lost her job and sought to earn income by providing child care. There were four other families in the apartment building who had small children and who could not find suitable child care. The defendant began looking after the children. The lease prohibited the operation of any commercial business on the premises. The landlord argued that the tenant was operating a day care business. The tenant took the position that she was only caring for children who already lived in the building, not bringing other children in from outside. She admitted she was getting paid for her services, but denied it was a business. Who would succeed?

INDEX